D0991563

THE INVINCIBLE IRON MAN

MY MONSTERS

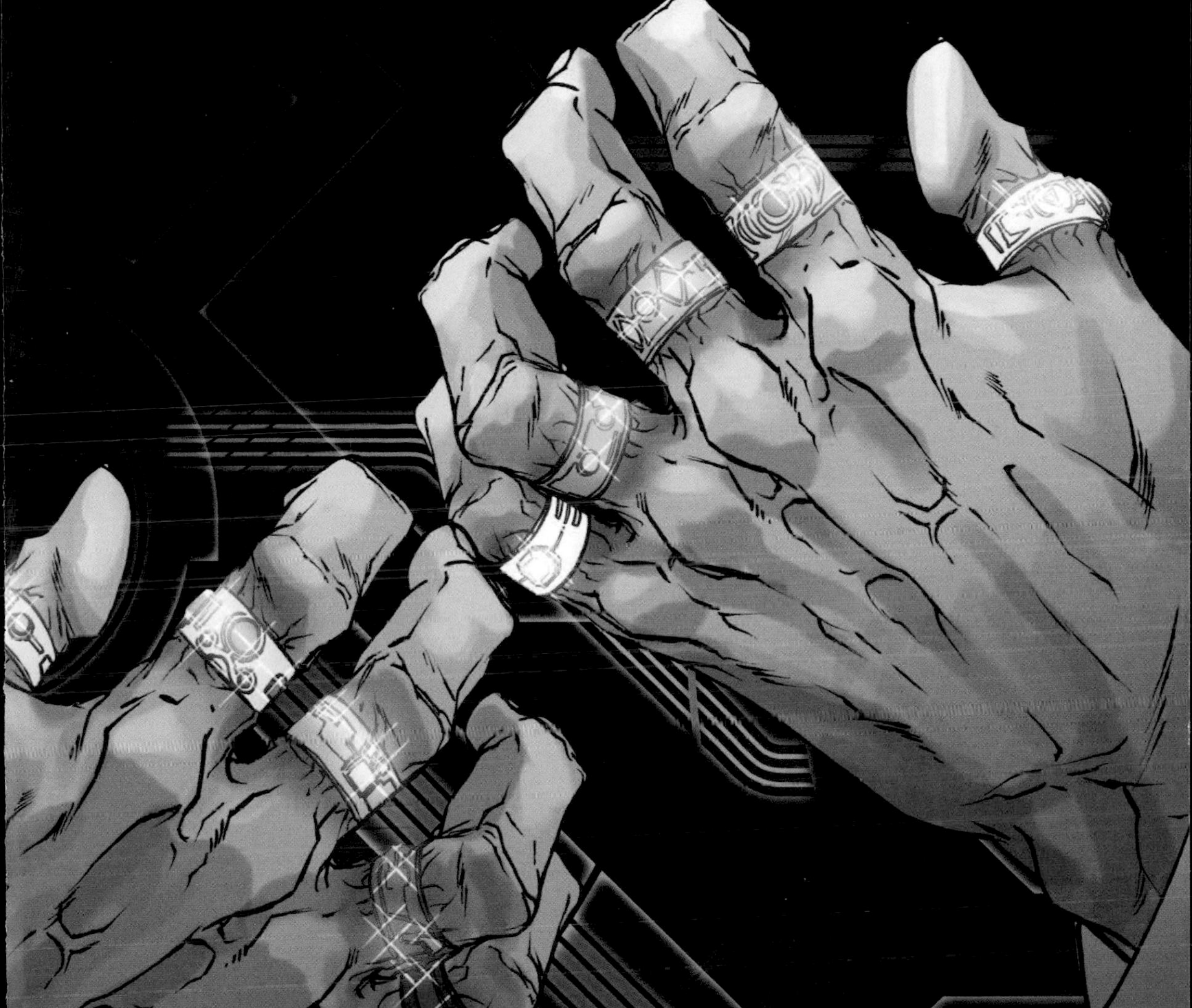

INVINCIBLE IRON MAN VOL. 7: MY MONSTERS. Contains material originally published in magazine form as INVINCIBLE IRON MAN #500, #500.1 and #503; and IRON MAN ANNUAL #1. First printing 2011. Hardcover ISBN# 978-0-7851-4836-4. Softcover ISBN# 978-0-7851-4837-1. Published by MARVEL WORLDWIDE, INC., a subsidiary of MARVEL ENTERTAINMENT, LLC. OFFICE OF PUBLICATION: 135 West 50th Street, New York, NY 10020. Hardcover: $19.99 per copy in the U.S. and $21.99 in Canada (GST #R127032852). Softcover: $15.99 per copy in the U.S. and $17.50 in Canada (GST #R127032852). Canadian Agreement #40668537. **Printed in the U.S.A.** ALAN FINE, EVP - Office of the President, Marvel Worldwide, Inc. and EVP & CMO Marvel Characters B.V.; DAN BUCKLEY, Publisher & President - Print, Animation & Digital Divisions; JOE QUESADA, Chief Creative Officer; JIM SOKOLOWSKI, Chief Operating Officer; DAVID BOGART, SVP of Business Affairs & Talent Management; TOM BREVOORT, SVP of Publishing; C.B. CEBULSKI, SVP of Creator & Content Development; DAVID GABRIEL, SVP of Publishing Sales & Circulation; MICHAEL PASCIULLO, SVP of Brand Planning & Communications; JIM O'KEEFE, VP of Operations & Logistics; DAN CARR, Executive Director of Publishing Technology; JUSTIN F. GABRIE, Director of Publishing & Editorial Operations; SUSAN CRESPI, Editorial Operations Manager; ALEX MORALES, Publishing Operations Manager; STAN LEE, Chairman Emeritus. For information regarding advertising in Marvel Comics or on Marvel.com, please contact John Dokes, SVP Integrated Sales and Marketing, at jdokes@marvel.com. For Marvel subscription inquiries, please call 800-217-9158. **Manufactured between 4/11/2011 and 5/9/2011 (hardcover), and 4/11/2011 and 10/3/2011 (softcover), by R.R. DONNELLEY, INC., SALEM, VA, USA.**

10 9 8 7 6 5 4 3 2 1

THE INVINCIBLE IRON MAN

MY MONSTERS

WRITER: **MATT FRACTION**

ANNUAL #1
ARTIST: **CARMINE DI GIANDOMENICO**
COLORS: **MATTHEW WILSON**

ISSUE #500.1
ARTIST: **SALVADOR LARROCA**
COLORS: **FRANK D'ARMATA**

"HOW I MET YOUR MOTHER"
ARTIST: **HOWARD CHAYKIN**
COLORS: **EDGAR DELGADO**

ISSUE #500
ART & COLOR, IRON MAN & SPIDER-MAN:
SALVADOR LARROCA & FRANK D'ARMATA
ART & COLOR, GINNY STARK: **KANO**
ART & COLOR, HOWARD STARK II: **NATHAN FOX & JAVIER RODRIGUEZ**
ART & COLOR, TONY STARK & THE MANDARIN:
CARMINE DI GIANDOMENICO & MATTHEW WILSON

LETTERS: **VC'S JOE CARAMAGNA**
COVER ART: **SALVADOR LARROCA** & **FRANK D'ARMATA**
EDITOR: **ALEJANDRO ARBONA**
SENIOR EDITOR: **STEPHEN WACKER**

COLLECTION EDITOR: **JENNIFER GRÜNWALD**
EDITORIAL ASSISTANTS: **JAMES EMMETT** & **JOE HOCHSTEIN**
ASSISTANT EDITORS: **ALEX STARBUCK** & **NELSON RIBEIRO**
EDITOR, SPECIAL PROJECTS: **MARK D. BEAZLEY**
SENIOR EDITOR, SPECIAL PROJECTS: **JEFF YOUNGQUIST**
SENIOR VICE PRESIDENT OF SALES: **DAVID GABRIEL**
SVP OF BRAND PLANNING & COMMUNICATIONS: **MICHAEL PASCIULLO**

EDITOR IN CHIEF: **AXEL ALONSO**
CHIEF CREATIVE OFFICER: **JOE QUESADA**
PUBLISHER: **DAN BUCKLEY**
EXECUTIVE PRODUCER: **ALAN FINE**

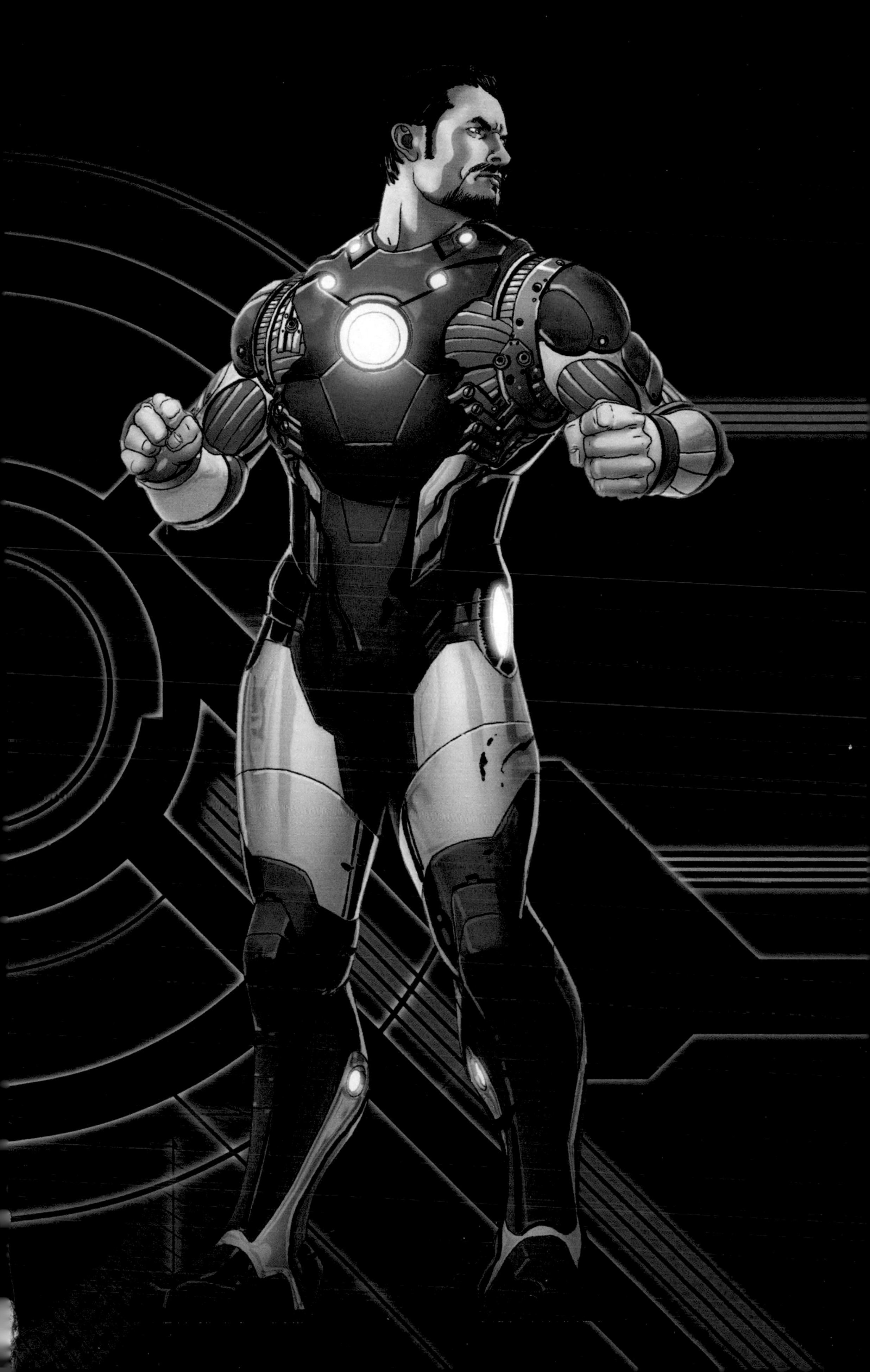

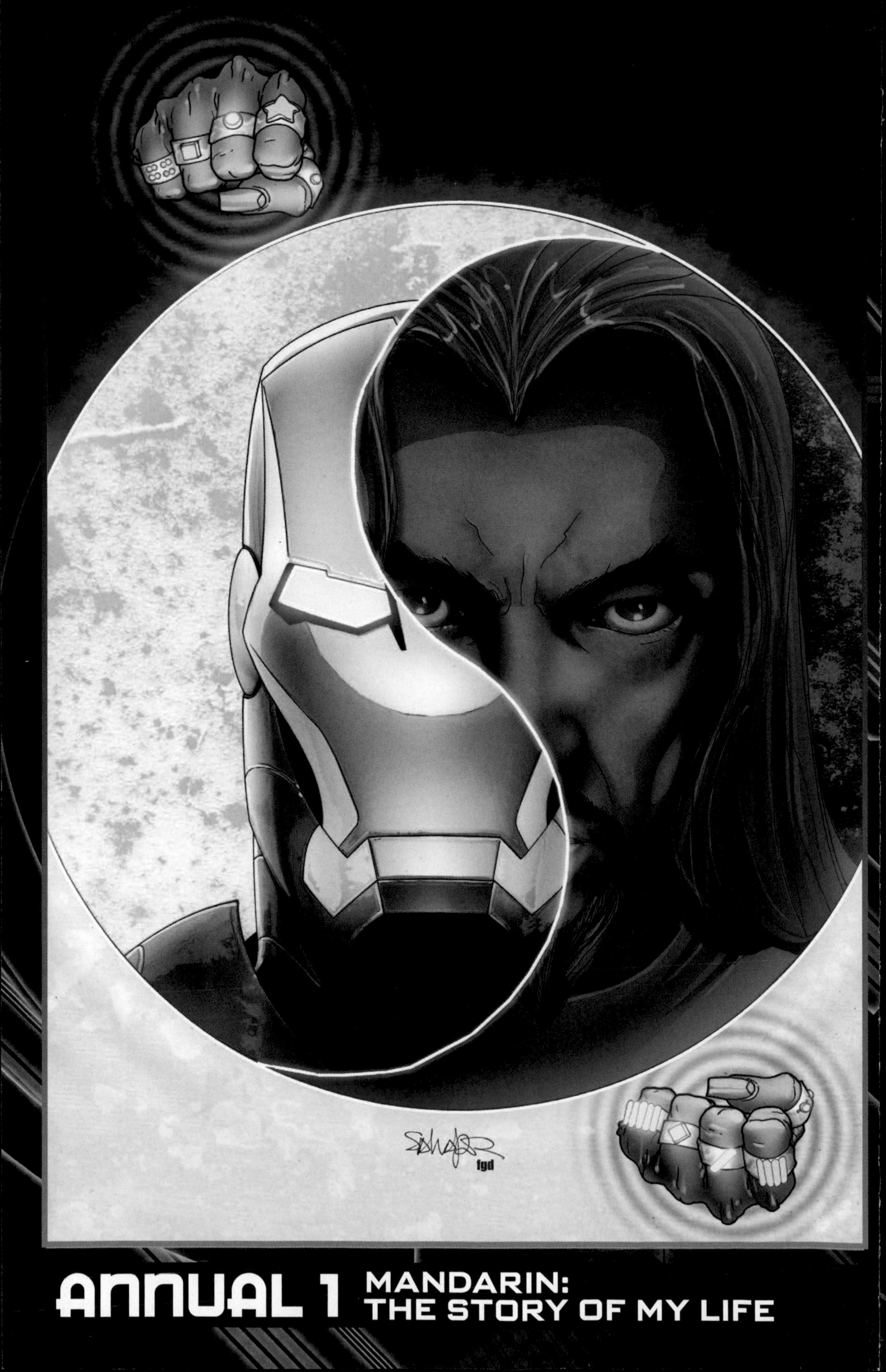

ANNUAL 1 MANDARIN: THE STORY OF MY LIFE

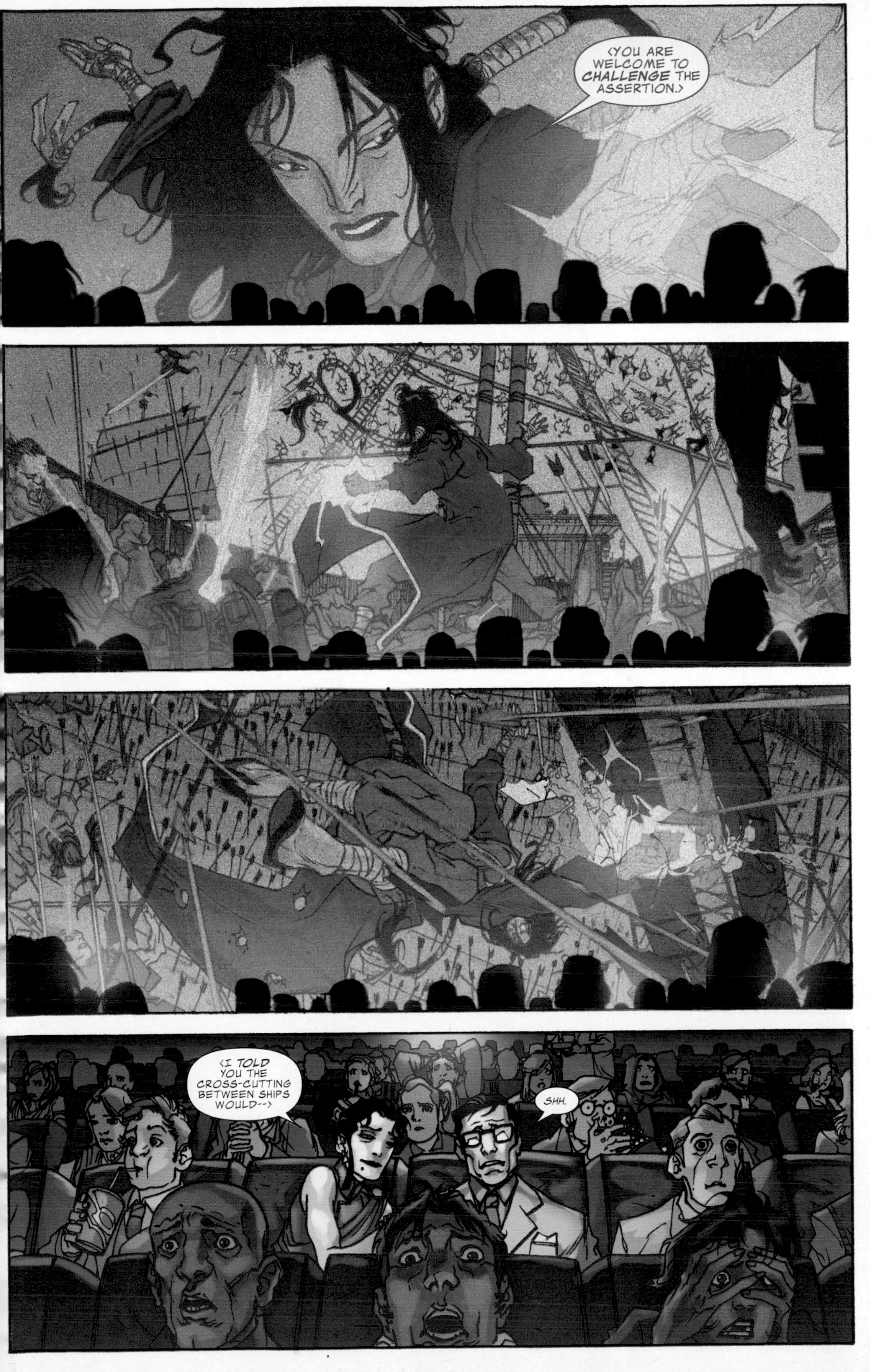
<YOU ARE WELCOME TO CHALLENGE THE ASSERTION.>
<I TOLD YOU THE CROSS-CUTTING BETWEEN SHIPS WOULD-->
SHH.

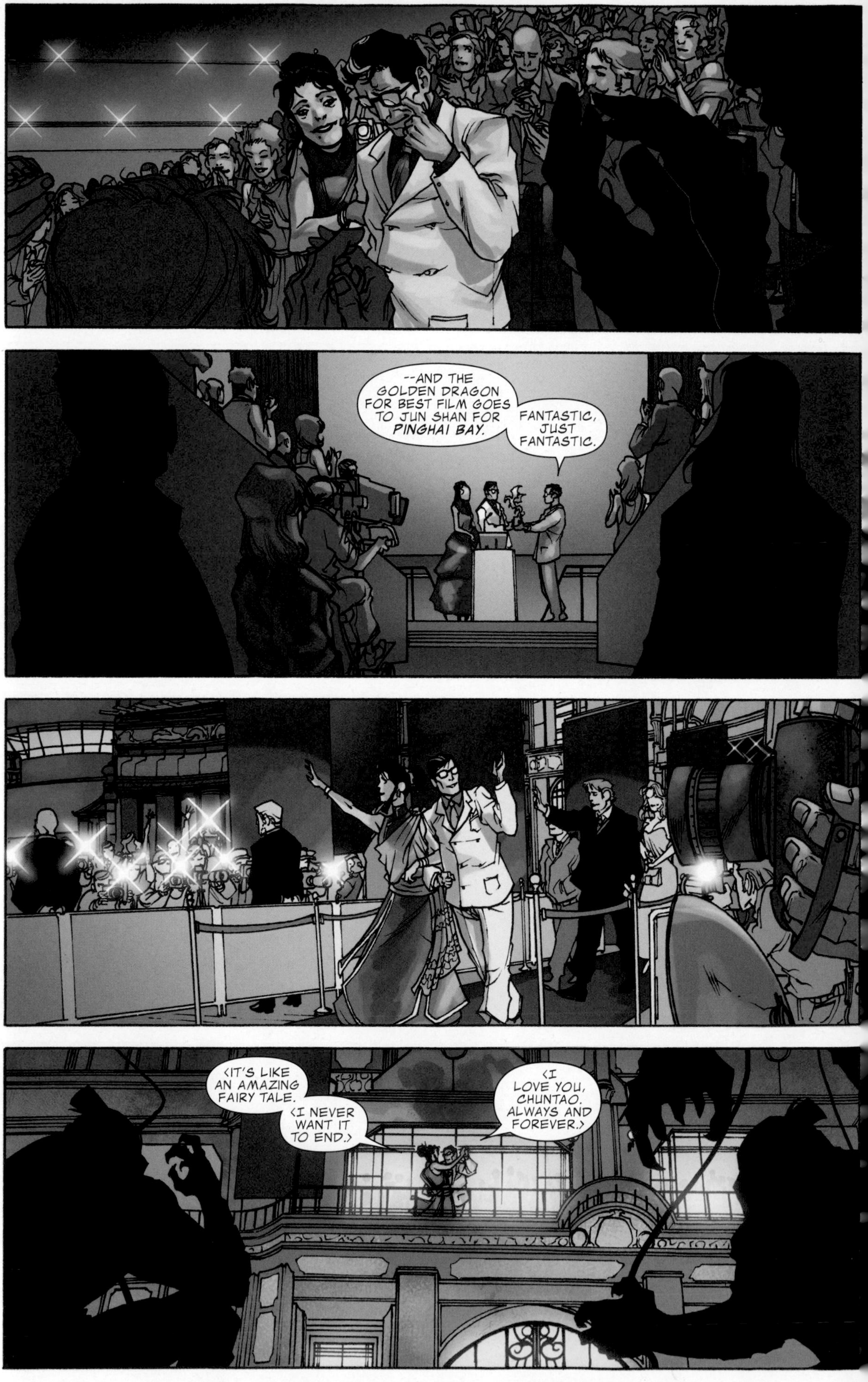
--AND THE GOLDEN DRAGON FOR BEST FILM GOES TO JUN SHAN FOR PINGHAI BAY.
FANTASTIC, JUST FANTASTIC.
<IT'S LIKE AN AMAZING FAIRY TALE.
<I NEVER WANT IT TO END.>
<I LOVE YOU, CHUNTAO. ALWAYS AND FOREVER.>

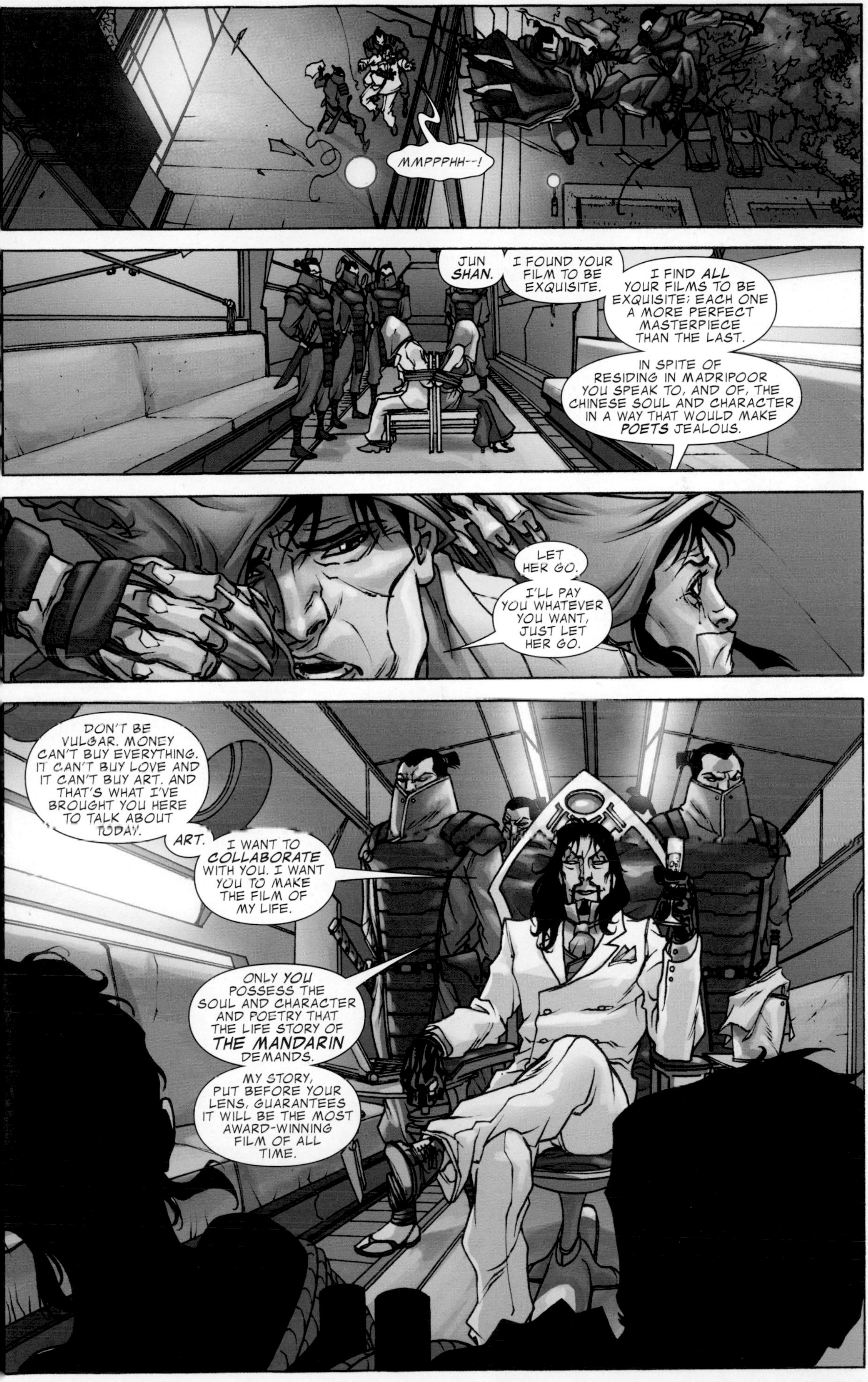

MMPPPHH--!
JUN SHAN.
I FOUND YOUR FILM TO BE EXQUISITE.
I FIND ALL YOUR FILMS TO BE EXQUISITE; EACH ONE A MORE PERFECT MASTERPIECE THAN THE LAST.
IN SPITE OF RESIDING IN MADRIPOOR YOU SPEAK TO, AND OF, THE CHINESE SOUL AND CHARACTER IN A WAY THAT WOULD MAKE POETS JEALOUS.
LET HER GO.
I'LL PAY YOU WHATEVER YOU WANT, JUST LET HER GO.
DON'T BE VULGAR. MONEY CAN'T BUY EVERYTHING. IT CAN'T BUY LOVE AND IT CAN'T BUY ART. AND THAT'S WHAT I'VE BROUGHT YOU HERE TO TALK ABOUT TODAY.
ART.
I WANT TO COLLABORATE WITH YOU. I WANT YOU TO MAKE THE FILM OF MY LIFE.
ONLY YOU POSSESS THE SOUL AND CHARACTER AND POETRY THAT THE LIFE STORY OF THE MANDARIN DEMANDS.
MY STORY, PUT BEFORE YOUR LENS, GUARANTEES IT WILL BE THE MOST AWARD-WINNING FILM OF ALL TIME.

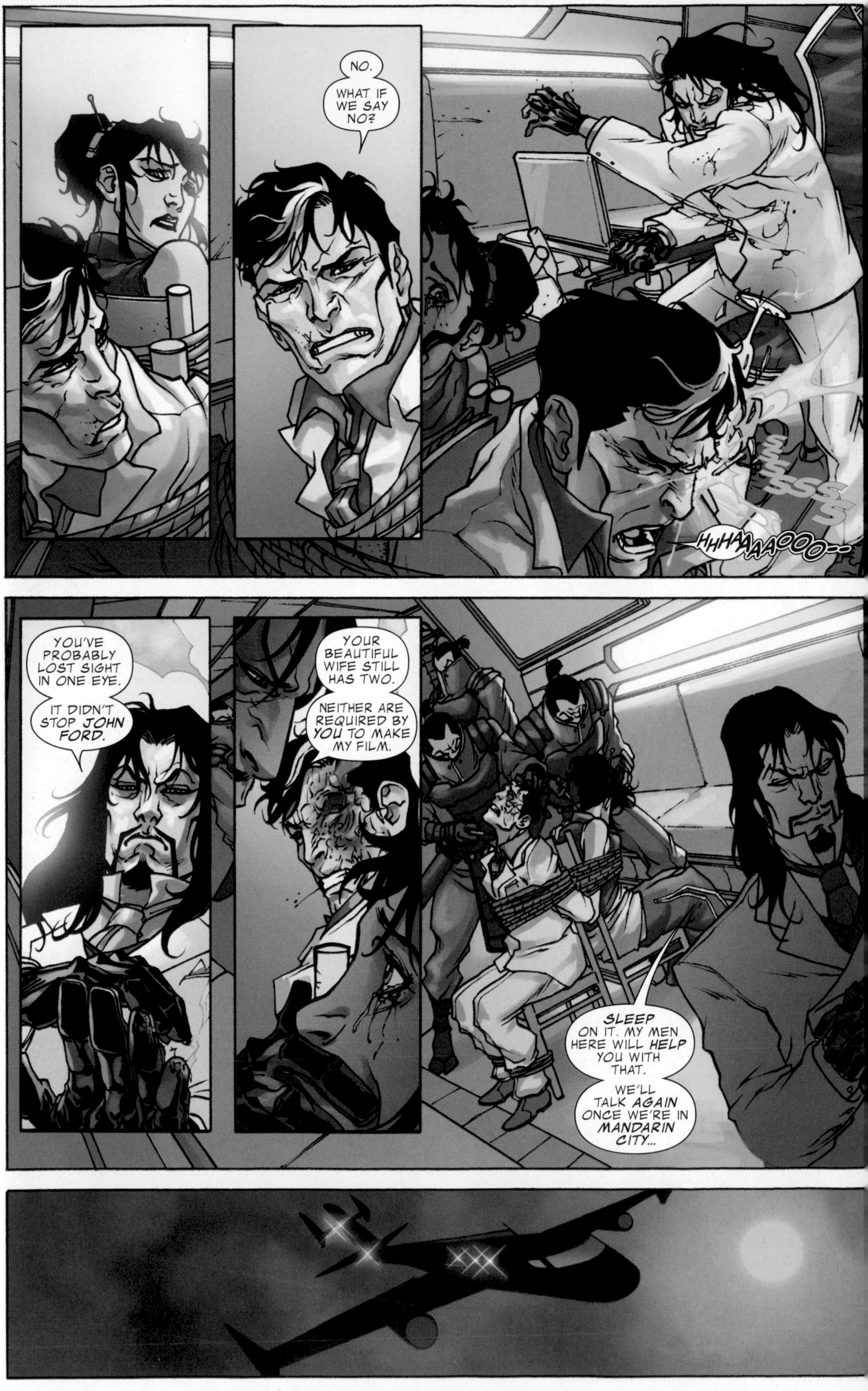
NO.
WHAT IF WE SAY NO?
SSSSSS
HHHAAAAOOO--
YOU'VE PROBABLY LOST SIGHT IN ONE EYE.
IT DIDN'T STOP JOHN FORD.
YOUR BEAUTIFUL WIFE STILL HAS TWO.
NEITHER ARE REQUIRED BY YOU TO MAKE MY FILM.
SLEEP ON IT. MY MEN HERE WILL HELP YOU WITH THAT.
WE'LL TALK AGAIN ONCE WE'RE IN MANDARIN CITY...

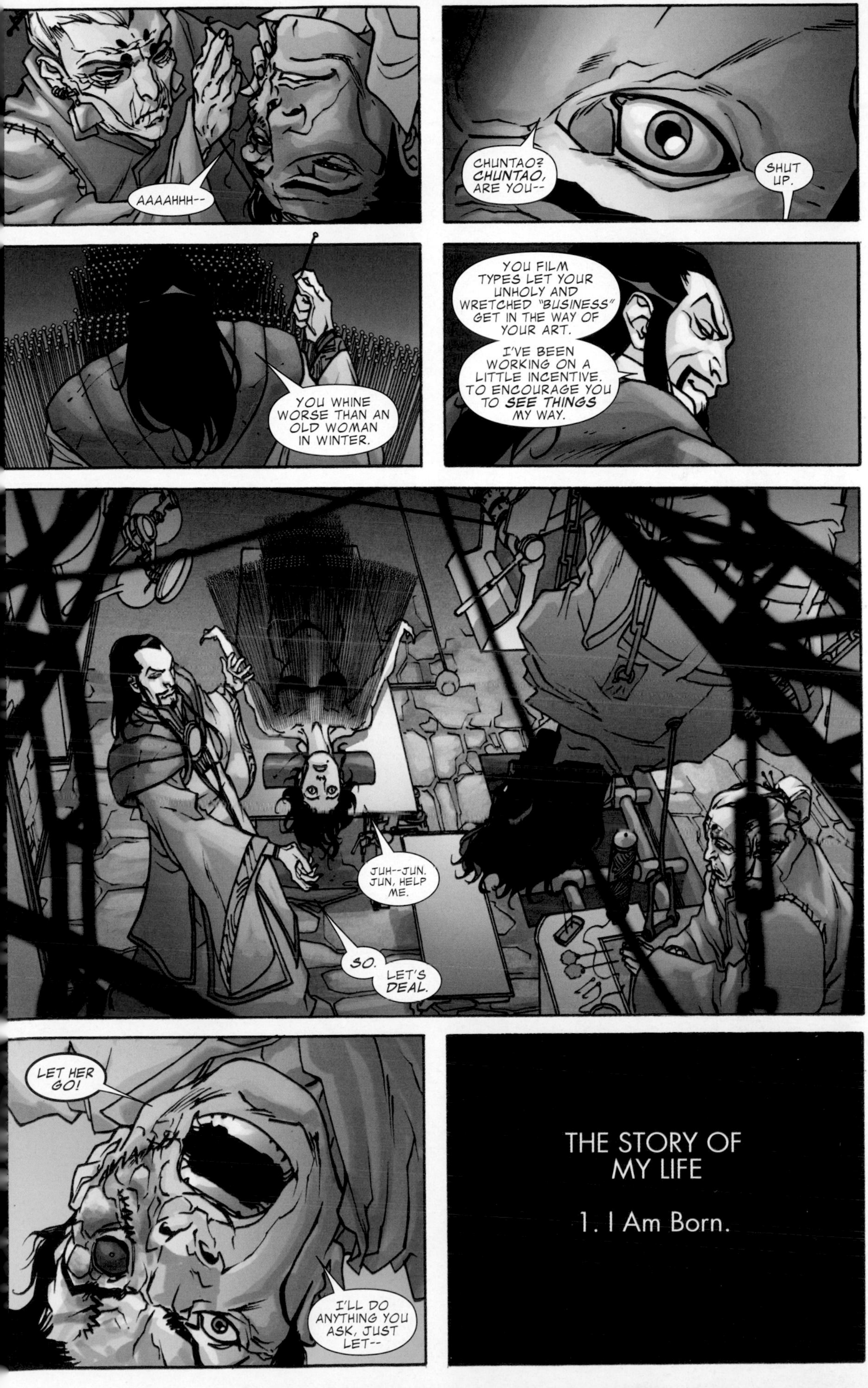

AAAAHHH--
CHUNTAO? CHUNTAO, ARE YOU--
SHUT UP.
YOU WHINE WORSE THAN AN OLD WOMAN IN WINTER.
YOU FILM TYPES LET YOUR UNHOLY AND WRETCHED "BUSINESS" GET IN THE WAY OF YOUR ART.
I'VE BEEN WORKING ON A LITTLE INCENTIVE. TO ENCOURAGE YOU TO SEE THINGS MY WAY.
JUH--JUN. JUN, HELP ME.
SO.
LET'S DEAL.
LET HER GO!
I'LL DO ANYTHING YOU ASK, JUST LET--
THE STORY OF MY LIFE
1. I Am Born.

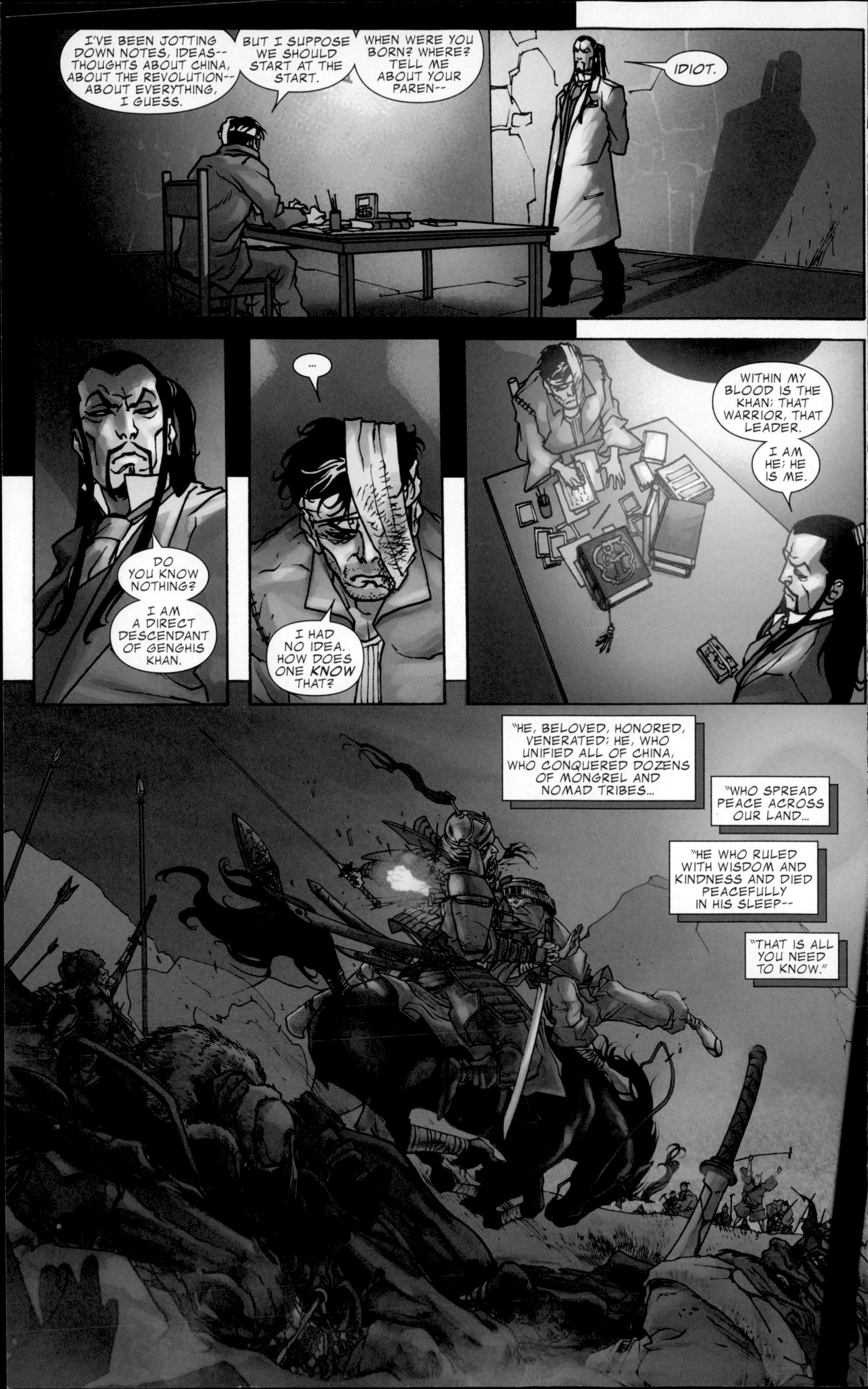
I'VE BEEN JOTTING DOWN NOTES, IDEAS-- THOUGHTS ABOUT CHINA, ABOUT THE REVOLUTION-- ABOUT EVERYTHING, I GUESS.
BUT I SUPPOSE WE SHOULD START AT THE START.
WHEN WERE YOU BORN? WHERE? TELL ME ABOUT YOUR PAREN--
IDIOT.
DO YOU KNOW NOTHING?
I AM A DIRECT DESCENDANT OF GENGHIS KHAN.
...
I HAD NO IDEA. HOW DOES ONE KNOW THAT?
WITHIN MY BLOOD IS THE KHAN; THAT WARRIOR, THAT LEADER.
I AM HE; HE IS ME.
"HE, BELOVED, HONORED, VENERATED; HE, WHO UNIFIED ALL OF CHINA, WHO CONQUERED DOZENS OF MONGREL AND NOMAD TRIBES...
"WHO SPREAD PEACE ACROSS OUR LAND...
"HE WHO RULED WITH WISDOM AND KINDNESS AND DIED PEACEFULLY IN HIS SLEEP--
"THAT IS ALL YOU NEED TO KNOW."

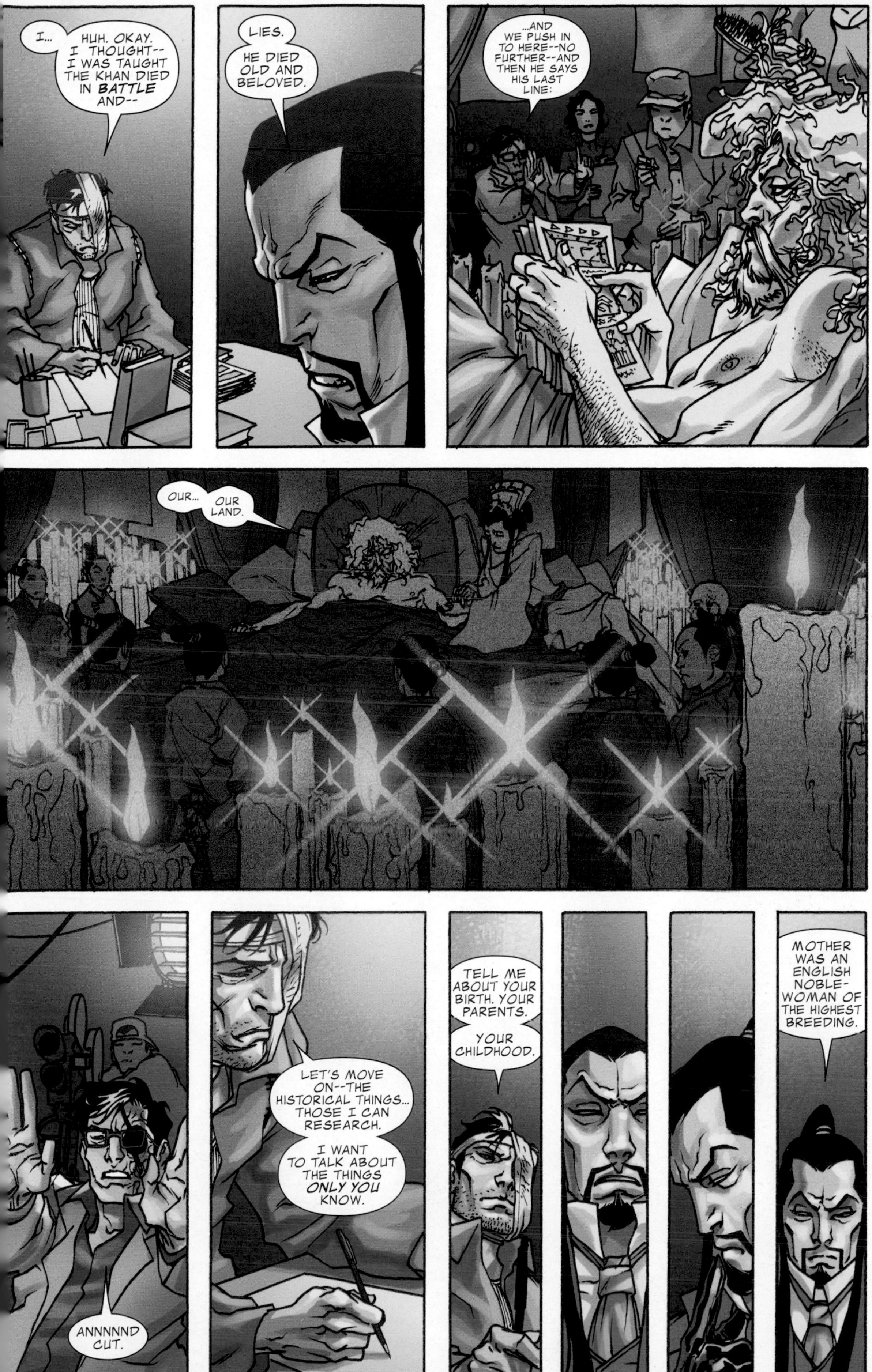
I...
HUH. OKAY. I THOUGHT-- I WAS TAUGHT THE KHAN DIED IN BATTLE AND--
LIES.
HE DIED OLD AND BELOVED.
...AND WE PUSH IN TO HERE--NO FURTHER--AND THEN HE SAYS HIS LAST LINE:
OUR... OUR LAND.
ANNNNND CUT.
LET'S MOVE ON--THE HISTORICAL THINGS... THOSE I CAN RESEARCH.
I WANT TO TALK ABOUT THE THINGS ONLY YOU KNOW.
TELL ME ABOUT YOUR BIRTH. YOUR PARENTS.
YOUR CHILDHOOD.
MOTHER WAS AN ENGLISH NOBLE-WOMAN OF THE HIGHEST BREEDING.

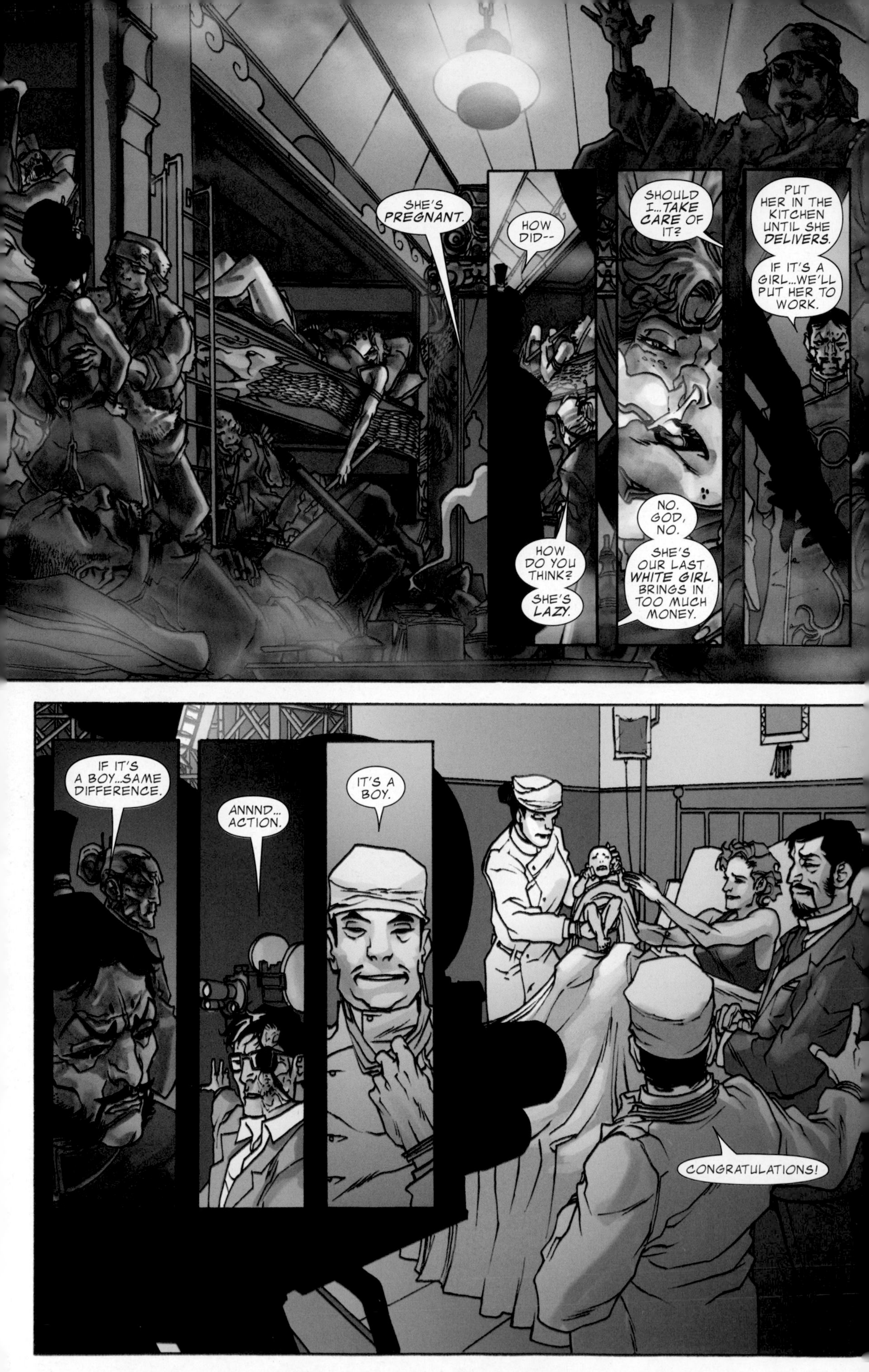
SHE'S PREGNANT.
HOW DID--
HOW DO YOU THINK?
SHE'S LAZY.
SHOULD I...TAKE CARE OF IT?
NO. GOD, NO.
SHE'S OUR LAST WHITE GIRL. BRINGS IN TOO MUCH MONEY.
PUT HER IN THE KITCHEN UNTIL SHE DELIVERS.
IF IT'S A GIRL...WE'LL PUT HER TO WORK.
IF IT'S A BOY...SAME DIFFERENCE.
ANNND... ACTION.
IT'S A BOY.
CONGRATULATIONS!

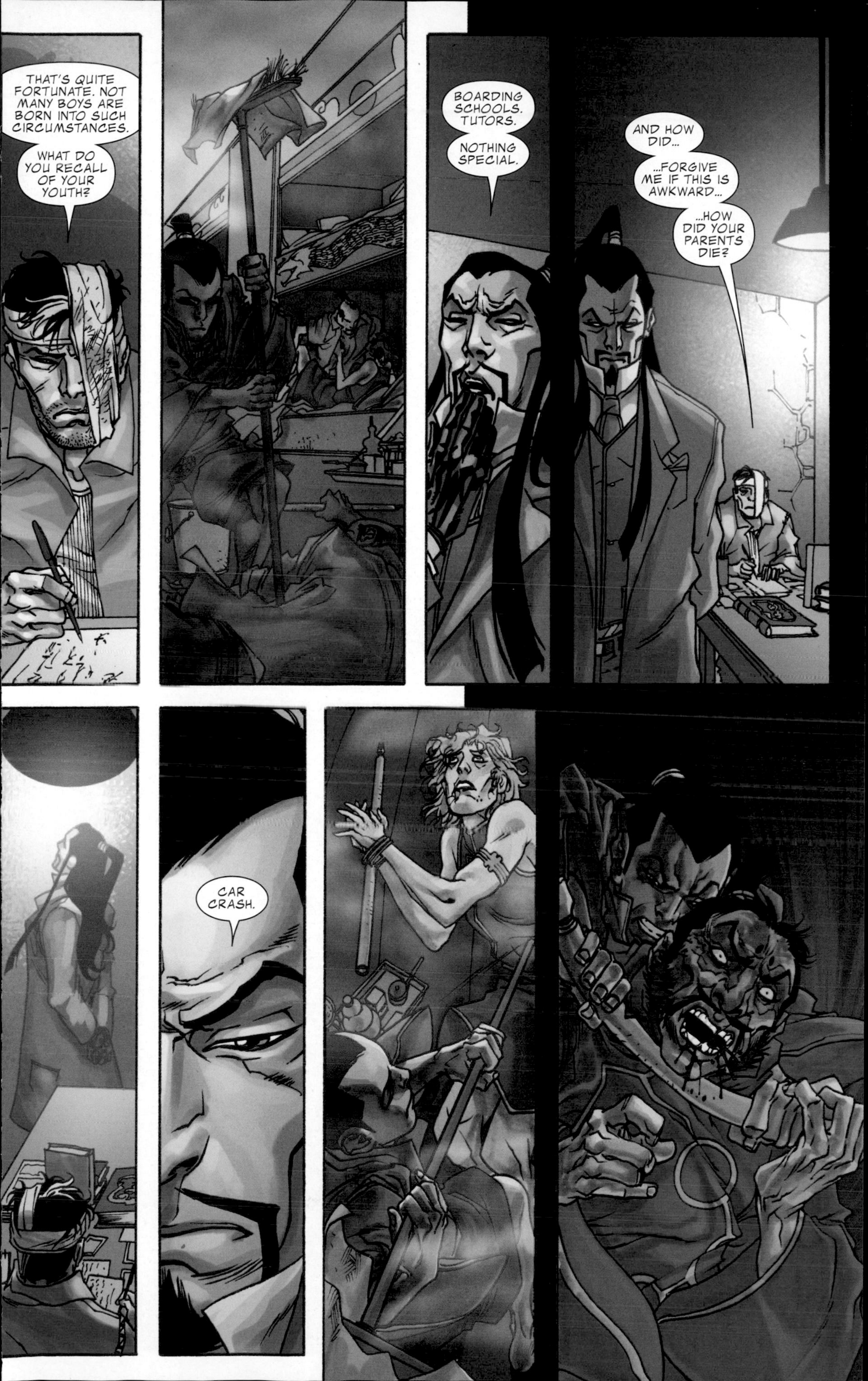
THAT'S QUITE FORTUNATE. NOT MANY BOYS ARE BORN INTO SUCH CIRCUMSTANCES.
WHAT DO YOU RECALL OF YOUR YOUTH?
BOARDING SCHOOLS. TUTORS.
NOTHING SPECIAL.
AND HOW DID...
...FORGIVE ME IF THIS IS AWKWARD...
...HOW DID YOUR PARENTS DIE?
CAR CRASH.

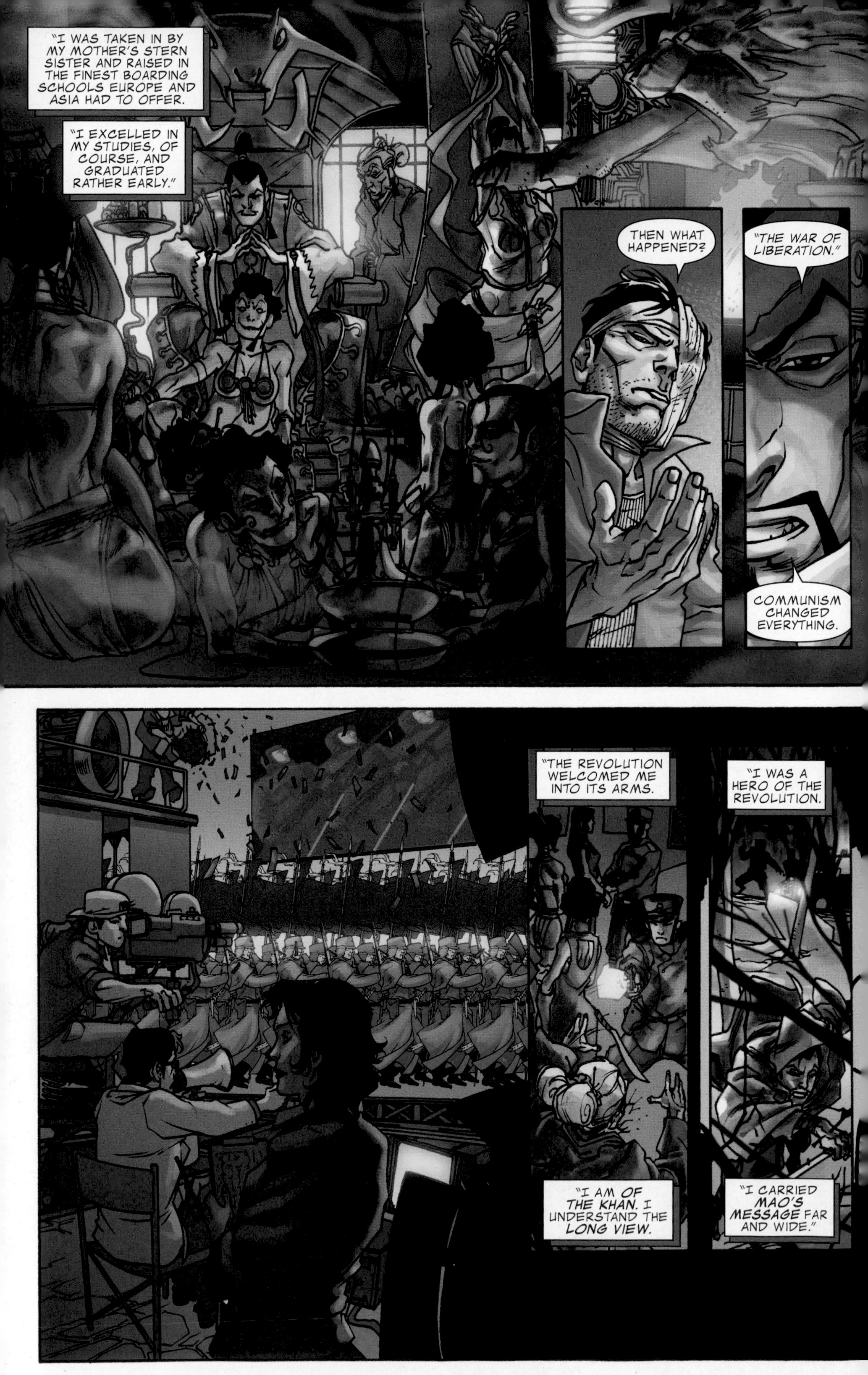
"I WAS TAKEN IN BY MY MOTHER'S STERN SISTER AND RAISED IN THE FINEST BOARDING SCHOOLS EUROPE AND ASIA HAD TO OFFER.
"I EXCELLED IN MY STUDIES, OF COURSE, AND GRADUATED RATHER EARLY."
THEN WHAT HAPPENED?
"THE WAR OF LIBERATION."
COMMUNISM CHANGED EVERYTHING.
"THE REVOLUTION WELCOMED ME INTO ITS ARMS.
"I AM OF THE KHAN. I UNDERSTAND THE LONG VIEW.
"I WAS A HERO OF THE REVOLUTION.
"I CARRIED MAO'S MESSAGE FAR AND WIDE."

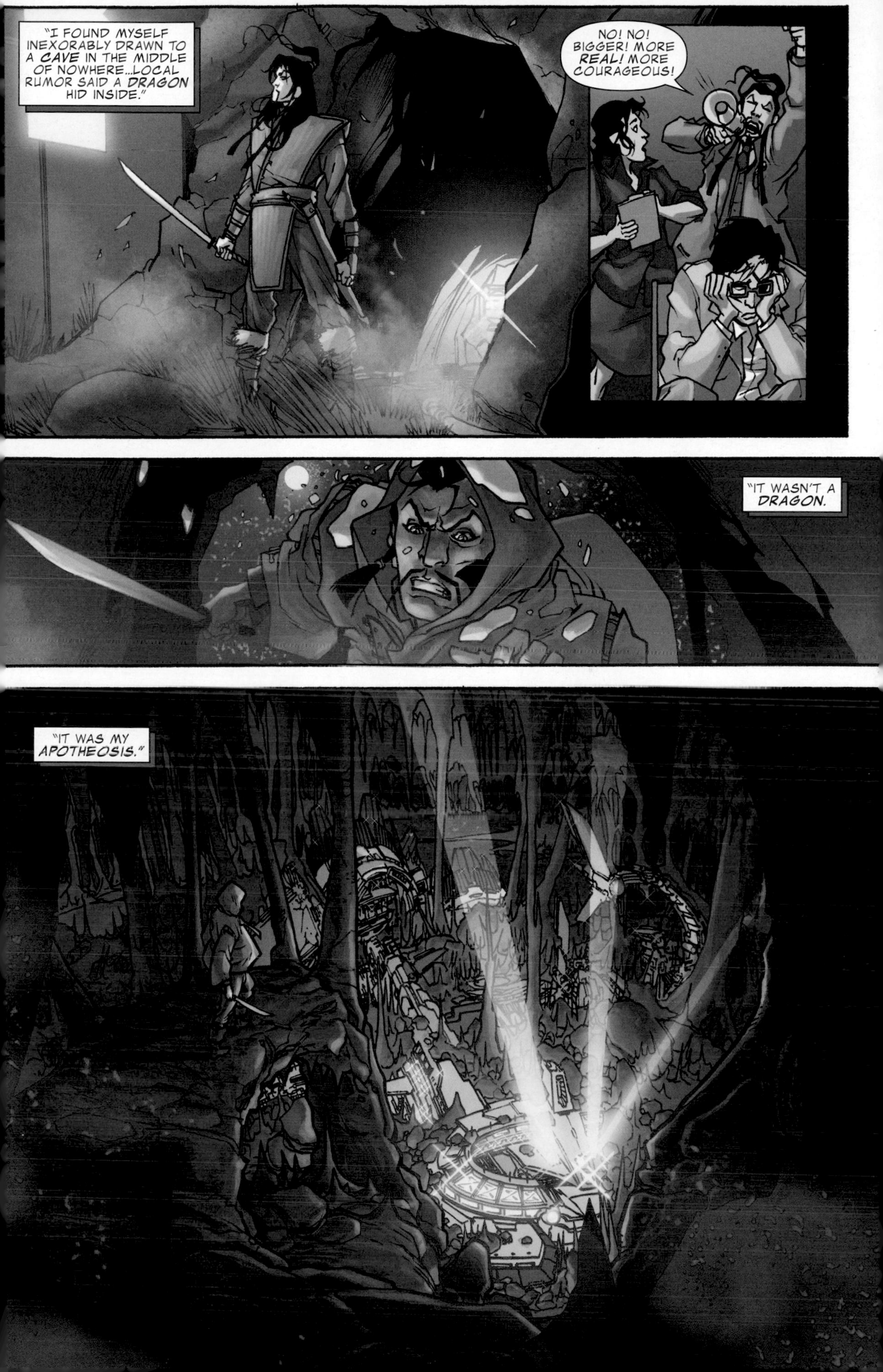
"I FOUND MYSELF INEXORABLY DRAWN TO A CAVE IN THE MIDDLE OF NOWHERE...LOCAL RUMOR SAID A DRAGON HID INSIDE."
NO! NO! BIGGER! MORE REAL! MORE COURAGEOUS!
"IT WASN'T A DRAGON.
"IT WAS MY APOTHEOSIS."

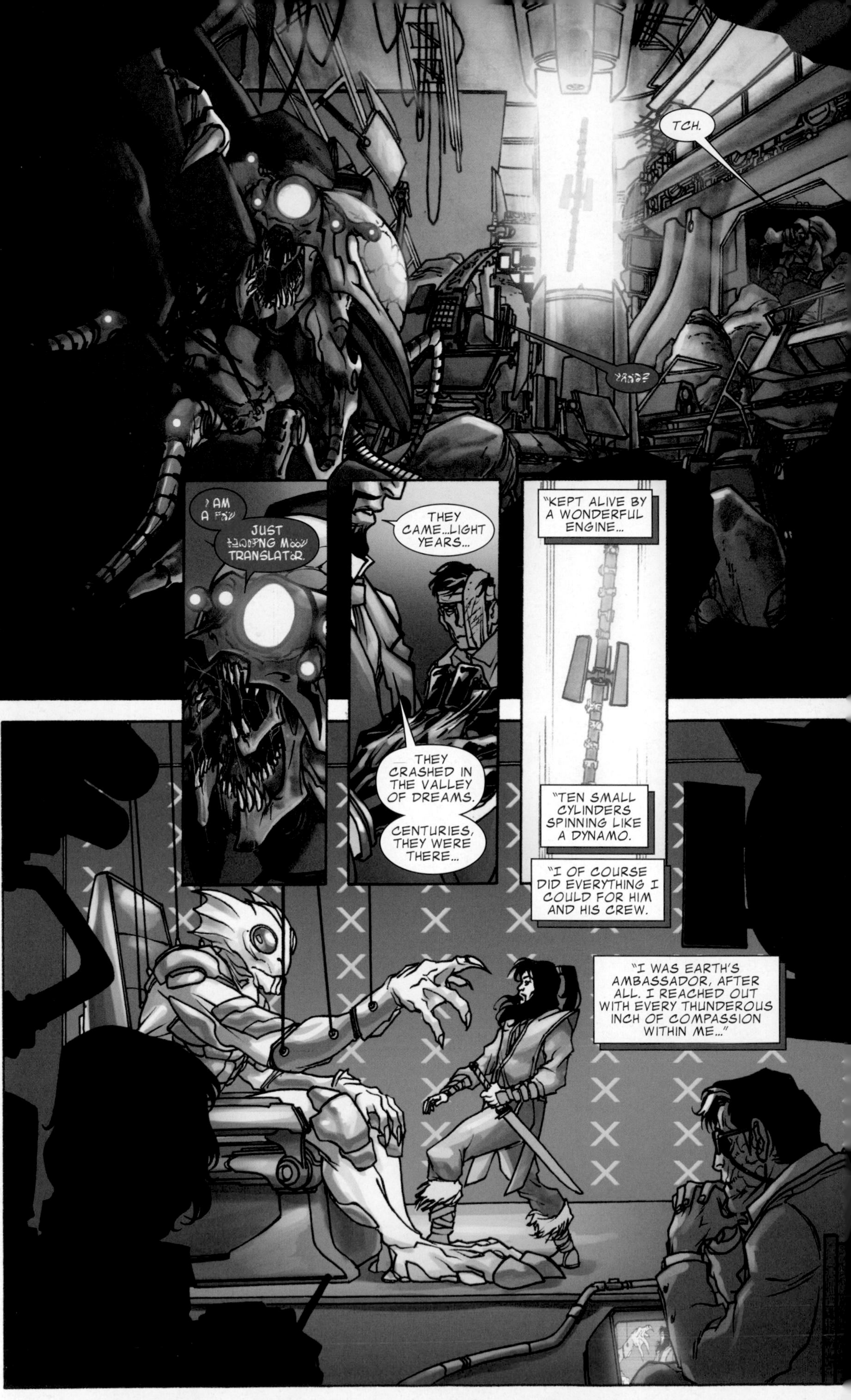
TCH.
AM A
JUST
TRANSLATOR.
THEY CAME...LIGHT YEARS...
THEY CRASHED IN THE VALLEY OF DREAMS.
CENTURIES, THEY WERE THERE...
"KEPT ALIVE BY A WONDERFUL ENGINE...
"TEN SMALL CYLINDERS SPINNING LIKE A DYNAMO.
"I OF COURSE DID EVERYTHING I COULD FOR HIM AND HIS CREW.
"I WAS EARTH'S AMBASSADOR, AFTER ALL. I REACHED OUT WITH EVERY THUNDEROUS INCH OF COMPASSION WITHIN ME..."

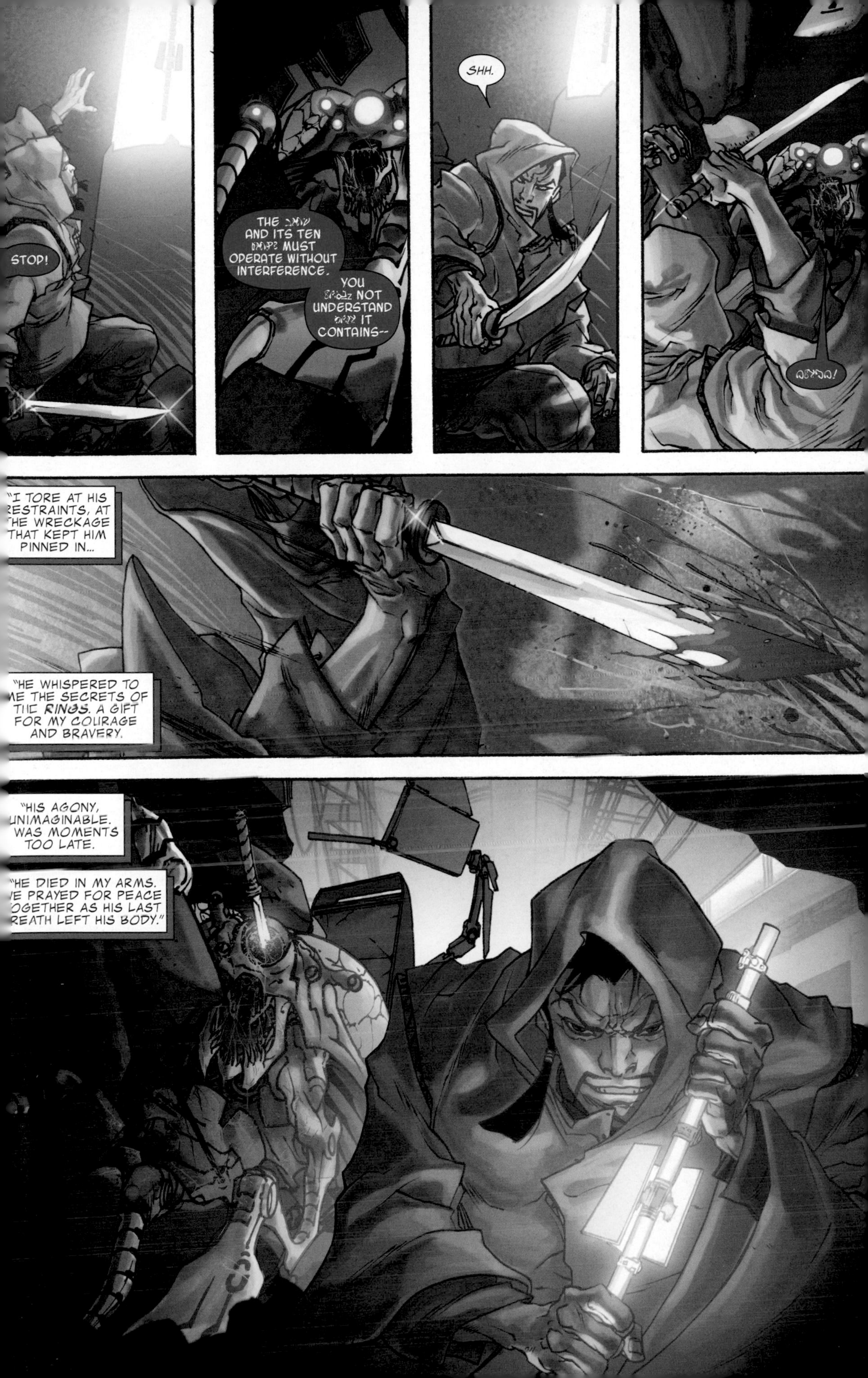
STOP!
THE [alien script] AND ITS TEN [alien script] MUST OPERATE WITHOUT INTERFERENCE.
YOU [alien script] NOT UNDERSTAND [alien script] IT CONTAINS--
SHH.
"I TORE AT HIS RESTRAINTS, AT THE WRECKAGE THAT KEPT HIM PINNED IN...
"HE WHISPERED TO ME THE SECRETS OF THE RINGS. A GIFT FOR MY COURAGE AND BRAVERY.
"HIS AGONY, UNIMAGINABLE. I WAS MOMENTS TOO LATE.
"HE DIED IN MY ARMS. WE PRAYED FOR PEACE TOGETHER AS HIS LAST BREATH LEFT HIS BODY."

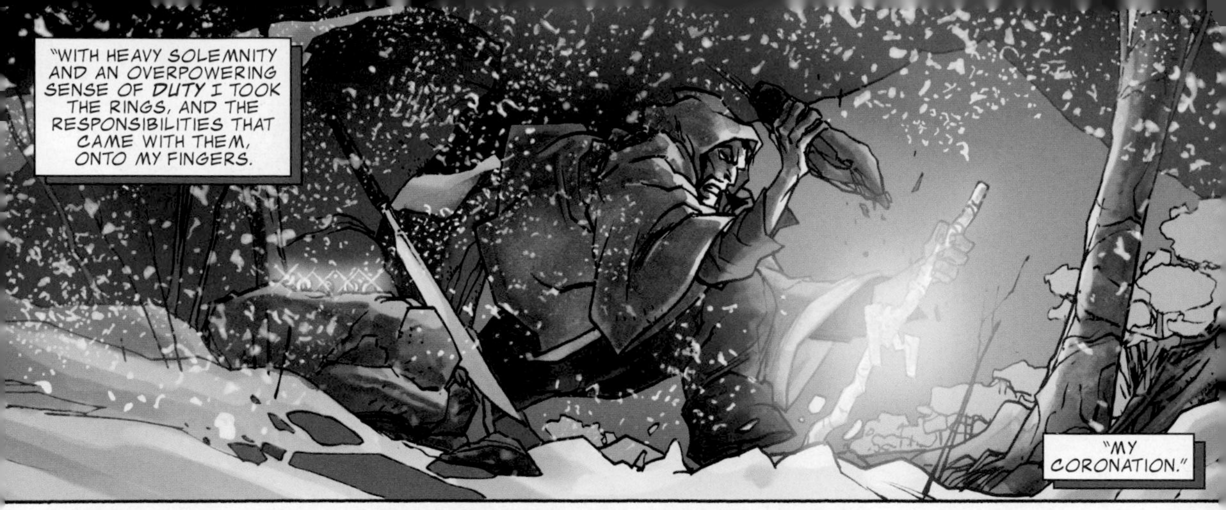
"WITH HEAVY SOLEMNITY AND AN OVERPOWERING SENSE OF DUTY I TOOK THE RINGS, AND THE RESPONSIBILITIES THAT CAME WITH THEM, ONTO MY FINGERS.
"MY CORONATION."

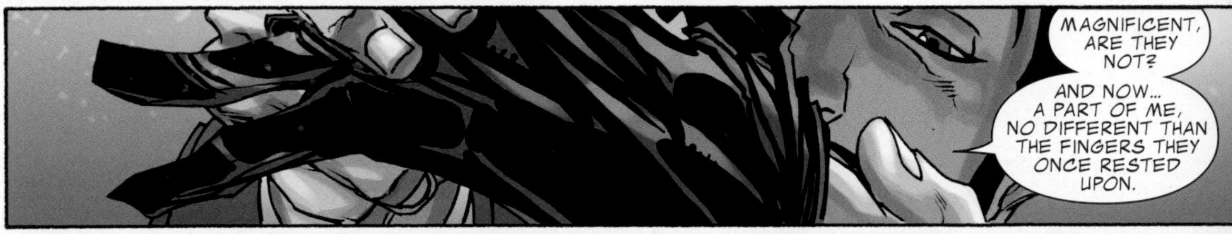
MAGNIFICENT, ARE THEY NOT?
AND NOW... A PART OF ME, NO DIFFERENT THAN THE FINGERS THEY ONCE RESTED UPON.

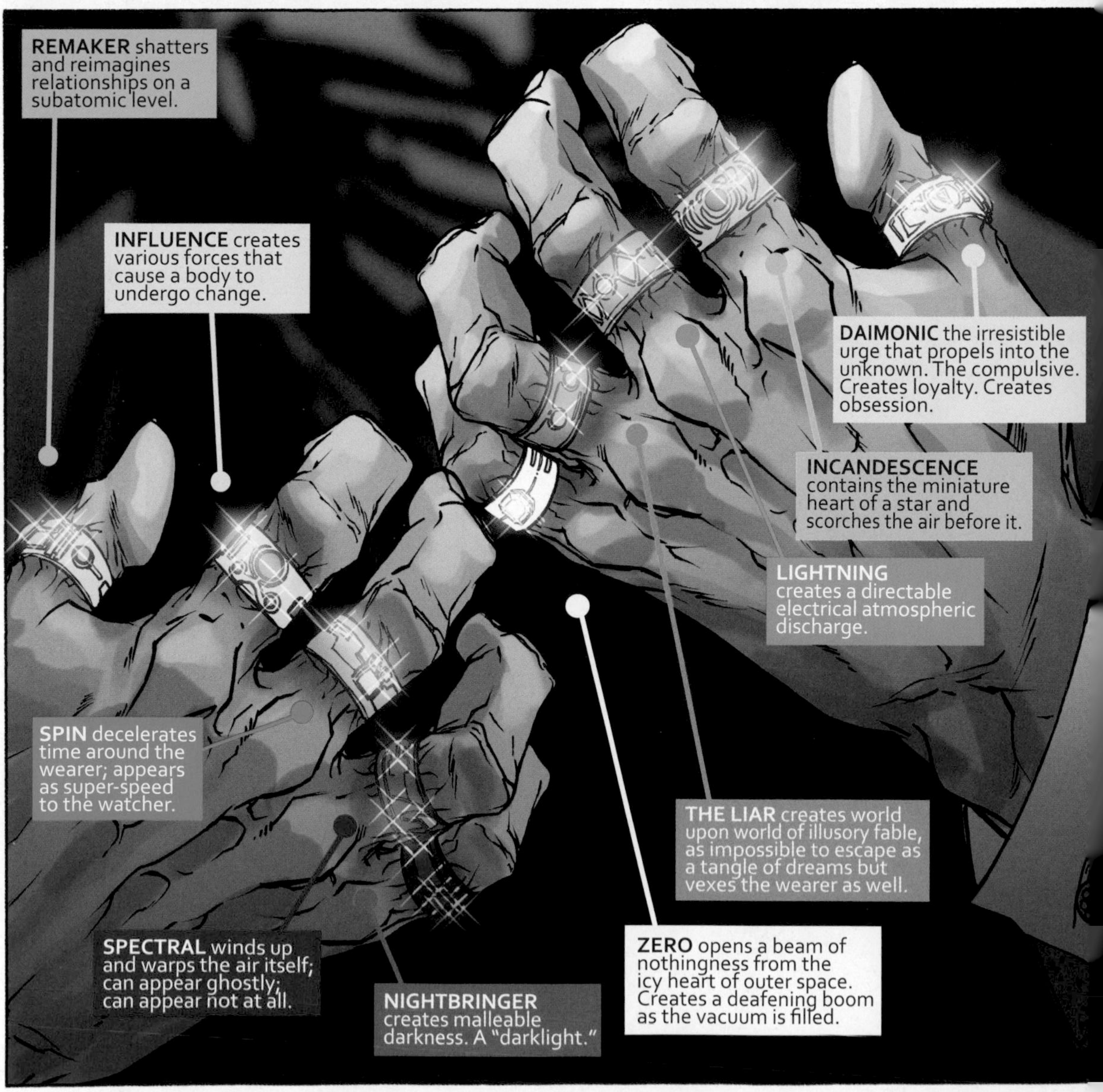
REMAKER shatters and reimagines relationships on a subatomic level.
INFLUENCE creates various forces that cause a body to undergo change.
DAIMONIC the irresistible urge that propels into the unknown. The compulsive. Creates loyalty. Creates obsession.
INCANDESCENCE contains the miniature heart of a star and scorches the air before it.
LIGHTNING creates a directable electrical atmospheric discharge.
SPIN decelerates time around the wearer; appears as super-speed to the watcher.
THE LIAR creates world upon world of illusory fable, as impossible to escape as a tangle of dreams but vexes the wearer as well.
SPECTRAL winds up and warps the air itself; can appear ghostly; can appear not at all.
NIGHTBRINGER creates malleable darkness. A "darklight."
ZERO opens a beam of nothingness from the icy heart of outer space. Creates a deafening boom as the vacuum is filled.

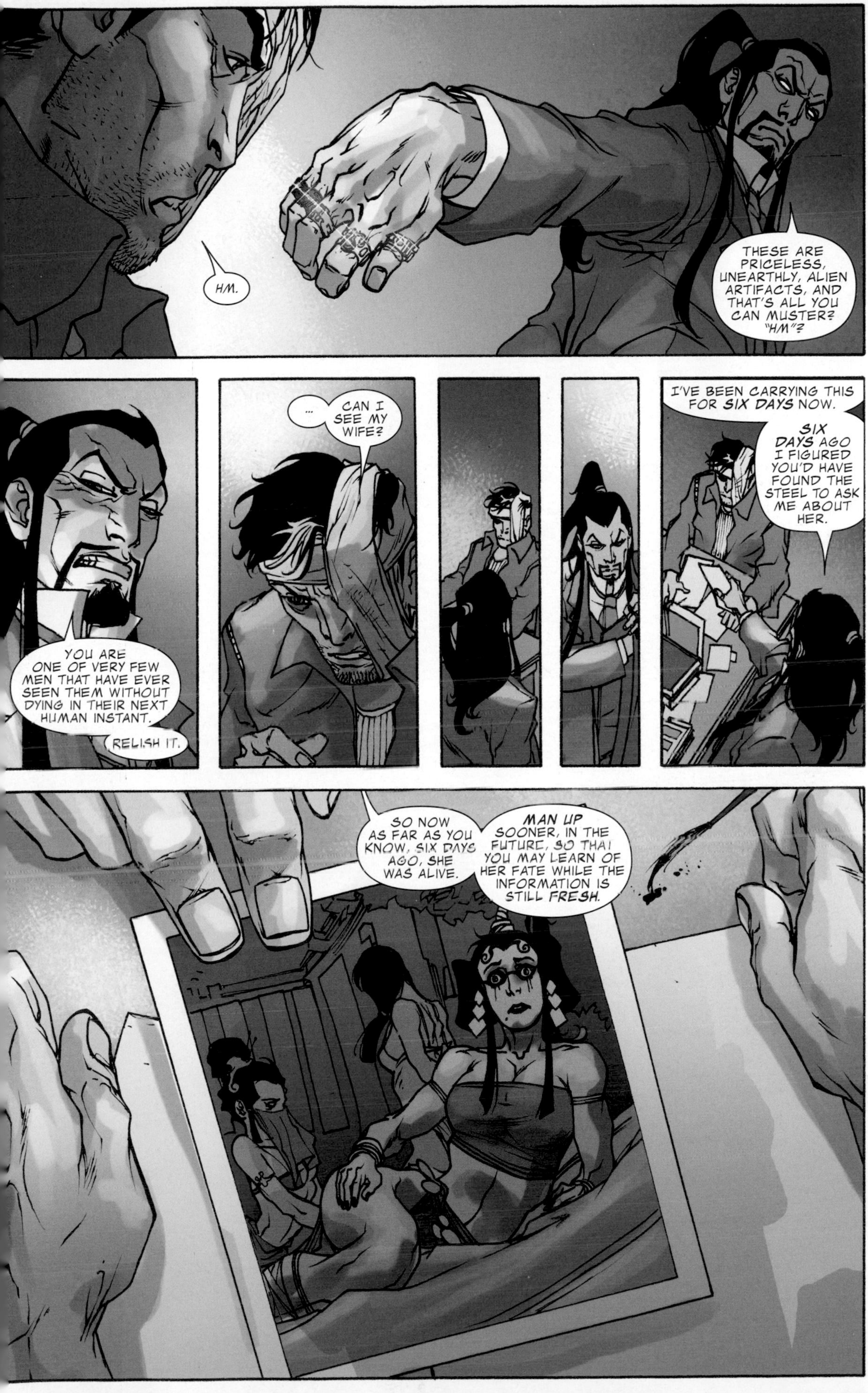
HM.
THESE ARE PRICELESS, UNEARTHLY, ALIEN ARTIFACTS, AND THAT'S ALL YOU CAN MUSTER? "HM"?
YOU ARE ONE OF VERY FEW MEN THAT HAVE EVER SEEN THEM WITHOUT DYING IN THEIR NEXT HUMAN INSTANT.
RELISH IT.
...
CAN I SEE MY WIFE?
I'VE BEEN CARRYING THIS FOR SIX DAYS NOW.
SIX DAYS AGO I FIGURED YOU'D HAVE FOUND THE STEEL TO ASK ME ABOUT HER.
SO NOW AS FAR AS YOU KNOW, SIX DAYS AGO, SHE WAS ALIVE.
MAN UP SOONER, IN THE FUTURE, SO THAT YOU MAY LEARN OF HER FATE WHILE THE INFORMATION IS STILL FRESH.

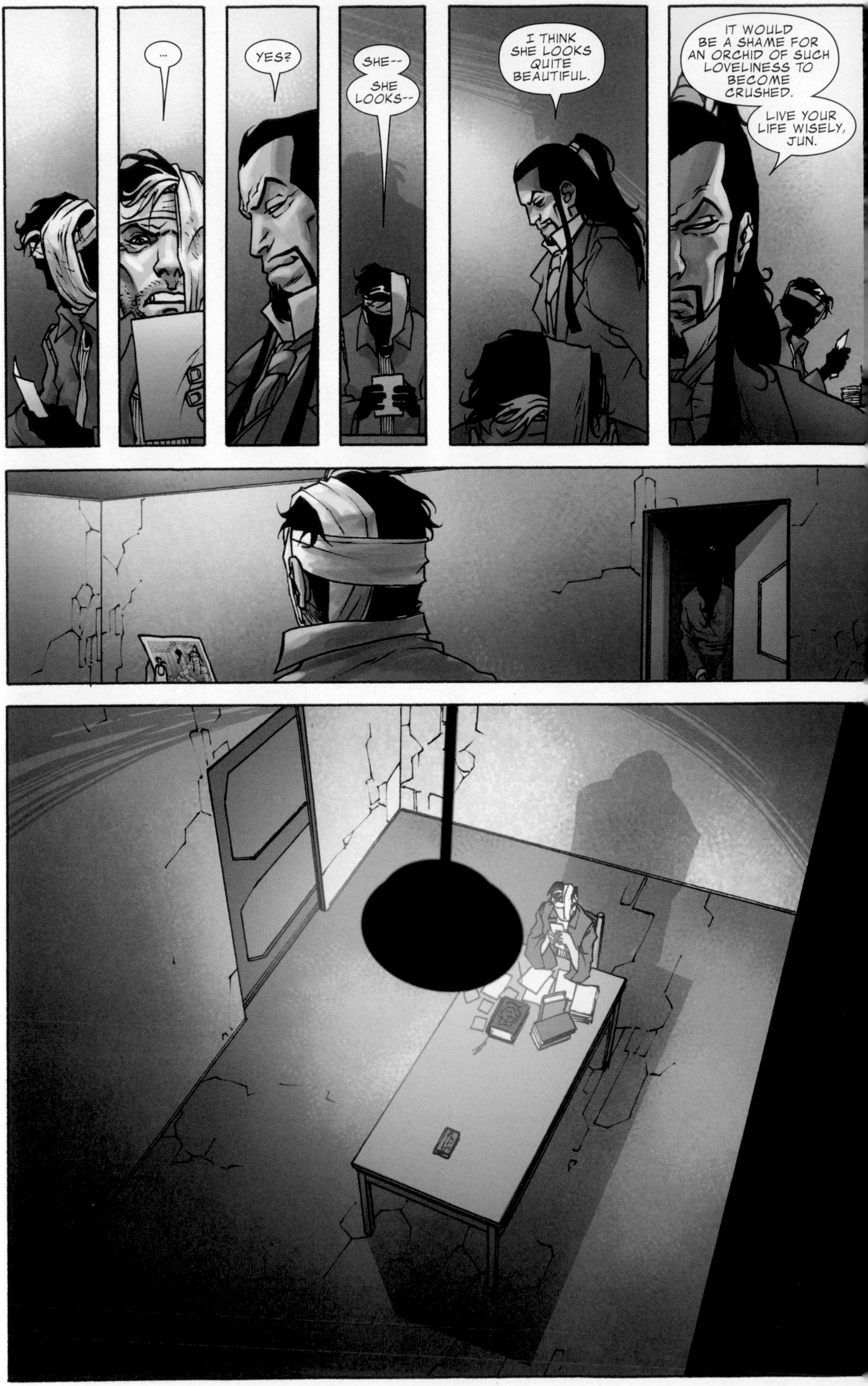
...
YES?
SHE--
SHE LOOKS--
I THINK SHE LOOKS QUITE BEAUTIFUL.
IT WOULD BE A SHAME FOR AN ORCHID OF SUCH LOVELINESS TO BECOME CRUSHED.
LIVE YOUR LIFE WISELY, JUN.

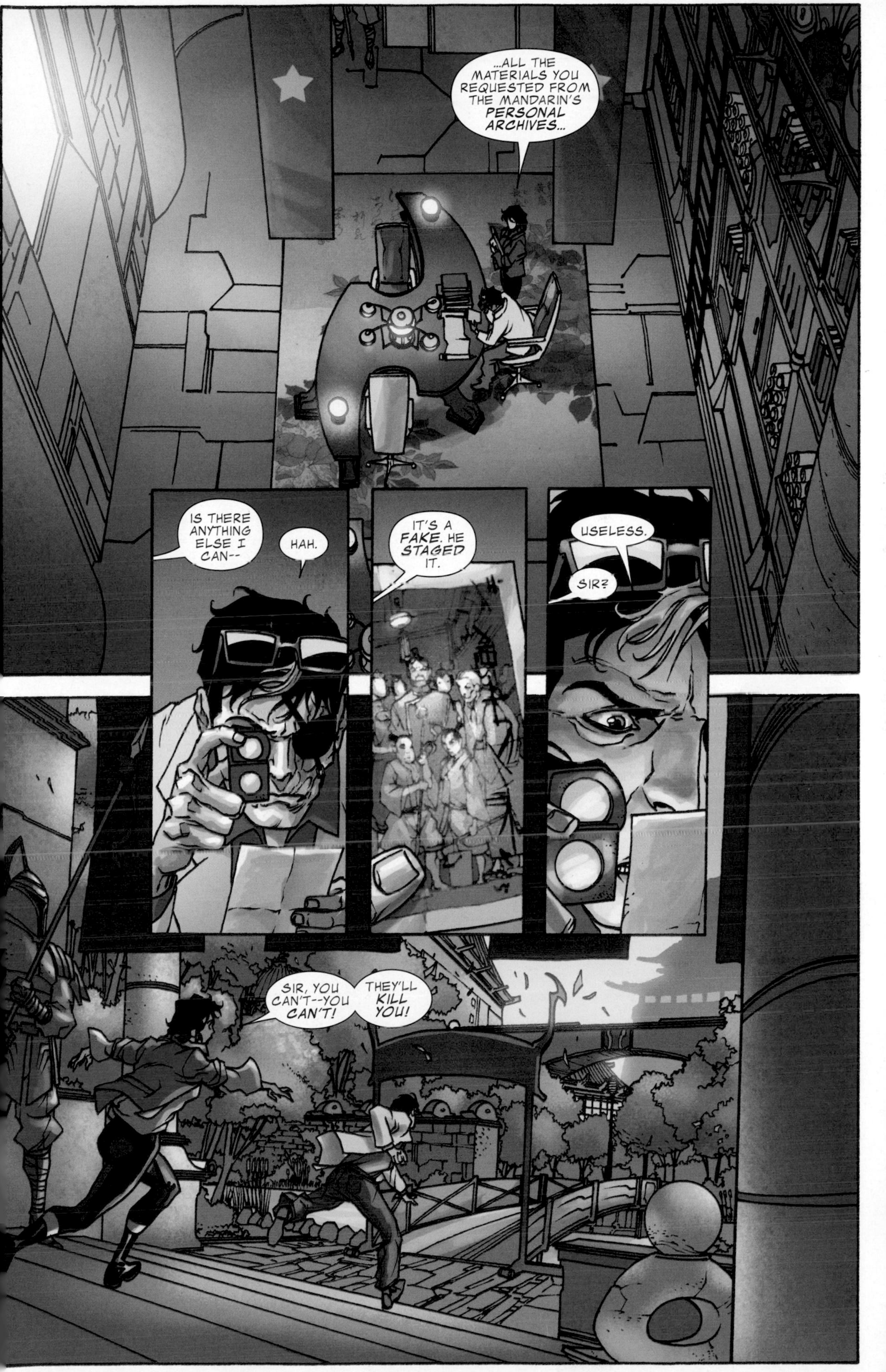
...ALL THE MATERIALS YOU REQUESTED FROM THE MANDARIN'S PERSONAL ARCHIVES...
IS THERE ANYTHING ELSE I CAN--
HAH.
IT'S A FAKE. HE STAGED IT.
USELESS.
SIR?
SIR, YOU CAN'T--YOU CAN'T!
THEY'LL KILL YOU!

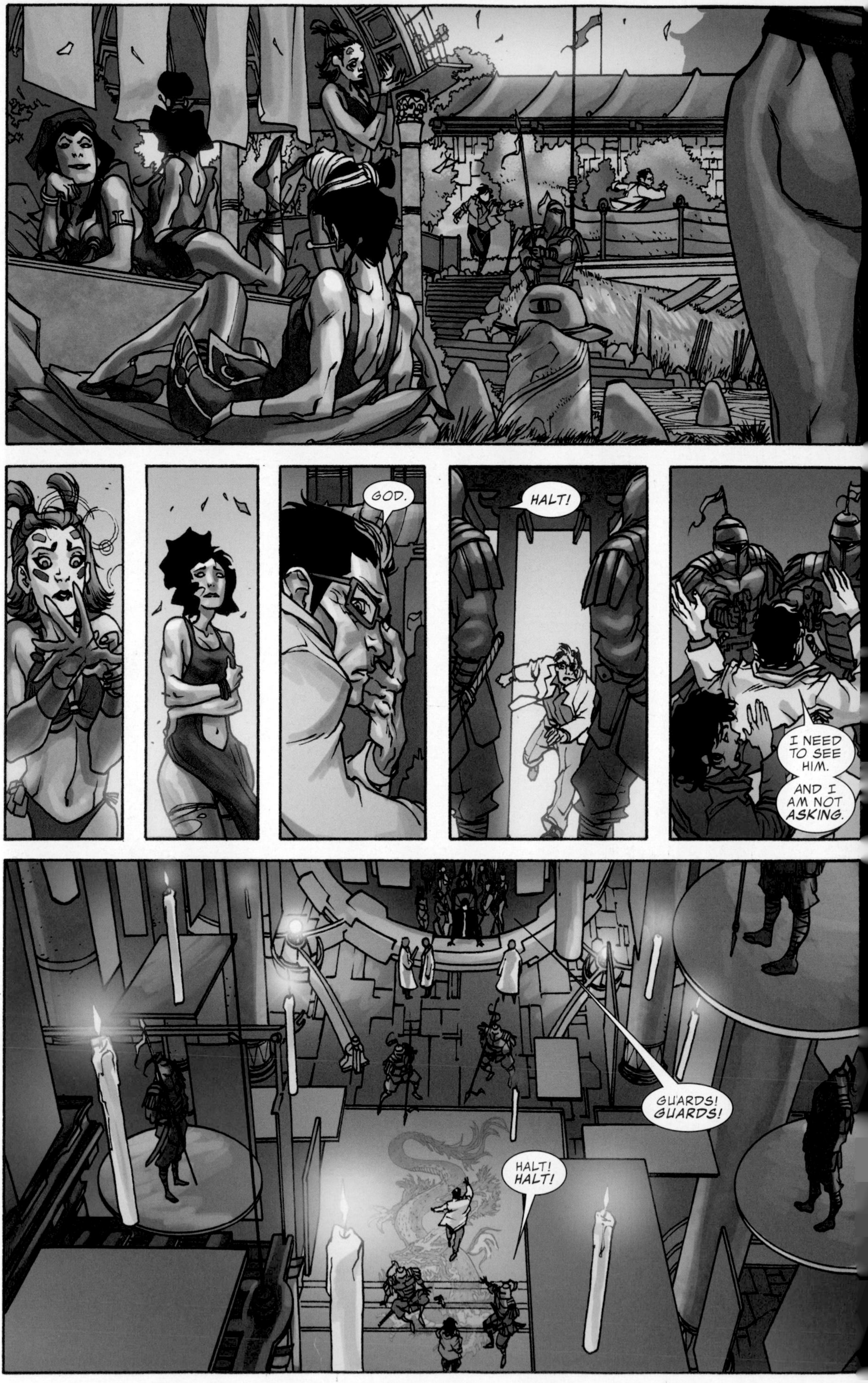
GOD.
HALT!
I NEED TO SEE HIM.
AND I AM NOT ASKING.
GUARDS! GUARDS!
HALT! HALT!

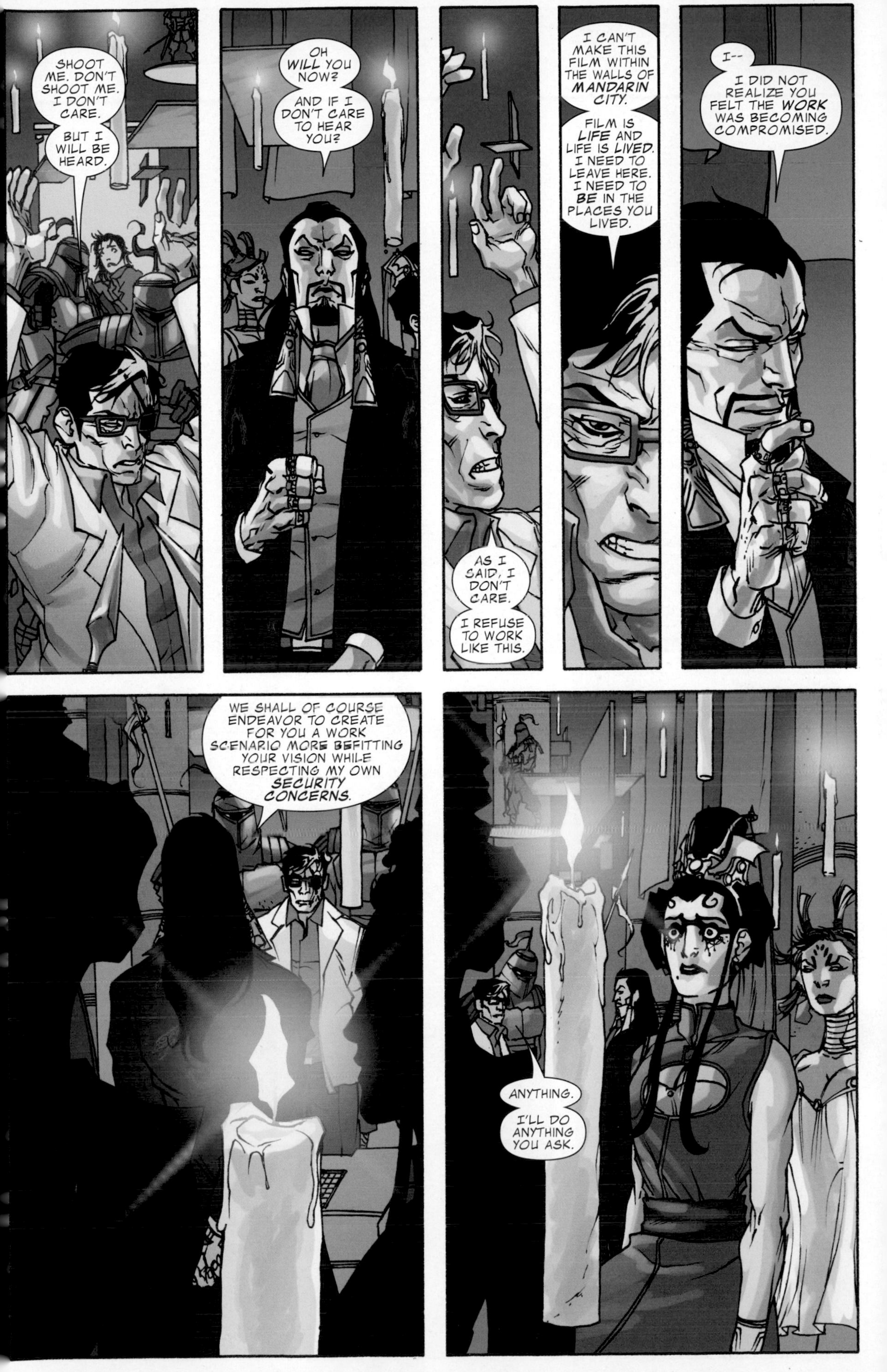
SHOOT ME. DON'T SHOOT ME. I DON'T CARE.
BUT I WILL BE HEARD.
OH WILL YOU NOW?
AND IF I DON'T CARE TO HEAR YOU?
I CAN'T MAKE THIS FILM WITHIN THE WALLS OF MANDARIN CITY.
FILM IS LIFE AND LIFE IS LIVED. I NEED TO LEAVE HERE. I NEED TO BE IN THE PLACES YOU LIVED.
AS I SAID, I DON'T CARE.
I REFUSE TO WORK LIKE THIS.
I--
I DID NOT REALIZE YOU FELT THE WORK WAS BECOMING COMPROMISED.
WE SHALL OF COURSE ENDEAVOR TO CREATE FOR YOU A WORK SCENARIO MORE BEFITTING YOUR VISION WHILE RESPECTING MY OWN SECURITY CONCERNS.
ANYTHING.
I'LL DO ANYTHING YOU ASK.

THE ASSISTANT STAYS. YOU GO.

WHOOP--

THREE HOURS.

OR WE SELL YOUR LITTLE HELPER GIRL AND KILL EVERYONE IN THE VILLAGE...

GOD.

JUN, WHAT HAVE YOU GOTTEN YOURSELF INTO...

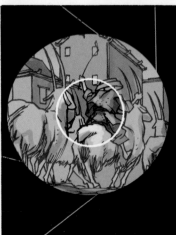

SO YOU REMEMBER HIM?

HOW COULD YOU FORGET THE HOMETOWN MONSTER THAT SLAUGHTERED YOUR FAMILY?

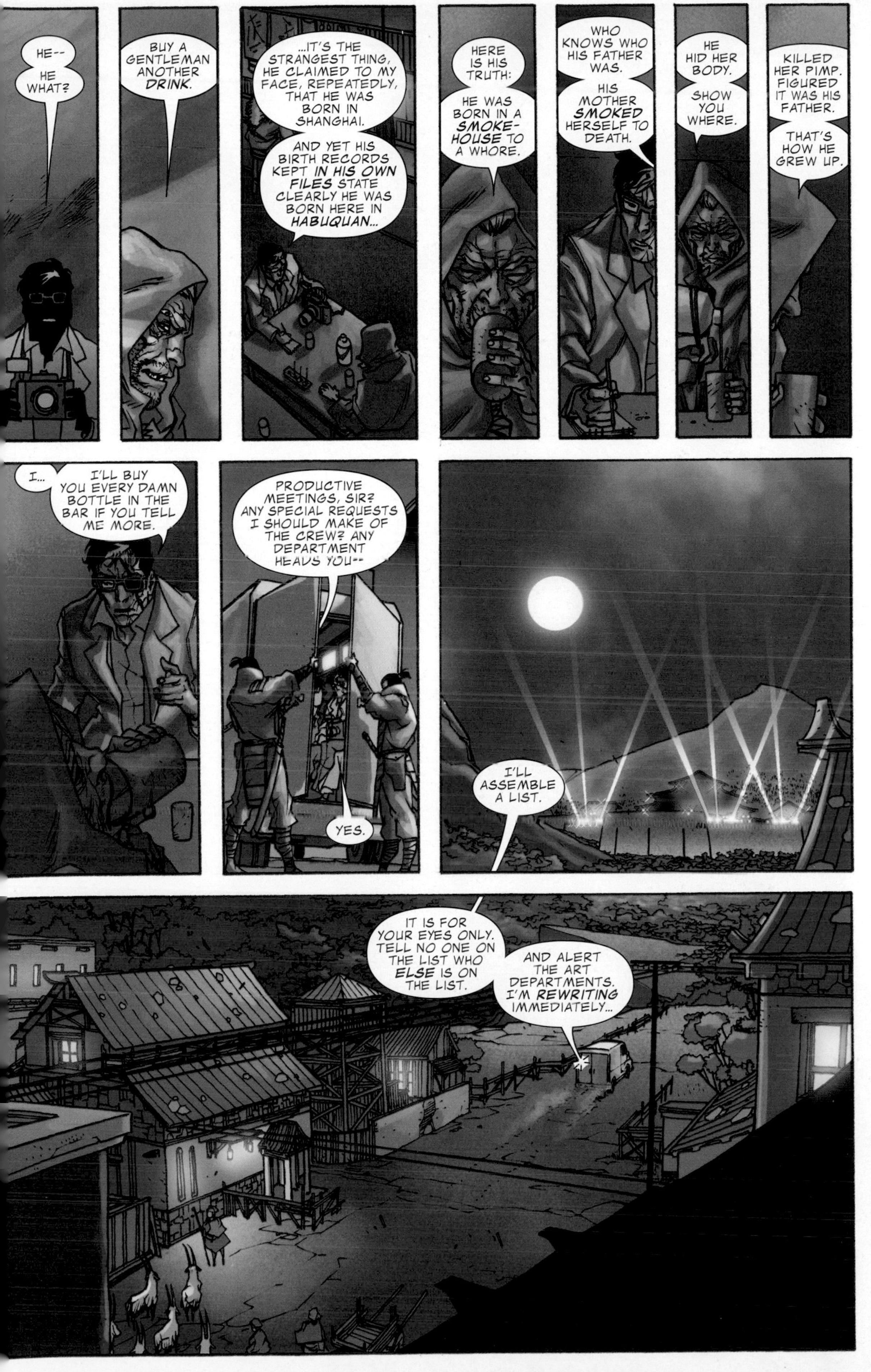
HE--
HE WHAT?
BUY A GENTLEMAN ANOTHER DRINK.
...IT'S THE STRANGEST THING, HE CLAIMED TO MY FACE, REPEATEDLY, THAT HE WAS BORN IN SHANGHAI.
AND YET HIS BIRTH RECORDS KEPT IN HIS OWN FILES STATE CLEARLY HE WAS BORN HERE IN HABUQUAN...
HERE IS HIS TRUTH:
HE WAS BORN IN A SMOKE-HOUSE TO A WHORE.
WHO KNOWS WHO HIS FATHER WAS.
HIS MOTHER SMOKED HERSELF TO DEATH.
HE HID HER BODY.
SHOW YOU WHERE.
KILLED HER PIMP. FIGURED IT WAS HIS FATHER.
THAT'S HOW HE GREW UP.
I...
I'LL BUY YOU EVERY DAMN BOTTLE IN THE BAR IF YOU TELL ME MORE.
PRODUCTIVE MEETINGS, SIR? ANY SPECIAL REQUESTS I SHOULD MAKE OF THE CREW? ANY DEPARTMENT HEADS YOU--
YES.
I'LL ASSEMBLE A LIST.
IT IS FOR YOUR EYES ONLY. TELL NO ONE ON THE LIST WHO ELSE IS ON THE LIST.
AND ALERT THE ART DEPARTMENTS. I'M REWRITING IMMEDIATELY...

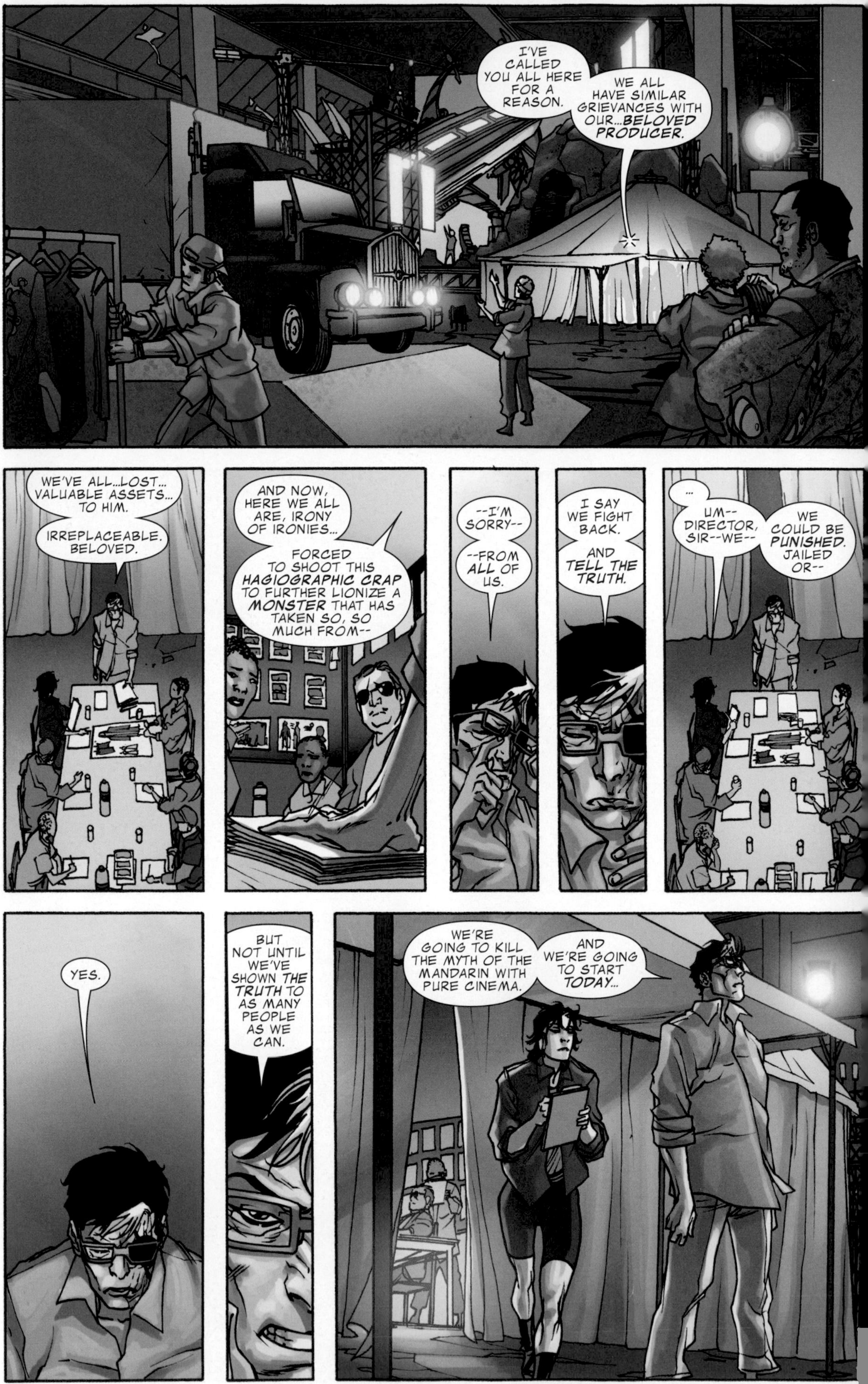
I'VE CALLED YOU ALL HERE FOR A REASON.
WE ALL HAVE SIMILAR GRIEVANCES WITH OUR...BELOVED PRODUCER.
WE'VE ALL...LOST... VALUABLE ASSETS... TO HIM.
IRREPLACEABLE. BELOVED.
AND NOW, HERE WE ALL ARE, IRONY OF IRONIES...
FORCED TO SHOOT THIS HAGIOGRAPHIC CRAP TO FURTHER LIONIZE A MONSTER THAT HAS TAKEN SO, SO MUCH FROM--
--I'M SORRY--
--FROM ALL OF US.
I SAY WE FIGHT BACK.
AND TELL THE TRUTH.
...
UM--DIRECTOR, SIR--WE--
WE COULD BE PUNISHED. JAILED OR--
YES.
BUT NOT UNTIL WE'VE SHOWN THE TRUTH TO AS MANY PEOPLE AS WE CAN.
WE'RE GOING TO KILL THE MYTH OF THE MANDARIN WITH PURE CINEMA.
AND WE'RE GOING TO START TODAY...

2. I Rise.

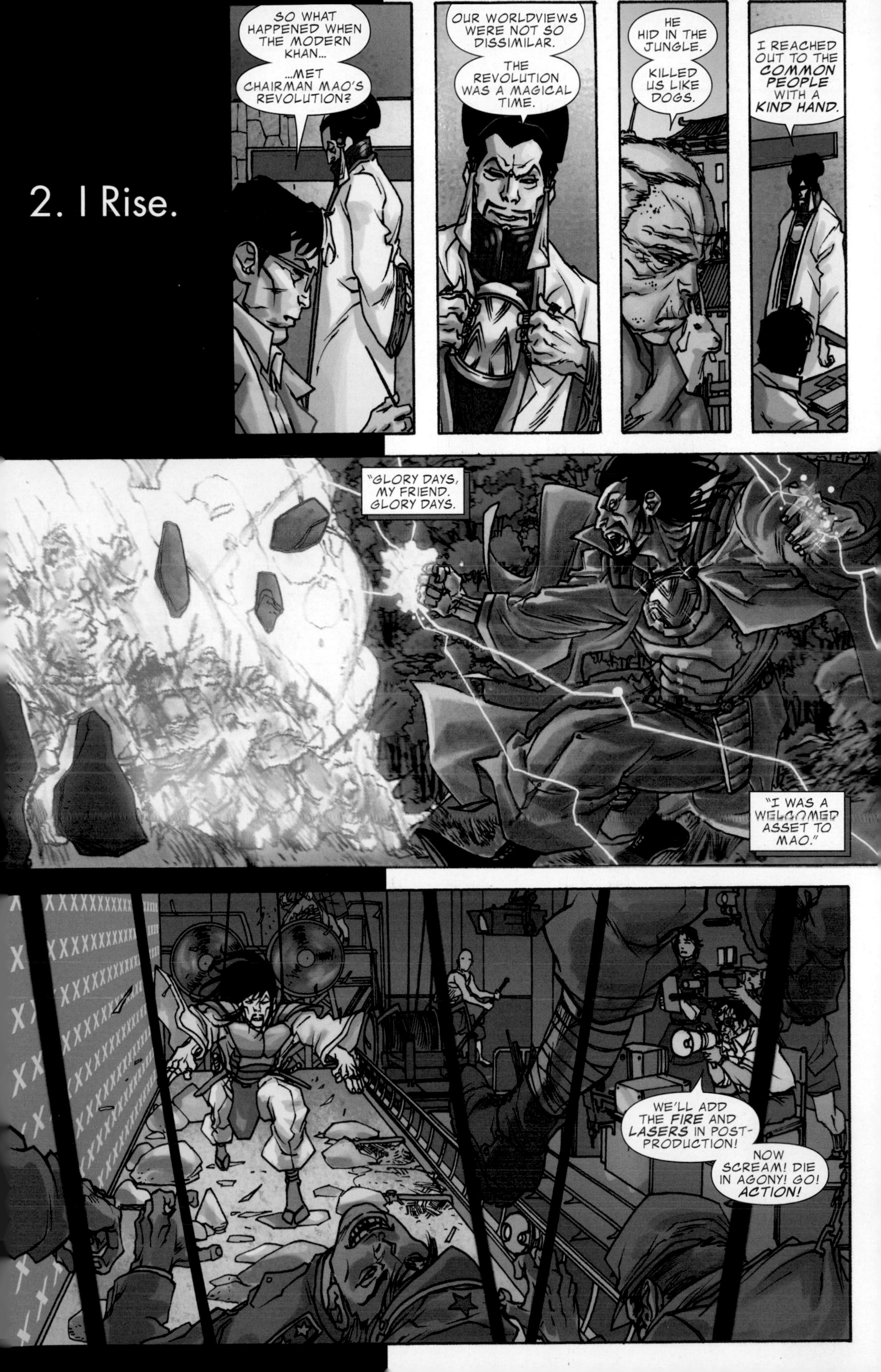
SO WHAT HAPPENED WHEN THE MODERN KHAN...
...MET CHAIRMAN MAO'S REVOLUTION?
OUR WORLDVIEWS WERE NOT SO DISSIMILAR.
THE REVOLUTION WAS A MAGICAL TIME.
HE HID IN THE JUNGLE.
KILLED US LIKE DOGS.
I REACHED OUT TO THE COMMON PEOPLE WITH A KIND HAND.
"GLORY DAYS, MY FRIEND. GLORY DAYS.
"I WAS A WELCOMED ASSET TO MAO."
WE'LL ADD THE FIRE AND LASERS IN POST-PRODUCTION!
NOW SCREAM! DIE IN AGONY! GO! ACTION!

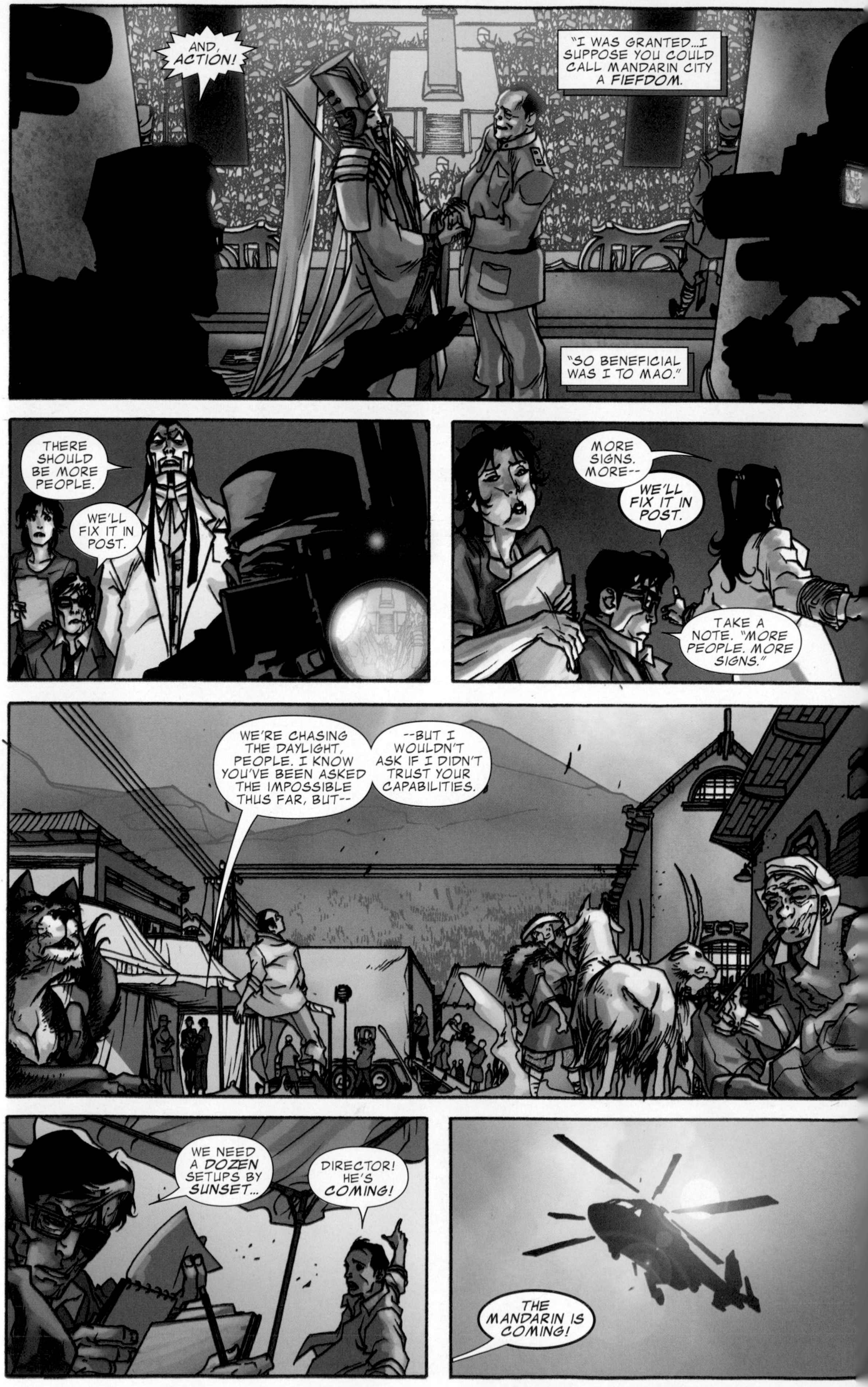
AND, ACTION!
"I WAS GRANTED...I SUPPOSE YOU COULD CALL MANDARIN CITY A FIEFDOM.
"SO BENEFICIAL WAS I TO MAO."
THERE SHOULD BE MORE PEOPLE.
WE'LL FIX IT IN POST.
MORE SIGNS. MORE--
WE'LL FIX IT IN POST.
TAKE A NOTE. "MORE PEOPLE. MORE SIGNS."
WE'RE CHASING THE DAYLIGHT, PEOPLE. I KNOW YOU'VE BEEN ASKED THE IMPOSSIBLE THUS FAR, BUT--
--BUT I WOULDN'T ASK IF I DIDN'T TRUST YOUR CAPABILITIES.
WE NEED A DOZEN SETUPS BY SUNSET...
DIRECTOR! HE'S COMING!
THE MANDARIN IS COMING!

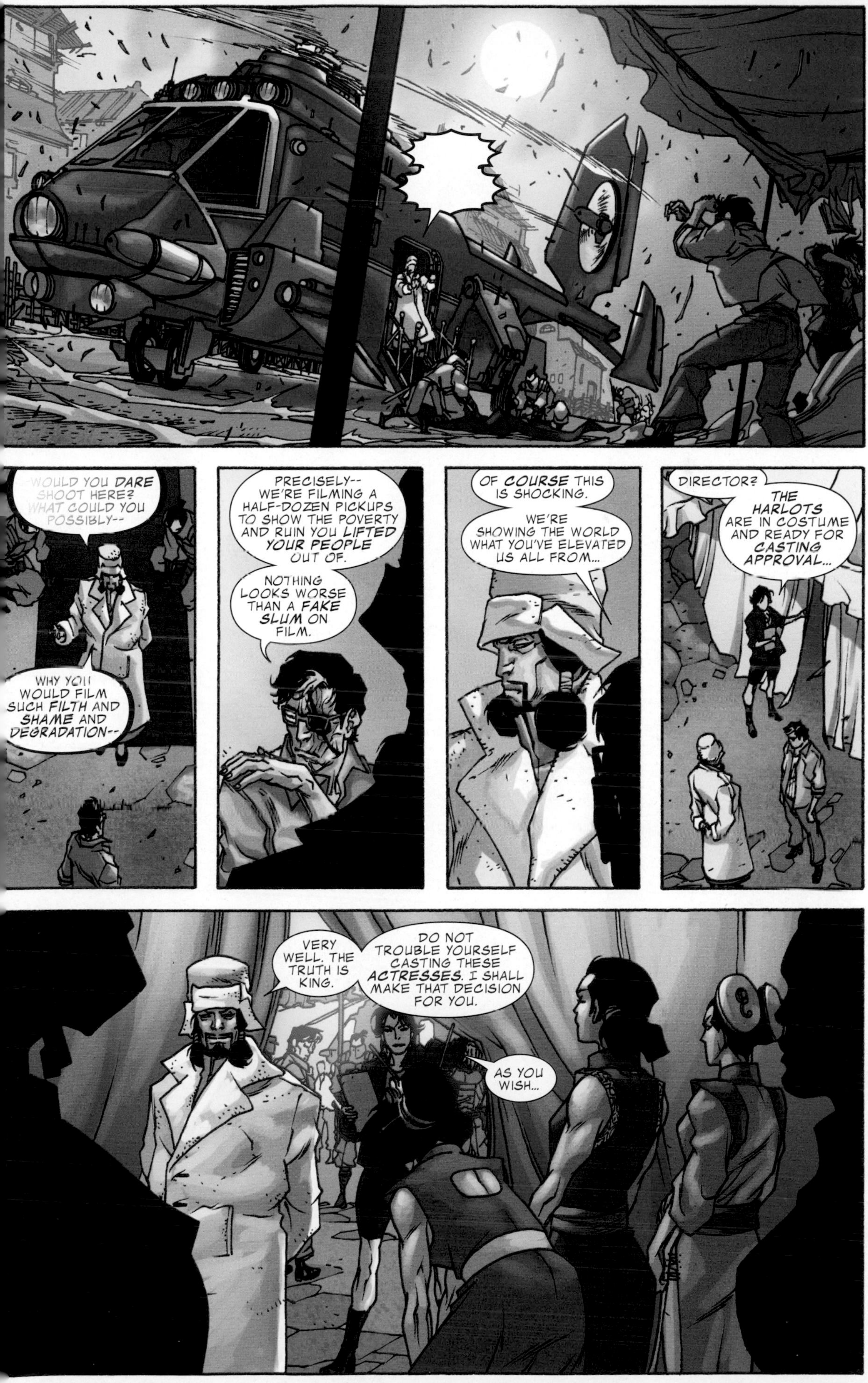
--WOULD YOU DARE SHOOT HERE? WHAT COULD YOU POSSIBLY--
WHY YOU WOULD FILM SUCH FILTH AND SHAME AND DEGRADATION--
PRECISELY-- WE'RE FILMING A HALF-DOZEN PICKUPS TO SHOW THE POVERTY AND RUIN YOU LIFTED YOUR PEOPLE OUT OF.
NOTHING LOOKS WORSE THAN A FAKE SLUM ON FILM.
OF COURSE THIS IS SHOCKING.
WE'RE SHOWING THE WORLD WHAT YOU'VE ELEVATED US ALL FROM...
DIRECTOR?
THE HARLOTS ARE IN COSTUME AND READY FOR CASTING APPROVAL...
VERY WELL. THE TRUTH IS KING.
DO NOT TROUBLE YOURSELF CASTING THESE ACTRESSES. I SHALL MAKE THAT DECISION FOR YOU.
AS YOU WISH...

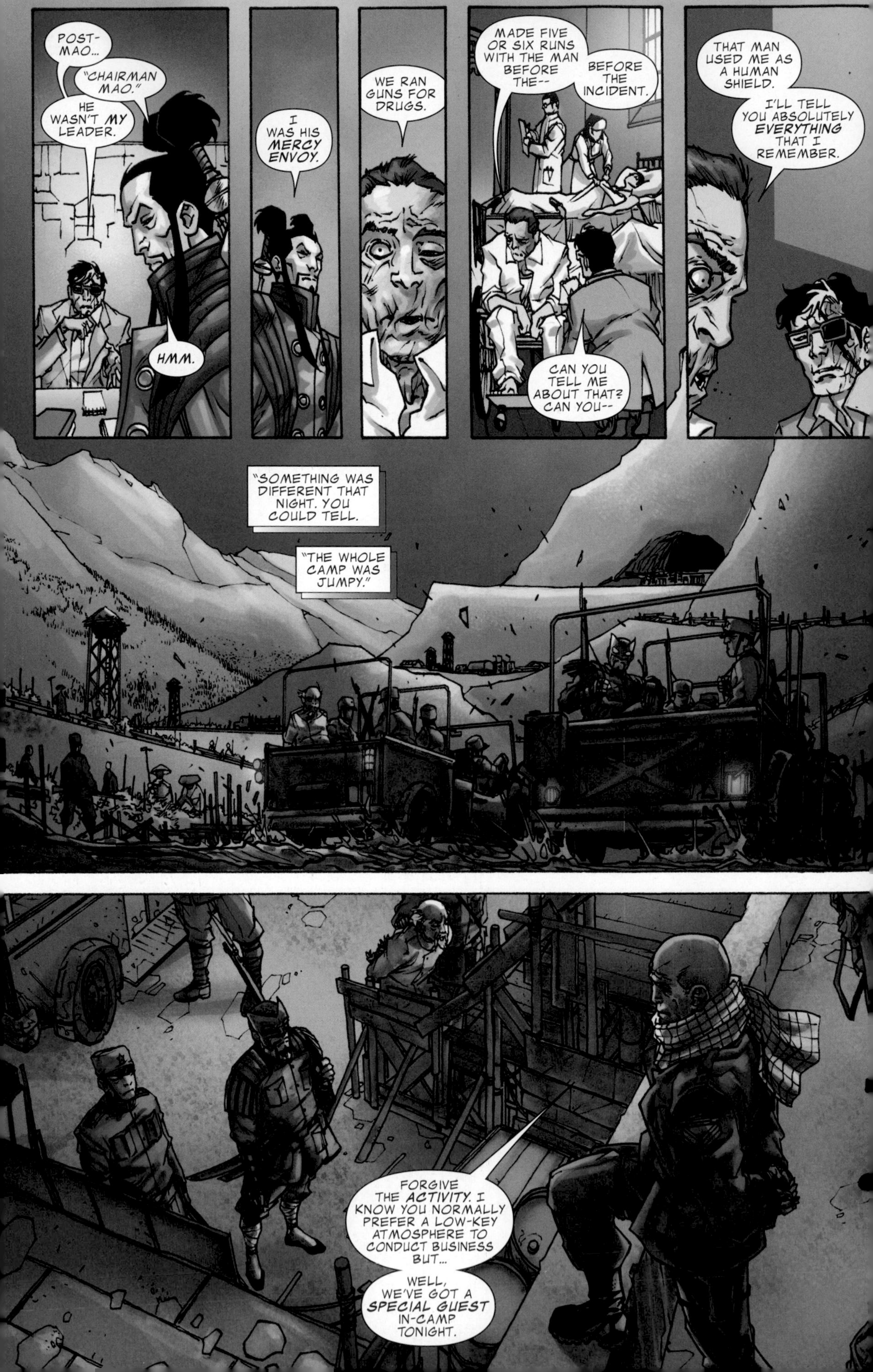
POST-MAO...
"CHAIRMAN MAO."
HE WASN'T **MY** LEADER.
HMM.
I WAS HIS ***MERCY ENVOY.***
WE RAN GUNS FOR DRUGS.
MADE FIVE OR SIX RUNS WITH THE MAN BEFORE THE--
BEFORE THE INCIDENT.
CAN YOU TELL ME ABOUT THAT? CAN YOU--
THAT MAN USED ME AS A HUMAN SHIELD.
I'LL TELL YOU ABSOLUTELY **EVERYTHING** THAT I REMEMBER.
"SOMETHING WAS DIFFERENT THAT NIGHT. YOU COULD TELL.
"THE WHOLE CAMP WAS JUMPY."
FORGIVE THE ***ACTIVITY.*** I KNOW YOU NORMALLY PREFER A LOW-KEY ATMOSPHERE TO CONDUCT BUSINESS BUT...
WELL, WE'VE GOT A ***SPECIAL GUEST*** IN-CAMP TONIGHT.

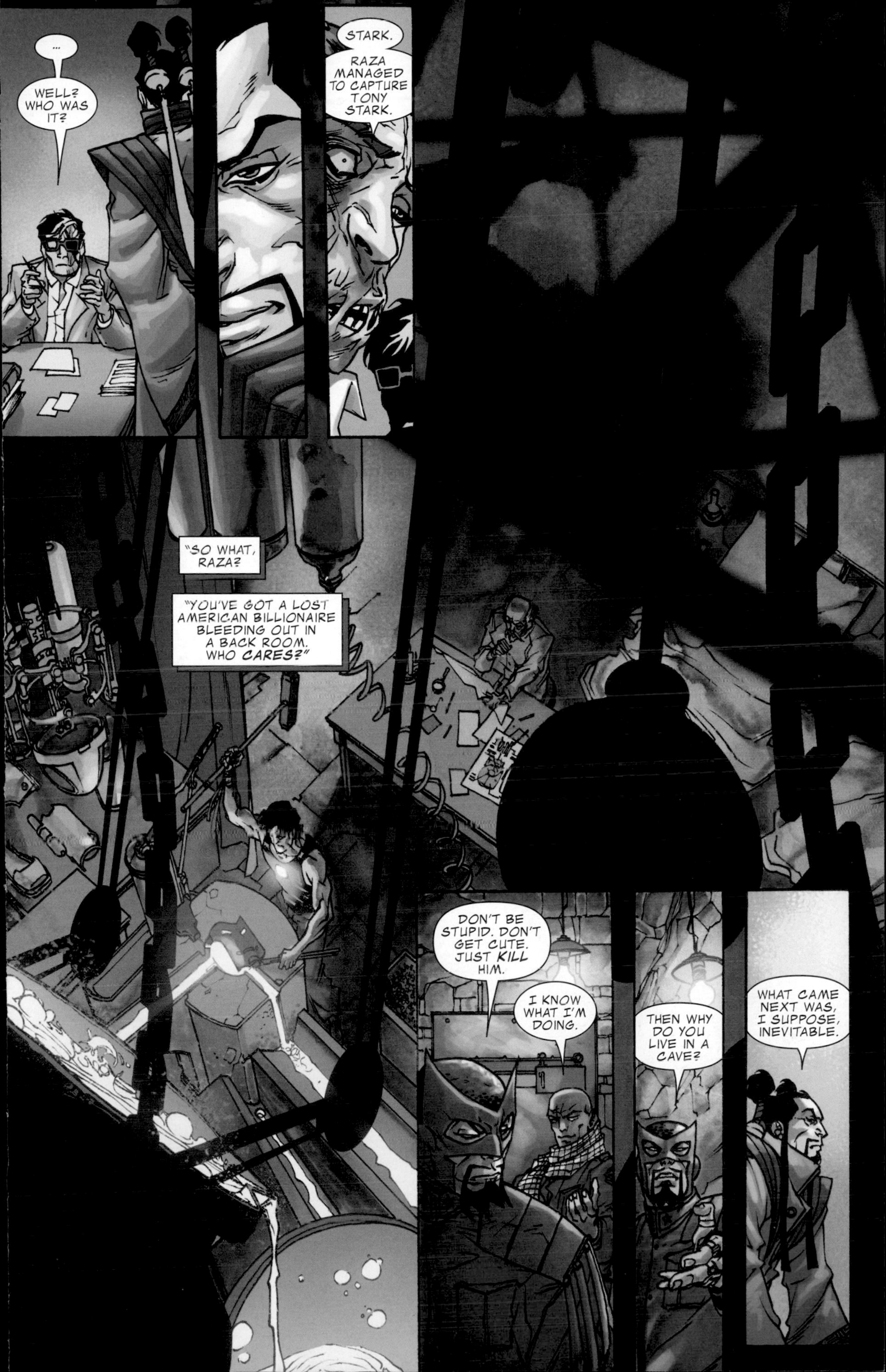
...
WELL? WHO WAS IT?
STARK.
RAZA MANAGED TO CAPTURE TONY STARK.
"SO WHAT, RAZA?
"YOU'VE GOT A LOST AMERICAN BILLIONAIRE BLEEDING OUT IN A BACK ROOM. WHO CARES?"
DON'T BE STUPID. DON'T GET CUTE. JUST KILL HIM.
I KNOW WHAT I'M DOING.
THEN WHY DO YOU LIVE IN A CAVE?
WHAT CAME NEXT WAS, I SUPPOSE, INEVITABLE.

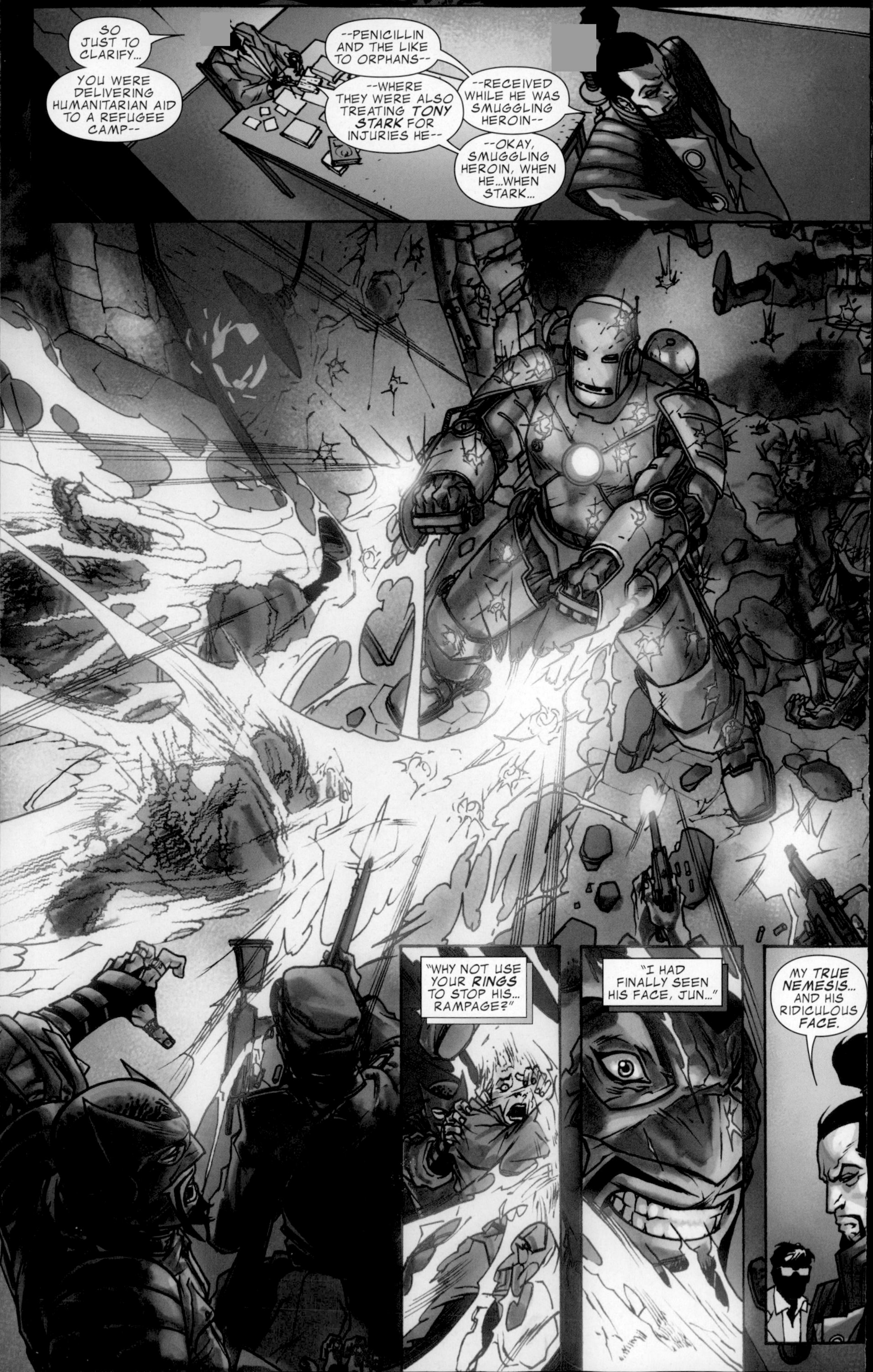
SO JUST TO CLARIFY...
YOU WERE DELIVERING HUMANITARIAN AID TO A REFUGEE CAMP--
--PENICILLIN AND THE LIKE TO ORPHANS--
--WHERE THEY WERE ALSO TREATING *TONY STARK* FOR INJURIES HE--
--RECEIVED WHILE HE WAS SMUGGLING HEROIN--
--OKAY, SMUGGLING HEROIN, WHEN HE...WHEN STARK...
"WHY NOT USE YOUR *RINGS* TO STOP HIS... RAMPAGE?"
"I HAD FINALLY SEEN HIS FACE, JUN..."
MY *TRUE NEMESIS*... AND HIS RIDICULOUS *FACE*.

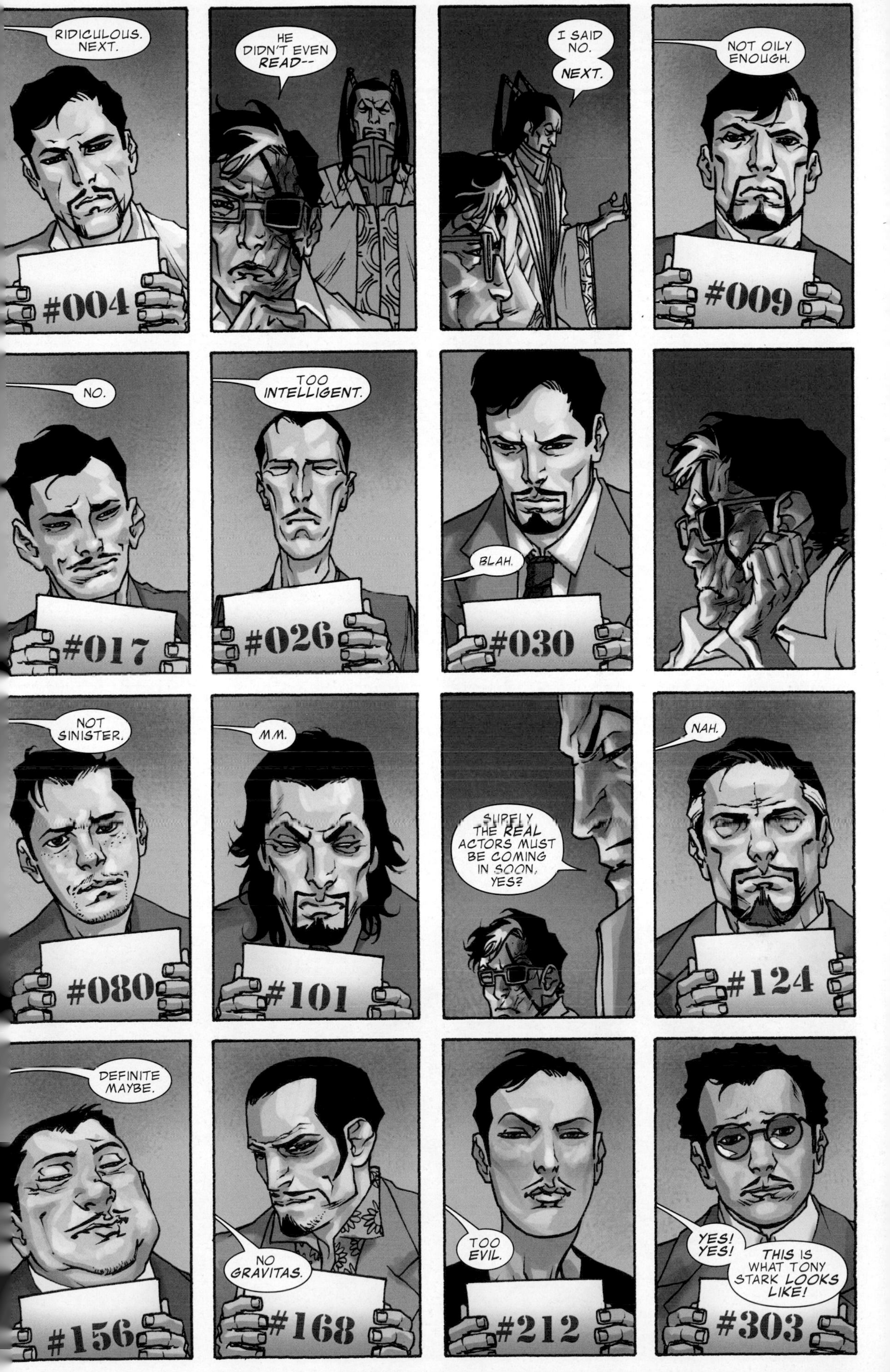
RIDICULOUS. NEXT.
#004
HE DIDN'T EVEN READ--
I SAID NO.
NEXT.
NOT OILY ENOUGH.
#009
NO.
#017
TOO INTELLIGENT.
#026
BLAH.
#030
NOT SINISTER.
#080
MM.
#101
SURELY THE REAL ACTORS MUST BE COMING IN SOON, YES?
NAH.
#124
DEFINITE MAYBE.
#156
NO GRAVITAS.
#168
TOO EVIL.
#212
YES! YES!
THIS IS WHAT TONY STARK LOOKS LIKE!
#303

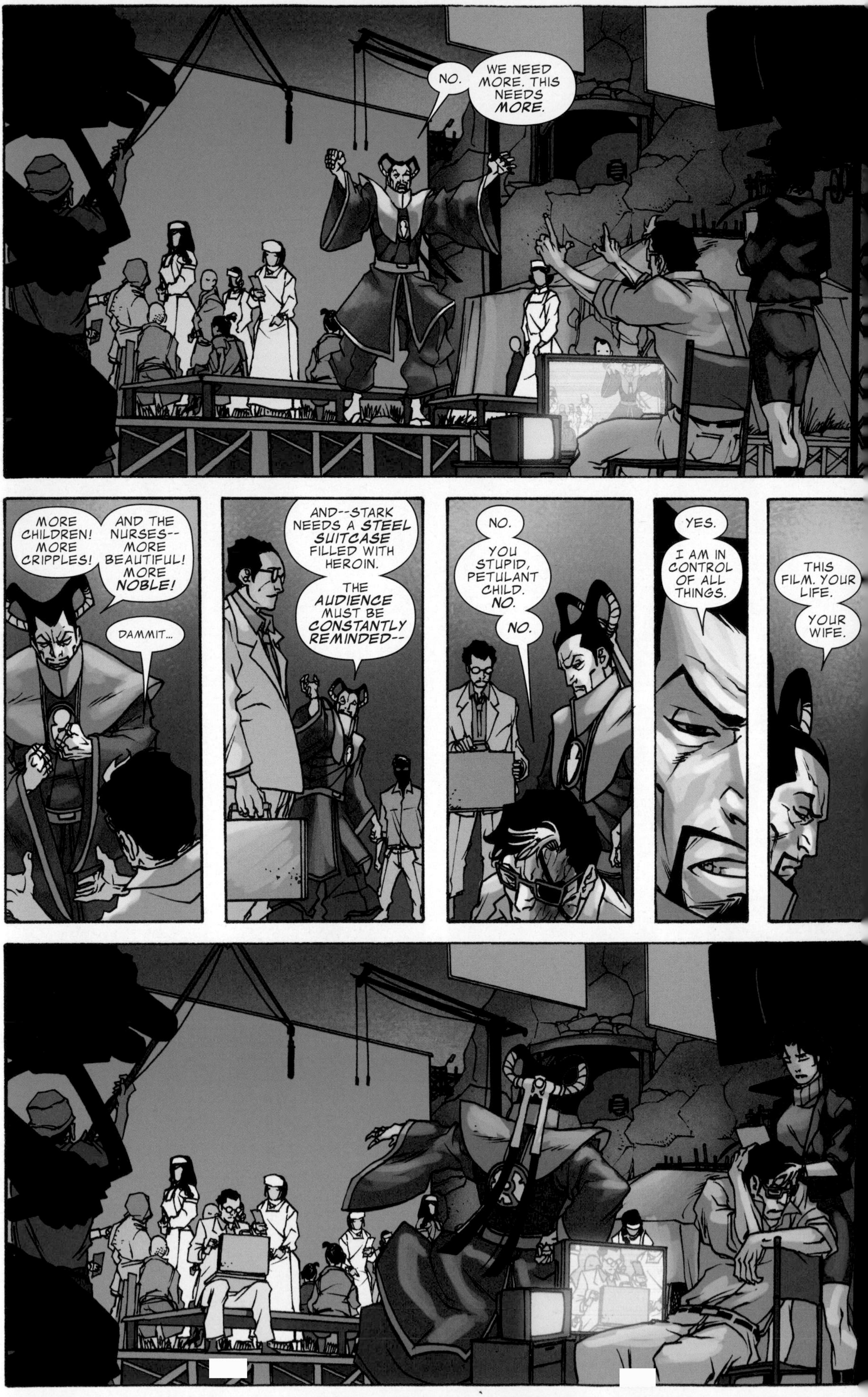
NO.
WE NEED MORE. THIS NEEDS MORE.
MORE CHILDREN! MORE CRIPPLES!
AND THE NURSES-- MORE BEAUTIFUL! MORE NOBLE!
DAMMIT...
AND--STARK NEEDS A STEEL SUITCASE FILLED WITH HEROIN.
THE AUDIENCE MUST BE CONSTANTLY REMINDED--
NO.
YOU STUPID, PETULANT CHILD. NO.
NO.
YES.
I AM IN CONTROL OF ALL THINGS.
THIS FILM. YOUR LIFE.
YOUR WIFE.

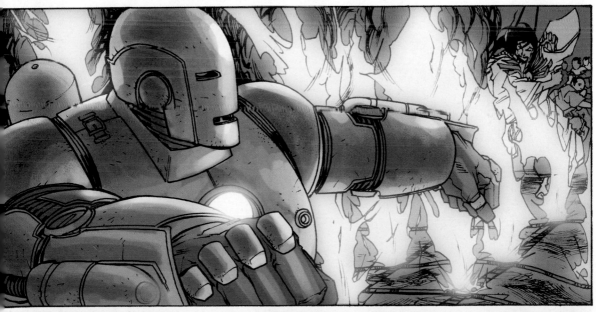

YES. YES, IT WAS JUST LIKE THIS...

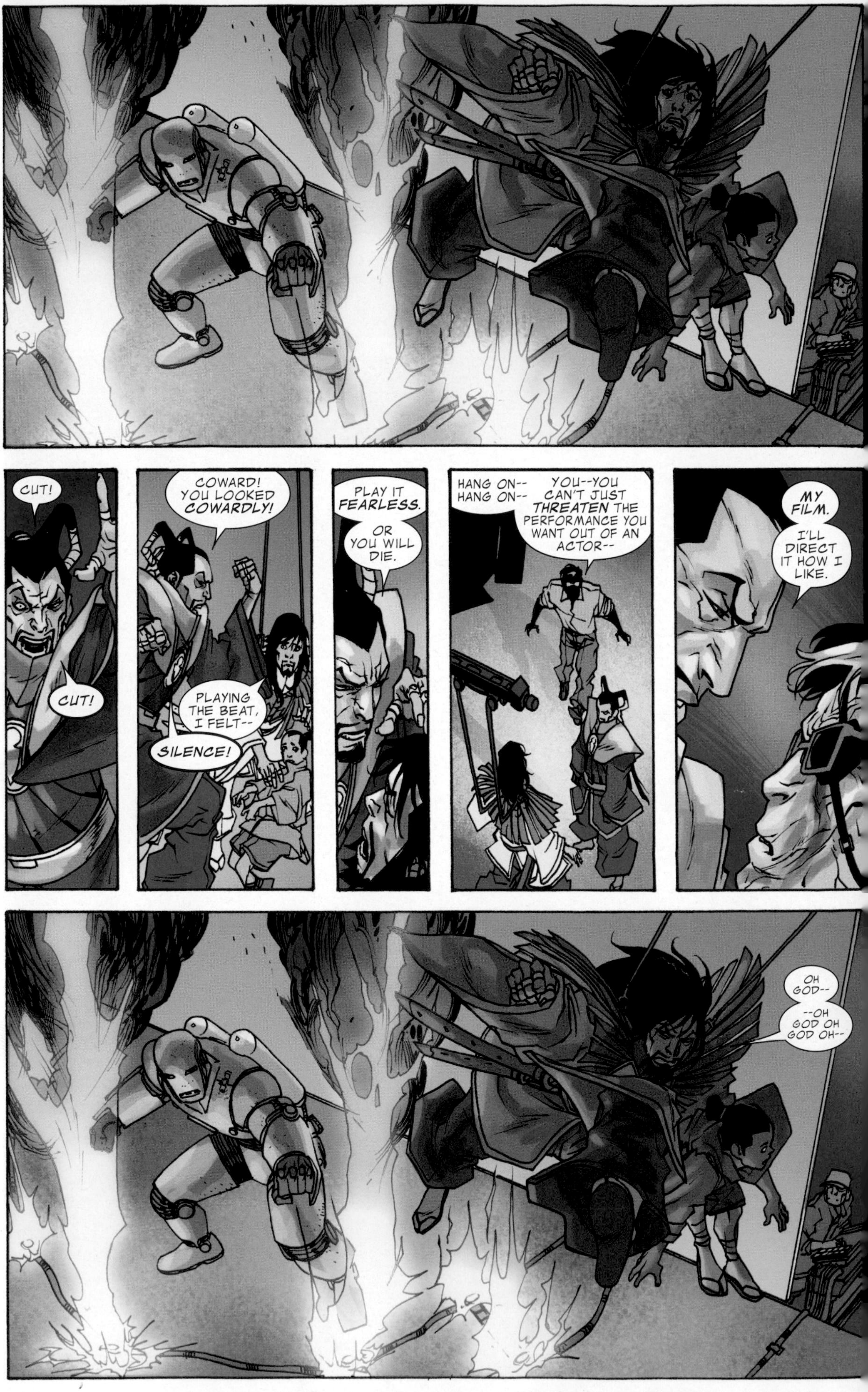
CUT!
CUT!
COWARD! YOU LOOKED COWARDLY!
PLAYING THE BEAT, I FELT--
SILENCE!
PLAY IT FEARLESS.
OR YOU WILL DIE.
HANG ON-- HANG ON--
YOU--YOU CAN'T JUST THREATEN THE PERFORMANCE YOU WANT OUT OF AN ACTOR--
MY FILM.
I'LL DIRECT IT HOW I LIKE.
OH GOD--
--OH GOD OH GOD OH--

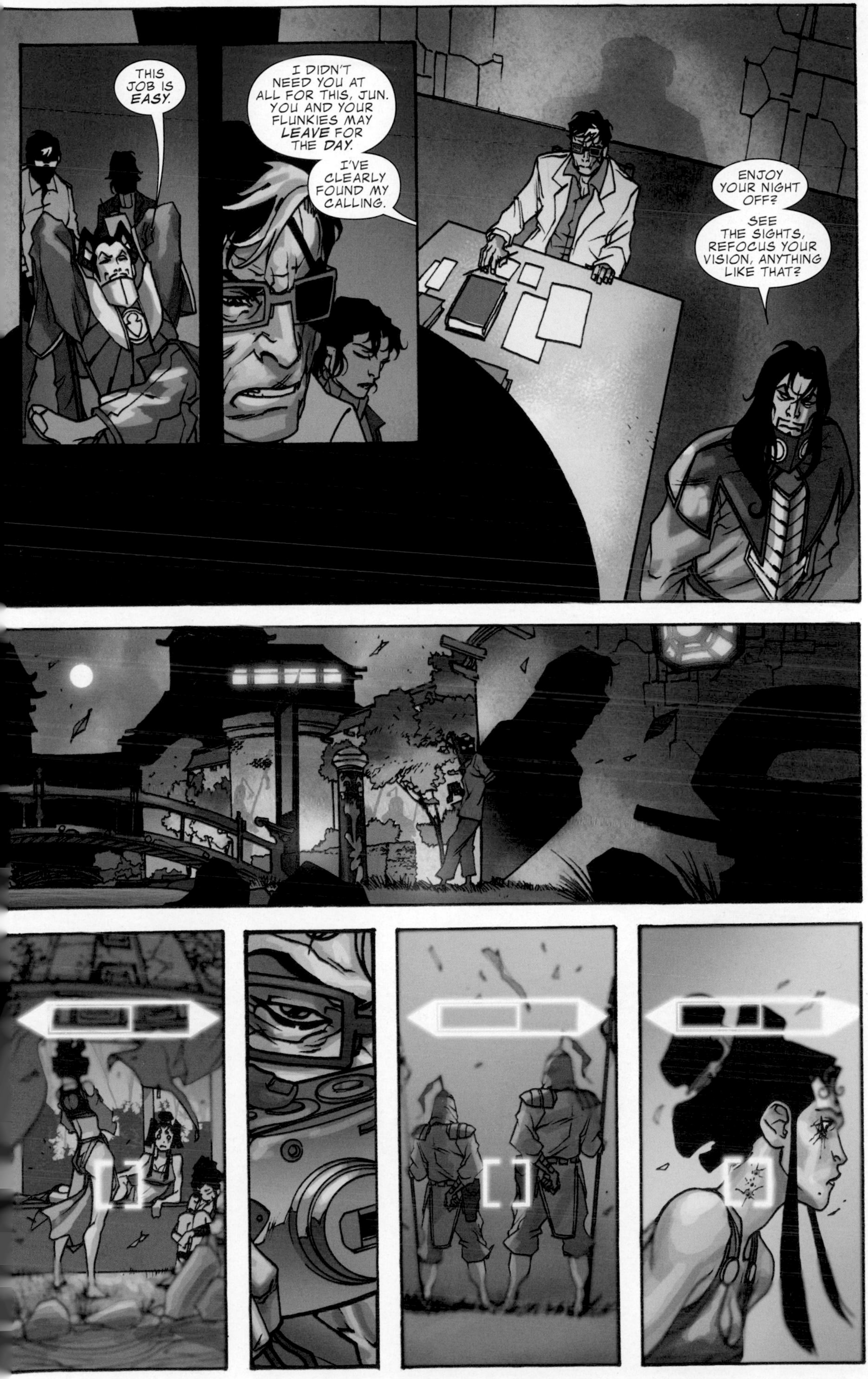
THIS JOB IS EASY.
I DIDN'T NEED YOU AT ALL FOR THIS, JUN. YOU AND YOUR FLUNKIES MAY LEAVE FOR THE DAY.
I'VE CLEARLY FOUND MY CALLING.
ENJOY YOUR NIGHT OFF?
SEE THE SIGHTS, REFOCUS YOUR VISION, ANYTHING LIKE THAT?

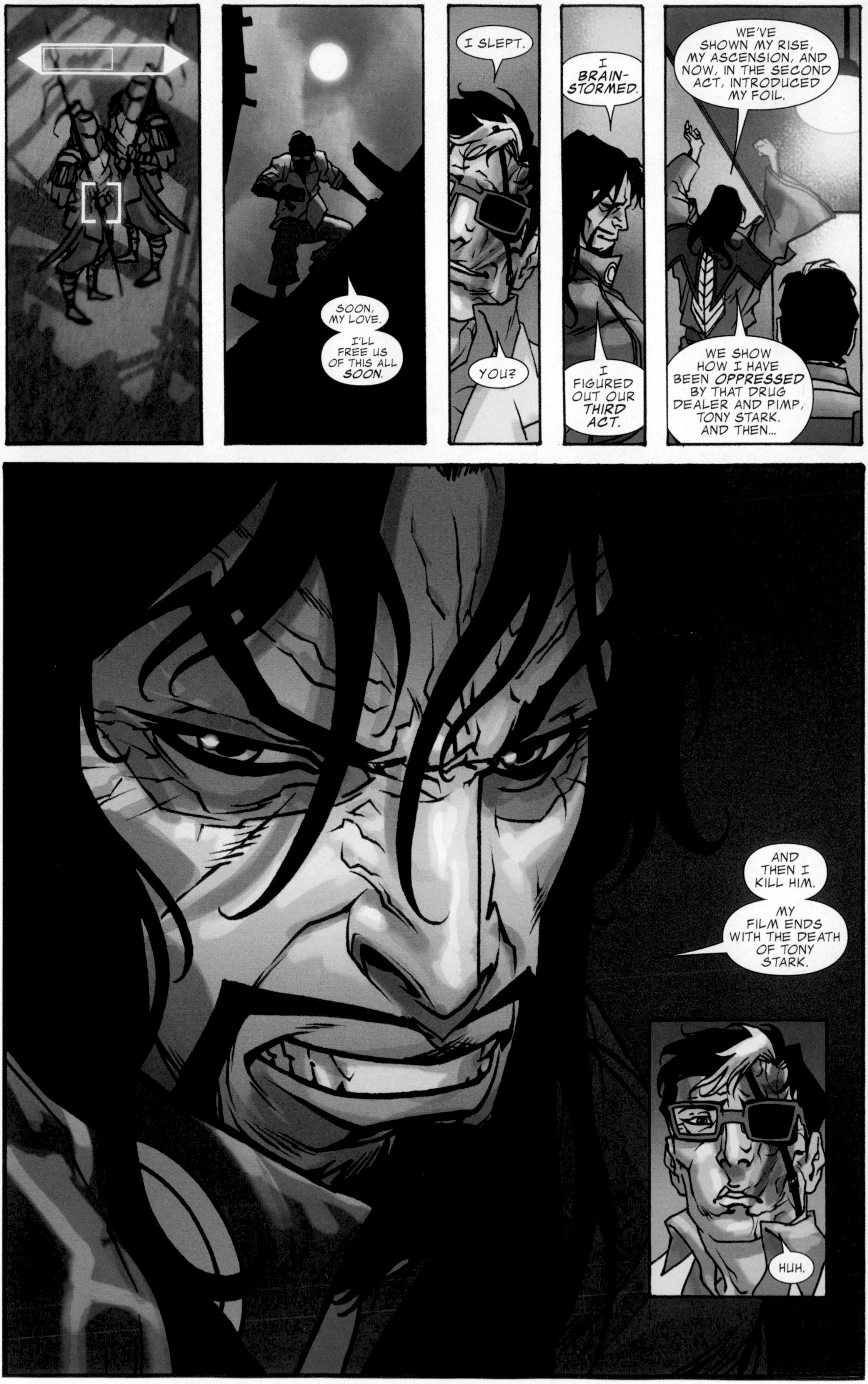

SOON, MY LOVE.
I'LL FREE US OF THIS ALL SOON.
I SLEPT.
YOU?
I BRAIN-STORMED.
I FIGURED OUT OUR THIRD ACT.
WE'VE SHOWN MY RISE, MY ASCENSION, AND NOW, IN THE SECOND ACT, INTRODUCED MY FOIL.
WE SHOW HOW I HAVE BEEN OPPRESSED BY THAT DRUG DEALER AND PIMP, TONY STARK. AND THEN...
AND THEN I KILL HIM.
MY FILM ENDS WITH THE DEATH OF TONY STARK.
HUH.

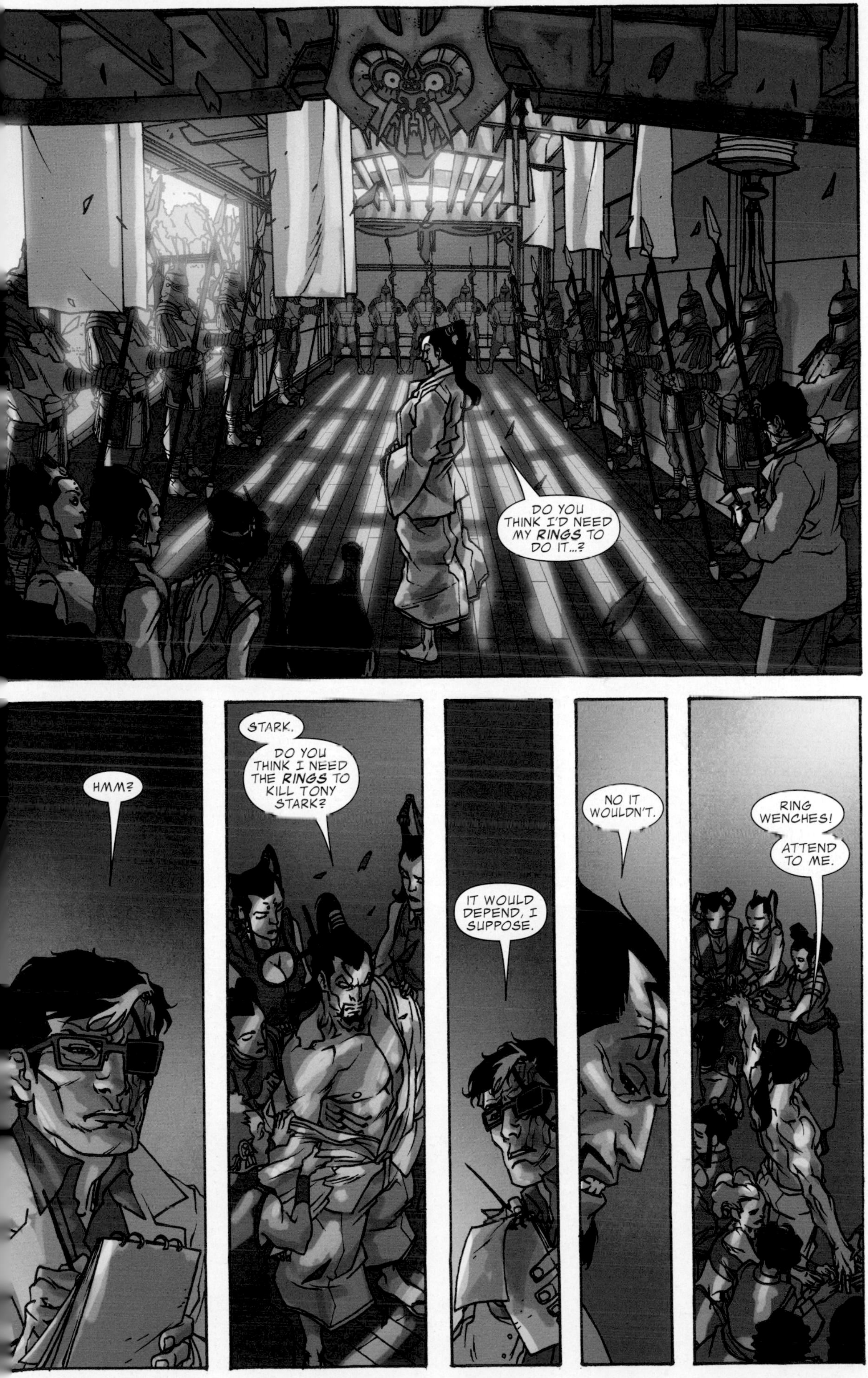
DO YOU THINK I'D NEED MY RINGS TO DO IT...?
HMM?
STARK.
DO YOU THINK I NEED THE RINGS TO KILL TONY STARK?
IT WOULD DEPEND, I SUPPOSE.
NO IT WOULDN'T.
RING WENCHES!
ATTEND TO ME.

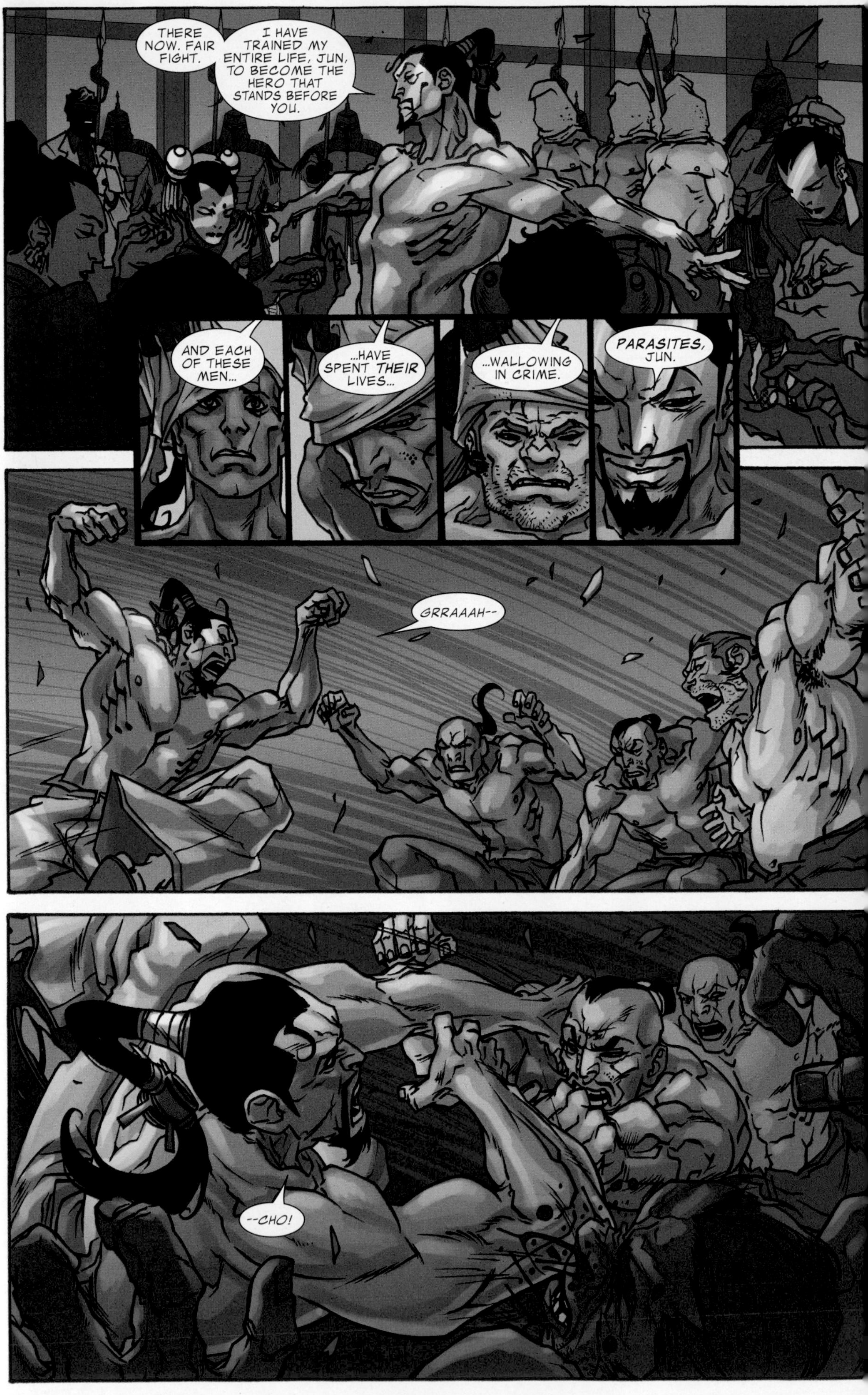
THERE NOW. FAIR FIGHT.
I HAVE TRAINED MY ENTIRE LIFE, JUN, TO BECOME THE HERO THAT STANDS BEFORE YOU.
AND EACH OF THESE MEN...
...HAVE SPENT THEIR LIVES...
...WALLOWING IN CRIME.
PARASITES, JUN.
GRRAAAH--
--CHO!

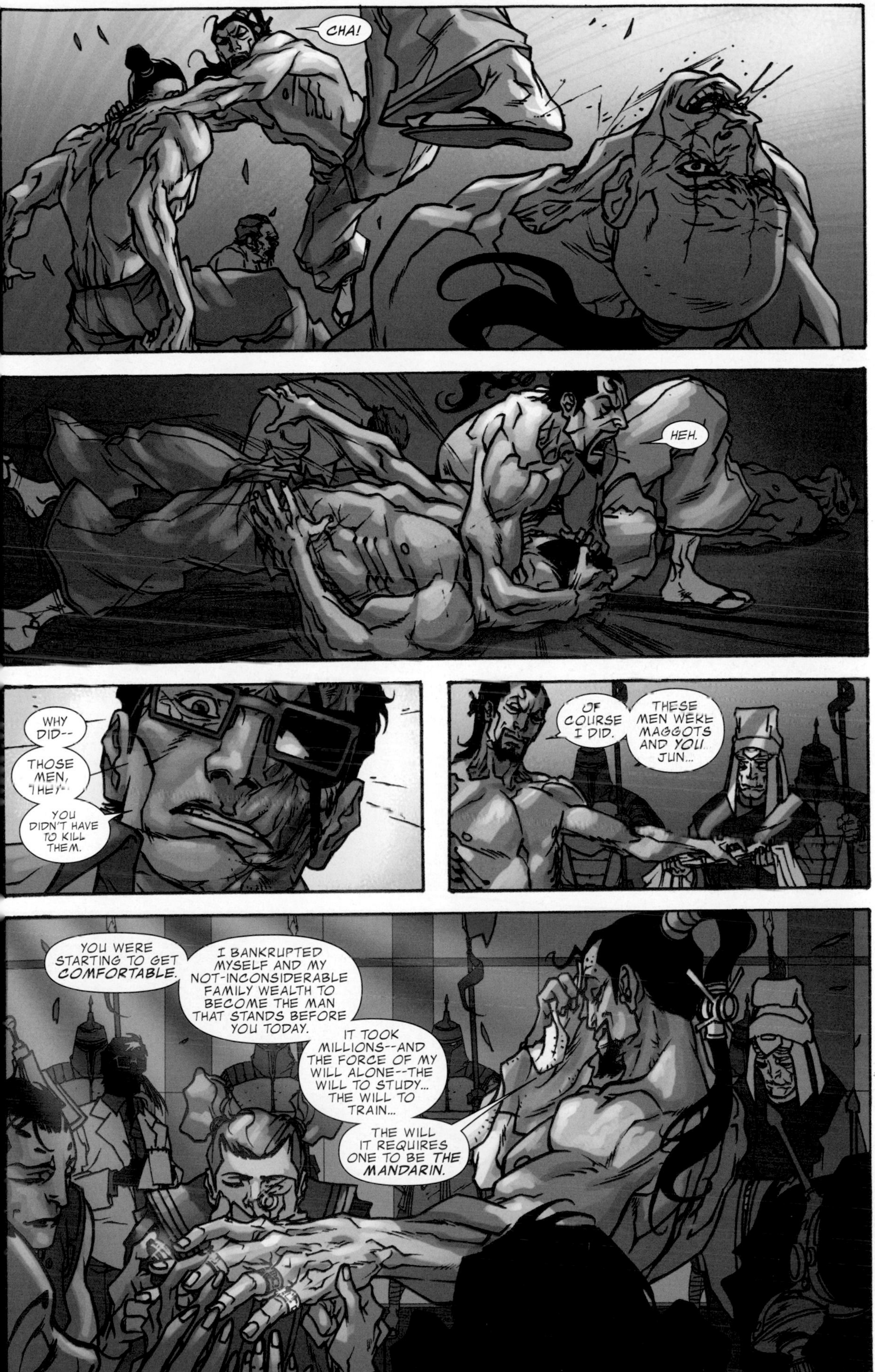
CHA!
HEH.
WHY DID--
THOSE MEN, THEY--
YOU DIDN'T HAVE TO KILL THEM.
OF COURSE I DID.
THESE MEN WERE MAGGOTS AND YOU, JUN...
YOU WERE STARTING TO GET COMFORTABLE.
I BANKRUPTED MYSELF AND MY NOT-INCONSIDERABLE FAMILY WEALTH TO BECOME THE MAN THAT STANDS BEFORE YOU TODAY.
IT TOOK MILLIONS--AND THE FORCE OF MY WILL ALONE--THE WILL TO STUDY... THE WILL TO TRAIN...
THE WILL IT REQUIRES ONE TO BE THE MANDARIN.

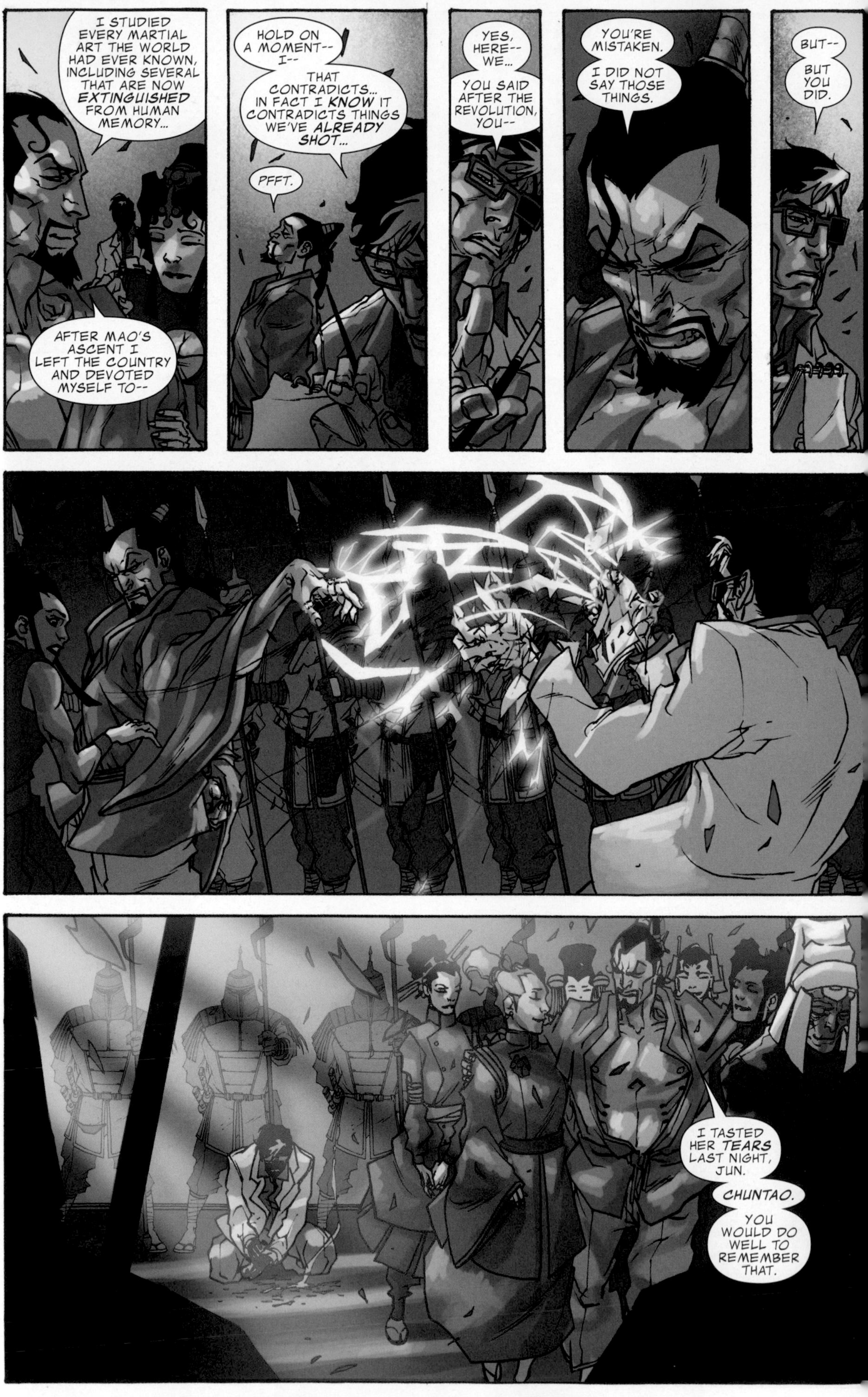
I STUDIED EVERY MARTIAL ART THE WORLD HAD EVER KNOWN, INCLUDING SEVERAL THAT ARE NOW **EXTINGUISHED** FROM HUMAN MEMORY...
AFTER MAO'S ASCENT I LEFT THE COUNTRY AND DEVOTED MYSELF TO--
HOLD ON A MOMENT-- I--
THAT CONTRADICTS... IN FACT I **KNOW** IT CONTRADICTS THINGS WE'VE **ALREADY SHOT**...
PFFT.
YES, HERE-- WE...
YOU SAID AFTER THE REVOLUTION, YOU--
YOU'RE MISTAKEN.
I DID NOT SAY THOSE THINGS.
BUT--
BUT YOU DID.
I TASTED HER **TEARS** LAST NIGHT, JUN.
CHUNTAO.
YOU WOULD DO WELL TO REMEMBER THAT.

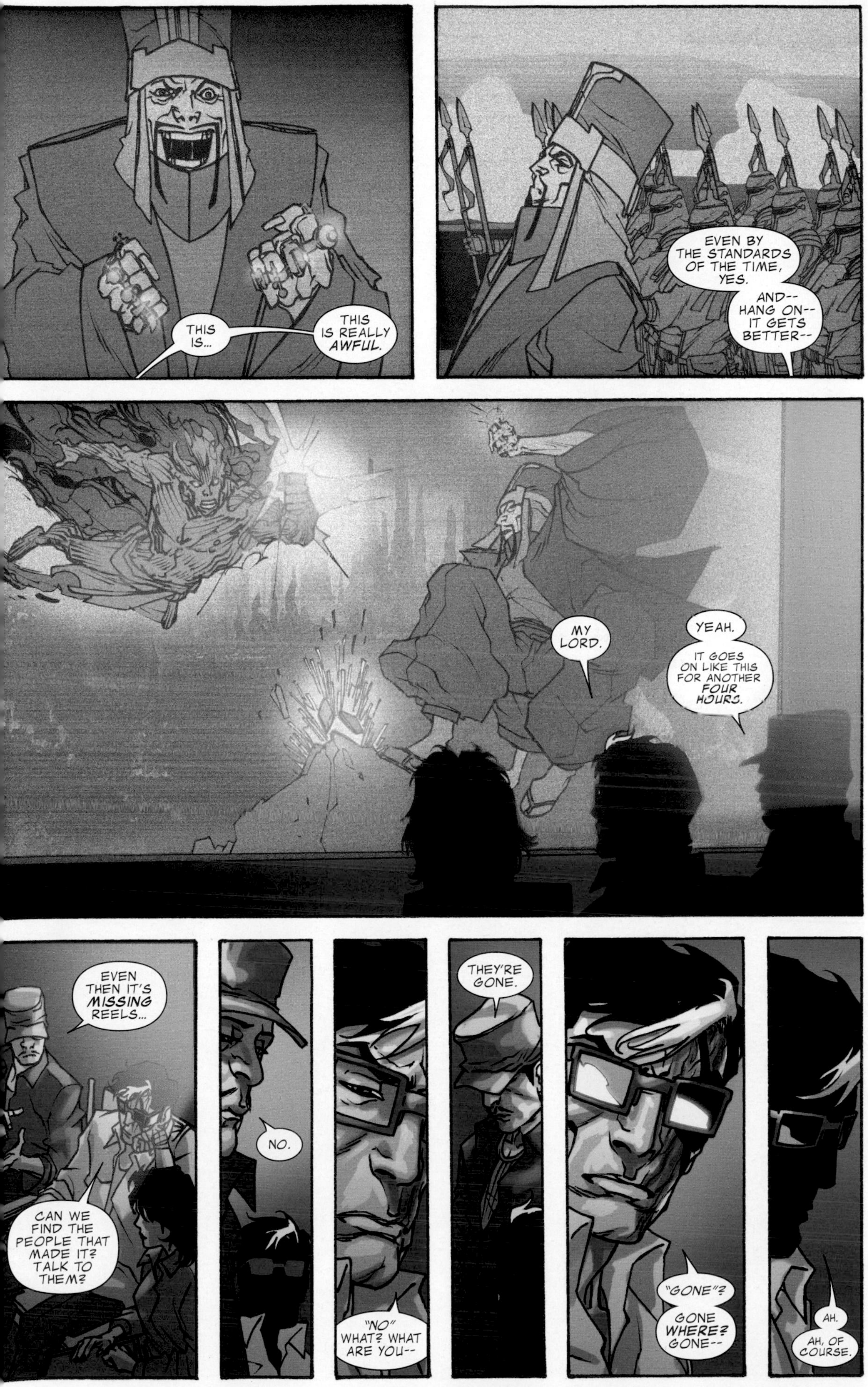
THIS IS...
THIS IS REALLY AWFUL.
EVEN BY THE STANDARDS OF THE TIME, YES.
AND-- HANG ON-- IT GETS BETTER--
MY LORD.
YEAH.
IT GOES ON LIKE THIS FOR ANOTHER FOUR HOURS.
EVEN THEN IT'S MISSING REELS...
CAN WE FIND THE PEOPLE THAT MADE IT? TALK TO THEM?
NO.
"NO" WHAT? WHAT ARE YOU--
THEY'RE GONE.
"GONE"?
GONE WHERE? GONE--
AH.
AH, OF COURSE.

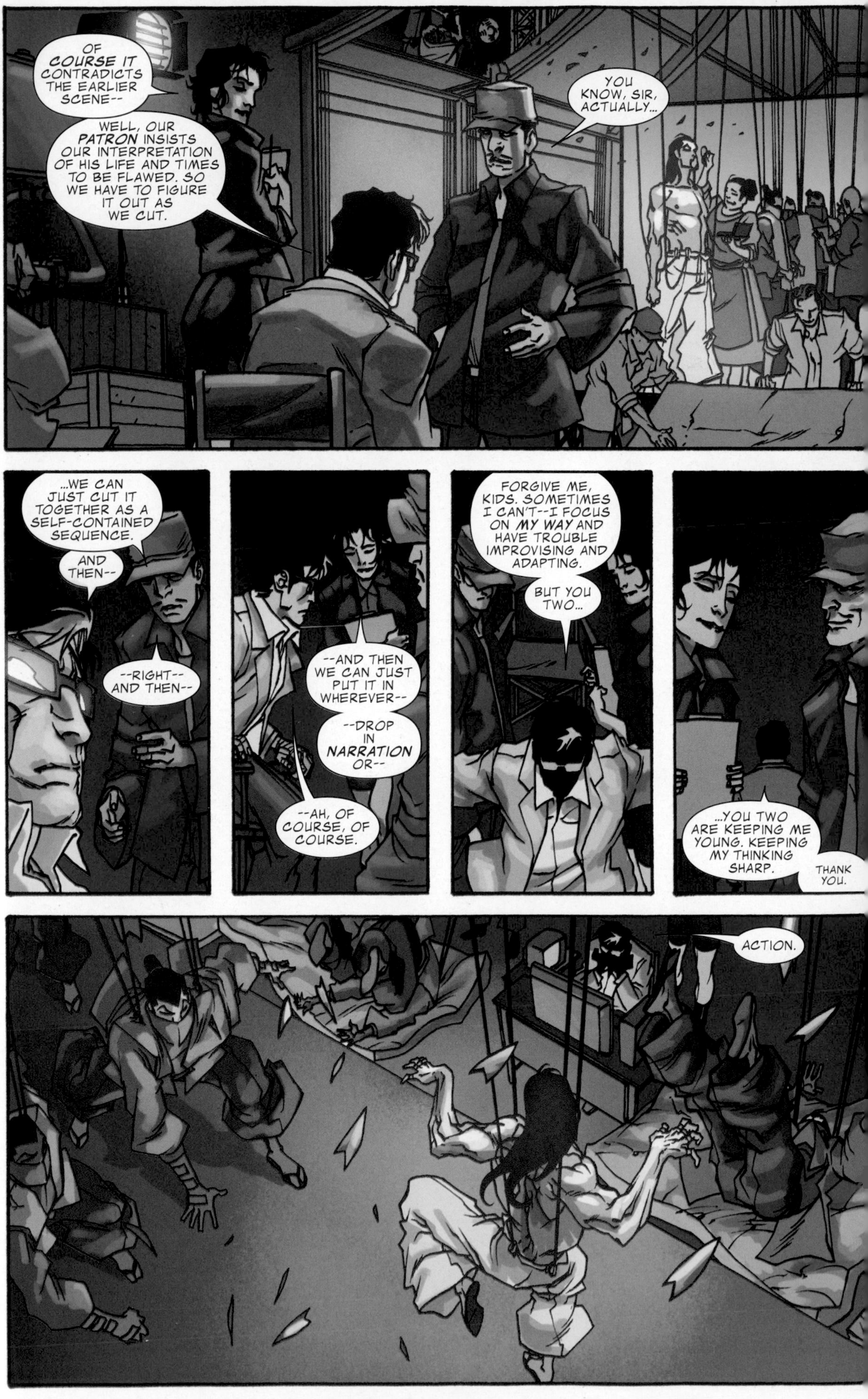
OF COURSE IT CONTRADICTS THE EARLIER SCENE--
WELL, OUR PATRON INSISTS OUR INTERPRETATION OF HIS LIFE AND TIMES TO BE FLAWED. SO WE HAVE TO FIGURE IT OUT AS WE CUT.
YOU KNOW, SIR, ACTUALLY...
...WE CAN JUST CUT IT TOGETHER AS A SELF-CONTAINED SEQUENCE.
AND THEN--
--RIGHT-- AND THEN--
--AND THEN WE CAN JUST PUT IT IN WHEREVER--
--DROP IN NARRATION OR--
--AH, OF COURSE, OF COURSE.
FORGIVE ME, KIDS. SOMETIMES I CAN'T--I FOCUS ON MY WAY AND HAVE TROUBLE IMPROVISING AND ADAPTING.
BUT YOU TWO...
...YOU TWO ARE KEEPING ME YOUNG. KEEPING MY THINKING SHARP.
THANK YOU.
ACTION.

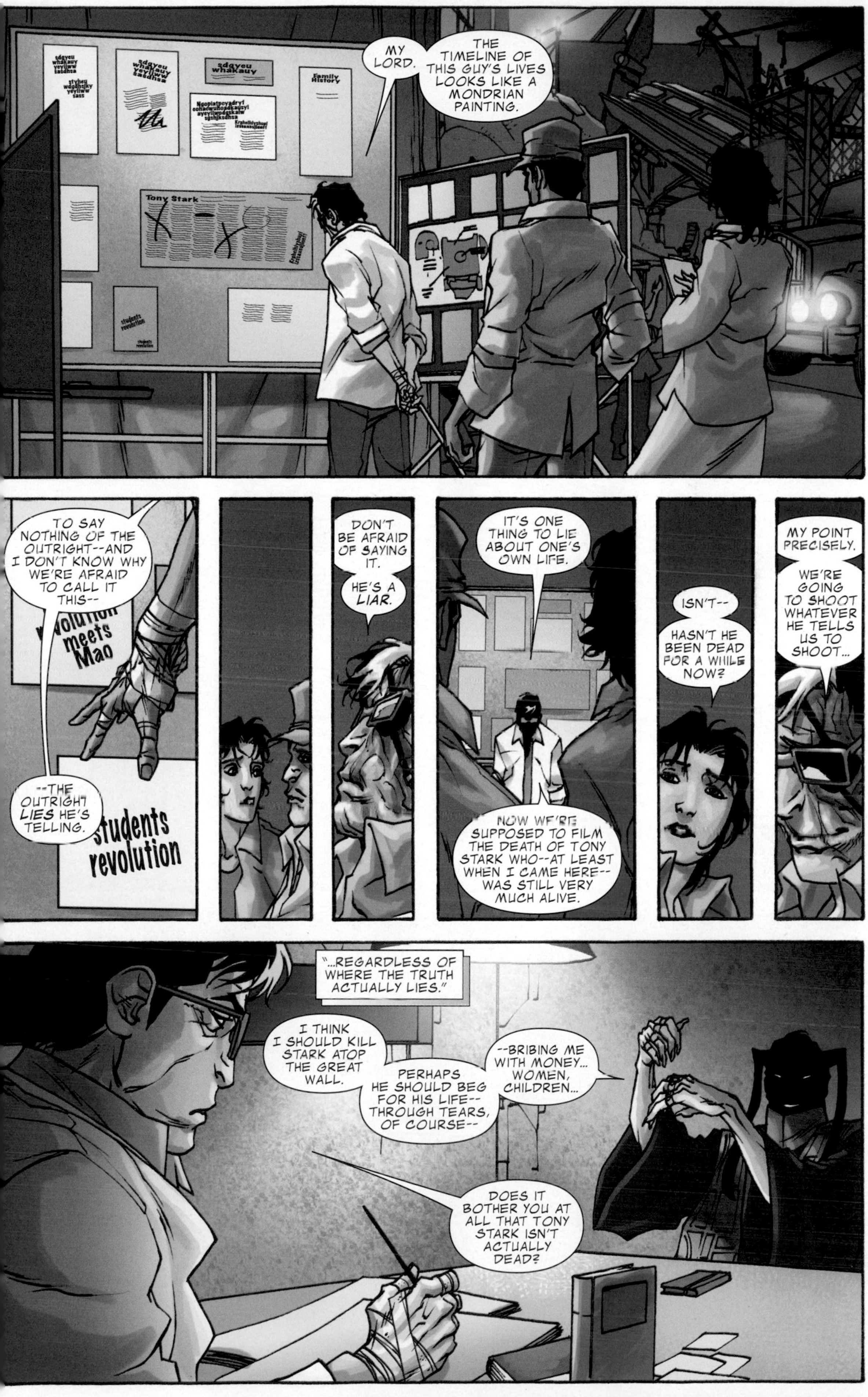
MY LORD.
THE TIMELINE OF THIS GUY'S LIVES LOOKS LIKE A MONDRIAN PAINTING.
TO SAY NOTHING OF THE OUTRIGHT--AND I DON'T KNOW WHY WE'RE AFRAID TO CALL IT THIS--
--THE OUTRIGHT LIES HE'S TELLING.
students revolution
DON'T BE AFRAID OF SAYING IT.
HE'S A LIAR.
IT'S ONE THING TO LIE ABOUT ONE'S OWN LIFE.
NOW WE'RE SUPPOSED TO FILM THE DEATH OF TONY STARK WHO--AT LEAST WHEN I CAME HERE--WAS STILL VERY MUCH ALIVE.
ISN'T--
HASN'T HE BEEN DEAD FOR A WHILE NOW?
MY POINT PRECISELY.
WE'RE GOING TO SHOOT WHATEVER HE TELLS US TO SHOOT...
"...REGARDLESS OF WHERE THE TRUTH ACTUALLY LIES."
I THINK I SHOULD KILL STARK ATOP THE GREAT WALL.
PERHAPS HE SHOULD BEG FOR HIS LIFE--THROUGH TEARS, OF COURSE--
--BRIBING ME WITH MONEY... WOMEN, CHILDREN...
DOES IT BOTHER YOU AT ALL THAT TONY STARK ISN'T ACTUALLY DEAD?

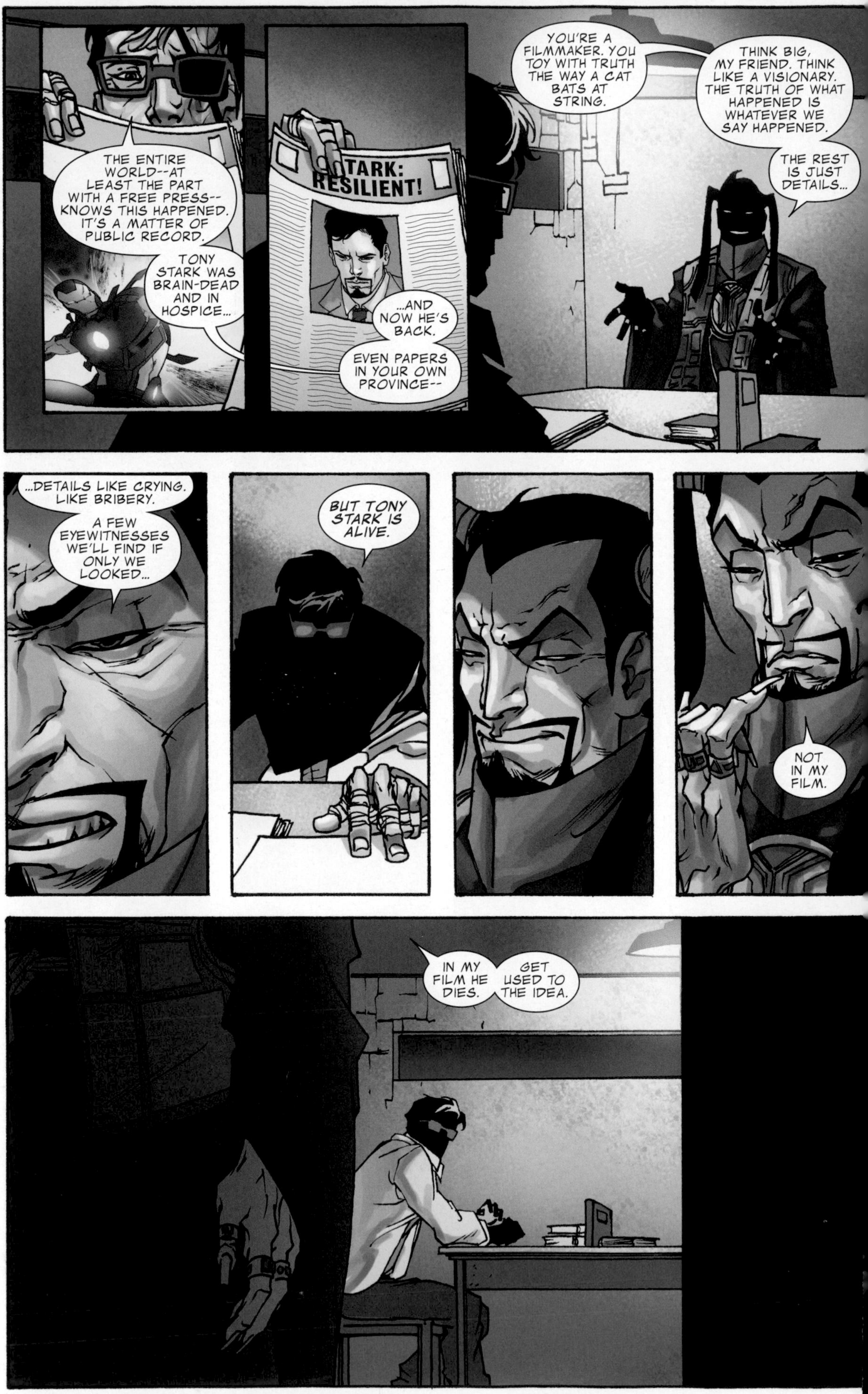
THE ENTIRE WORLD--AT LEAST THE PART WITH A FREE PRESS--KNOWS THIS HAPPENED. IT'S A MATTER OF PUBLIC RECORD.
TONY STARK WAS BRAIN-DEAD AND IN HOSPICE...
STARK: RESILIENT!
...AND NOW HE'S BACK.
EVEN PAPERS IN YOUR OWN PROVINCE--
YOU'RE A FILMMAKER. YOU TOY WITH TRUTH THE WAY A CAT BATS AT STRING.
THINK BIG, MY FRIEND. THINK LIKE A VISIONARY. THE TRUTH OF WHAT HAPPENED IS WHATEVER WE SAY HAPPENED.
THE REST IS JUST DETAILS...
...DETAILS LIKE CRYING. LIKE BRIBERY.
A FEW EYEWITNESSES WE'LL FIND IF ONLY WE LOOKED...
BUT TONY STARK IS ALIVE.
NOT IN MY FILM.
IN MY FILM HE DIES.
GET USED TO THE IDEA.

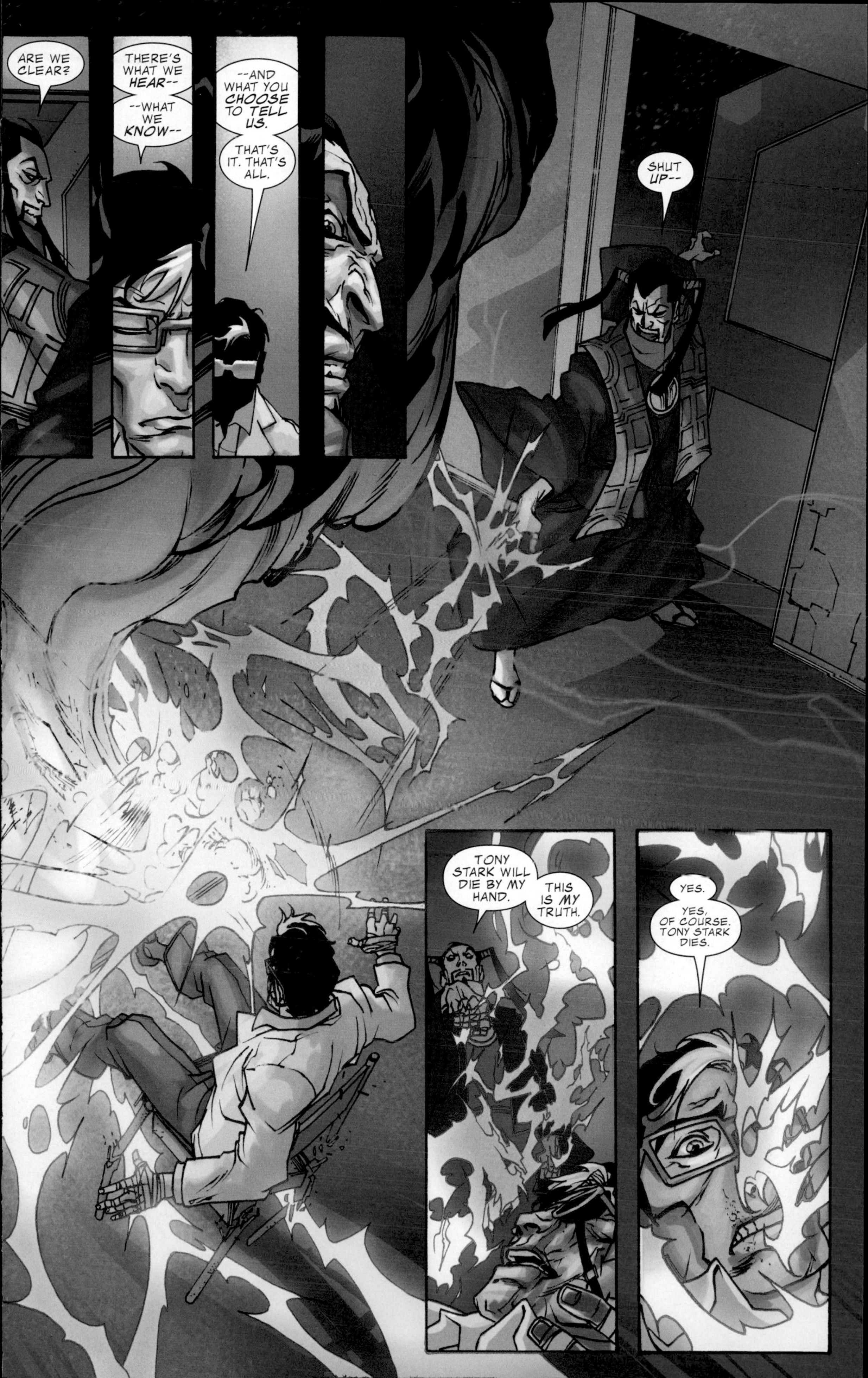
ARE WE CLEAR?
THERE'S WHAT WE HEAR--
--WHAT WE KNOW--
--AND WHAT YOU CHOOSE TO TELL US.
THAT'S IT. THAT'S ALL.
SHUT UP--
TONY STARK WILL DIE BY MY HAND.
THIS IS MY TRUTH.
YES.
YES, OF COURSE. TONY STARK DIES.

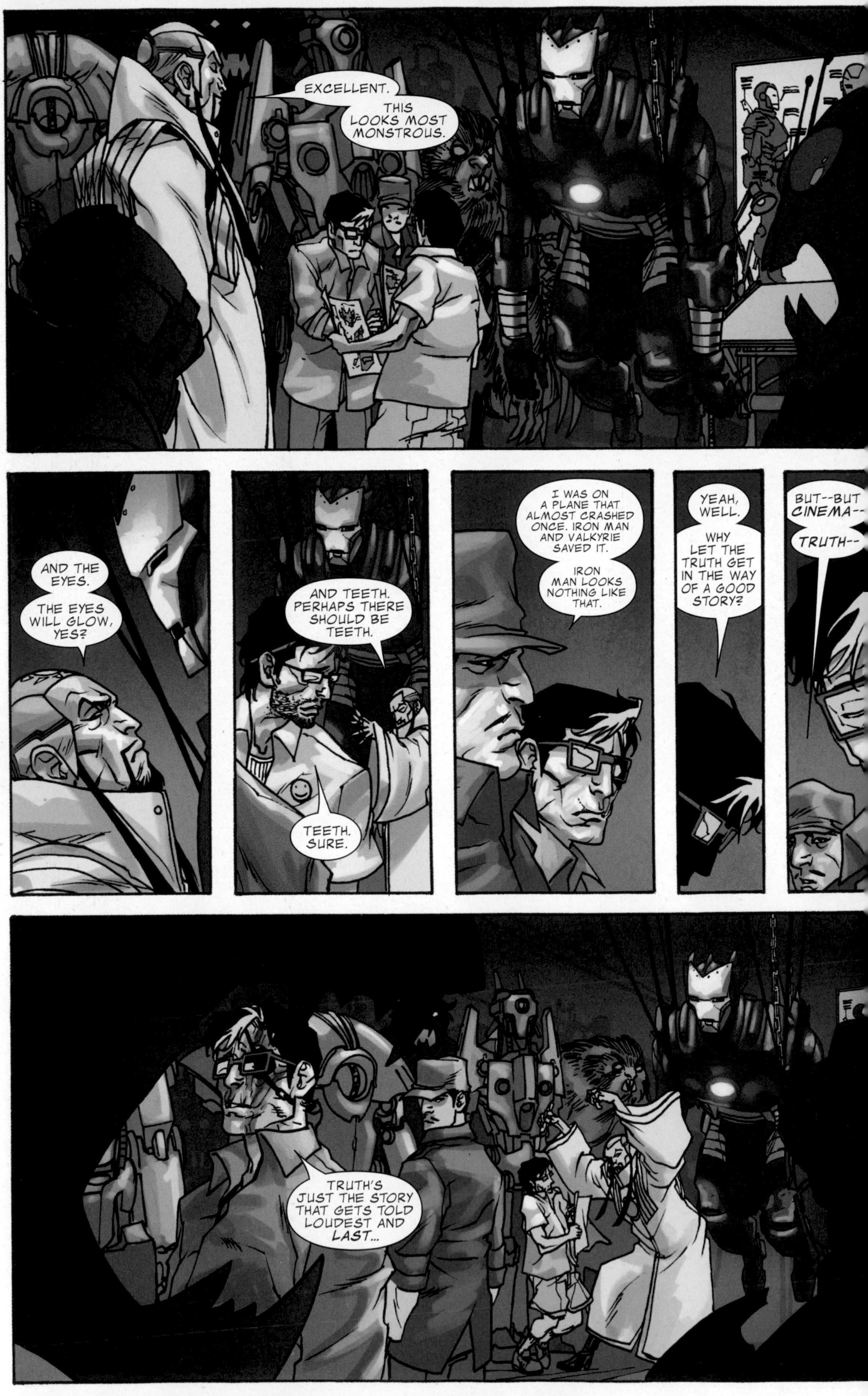
EXCELLENT.
THIS LOOKS MOST MONSTROUS.
AND THE EYES.
THE EYES WILL GLOW, YES?
AND TEETH. PERHAPS THERE SHOULD BE TEETH.
TEETH. SURE.
I WAS ON A PLANE THAT ALMOST CRASHED ONCE. IRON MAN AND VALKYRIE SAVED IT.
IRON MAN LOOKS NOTHING LIKE THAT.
YEAH, WELL.
WHY LET THE TRUTH GET IN THE WAY OF A GOOD STORY?
BUT--BUT CINEMA--
TRUTH--
TRUTH'S JUST THE STORY THAT GETS TOLD LOUDEST AND LAST...

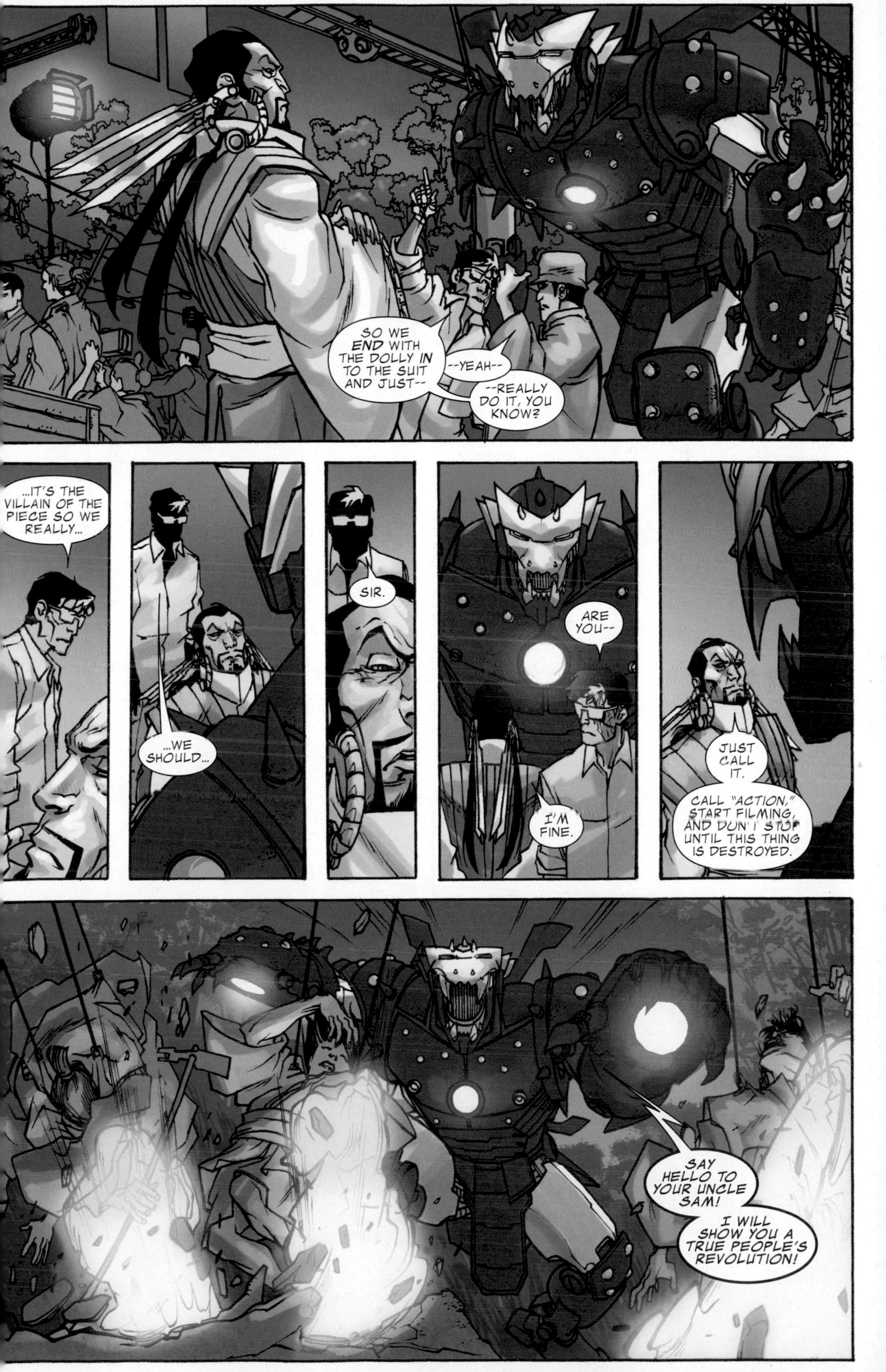
SO WE END WITH THE DOLLY IN TO THE SUIT AND JUST--
--YEAH--
--REALLY DO IT, YOU KNOW?
...IT'S THE VILLAIN OF THE PIECE SO WE REALLY...
...WE SHOULD...
SIR.
ARE YOU--
I'M FINE.
JUST CALL IT.
CALL "ACTION," START FILMING, AND DON'T STOP UNTIL THIS THING IS DESTROYED.
SAY HELLO TO YOUR UNCLE SAM!
I WILL SHOW YOU A TRUE PEOPLE'S REVOLUTION!

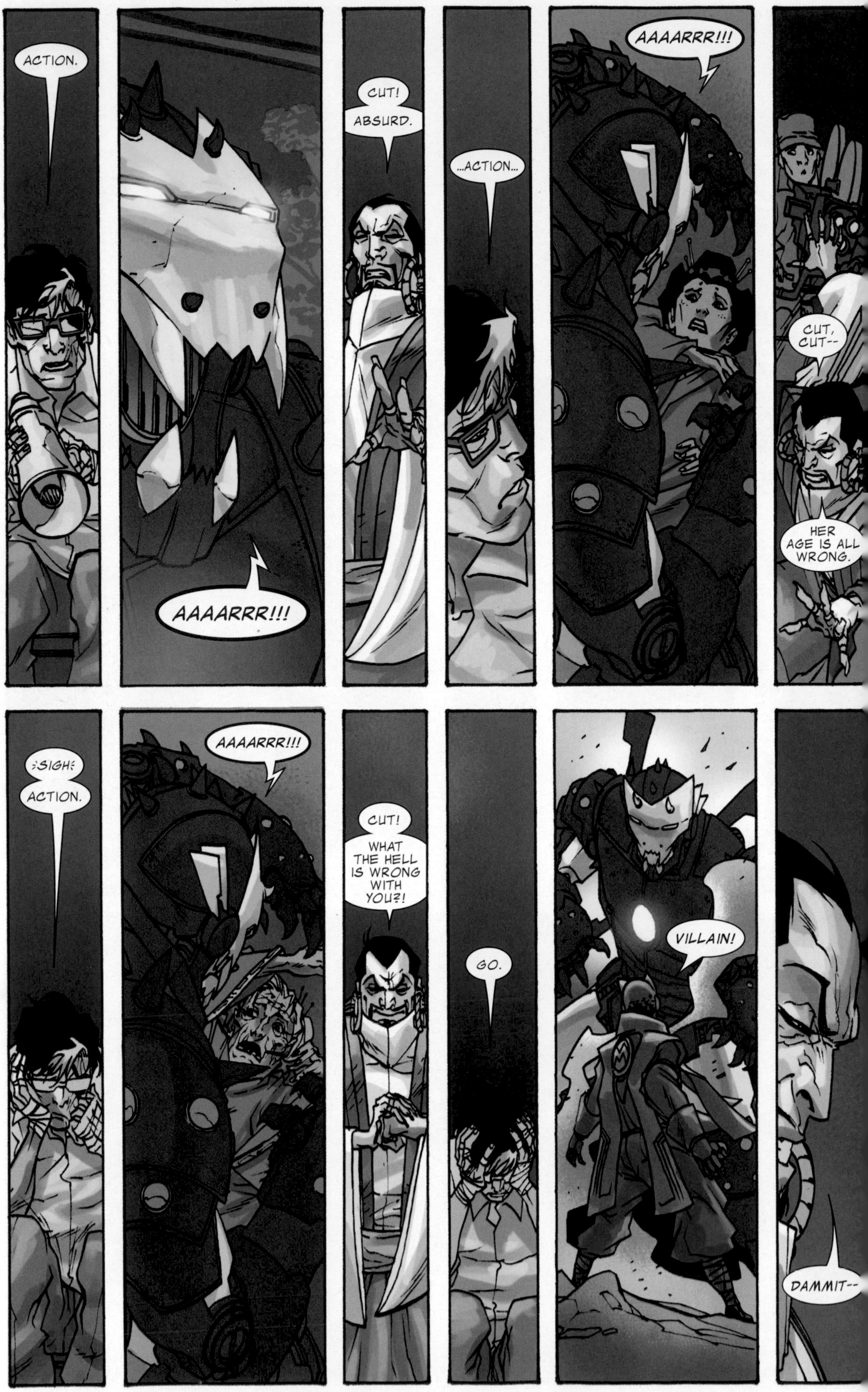
ACTION.
AAAARRR!!!
CUT! ABSURD.
...ACTION...
AAAARRR!!!
CUT, CUT--
HER AGE IS ALL WRONG.
SIGH
ACTION.
AAAARRR!!!
CUT! WHAT THE HELL IS WRONG WITH YOU?!
GO.
VILLAIN!
DAMMIT--

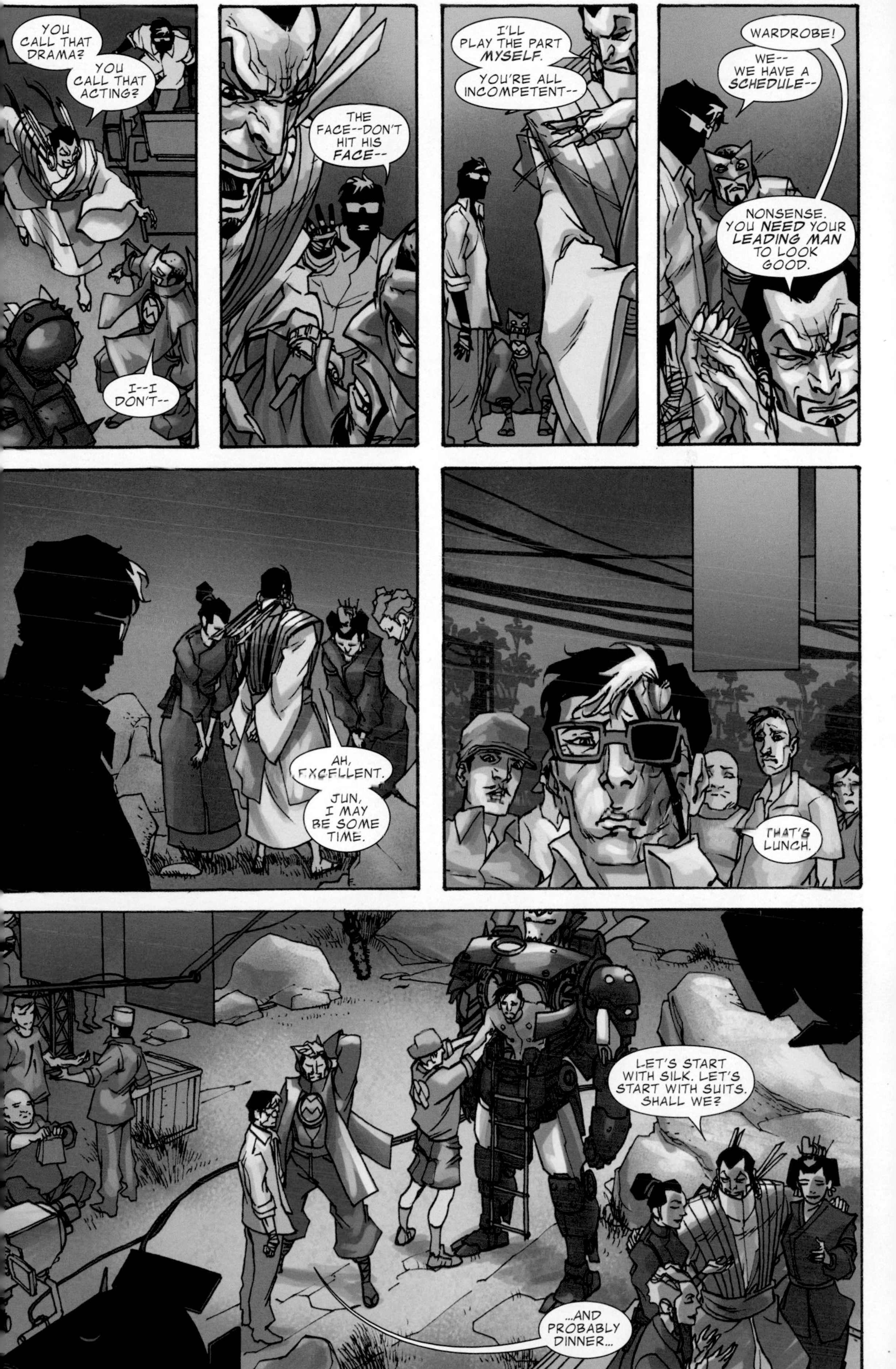
YOU CALL THAT DRAMA?
YOU CALL THAT ACTING?
I--I DON'T--
THE FACE--DON'T HIT HIS FACE--
I'LL PLAY THE PART MYSELF.
YOU'RE ALL INCOMPETENT--
WARDROBE!
WE-- WE HAVE A SCHEDULE--
NONSENSE. YOU NEED YOUR LEADING MAN TO LOOK GOOD.
AH, EXCELLENT.
JUN, I MAY BE SOME TIME.
THAT'S LUNCH.
LET'S START WITH SILK. LET'S START WITH SUITS. SHALL WE?
...AND PROBABLY DINNER...

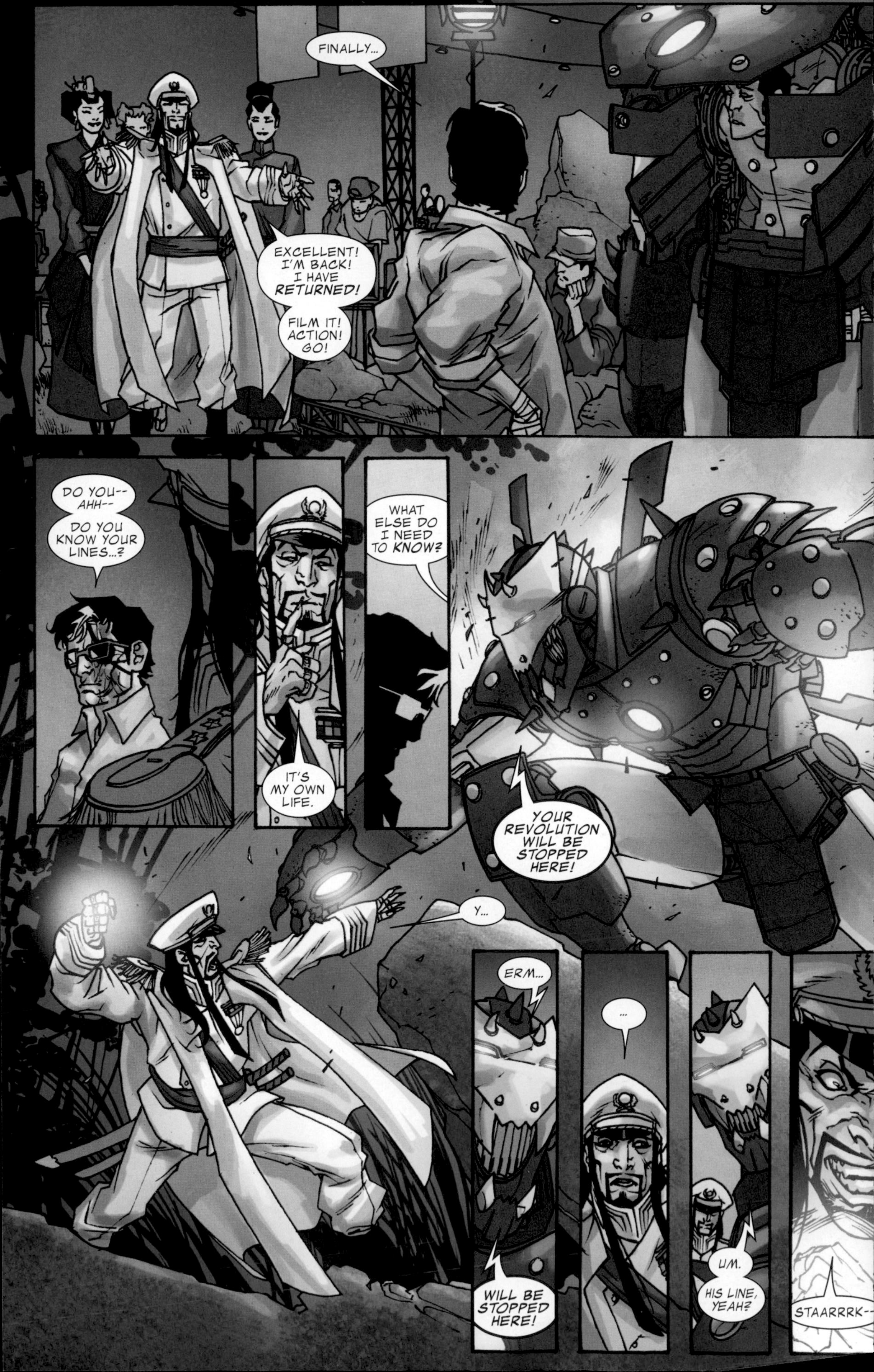
FINALLY...
EXCELLENT! I'M BACK! I HAVE RETURNED!
FILM IT! ACTION! GO!
DO YOU-- AHH-- DO YOU KNOW YOUR LINES...?
WHAT ELSE DO I NEED TO KNOW?
IT'S MY OWN LIFE.
YOUR REVOLUTION WILL BE STOPPED HERE!
Y...
ERM...
WILL BE STOPPED HERE!
...
UM.
HIS LINE, YEAH?
STAARRRK--

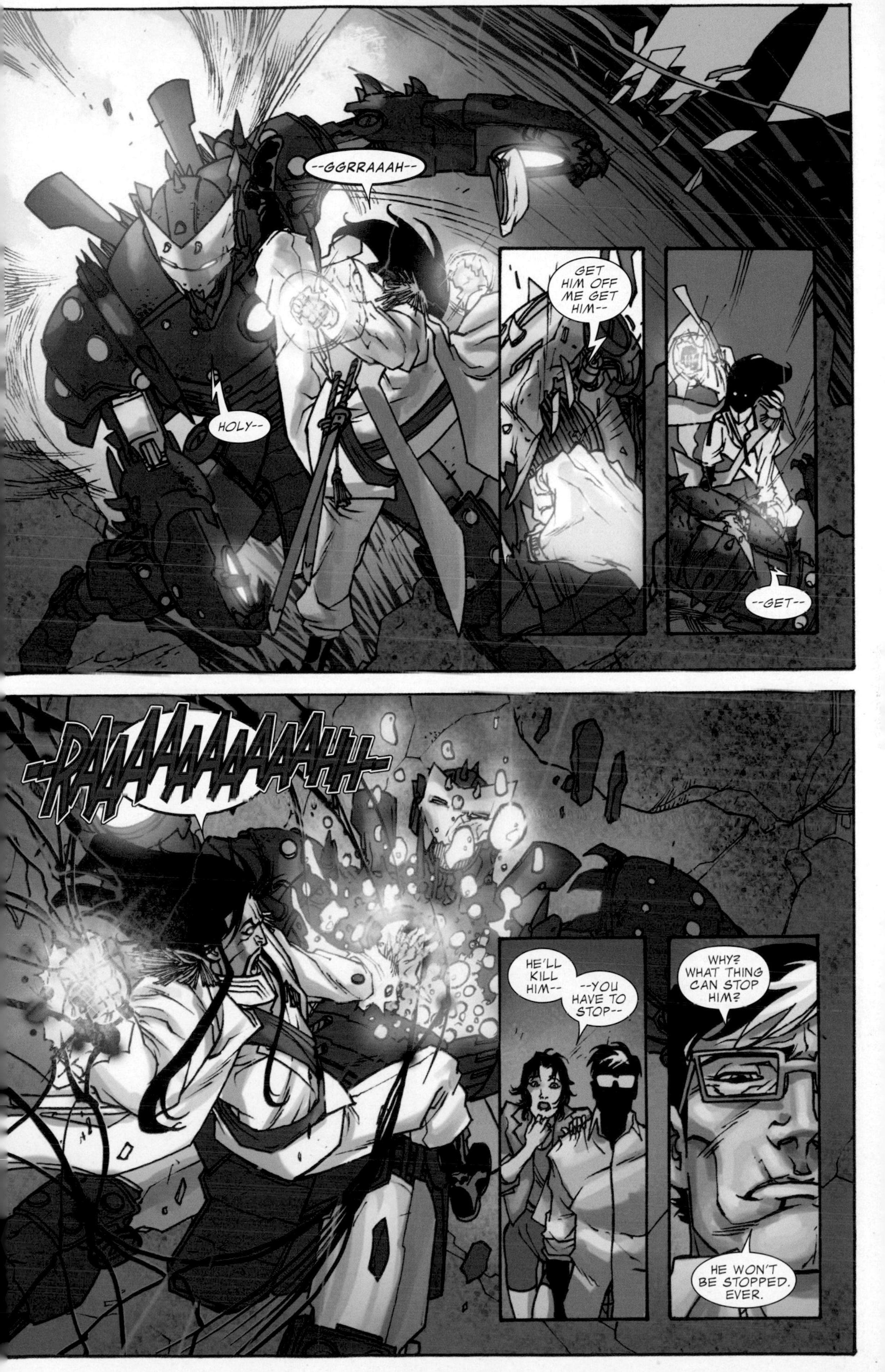
--GGRRAAAH--
HOLY--
GET HIM OFF ME GET HIM--
--GET--
RAAAAAAAAAHH
HE'LL KILL HIM--
--YOU HAVE TO STOP--
WHY? WHAT THING CAN STOP HIM?
HE WON'T BE STOPPED. EVER.

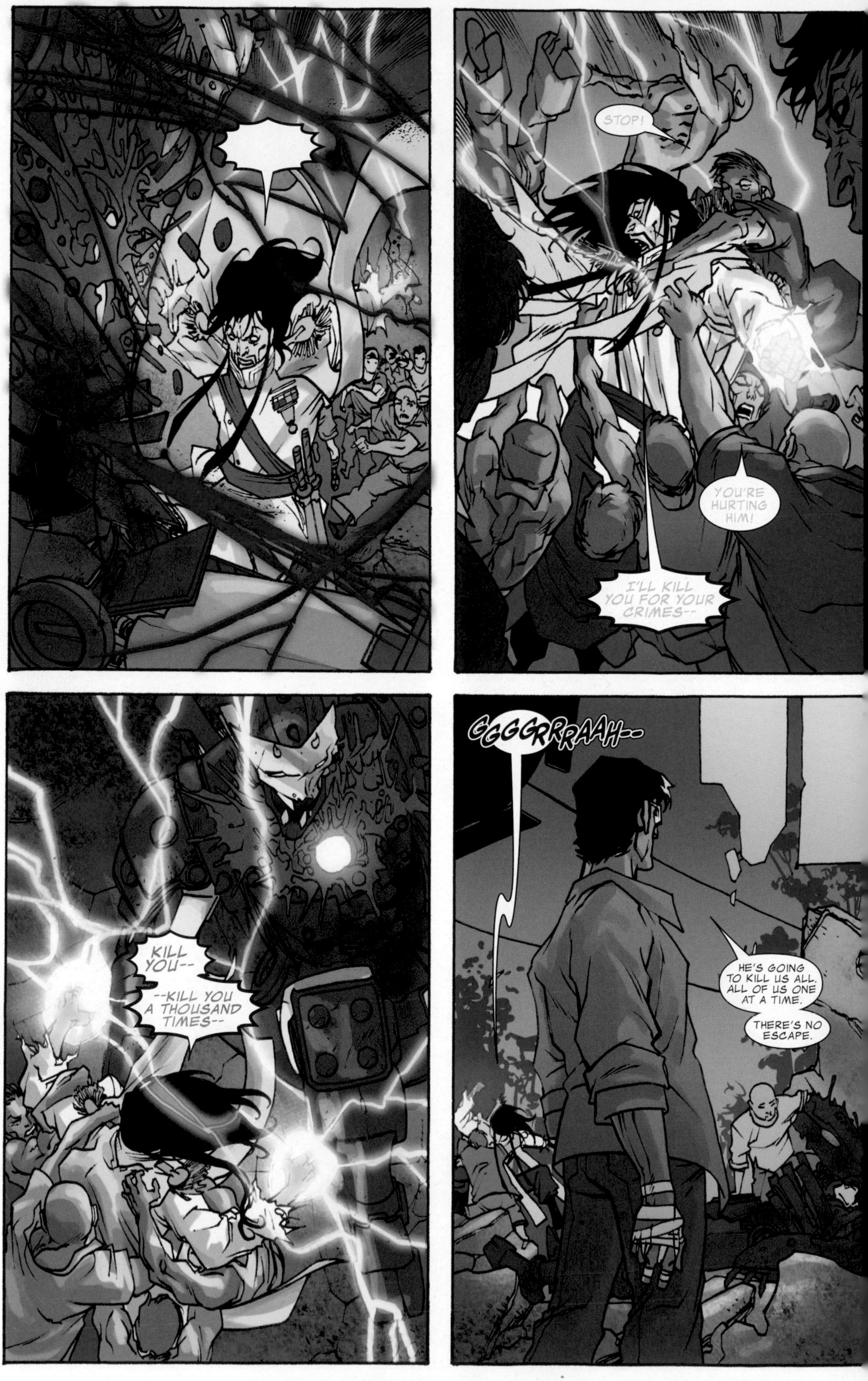
STOP!
YOU'RE HURTING HIM!
I'LL KILL YOU FOR YOUR CRIMES--
KILL YOU--
--KILL YOU A THOUSAND TIMES--
GGGGRRRAAH--
HE'S GOING TO KILL US ALL. ALL OF US ONE AT A TIME.
THERE'S NO ESCAPE.

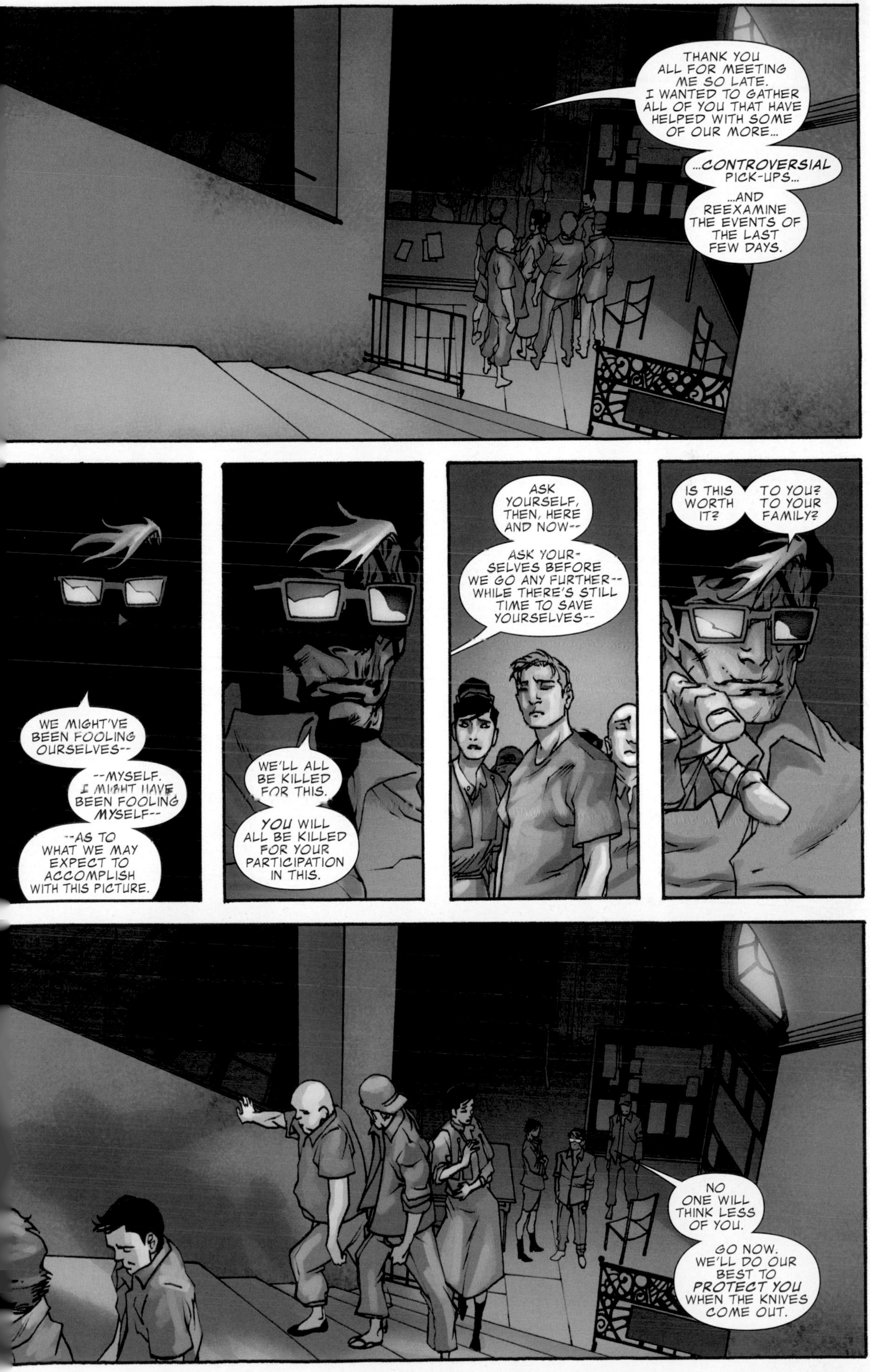
THANK YOU ALL FOR MEETING ME SO LATE. I WANTED TO GATHER ALL OF YOU THAT HAVE HELPED WITH SOME OF OUR MORE...
...CONTROVERSIAL PICK-UPS...
...AND REEXAMINE THE EVENTS OF THE LAST FEW DAYS.
WE MIGHT'VE BEEN FOOLING OURSELVES--
--MYSELF. I MIGHT HAVE BEEN FOOLING MYSELF--
--AS TO WHAT WE MAY EXPECT TO ACCOMPLISH WITH THIS PICTURE.
WE'LL ALL BE KILLED FOR THIS.
YOU WILL ALL BE KILLED FOR YOUR PARTICIPATION IN THIS.
ASK YOURSELF, THEN, HERE AND NOW--
ASK YOURSELVES BEFORE WE GO ANY FURTHER--WHILE THERE'S STILL TIME TO SAVE YOURSELVES--
IS THIS WORTH IT?
TO YOU? TO YOUR FAMILY?
NO ONE WILL THINK LESS OF YOU.
GO NOW. WE'LL DO OUR BEST TO PROTECT YOU WHEN THE KNIVES COME OUT.

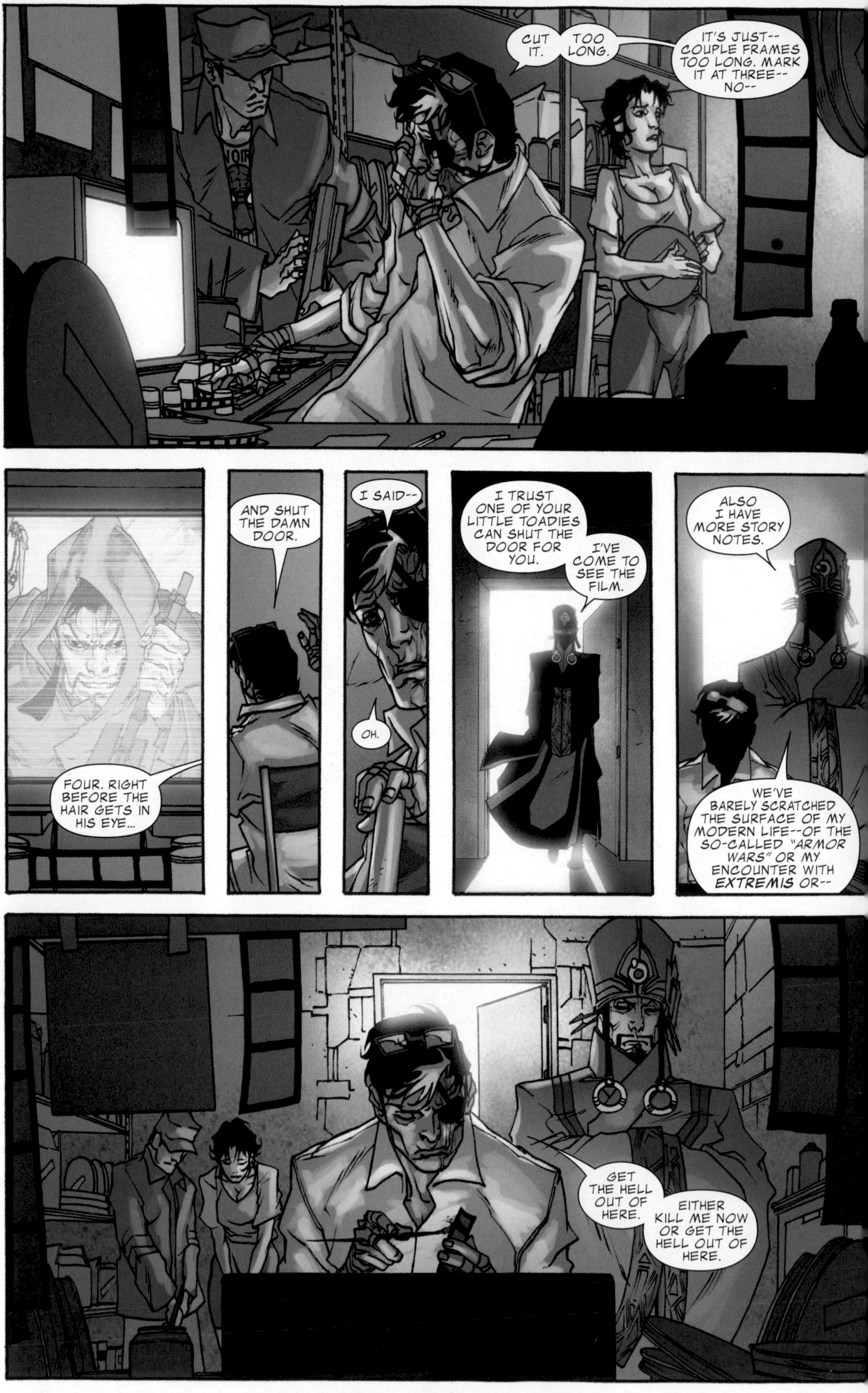
IT'S JUST-- COUPLE FRAMES TOO LONG. MARK IT AT THREE-- NO--
TOO LONG.
CUT IT.
FOUR. RIGHT BEFORE THE HAIR GETS IN HIS EYE...
AND SHUT THE DAMN DOOR.
I SAID--
OH.
I TRUST ONE OF YOUR LITTLE TOADIES CAN SHUT THE DOOR FOR YOU.
I'VE COME TO SEE THE FILM.
ALSO I HAVE MORE STORY NOTES.
WE'VE BARELY SCRATCHED THE SURFACE OF MY MODERN LIFE--OF THE SO-CALLED "ARMOR WARS" OR MY ENCOUNTER WITH EXTREMIS OR--
GET THE HELL OUT OF HERE.
EITHER KILL ME NOW OR GET THE HELL OUT OF HERE.

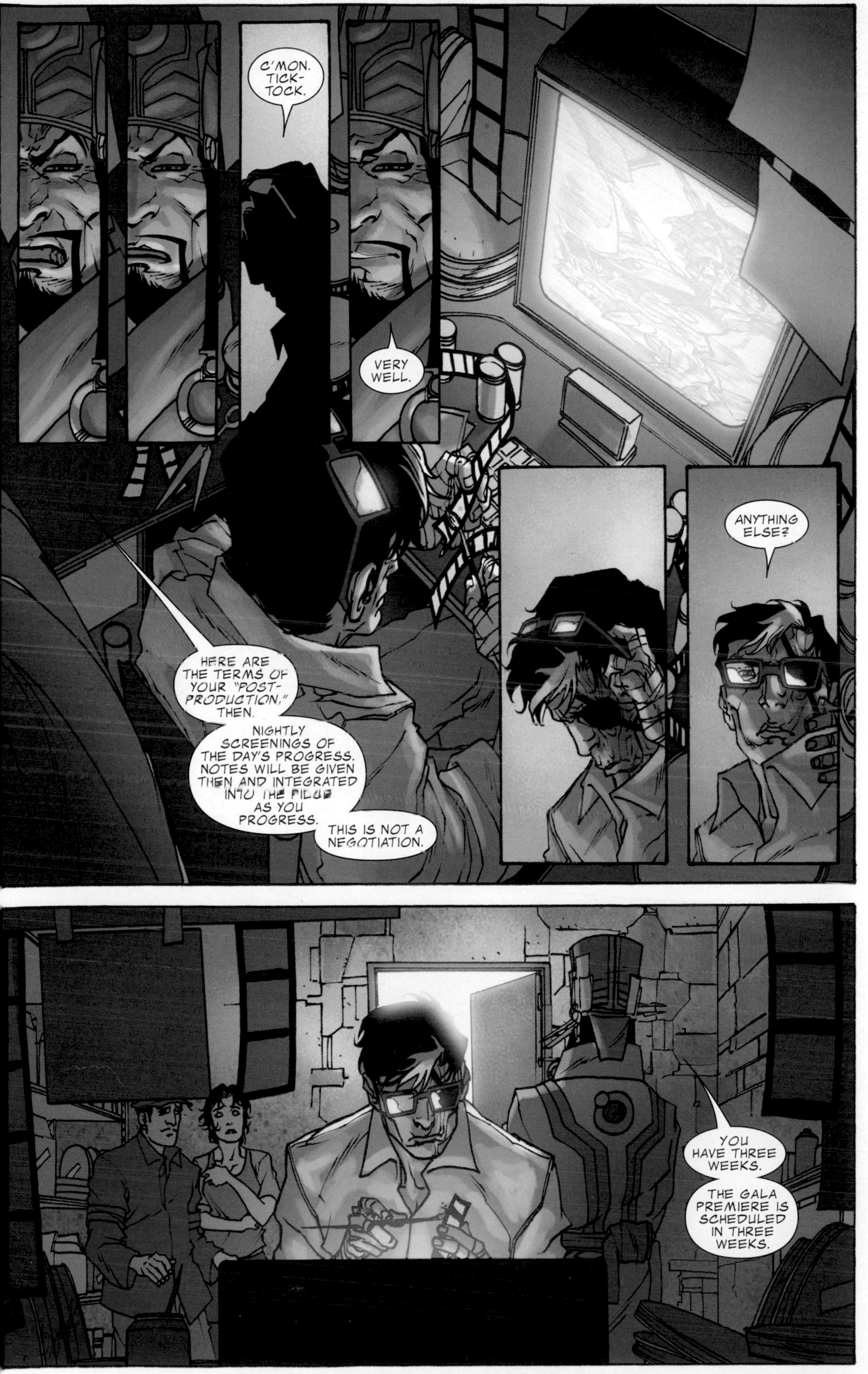
C'MON. TICK-TOCK.
VERY WELL.
HERE ARE THE TERMS OF YOUR "POST-PRODUCTION," THEN.
NIGHTLY SCREENINGS OF THE DAY'S PROGRESS. NOTES WILL BE GIVEN THEN AND INTEGRATED INTO THE FILM AS YOU PROGRESS.
THIS IS NOT A NEGOTIATION.
ANYTHING ELSE?
YOU HAVE THREE WEEKS.
THE GALA PREMIERE IS SCHEDULED IN THREE WEEKS.

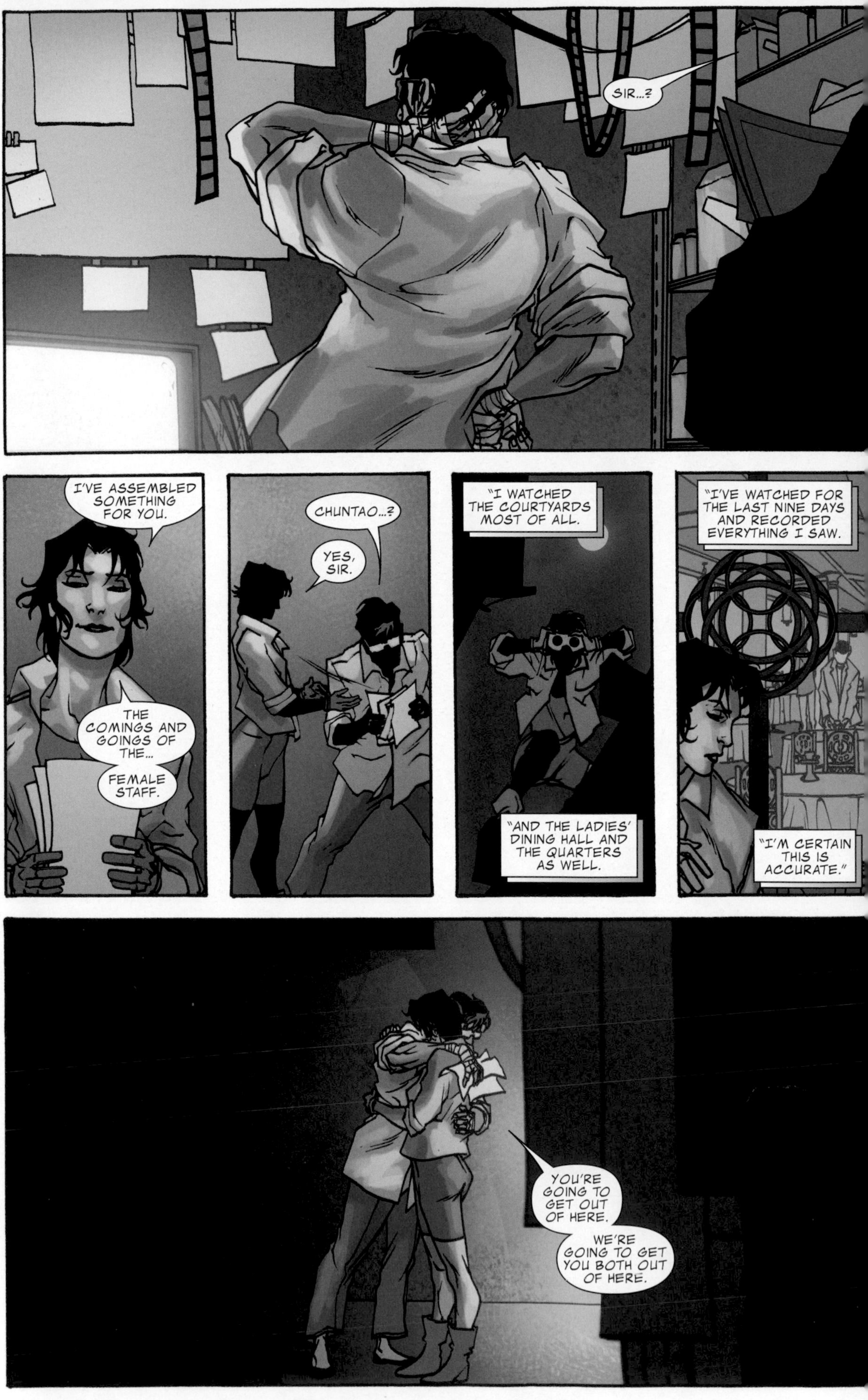
SIR...?
I'VE ASSEMBLED SOMETHING FOR YOU.
THE COMINGS AND GOINGS OF THE...
FEMALE STAFF.
CHUNTAO...?
YES, SIR.
"I WATCHED THE COURTYARDS MOST OF ALL.
"AND THE LADIES' DINING HALL AND THE QUARTERS AS WELL.
"I'VE WATCHED FOR THE LAST NINE DAYS AND RECORDED EVERYTHING I SAW.
"I'M CERTAIN THIS IS ACCURATE."
YOU'RE GOING TO GET OUT OF HERE.
WE'RE GOING TO GET YOU BOTH OUT OF HERE.

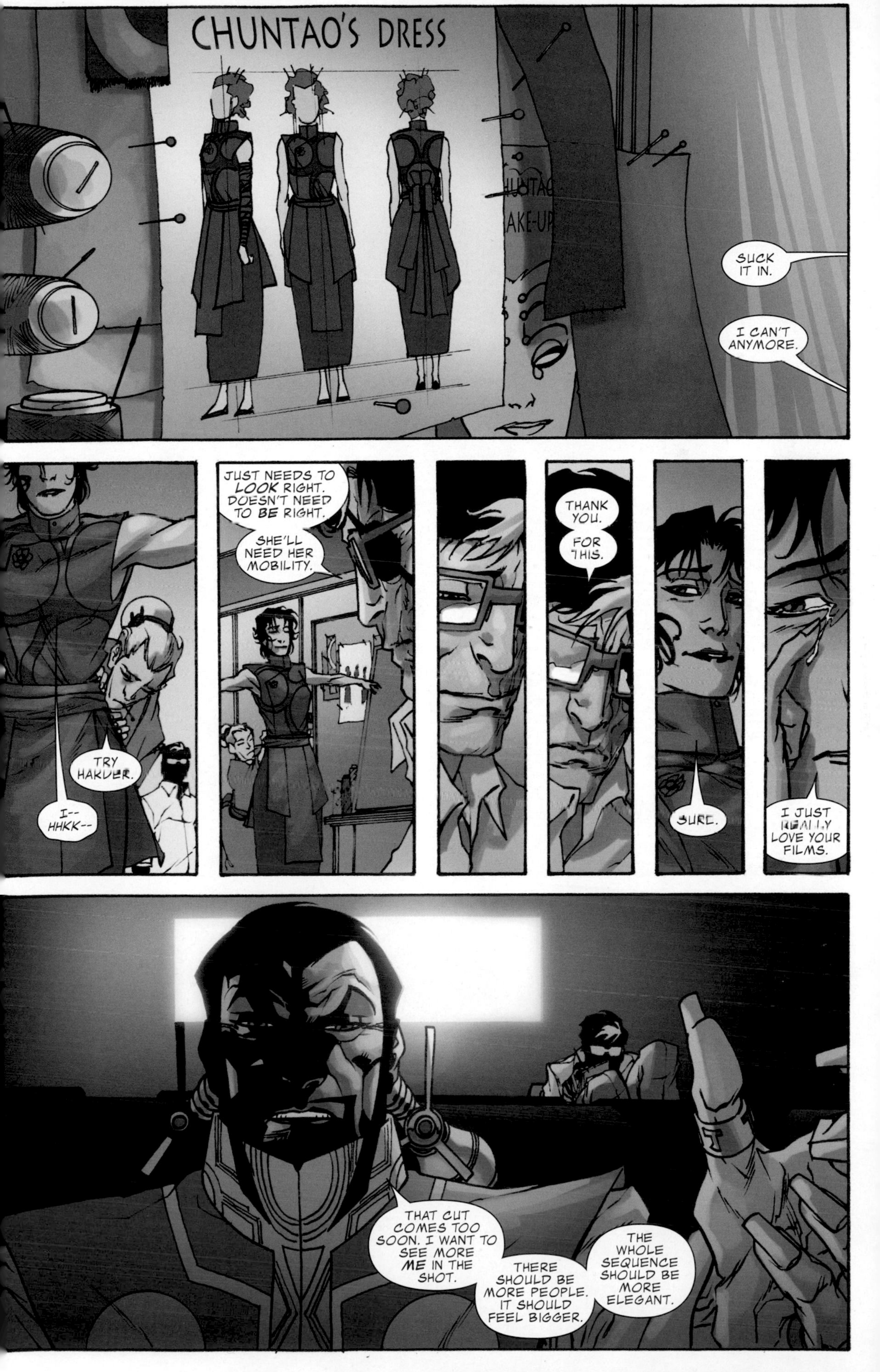
CHUNTAO'S DRESS
SUCK IT IN.
I CAN'T ANYMORE.
TRY HARDER.
I-- HHKK--
JUST NEEDS TO LOOK RIGHT. DOESN'T NEED TO BE RIGHT.
SHE'LL NEED HER MOBILITY.
THANK YOU.
FOR THIS.
SURE.
I JUST REALLY LOVE YOUR FILMS.
THAT CUT COMES TOO SOON. I WANT TO SEE MORE ME IN THE SHOT.
THERE SHOULD BE MORE PEOPLE. IT SHOULD FEEL BIGGER.
THE WHOLE SEQUENCE SHOULD BE MORE ELEGANT.

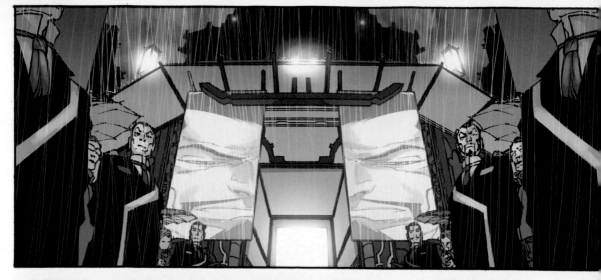

I HAVE ARRIVED.

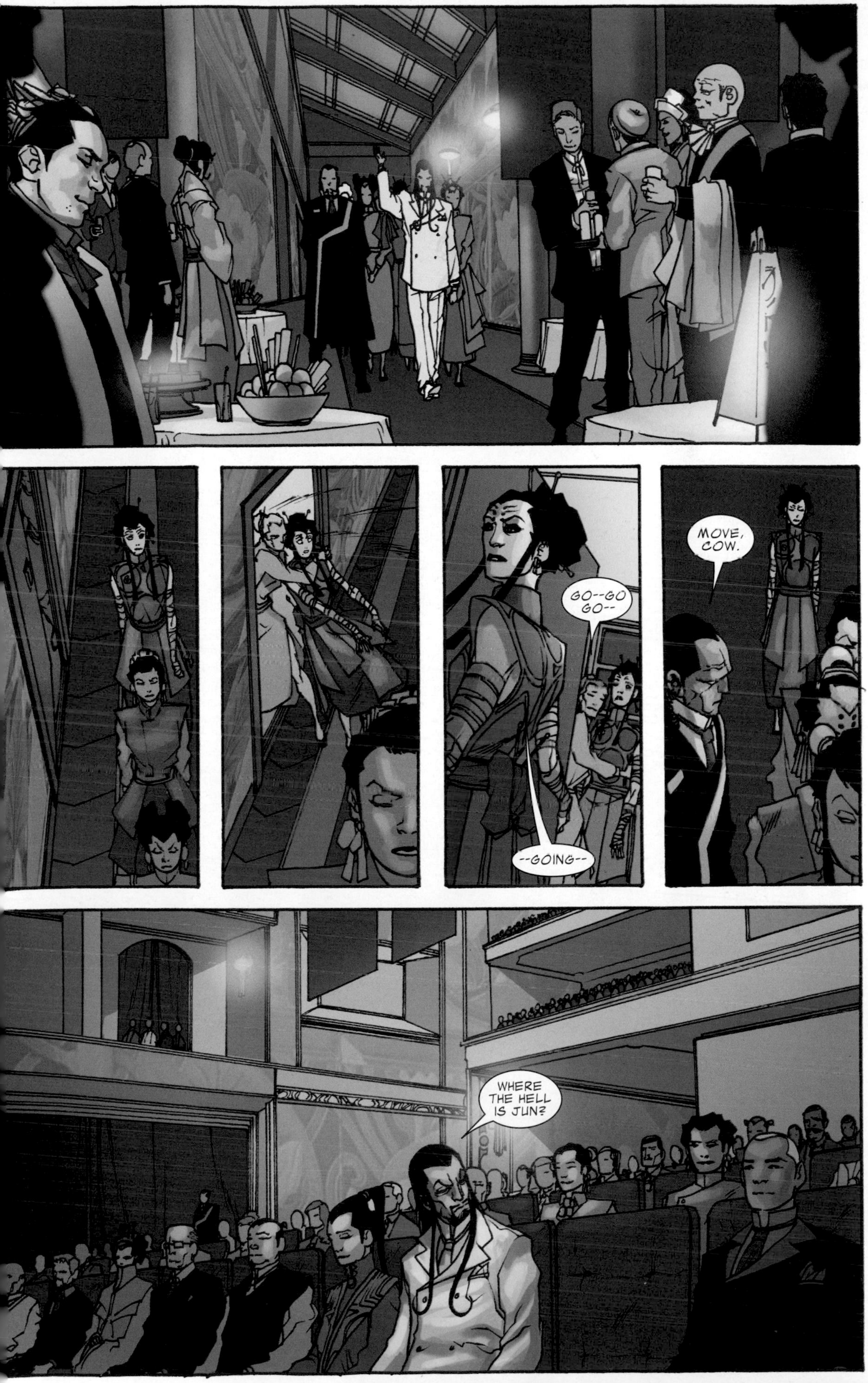
GO--GO
GO--
--GOING--
MOVE, COW.
WHERE THE HELL IS JUN?

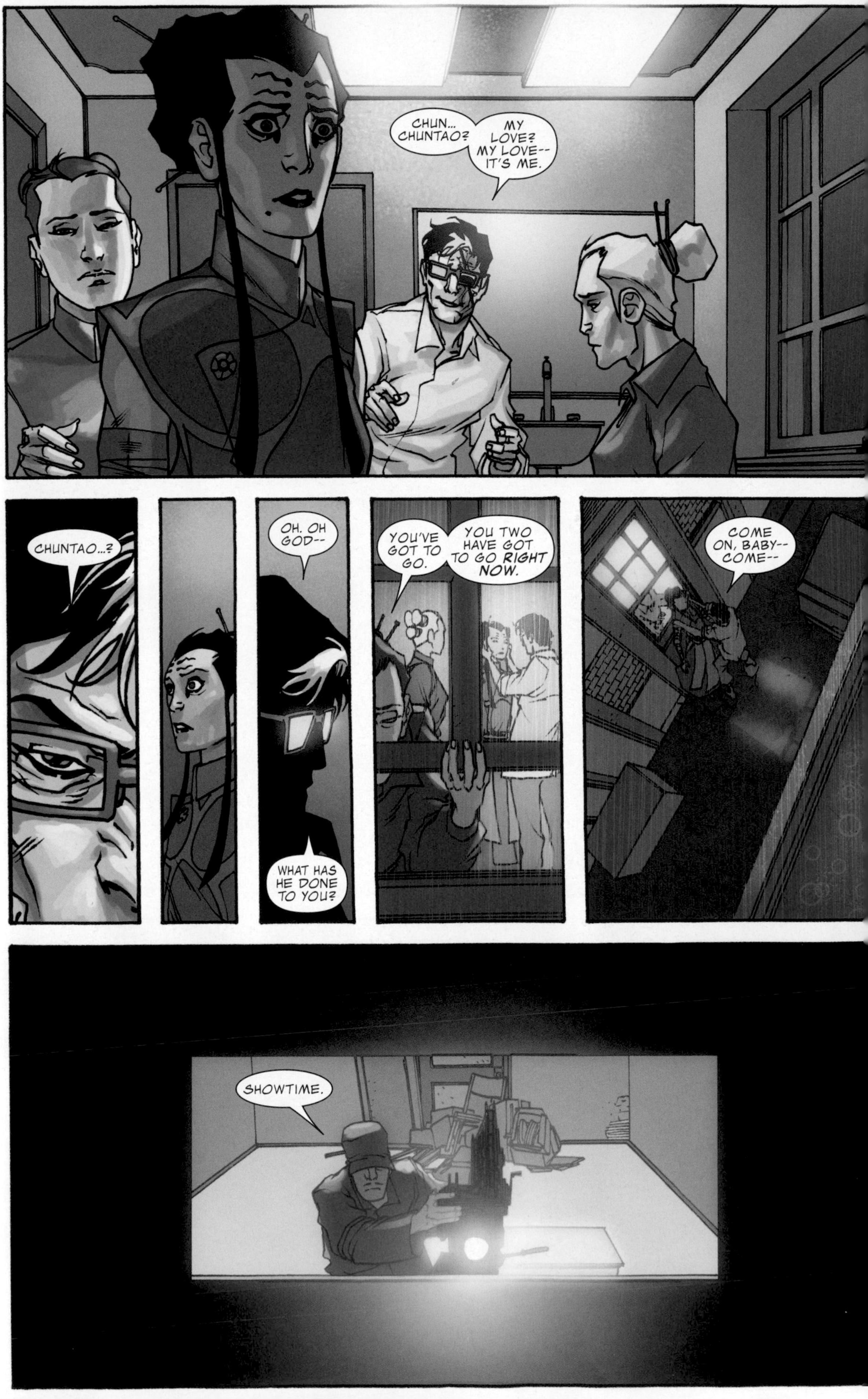
CHUN... CHUNTAO?
MY LOVE? MY LOVE-- IT'S ME.
CHUNTAO...?
OH. OH GOD--
WHAT HAS HE DONE TO YOU?
YOU'VE GOT TO GO.
YOU TWO HAVE GOT TO GO RIGHT NOW.
COME ON, BABY-- COME--
SHOWTIME.

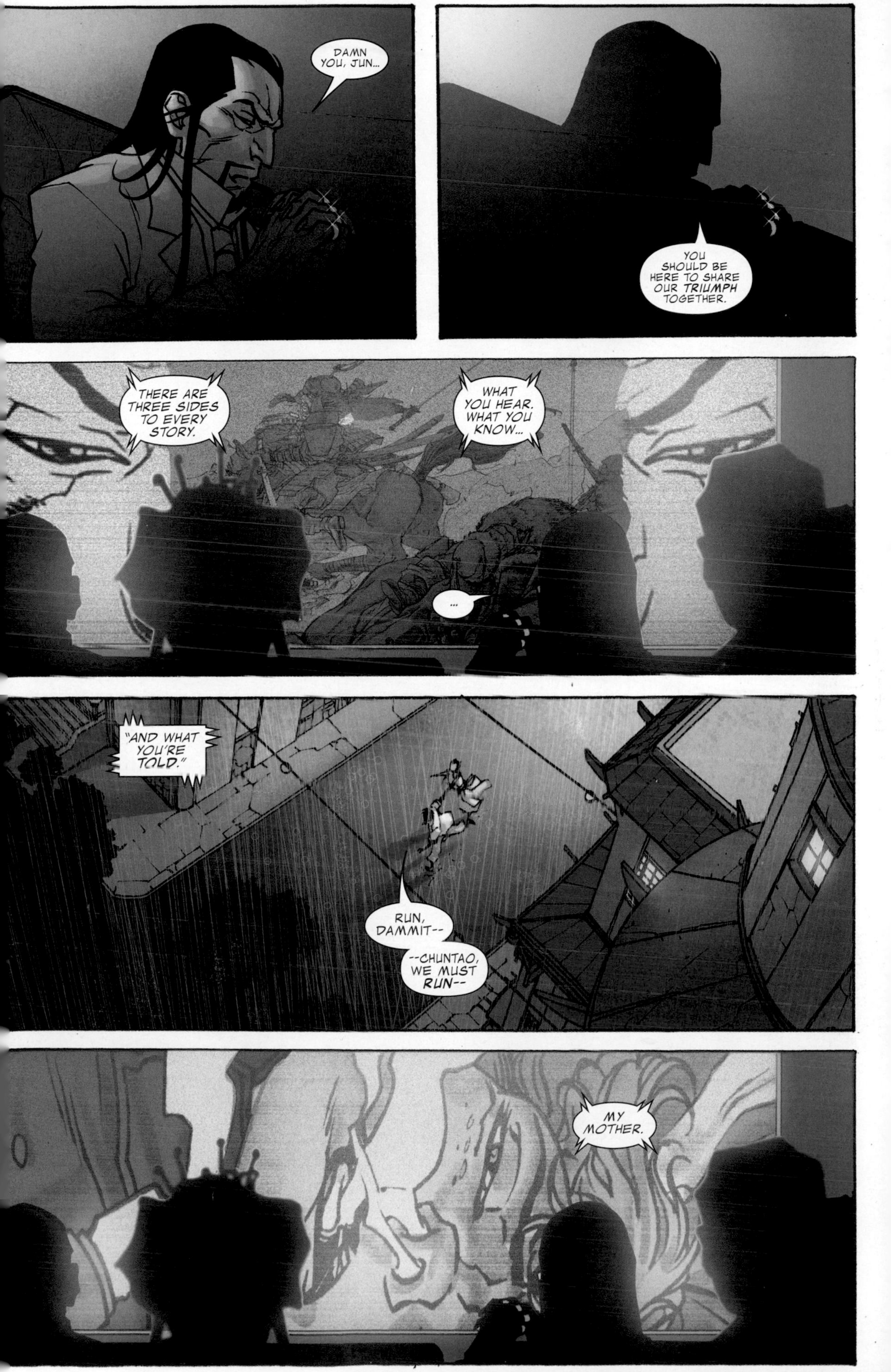
DAMN YOU, JUN...
YOU SHOULD BE HERE TO SHARE OUR *TRIUMPH* TOGETHER.
THERE ARE THREE SIDES TO EVERY STORY.
WHAT YOU HEAR. WHAT YOU KNOW...
...
"AND WHAT YOU'RE *TOLD*."
RUN, DAMMIT--
--CHUNTAO, WE MUST *RUN*--
MY MOTHER.

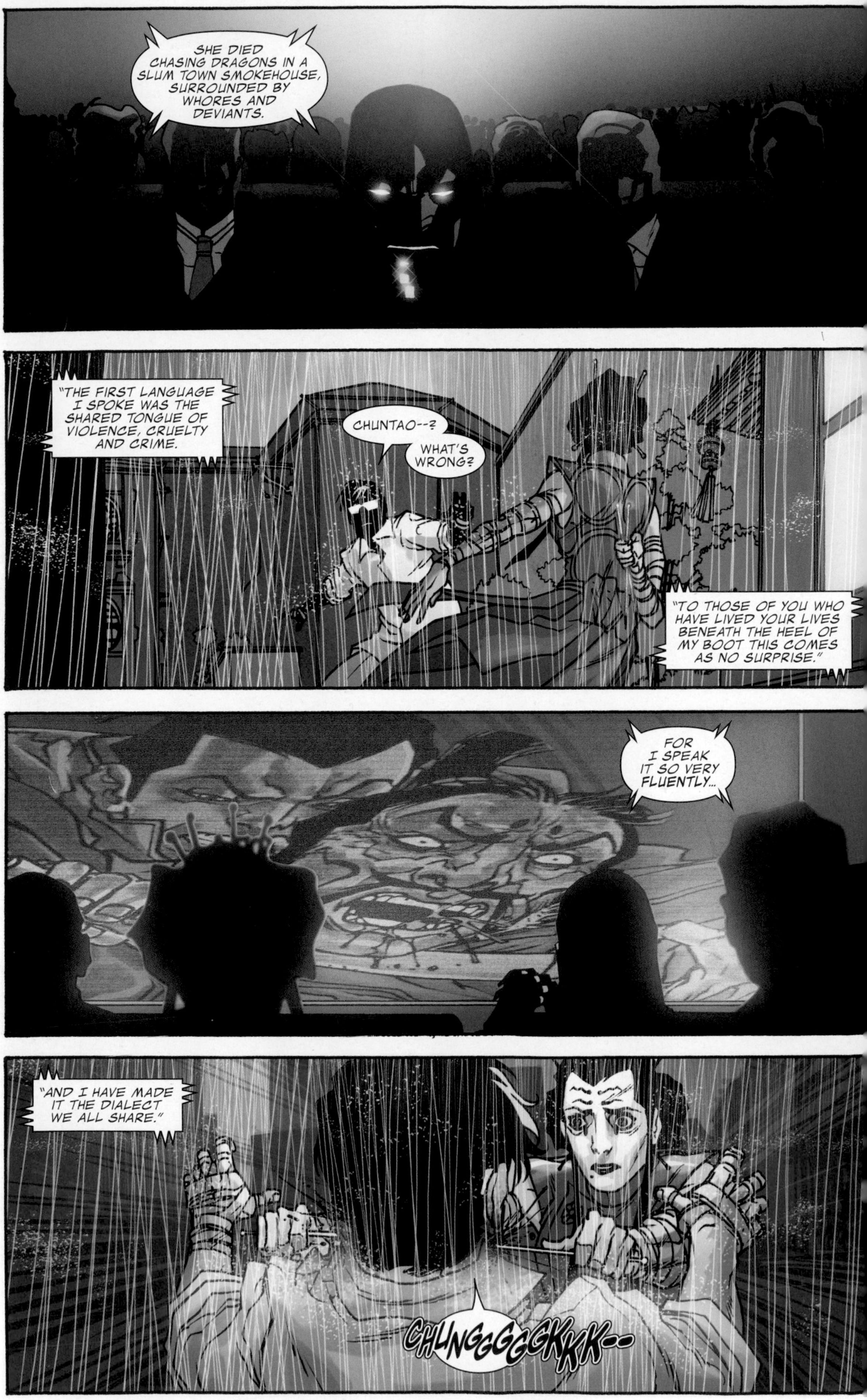
SHE DIED CHASING DRAGONS IN A SLUM TOWN SMOKEHOUSE, SURROUNDED BY WHORES AND DEVIANTS.
"THE FIRST LANGUAGE I SPOKE WAS THE SHARED TONGUE OF VIOLENCE, CRUELTY AND CRIME.
CHUNTAO--?
WHAT'S WRONG?
"TO THOSE OF YOU WHO HAVE LIVED YOUR LIVES BENEATH THE HEEL OF MY BOOT THIS COMES AS NO SURPRISE."
FOR I SPEAK IT SO VERY FLUENTLY...
"AND I HAVE MADE IT THE DIALECT WE ALL SHARE."
CHUNGGGGGKKKK--

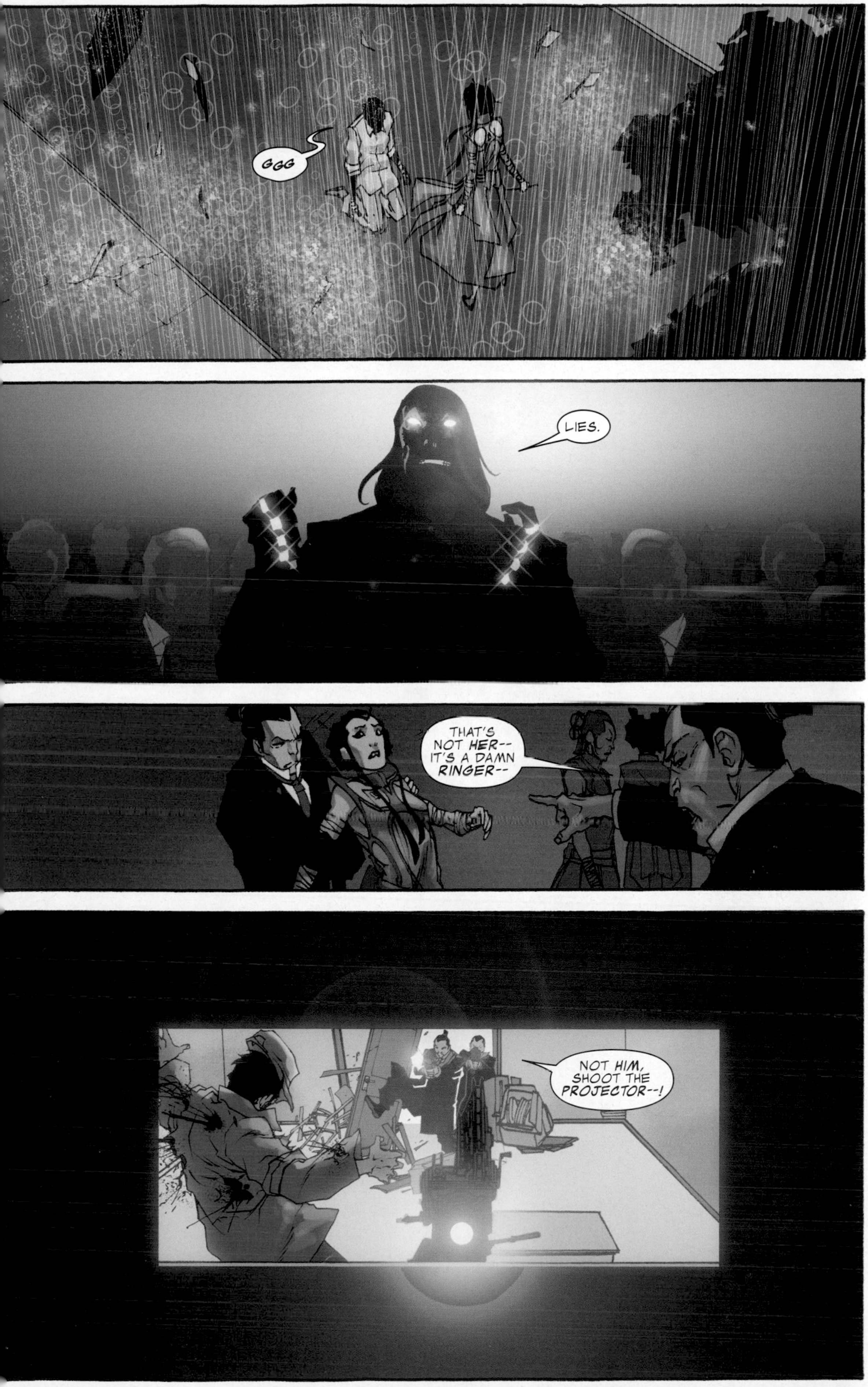
GGG
LIES.
THAT'S NOT HER-- IT'S A DAMN RINGER--
NOT HIM, SHOOT THE PROJECTOR--!

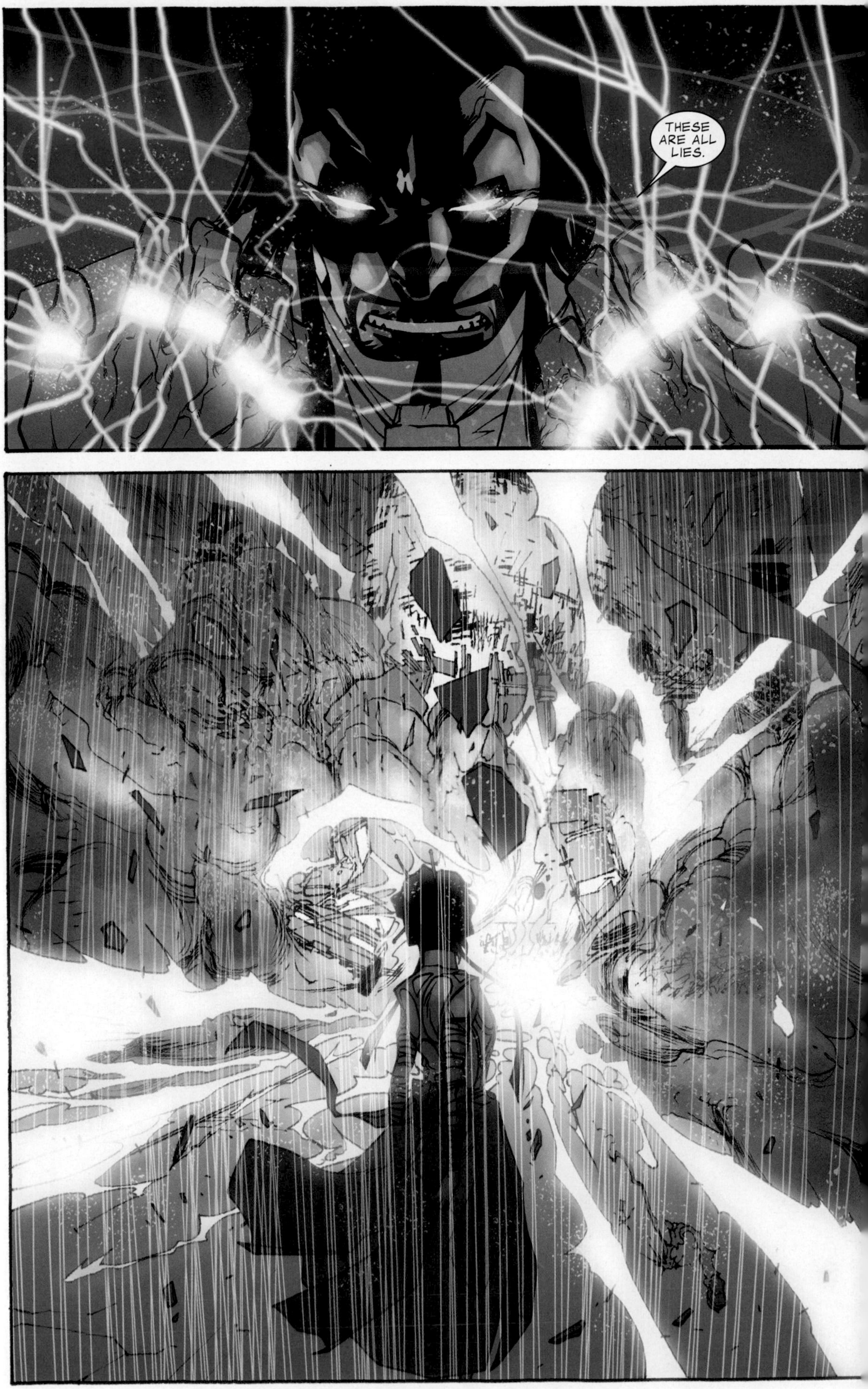
THESE ARE ALL LIES.

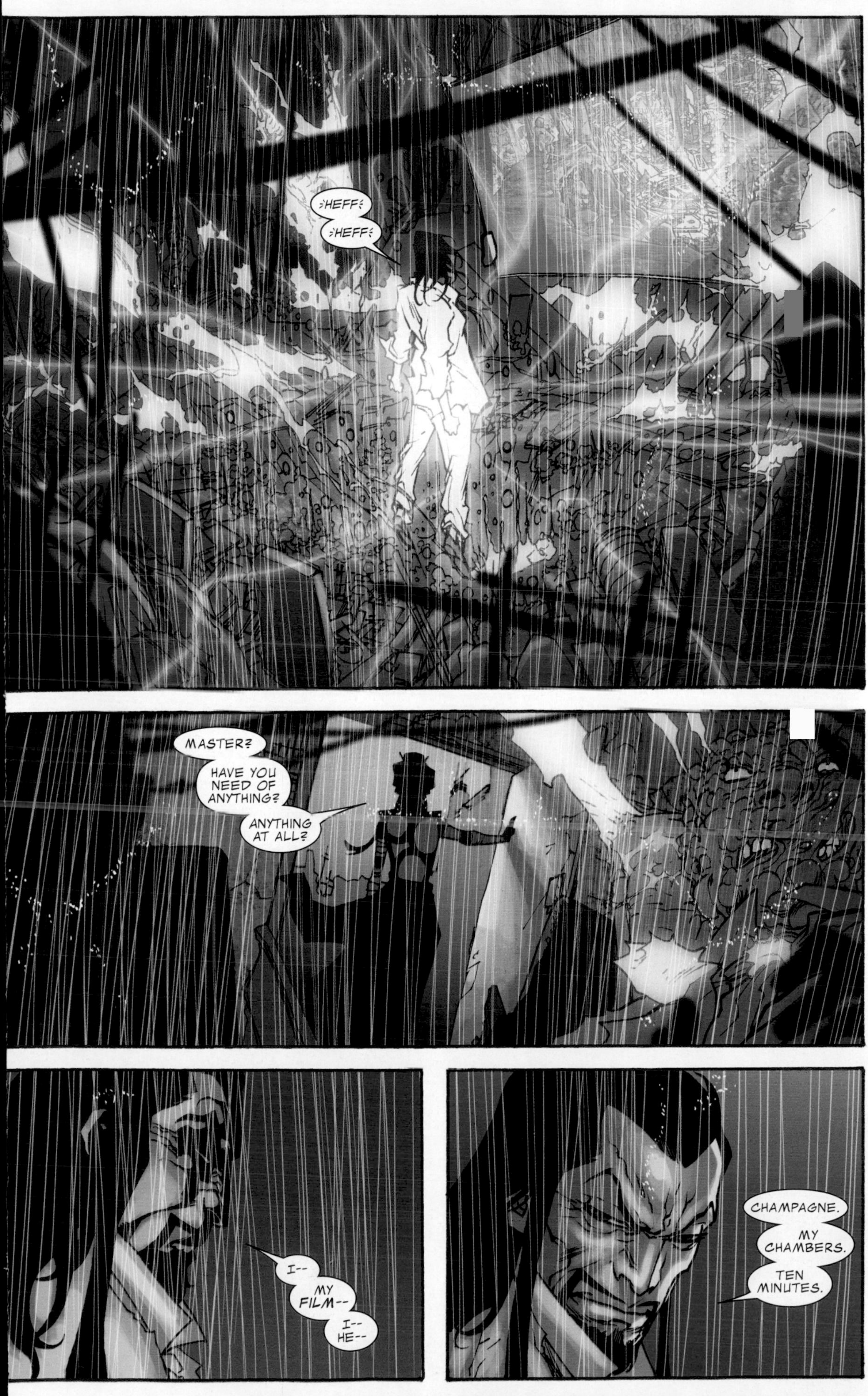
HEFF
HEFF
MASTER?
HAVE YOU NEED OF ANYTHING?
ANYTHING AT ALL?
I-- MY FILM-- I-- HE--
CHAMPAGNE.
MY CHAMBERS.
TEN MINUTES.

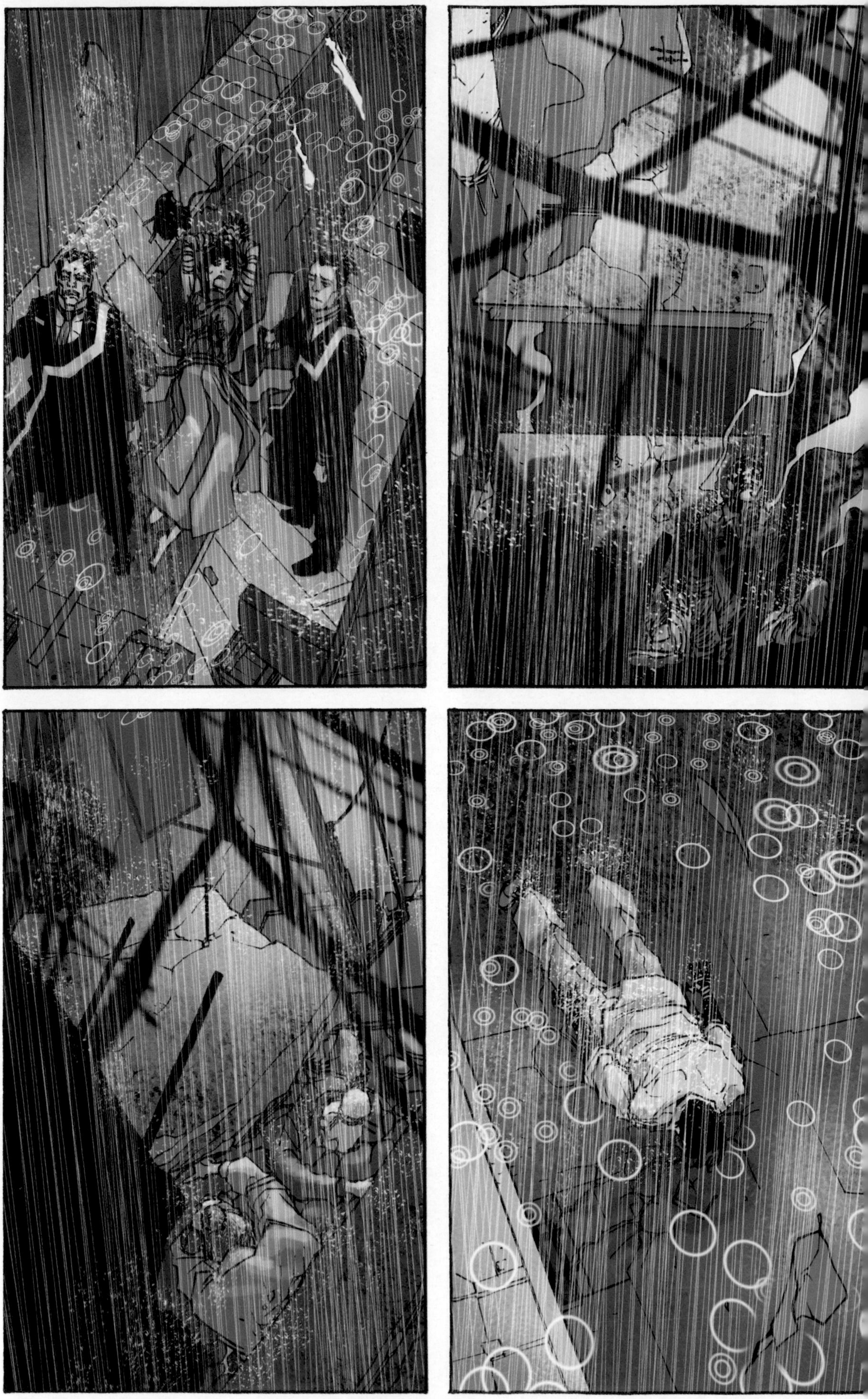

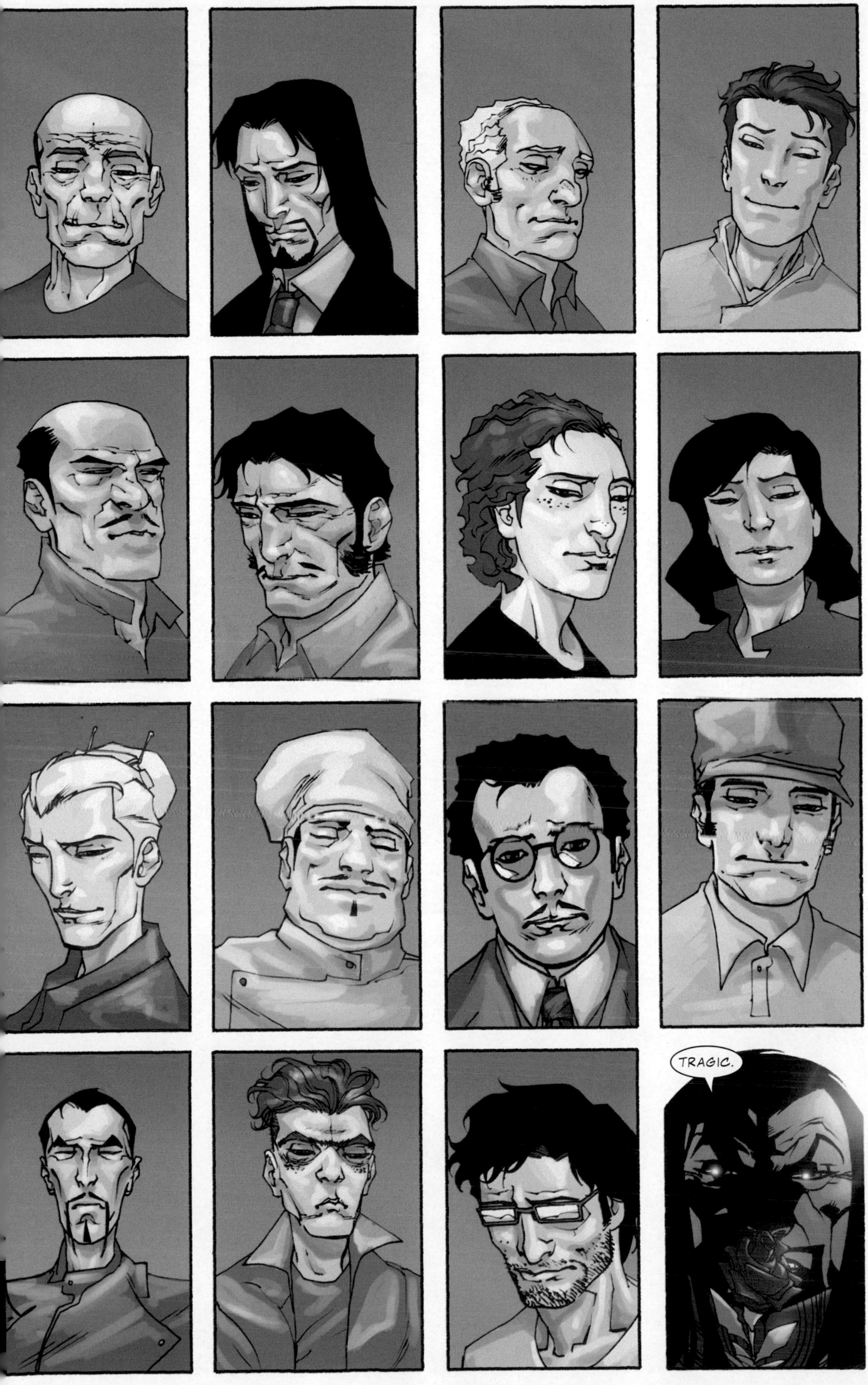
TRAGIC.

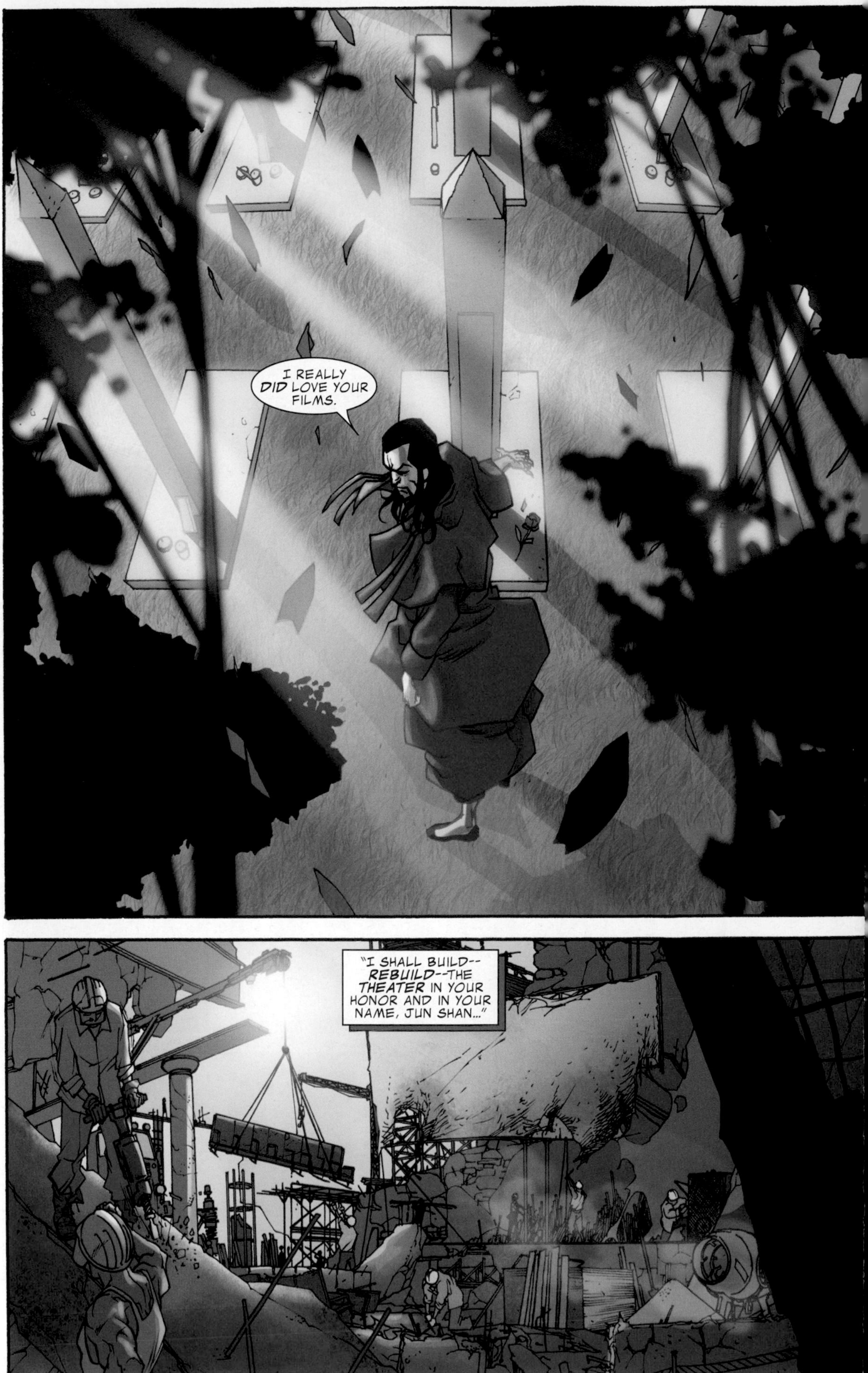
I REALLY DID LOVE YOUR FILMS.
"I SHALL BUILD-- REBUILD--THE THEATER IN YOUR HONOR AND IN YOUR NAME, JUN SHAN..."

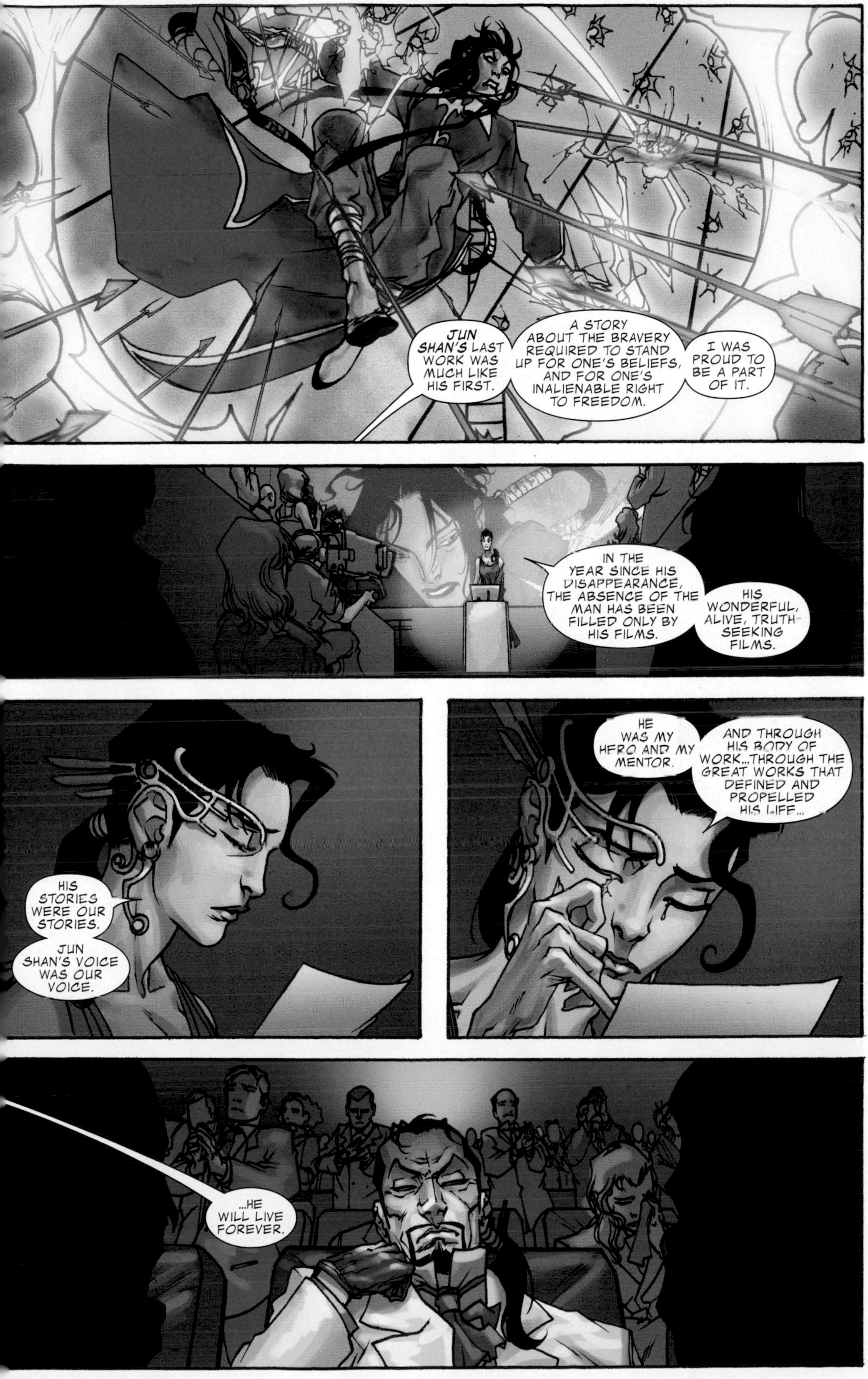
JUN SHAN'S LAST WORK WAS MUCH LIKE HIS FIRST.
A STORY ABOUT THE BRAVERY REQUIRED TO STAND UP FOR ONE'S BELIEFS, AND FOR ONE'S INALIENABLE RIGHT TO FREEDOM.
I WAS PROUD TO BE A PART OF IT.
IN THE YEAR SINCE HIS DISAPPEARANCE, THE ABSENCE OF THE MAN HAS BEEN FILLED ONLY BY HIS FILMS.
HIS WONDERFUL, ALIVE, TRUTH-SEEKING FILMS.
HIS STORIES WERE OUR STORIES.
JUN SHAN'S VOICE WAS OUR VOICE.
HE WAS MY HERO AND MY MENTOR.
AND THROUGH HIS BODY OF WORK...THROUGH THE GREAT WORKS THAT DEFINED AND PROPELLED HIS LIFE...
...HE WILL LIVE FOREVER.

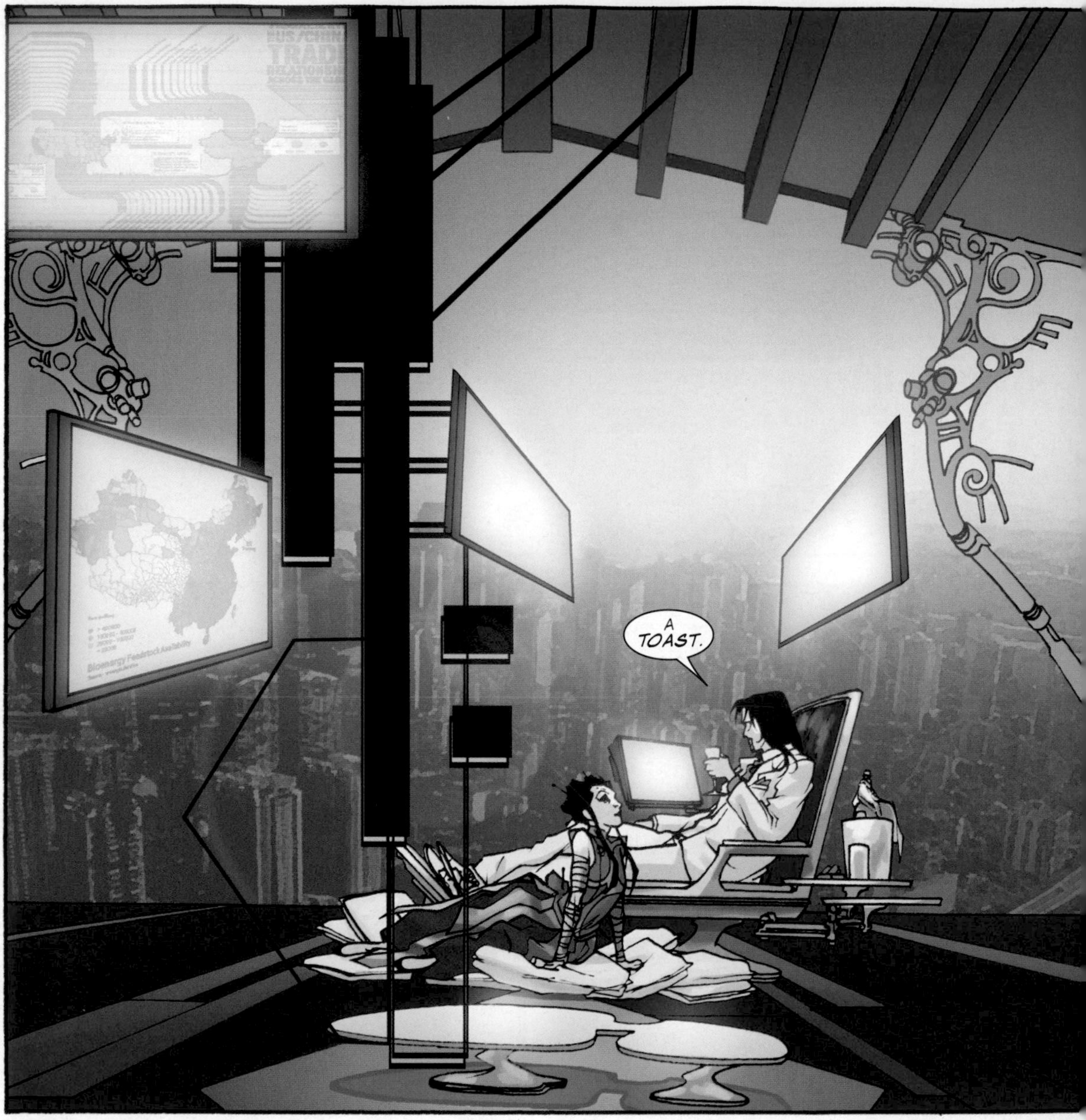
Bioenergy Feedstock Availability
A TOAST.

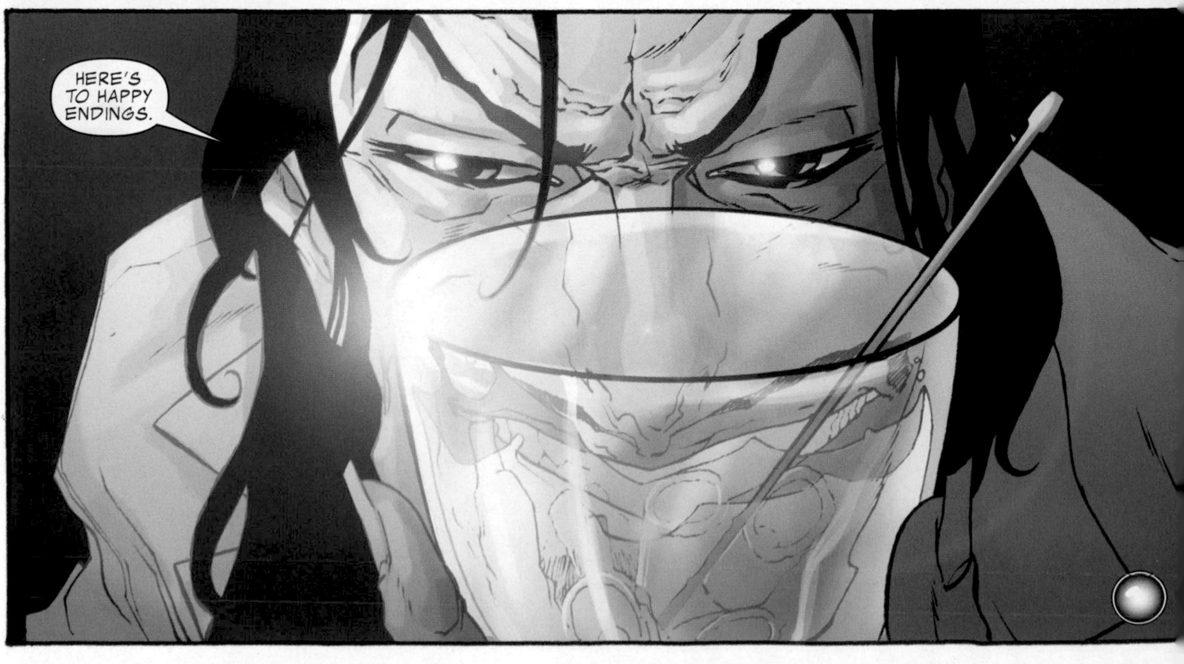
HERE'S TO HAPPY ENDINGS.

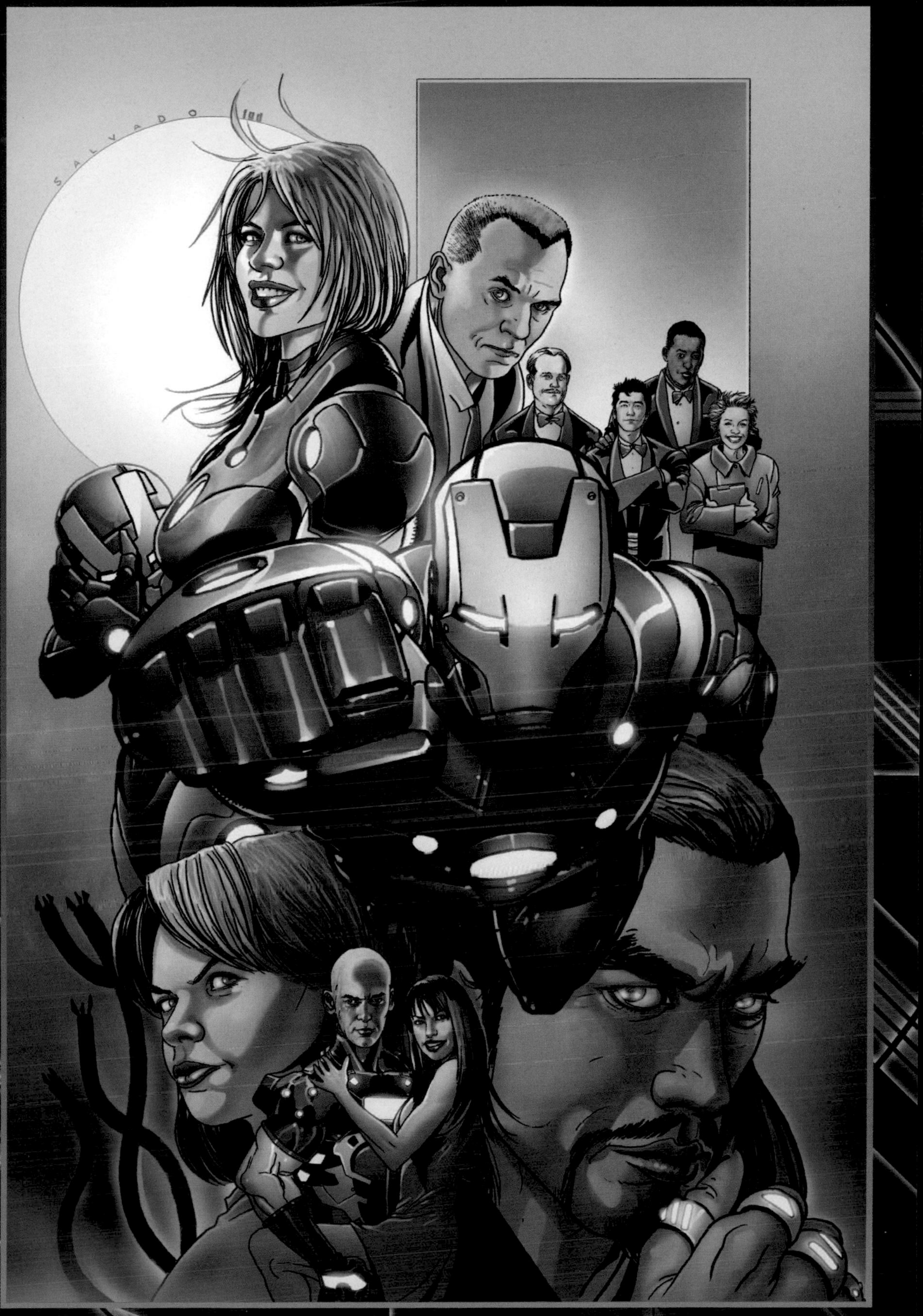

WHAT IT WAS LIKE, WHAT HAPPENED, AND WHAT IT'S LIKE NOW **500.1**

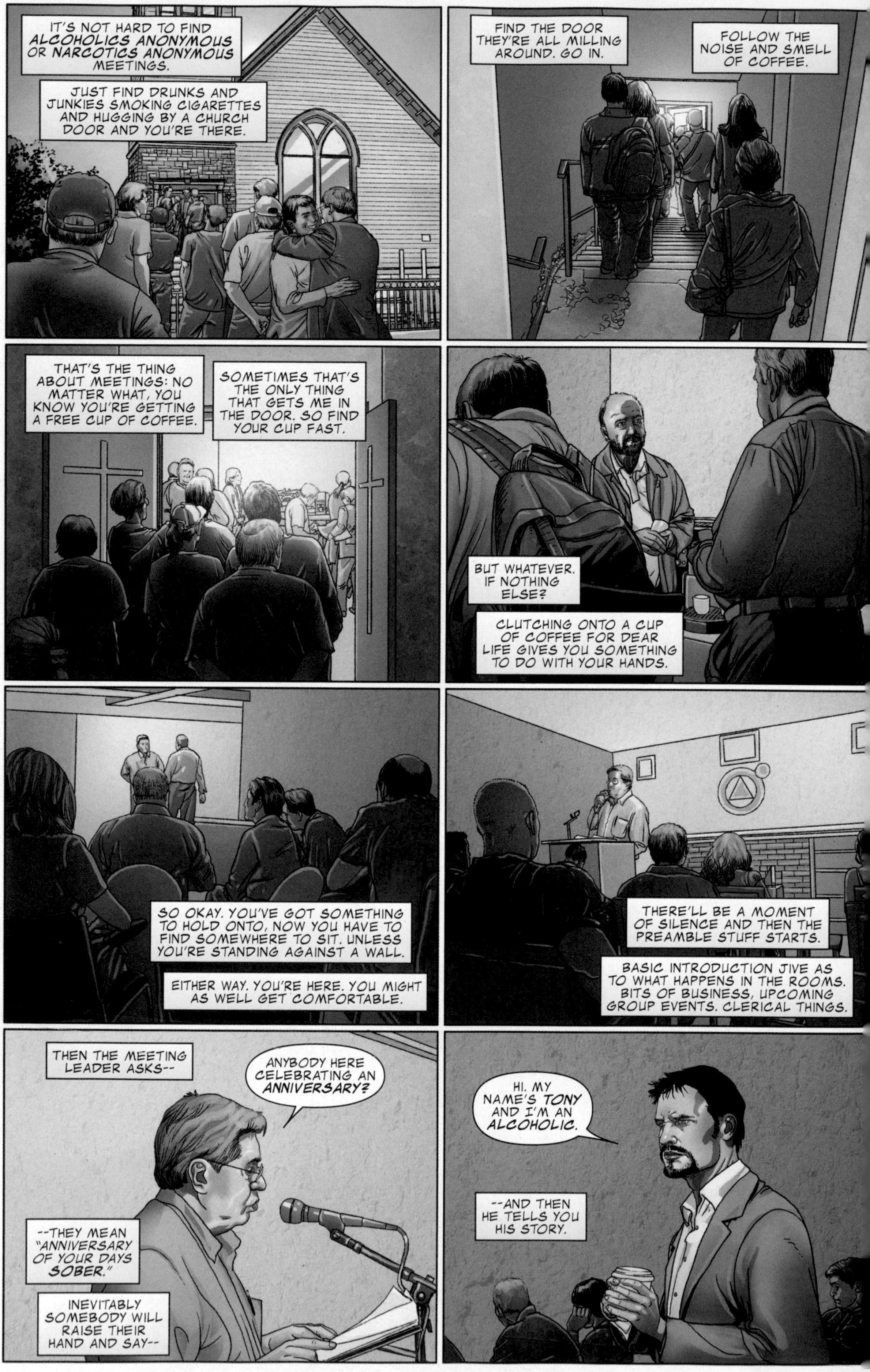

IT'S NOT HARD TO FIND ALCOHOLICS ANONYMOUS OR NARCOTICS ANONYMOUS MEETINGS.
JUST FIND DRUNKS AND JUNKIES SMOKING CIGARETTES AND HUGGING BY A CHURCH DOOR AND YOU'RE THERE.
FIND THE DOOR THEY'RE ALL MILLING AROUND. GO IN.
FOLLOW THE NOISE AND SMELL OF COFFEE.
THAT'S THE THING ABOUT MEETINGS: NO MATTER WHAT, YOU KNOW YOU'RE GETTING A FREE CUP OF COFFEE.
SOMETIMES THAT'S THE ONLY THING THAT GETS ME IN THE DOOR. SO FIND YOUR CUP FAST.
BUT WHATEVER. IF NOTHING ELSE?
CLUTCHING ONTO A CUP OF COFFEE FOR DEAR LIFE GIVES YOU SOMETHING TO DO WITH YOUR HANDS.
SO OKAY. YOU'VE GOT SOMETHING TO HOLD ONTO, NOW YOU HAVE TO FIND SOMEWHERE TO SIT. UNLESS YOU'RE STANDING AGAINST A WALL.
EITHER WAY. YOU'RE HERE. YOU MIGHT AS WELL GET COMFORTABLE.
THERE'LL BE A MOMENT OF SILENCE AND THEN THE PREAMBLE STUFF STARTS.
BASIC INTRODUCTION JIVE AS TO WHAT HAPPENS IN THE ROOMS. BITS OF BUSINESS, UPCOMING GROUP EVENTS. CLERICAL THINGS.
THEN THE MEETING LEADER ASKS--
ANYBODY HERE CELEBRATING AN ANNIVERSARY?
--THEY MEAN "ANNIVERSARY OF YOUR DAYS SOBER."
INEVITABLY SOMEBODY WILL RAISE THEIR HAND AND SAY--
HI. MY NAME'S TONY AND I'M AN ALCOHOLIC.
--AND THEN HE TELLS YOU HIS STORY.

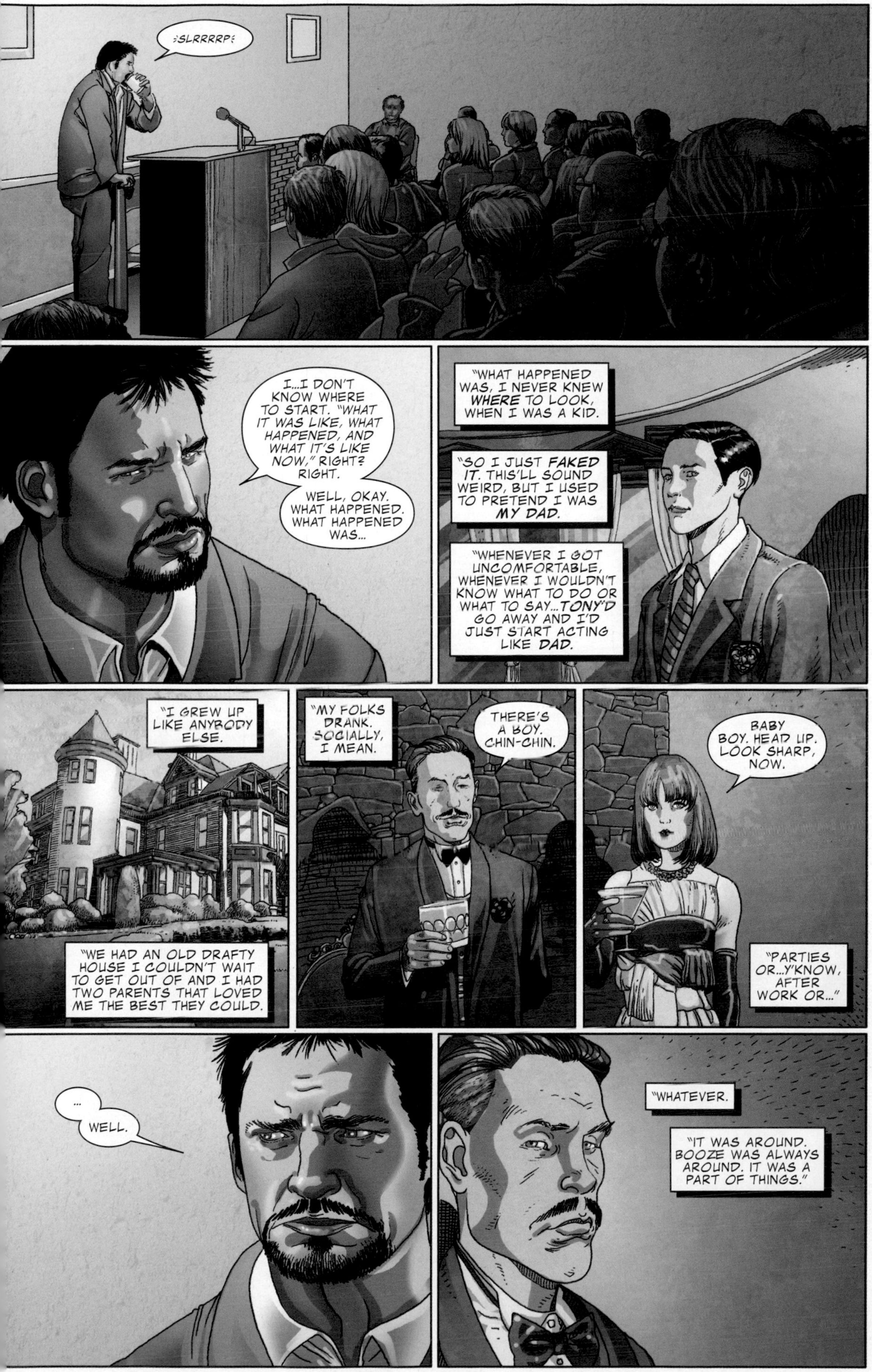

SLRRRRP
I...I DON'T KNOW WHERE TO START. "WHAT IT WAS LIKE, WHAT HAPPENED, AND WHAT IT'S LIKE NOW," RIGHT? RIGHT.
WELL, OKAY. WHAT HAPPENED. WHAT HAPPENED WAS...
"WHAT HAPPENED WAS, I NEVER KNEW WHERE TO LOOK, WHEN I WAS A KID.
"SO I JUST FAKED IT. THIS'LL SOUND WEIRD, BUT I USED TO PRETEND I WAS MY DAD.
"WHENEVER I GOT UNCOMFORTABLE, WHENEVER I WOULDN'T KNOW WHAT TO DO OR WHAT TO SAY...TONY'D GO AWAY AND I'D JUST START ACTING LIKE DAD.
"I GREW UP LIKE ANYBODY ELSE.
"WE HAD AN OLD DRAFTY HOUSE I COULDN'T WAIT TO GET OUT OF AND I HAD TWO PARENTS THAT LOVED ME THE BEST THEY COULD.
"MY FOLKS DRANK. SOCIALLY, I MEAN.
THERE'S A BOY. CHIN-CHIN.
BABY BOY. HEAD UP. LOOK SHARP, NOW.
"PARTIES OR...Y'KNOW, AFTER WORK OR..."
... WELL.
"WHATEVER.
"IT WAS AROUND. BOOZE WAS ALWAYS AROUND. IT WAS A PART OF THINGS."

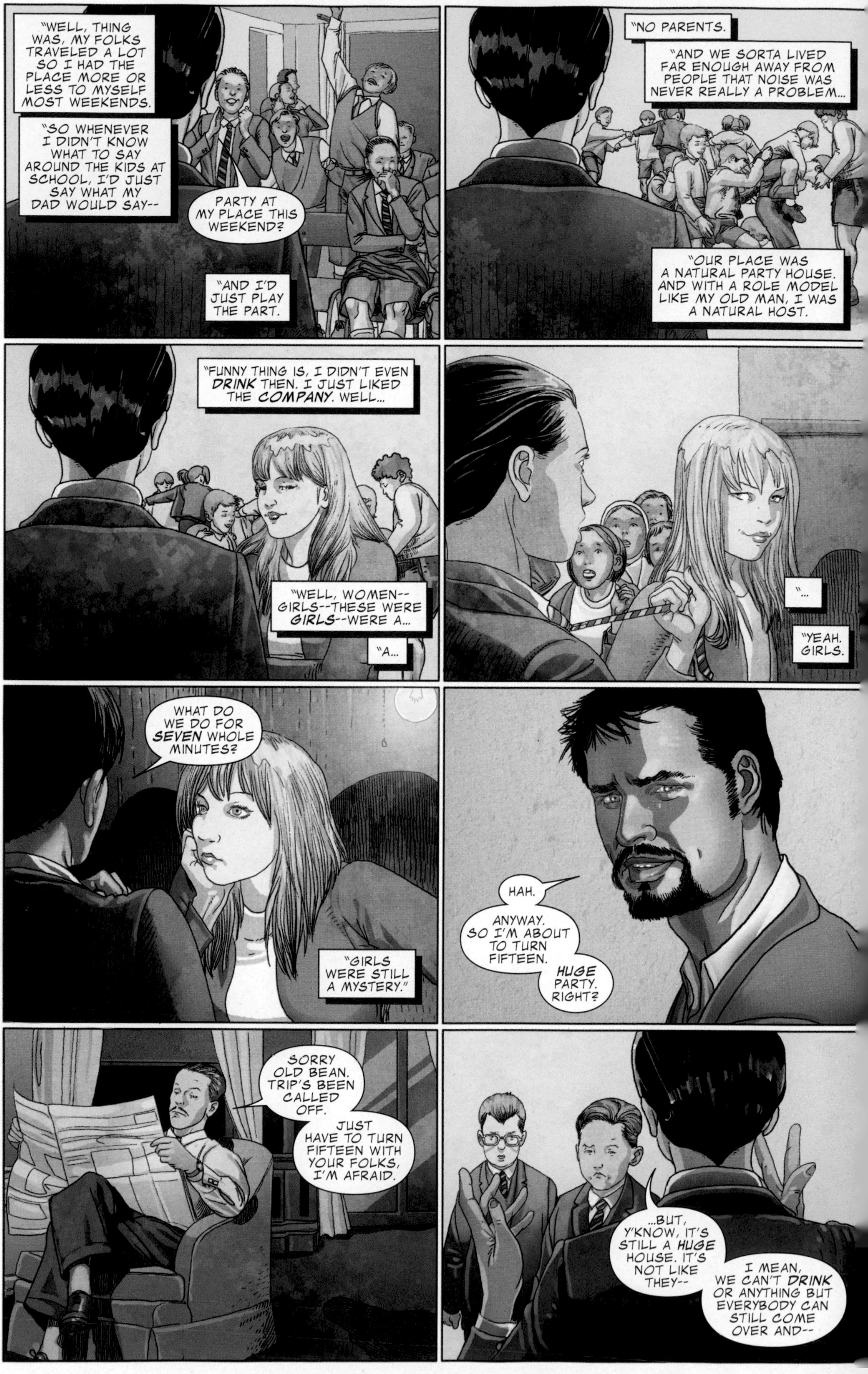
"WELL, THING WAS, MY FOLKS TRAVELED A LOT SO I HAD THE PLACE MORE OR LESS TO MYSELF MOST WEEKENDS.
"SO WHENEVER I DIDN'T KNOW WHAT TO SAY AROUND THE KIDS AT SCHOOL, I'D JUST SAY WHAT MY DAD WOULD SAY--
PARTY AT MY PLACE THIS WEEKEND?
"AND I'D JUST PLAY THE PART.
"NO PARENTS.
"AND WE SORTA LIVED FAR ENOUGH AWAY FROM PEOPLE THAT NOISE WAS NEVER REALLY A PROBLEM...
"OUR PLACE WAS A NATURAL PARTY HOUSE. AND WITH A ROLE MODEL LIKE MY OLD MAN, I WAS A NATURAL HOST.
"FUNNY THING IS, I DIDN'T EVEN DRINK THEN. I JUST LIKED THE COMPANY. WELL...
"WELL, WOMEN--GIRLS--THESE WERE GIRLS--WERE A...
"A...
"...
"YEAH. GIRLS.
WHAT DO WE DO FOR SEVEN WHOLE MINUTES?
"GIRLS WERE STILL A MYSTERY."
HAH.
ANYWAY. SO I'M ABOUT TO TURN FIFTEEN.
HUGE PARTY. RIGHT?
SORRY OLD BEAN. TRIP'S BEEN CALLED OFF.
JUST HAVE TO TURN FIFTEEN WITH YOUR FOLKS, I'M AFRAID.
...BUT, Y'KNOW, IT'S STILL A HUGE HOUSE. IT'S NOT LIKE THEY--
I MEAN, WE CAN'T DRINK OR ANYTHING BUT EVERYBODY CAN STILL COME OVER AND--

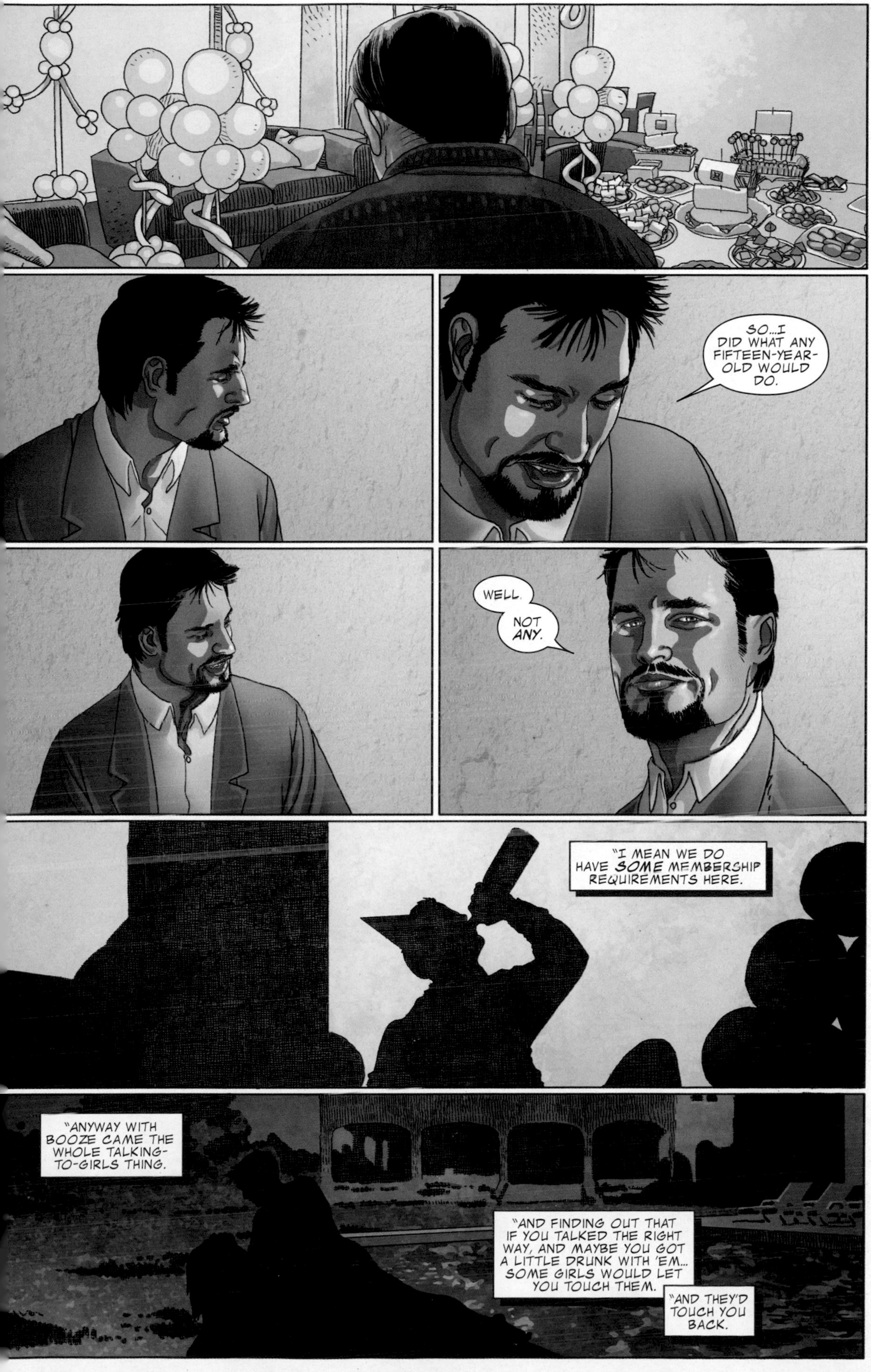
SO...I DID WHAT ANY FIFTEEN-YEAR-OLD WOULD DO.
WELL.
NOT ANY.
"I MEAN WE DO HAVE SOME MEMBERSHIP REQUIREMENTS HERE.
"ANYWAY WITH BOOZE CAME THE WHOLE TALKING-TO-GIRLS THING.
"AND FINDING OUT THAT IF YOU TALKED THE RIGHT WAY, AND MAYBE YOU GOT A LITTLE DRUNK WITH 'EM... SOME GIRLS WOULD LET YOU TOUCH THEM.
"AND THEY'D TOUCH YOU BACK.

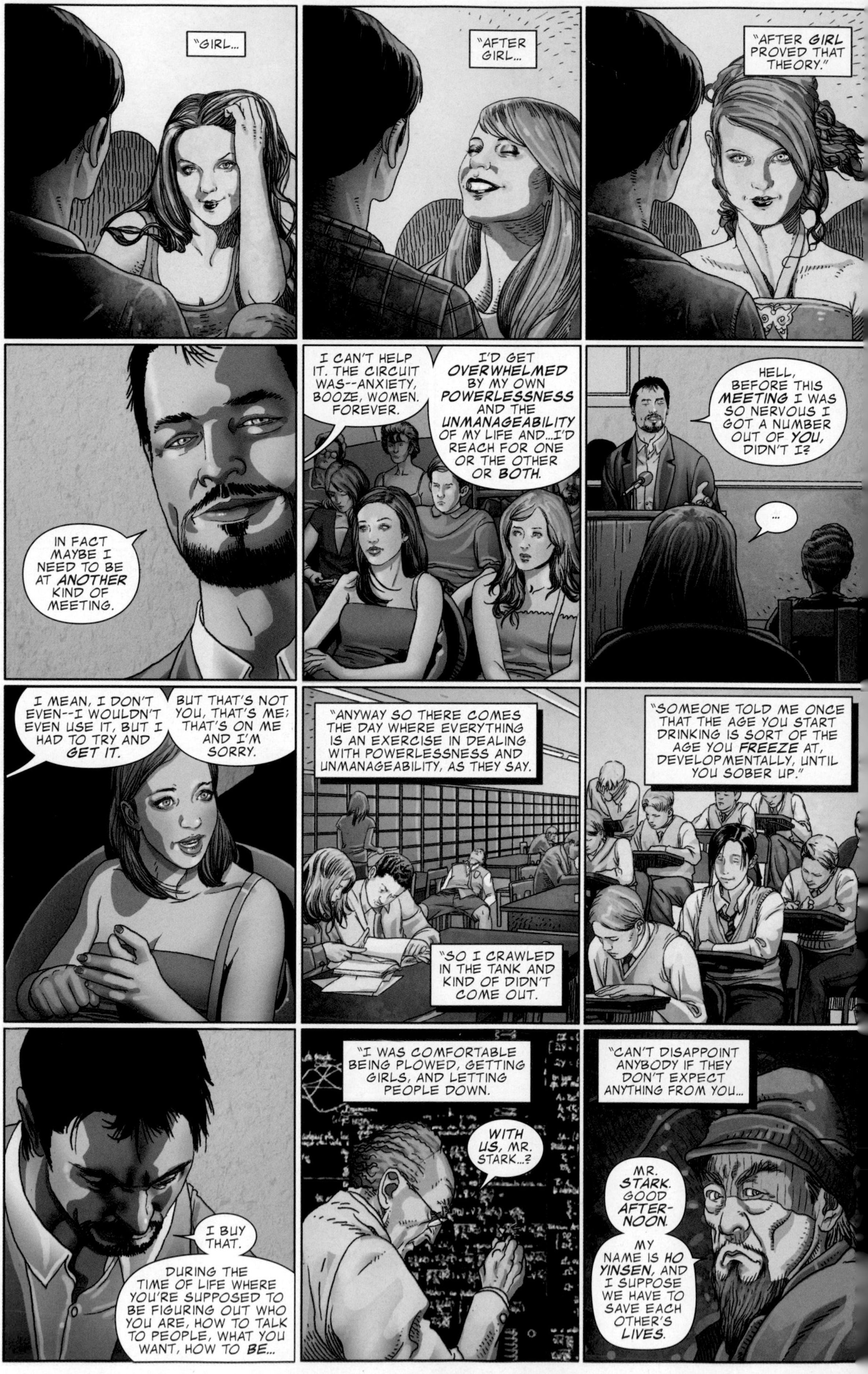
"GIRL...
"AFTER GIRL...
"AFTER GIRL PROVED THAT THEORY."
IN FACT MAYBE I NEED TO BE AT ANOTHER KIND OF MEETING.
I CAN'T HELP IT. THE CIRCUIT WAS--ANXIETY, BOOZE, WOMEN. FOREVER.
I'D GET OVERWHELMED BY MY OWN POWERLESSNESS AND THE UNMANAGEABILITY OF MY LIFE AND...I'D REACH FOR ONE OR THE OTHER OR BOTH.
HELL, BEFORE THIS MEETING I WAS SO NERVOUS I GOT A NUMBER OUT OF YOU, DIDN'T I?
...
I MEAN, I DON'T EVEN--I WOULDN'T EVEN USE IT, BUT I HAD TO TRY AND GET IT.
BUT THAT'S NOT YOU, THAT'S ME; THAT'S ON ME AND I'M SORRY.
"ANYWAY SO THERE COMES THE DAY WHERE EVERYTHING IS AN EXERCISE IN DEALING WITH POWERLESSNESS AND UNMANAGEABILITY, AS THEY SAY.
"SO I CRAWLED IN THE TANK AND KIND OF DIDN'T COME OUT.
"SOMEONE TOLD ME ONCE THAT THE AGE YOU START DRINKING IS SORT OF THE AGE YOU FREEZE AT, DEVELOPMENTALLY, UNTIL YOU SOBER UP."
I BUY THAT.
DURING THE TIME OF LIFE WHERE YOU'RE SUPPOSED TO BE FIGURING OUT WHO YOU ARE, HOW TO TALK TO PEOPLE, WHAT YOU WANT, HOW TO BE...
"I WAS COMFORTABLE BEING PLOWED, GETTING GIRLS, AND LETTING PEOPLE DOWN.
WITH US, MR. STARK...?
"CAN'T DISAPPOINT ANYBODY IF THEY DON'T EXPECT ANYTHING FROM YOU...
MR. STARK. GOOD AFTER-NOON.
MY NAME IS HO YINSEN, AND I SUPPOSE WE HAVE TO SAVE EACH OTHER'S LIVES.

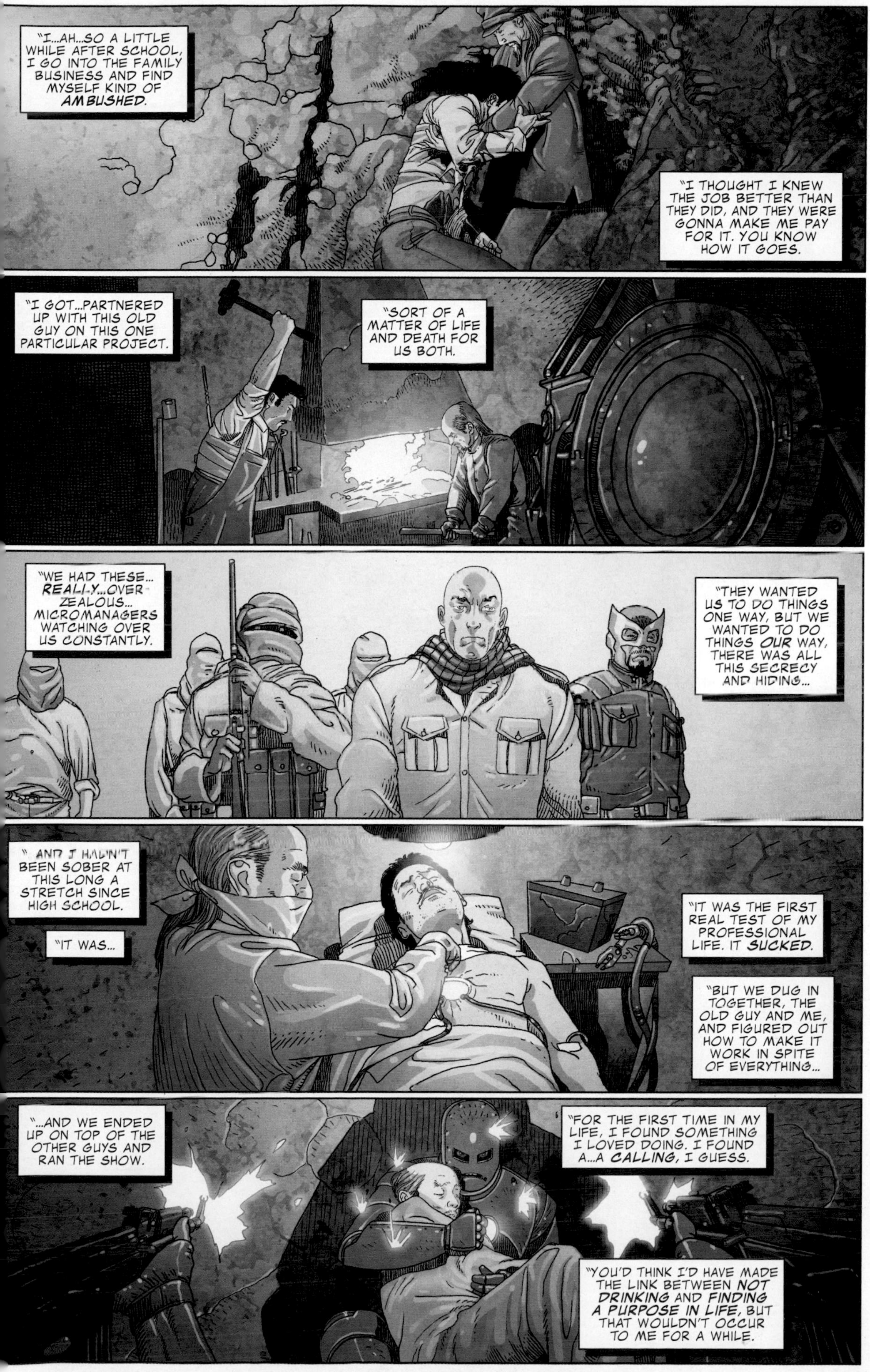
"I...AH...SO A LITTLE WHILE AFTER SCHOOL, I GO INTO THE FAMILY BUSINESS AND FIND MYSELF KIND OF AMBUSHED.
"I THOUGHT I KNEW THE JOB BETTER THAN THEY DID, AND THEY WERE GONNA MAKE ME PAY FOR IT. YOU KNOW HOW IT GOES.
"I GOT...PARTNERED UP WITH THIS OLD GUY ON THIS ONE PARTICULAR PROJECT.
"SORT OF A MATTER OF LIFE AND DEATH FOR US BOTH.
"WE HAD THESE... REALLY...OVER ZEALOUS... MICROMANAGERS WATCHING OVER US CONSTANTLY.
"THEY WANTED US TO DO THINGS ONE WAY, BUT WE WANTED TO DO THINGS OUR WAY, THERE WAS ALL THIS SECRECY AND HIDING...
"...AND I HADN'T BEEN SOBER AT THIS LONG A STRETCH SINCE HIGH SCHOOL.
"IT WAS...
"IT WAS THE FIRST REAL TEST OF MY PROFESSIONAL LIFE. IT SUCKED.
"BUT WE DUG IN TOGETHER, THE OLD GUY AND ME, AND FIGURED OUT HOW TO MAKE IT WORK IN SPITE OF EVERYTHING...
"...AND WE ENDED UP ON TOP OF THE OTHER GUYS AND RAN THE SHOW.
"FOR THE FIRST TIME IN MY LIFE, I FOUND SOMETHING I LOVED DOING. I FOUND A...A CALLING, I GUESS.
"YOU'D THINK I'D HAVE MADE THE LINK BETWEEN NOT DRINKING AND FINDING A PURPOSE IN LIFE, BUT THAT WOULDN'T OCCUR TO ME FOR A WHILE.

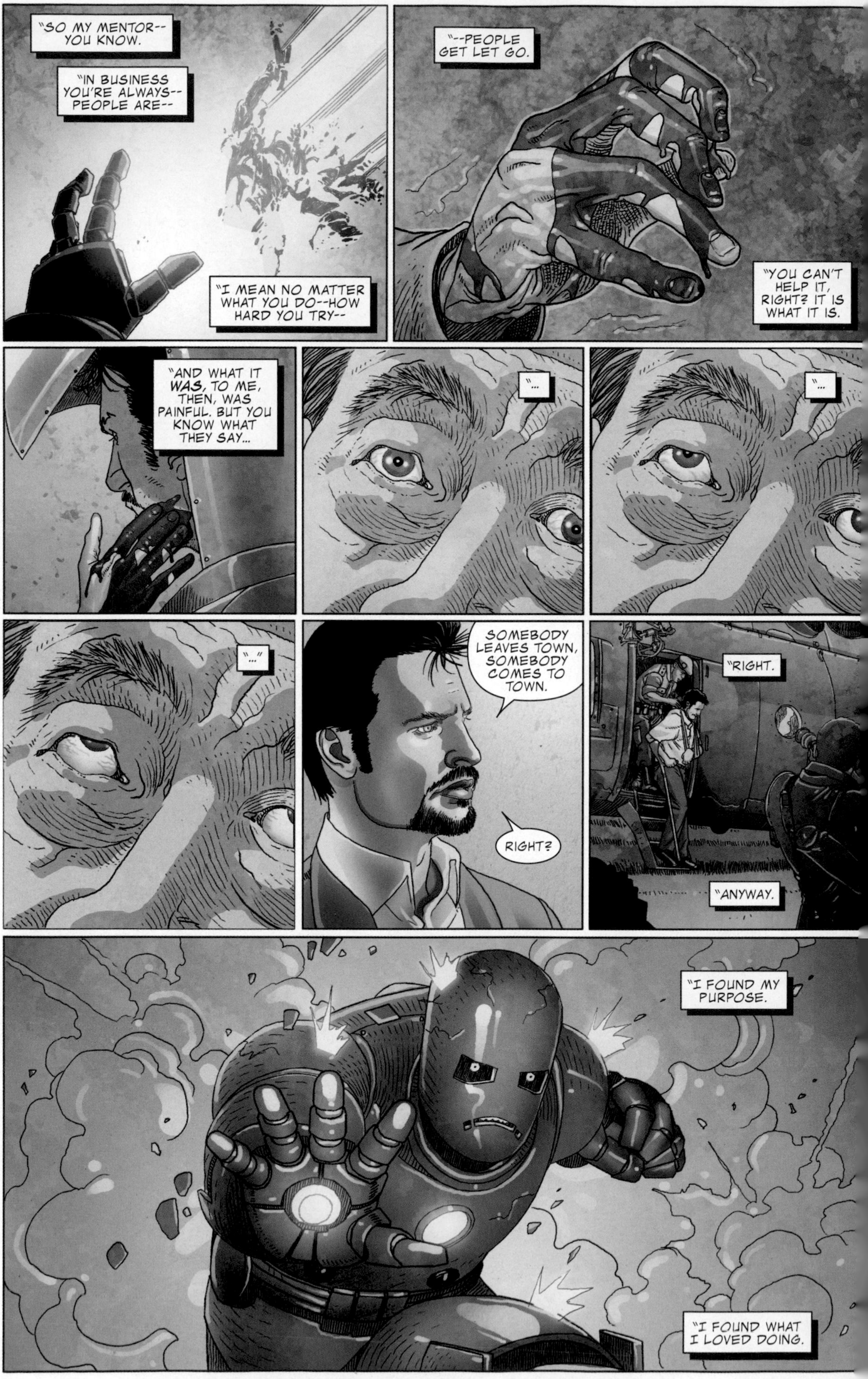
"SO MY MENTOR-- YOU KNOW.
"IN BUSINESS YOU'RE ALWAYS-- PEOPLE ARE--
"I MEAN NO MATTER WHAT YOU DO--HOW HARD YOU TRY--
"--PEOPLE GET LET GO.
"YOU CAN'T HELP IT, RIGHT? IT IS WHAT IT IS.
"AND WHAT IT WAS, TO ME, THEN, WAS PAINFUL. BUT YOU KNOW WHAT THEY SAY...
"...
"...
"..."
SOMEBODY LEAVES TOWN, SOMEBODY COMES TO TOWN.
RIGHT?
"RIGHT.
"ANYWAY.
"I FOUND MY PURPOSE.
"I FOUND WHAT I LOVED DOING.

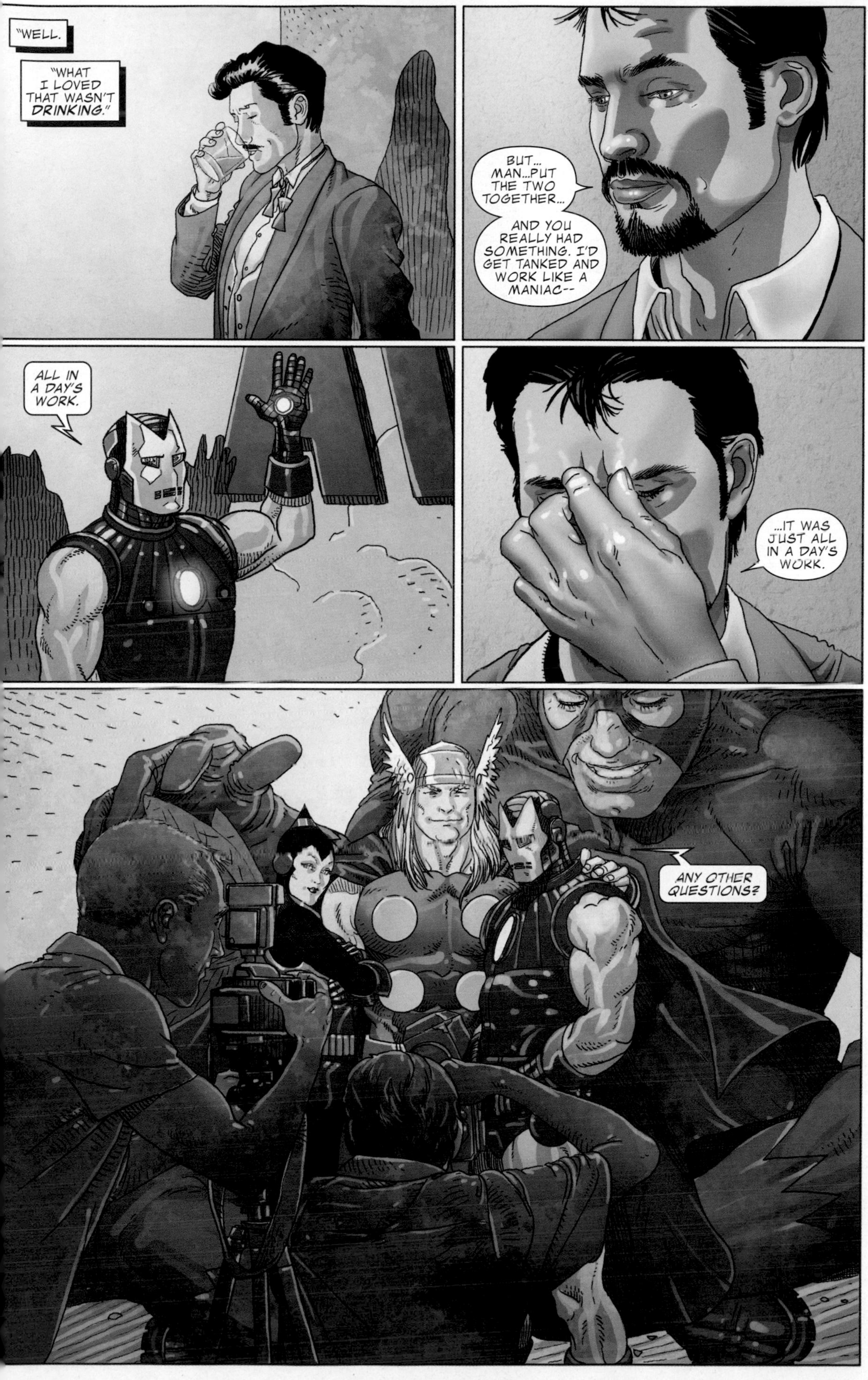
"WELL.
"WHAT I LOVED THAT WASN'T DRINKING."
BUT... MAN...PUT THE TWO TOGETHER...
AND YOU REALLY HAD SOMETHING. I'D GET TANKED AND WORK LIKE A MANIAC--
ALL IN A DAY'S WORK.
...IT WAS JUST ALL IN A DAY'S WORK.
ANY OTHER QUESTIONS?

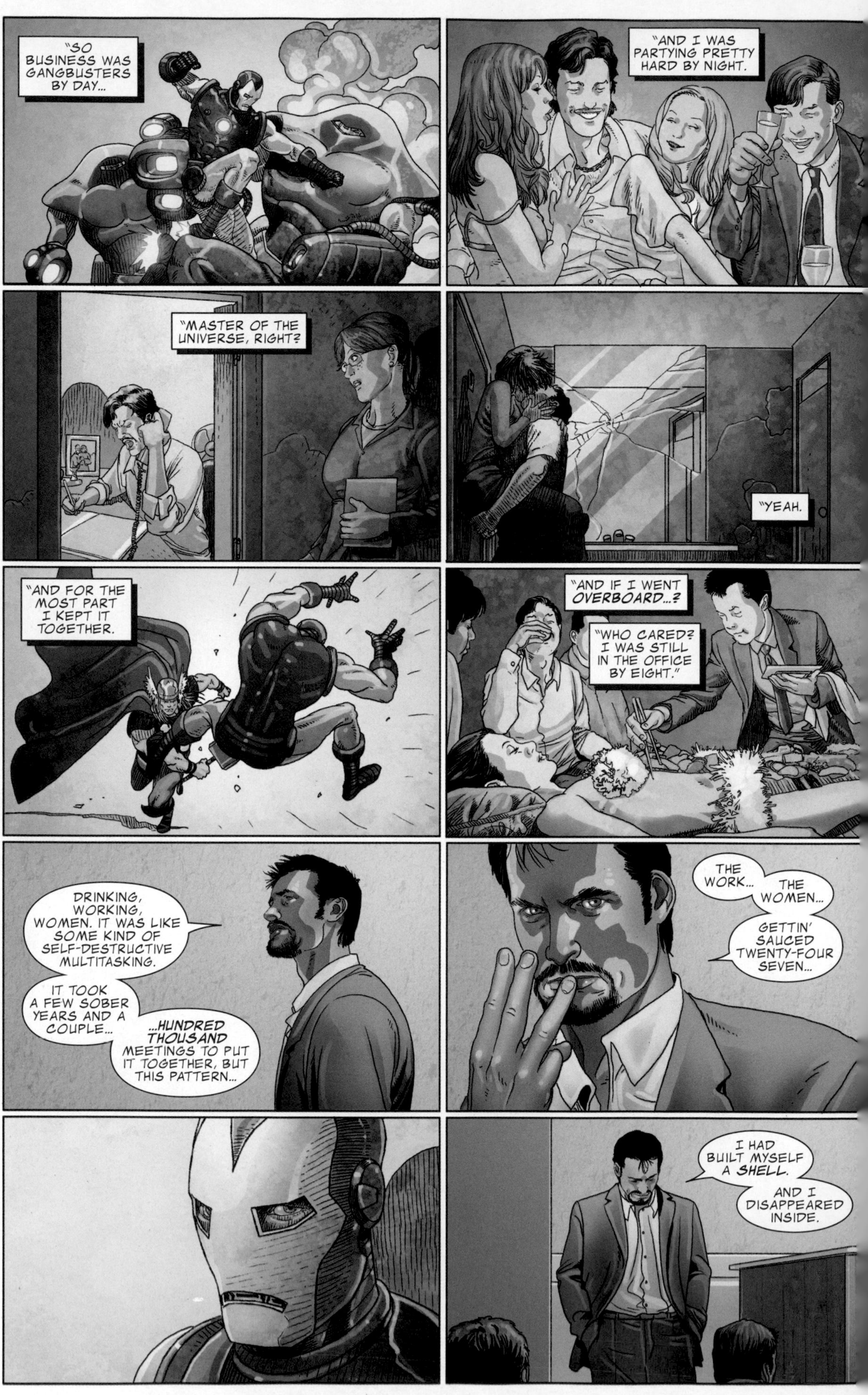
"SO BUSINESS WAS GANGBUSTERS BY DAY...
"AND I WAS PARTYING PRETTY HARD BY NIGHT.
"MASTER OF THE UNIVERSE, RIGHT?
"YEAH.
"AND FOR THE MOST PART I KEPT IT TOGETHER.
"AND IF I WENT **OVERBOARD**...?
"WHO CARED? I WAS STILL IN THE OFFICE BY EIGHT."
DRINKING, WORKING, WOMEN. IT WAS LIKE SOME KIND OF SELF-DESTRUCTIVE MULTITASKING.
IT TOOK A FEW SOBER YEARS AND A COUPLE...
...**HUNDRED THOUSAND** MEETINGS TO PUT IT TOGETHER, BUT THIS PATTERN...
THE WORK...
THE WOMEN...
GETTIN' SAUCED TWENTY-FOUR SEVEN...
I HAD BUILT MYSELF A **SHELL**.
AND I DISAPPEARED INSIDE.

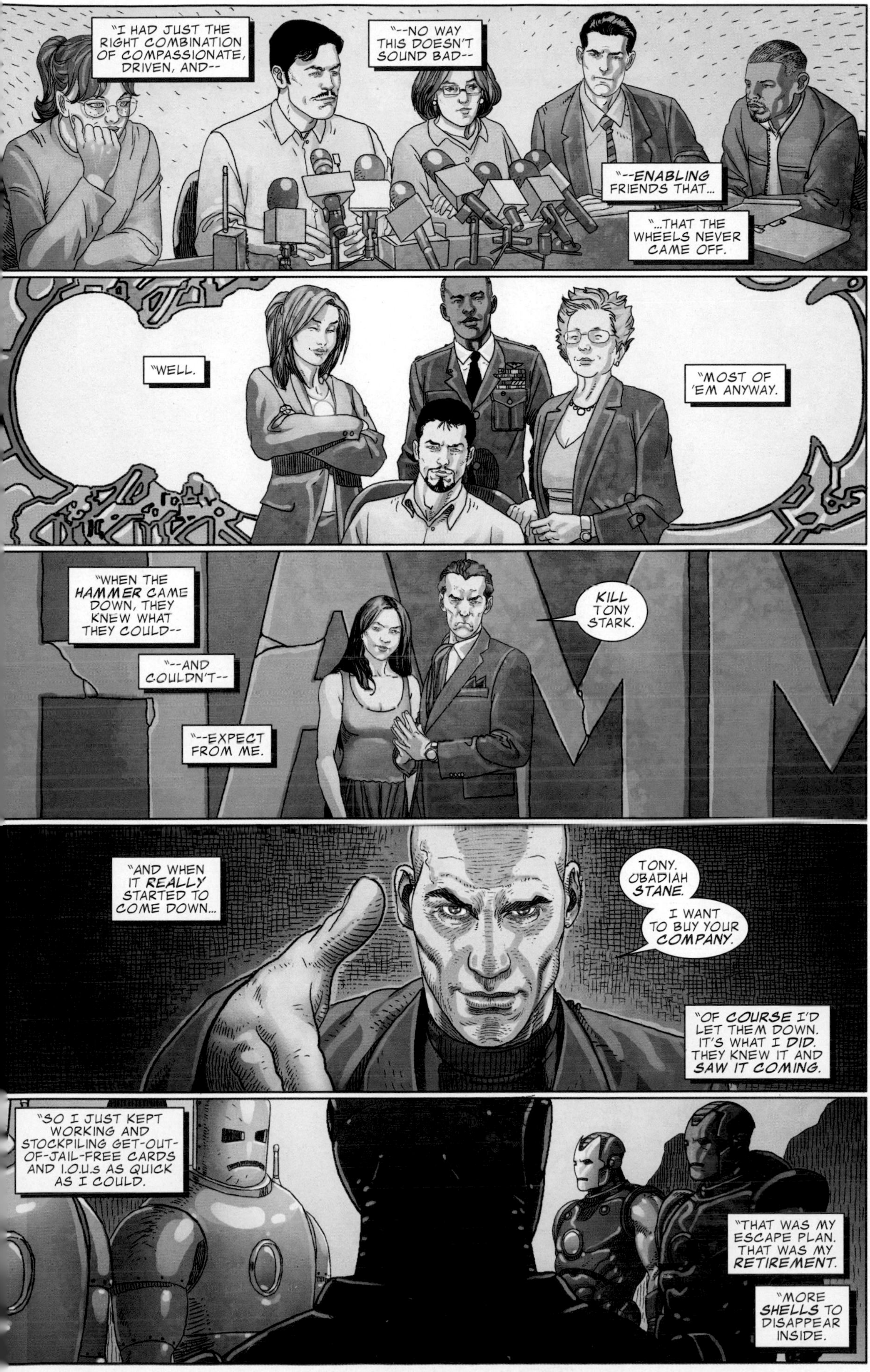
"I HAD JUST THE RIGHT COMBINATION OF COMPASSIONATE, DRIVEN, AND--
"--NO WAY THIS DOESN'T SOUND BAD--
"--ENABLING FRIENDS THAT...
"...THAT THE WHEELS NEVER CAME OFF.
"WELL.
"MOST OF 'EM ANYWAY.
"WHEN THE HAMMER CAME DOWN, THEY KNEW WHAT THEY COULD--
"--AND COULDN'T--
"--EXPECT FROM ME.
KILL TONY STARK.
"AND WHEN IT REALLY STARTED TO COME DOWN...
TONY. OBADIAH STANE.
I WANT TO BUY YOUR COMPANY.
"OF COURSE I'D LET THEM DOWN. IT'S WHAT I DID. THEY KNEW IT AND SAW IT COMING.
"SO I JUST KEPT WORKING AND STOCKPILING GET-OUT-OF-JAIL-FREE CARDS AND I.O.U.s AS QUICK AS I COULD.
"THAT WAS MY ESCAPE PLAN. THAT WAS MY RETIREMENT.
"MORE SHELLS TO DISAPPEAR INSIDE.

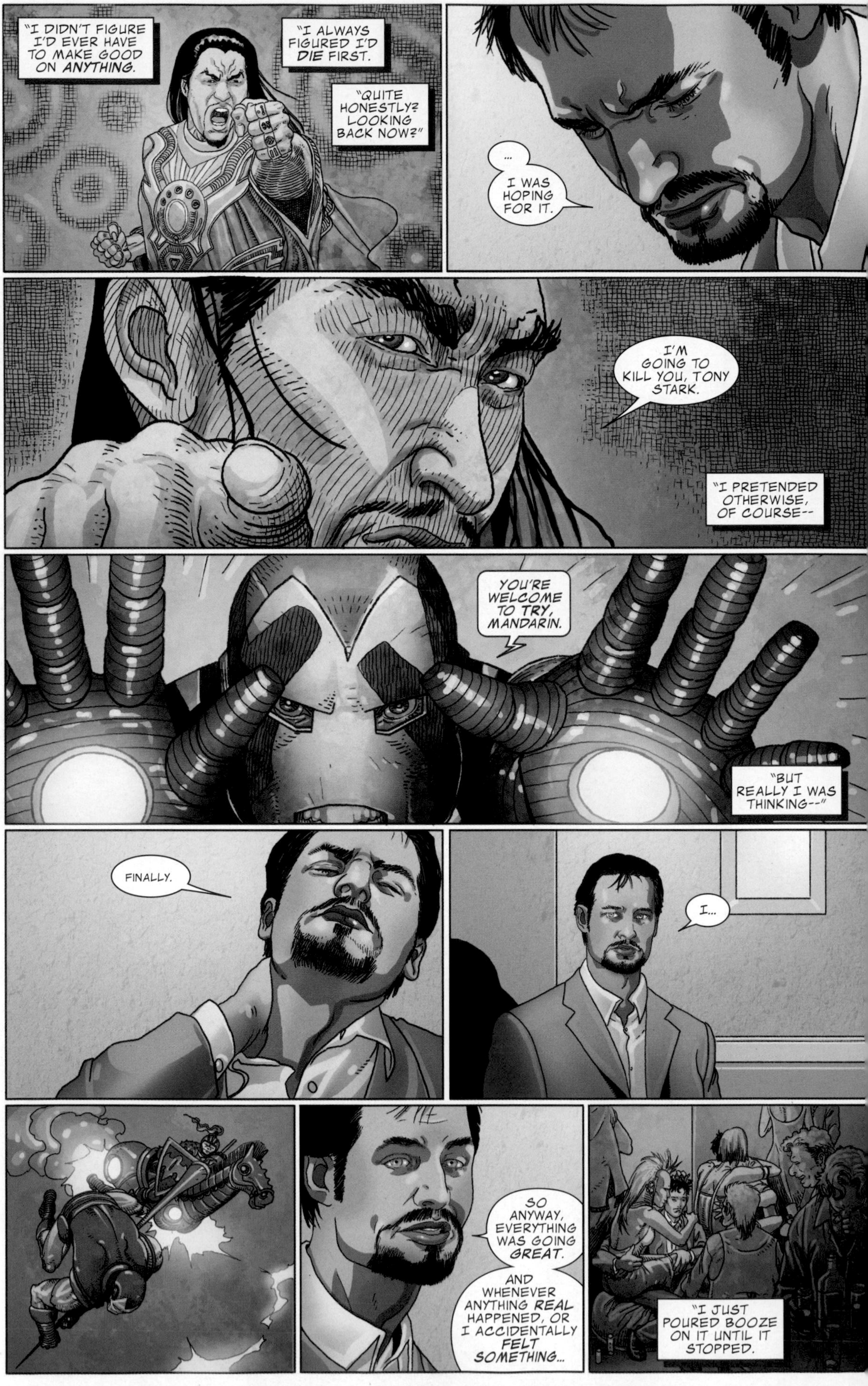
"I DIDN'T FIGURE I'D EVER HAVE TO MAKE GOOD ON ANYTHING.
"I ALWAYS FIGURED I'D DIE FIRST.
"QUITE HONESTLY? LOOKING BACK NOW?"
... I WAS HOPING FOR IT.
I'M GOING TO KILL YOU, TONY STARK.
"I PRETENDED OTHERWISE, OF COURSE--
YOU'RE WELCOME TO TRY, MANDARIN.
"BUT REALLY I WAS THINKING--"
FINALLY.
I...
SO ANYWAY, EVERYTHING WAS GOING GREAT.
AND WHENEVER ANYTHING REAL HAPPENED, OR I ACCIDENTALLY FELT SOMETHING...
"I JUST POURED BOOZE ON IT UNTIL IT STOPPED.

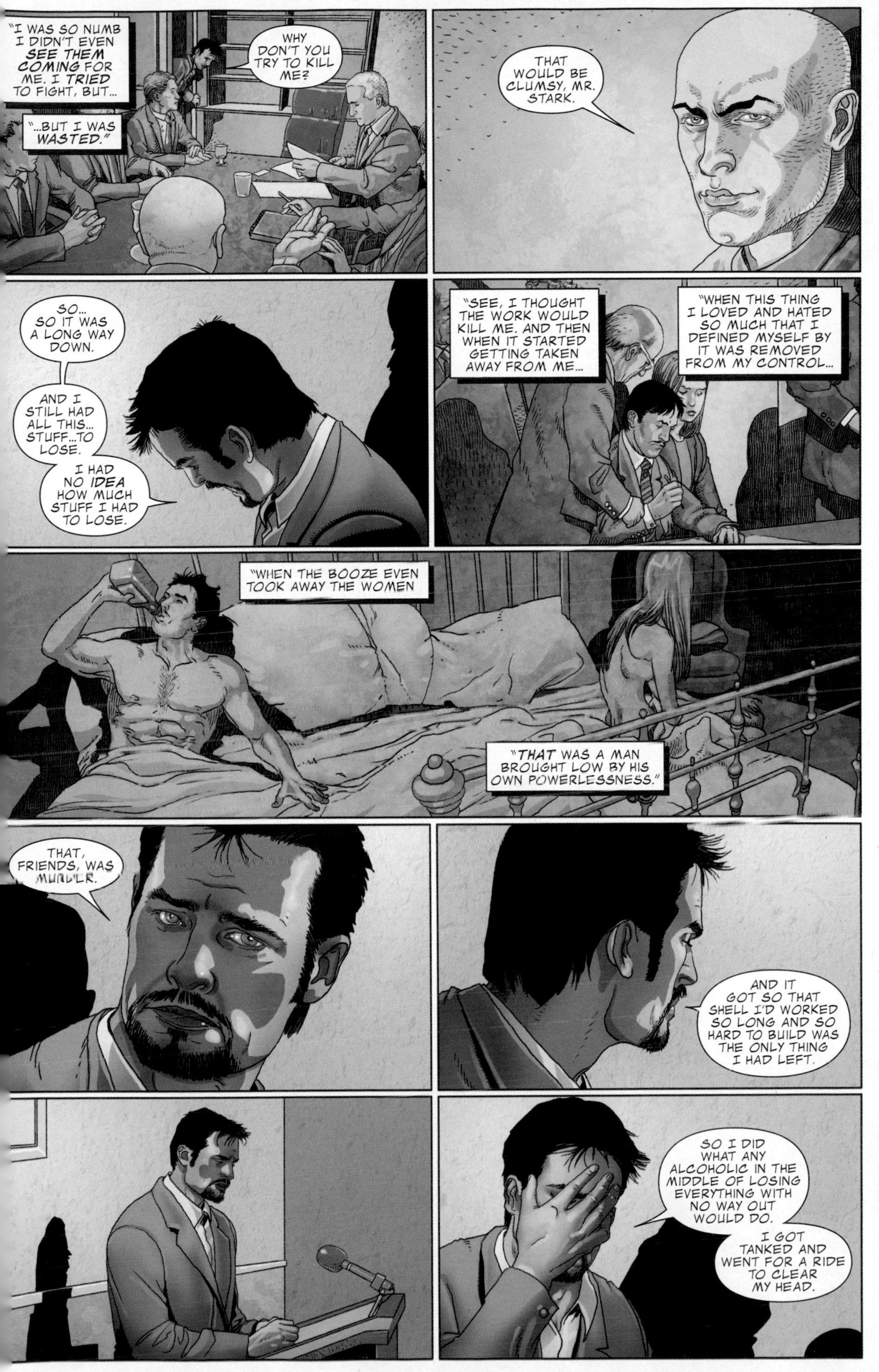
"I WAS SO NUMB I DIDN'T EVEN SEE THEM COMING FOR ME. I TRIED TO FIGHT, BUT...
"...BUT I WAS WASTED."
WHY DON'T YOU TRY TO KILL ME?
THAT WOULD BE CLUMSY, MR. STARK.
SO... SO IT WAS A LONG WAY DOWN.
AND I STILL HAD ALL THIS... STUFF...TO LOSE.
I HAD NO IDEA HOW MUCH STUFF I HAD TO LOSE.
"SEE, I THOUGHT THE WORK WOULD KILL ME. AND THEN WHEN IT STARTED GETTING TAKEN AWAY FROM ME...
"WHEN THIS THING I LOVED AND HATED SO MUCH THAT I DEFINED MYSELF BY IT WAS REMOVED FROM MY CONTROL...
"WHEN THE BOOZE EVEN TOOK AWAY THE WOMEN
"THAT WAS A MAN BROUGHT LOW BY HIS OWN POWERLESSNESS."
THAT, FRIENDS, WAS MURDER.
AND IT GOT SO THAT SHELL I'D WORKED SO LONG AND SO HARD TO BUILD WAS THE ONLY THING I HAD LEFT.
SO I DID WHAT ANY ALCOHOLIC IN THE MIDDLE OF LOSING EVERYTHING WITH NO WAY OUT WOULD DO.
I GOT TANKED AND WENT FOR A RIDE TO CLEAR MY HEAD.

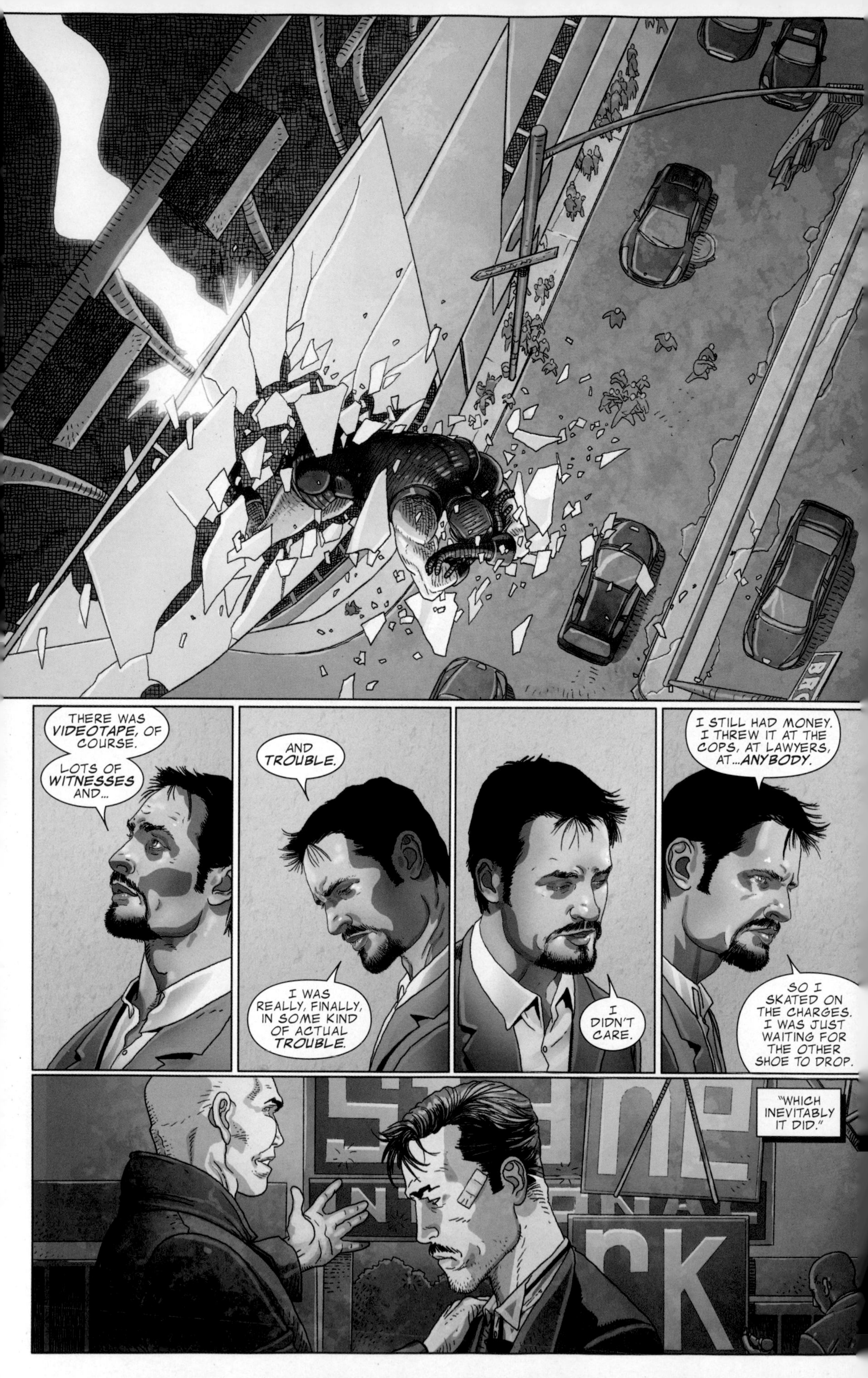

THERE WAS VIDEOTAPE, OF COURSE.
LOTS OF WITNESSES AND...
AND TROUBLE.
I WAS REALLY, FINALLY, IN SOME KIND OF ACTUAL TROUBLE.
I DIDN'T CARE.
I STILL HAD MONEY. I THREW IT AT THE COPS, AT LAWYERS, AT...ANYBODY.
SO I SKATED ON THE CHARGES. I WAS JUST WAITING FOR THE OTHER SHOE TO DROP.
"WHICH INEVITABLY IT DID."

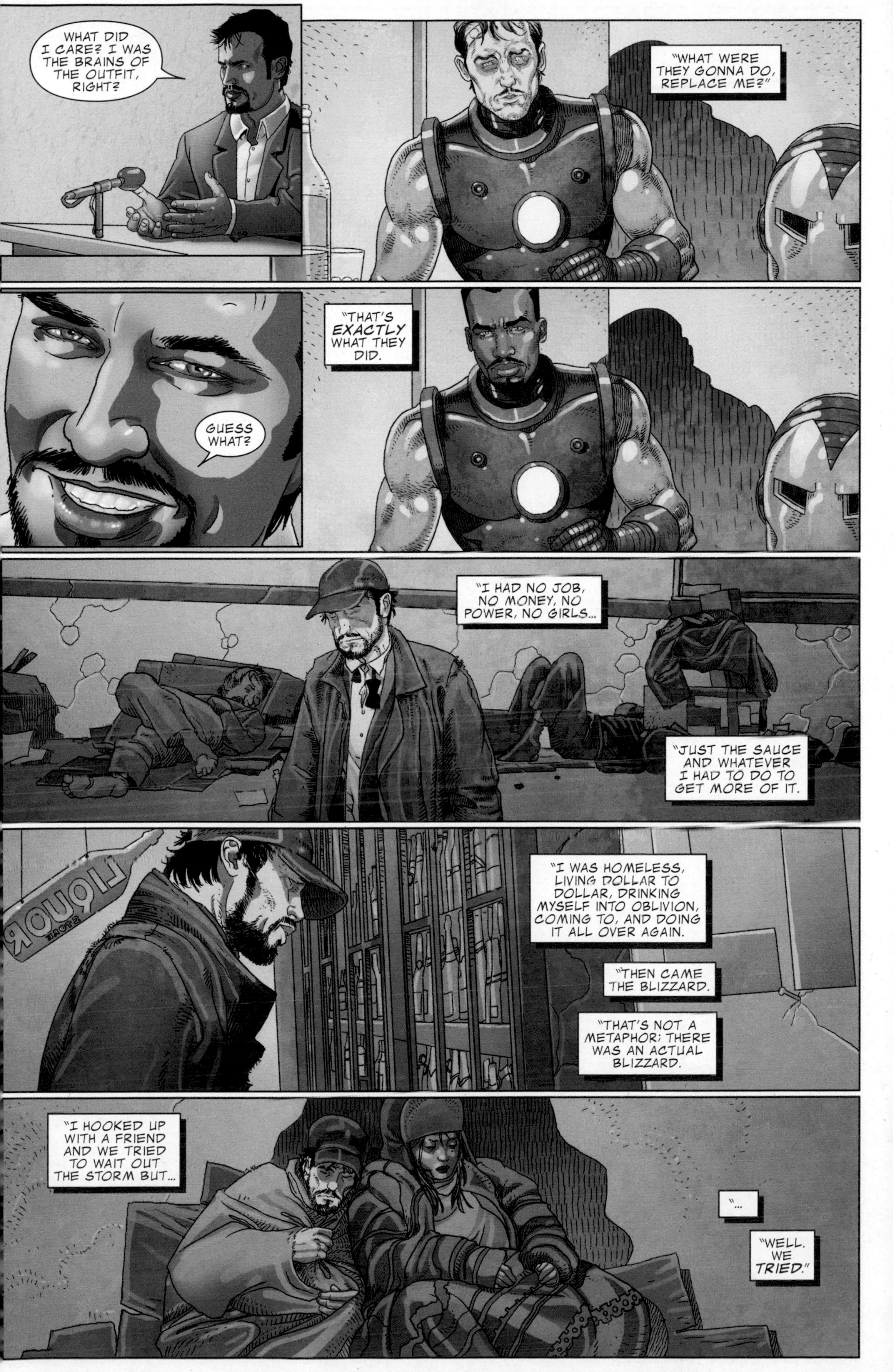
WHAT DID I CARE? I WAS THE BRAINS OF THE OUTFIT, RIGHT?
"WHAT WERE THEY GONNA DO, REPLACE ME?"
"THAT'S *EXACTLY* WHAT THEY DID.
GUESS WHAT?
"I HAD NO JOB, NO MONEY, NO POWER, NO GIRLS...
"JUST THE SAUCE AND WHATEVER I HAD TO DO TO GET MORE OF IT.
LIQUOR
"I WAS HOMELESS, LIVING DOLLAR TO DOLLAR, DRINKING MYSELF INTO OBLIVION, COMING TO, AND DOING IT ALL OVER AGAIN.
"THEN CAME THE BLIZZARD.
"THAT'S NOT A METAPHOR; THERE WAS AN ACTUAL BLIZZARD.
"I HOOKED UP WITH A FRIEND AND WE TRIED TO WAIT OUT THE STORM BUT...
"...
"WELL. WE *TRIED*."

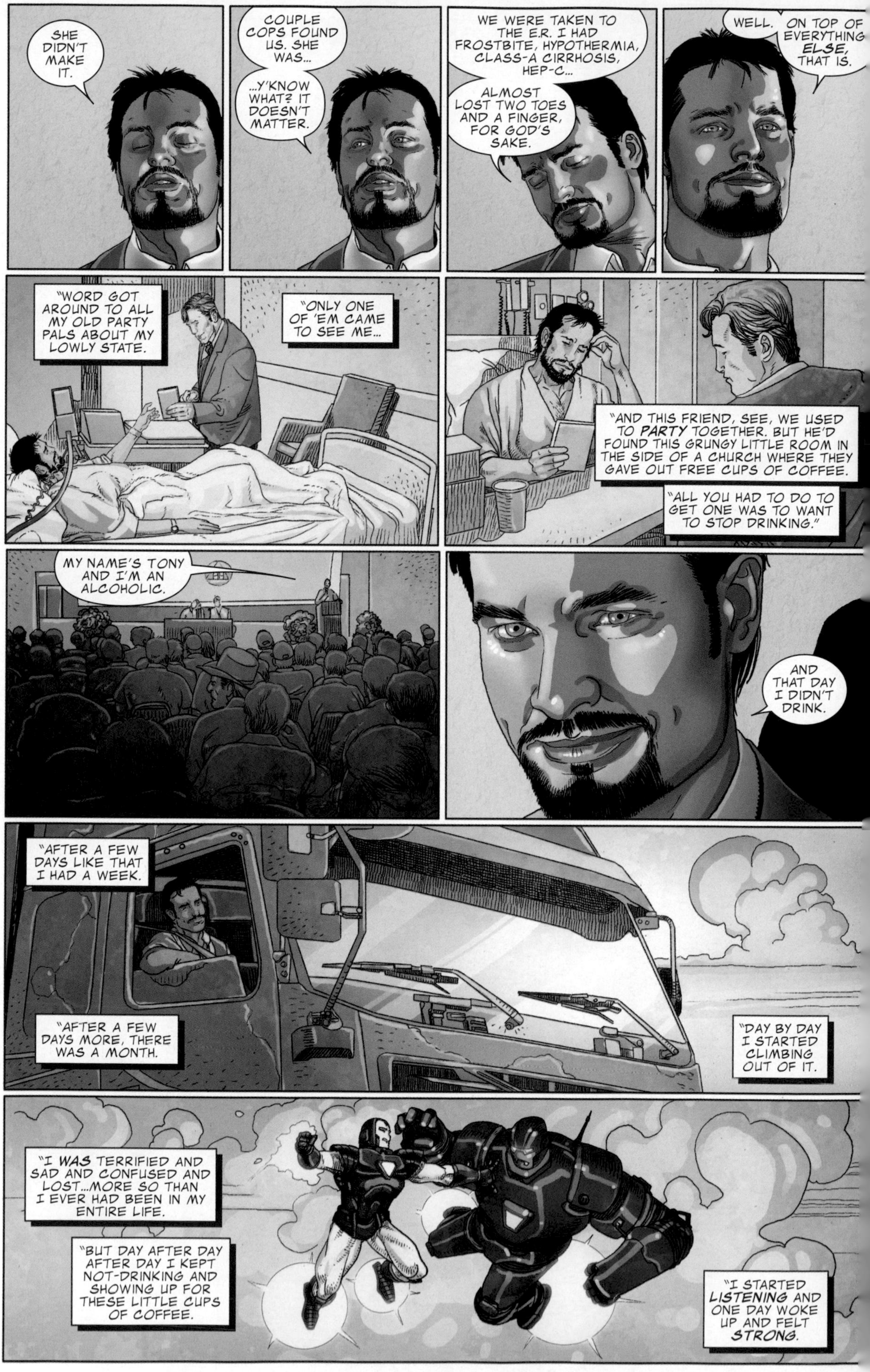
SHE DIDN'T MAKE IT.
COUPLE COPS FOUND US. SHE WAS...
...Y'KNOW WHAT? IT DOESN'T MATTER.
WE WERE TAKEN TO THE E.R. I HAD FROSTBITE, HYPOTHERMIA, CLASS-A CIRRHOSIS, HEP-C...
ALMOST LOST TWO TOES AND A FINGER, FOR GOD'S SAKE.
WELL.
ON TOP OF EVERYTHING ELSE, THAT IS.
"WORD GOT AROUND TO ALL MY OLD PARTY PALS ABOUT MY LOWLY STATE.
"ONLY ONE OF 'EM CAME TO SEE ME...
"AND THIS FRIEND, SEE, WE USED TO PARTY TOGETHER. BUT HE'D FOUND THIS GRUNGY LITTLE ROOM IN THE SIDE OF A CHURCH WHERE THEY GAVE OUT FREE CUPS OF COFFEE.
"ALL YOU HAD TO DO TO GET ONE WAS TO WANT TO STOP DRINKING."
MY NAME'S TONY AND I'M AN ALCOHOLIC.
AND THAT DAY I DIDN'T DRINK.
"AFTER A FEW DAYS LIKE THAT I HAD A WEEK.
"AFTER A FEW DAYS MORE, THERE WAS A MONTH.
"DAY BY DAY I STARTED CLIMBING OUT OF IT.
"I WAS TERRIFIED AND SAD AND CONFUSED AND LOST...MORE SO THAN I EVER HAD BEEN IN MY ENTIRE LIFE.
"BUT DAY AFTER DAY AFTER DAY I KEPT NOT-DRINKING AND SHOWING UP FOR THESE LITTLE CUPS OF COFFEE.
"I STARTED LISTENING AND ONE DAY WOKE UP AND FELT STRONG.

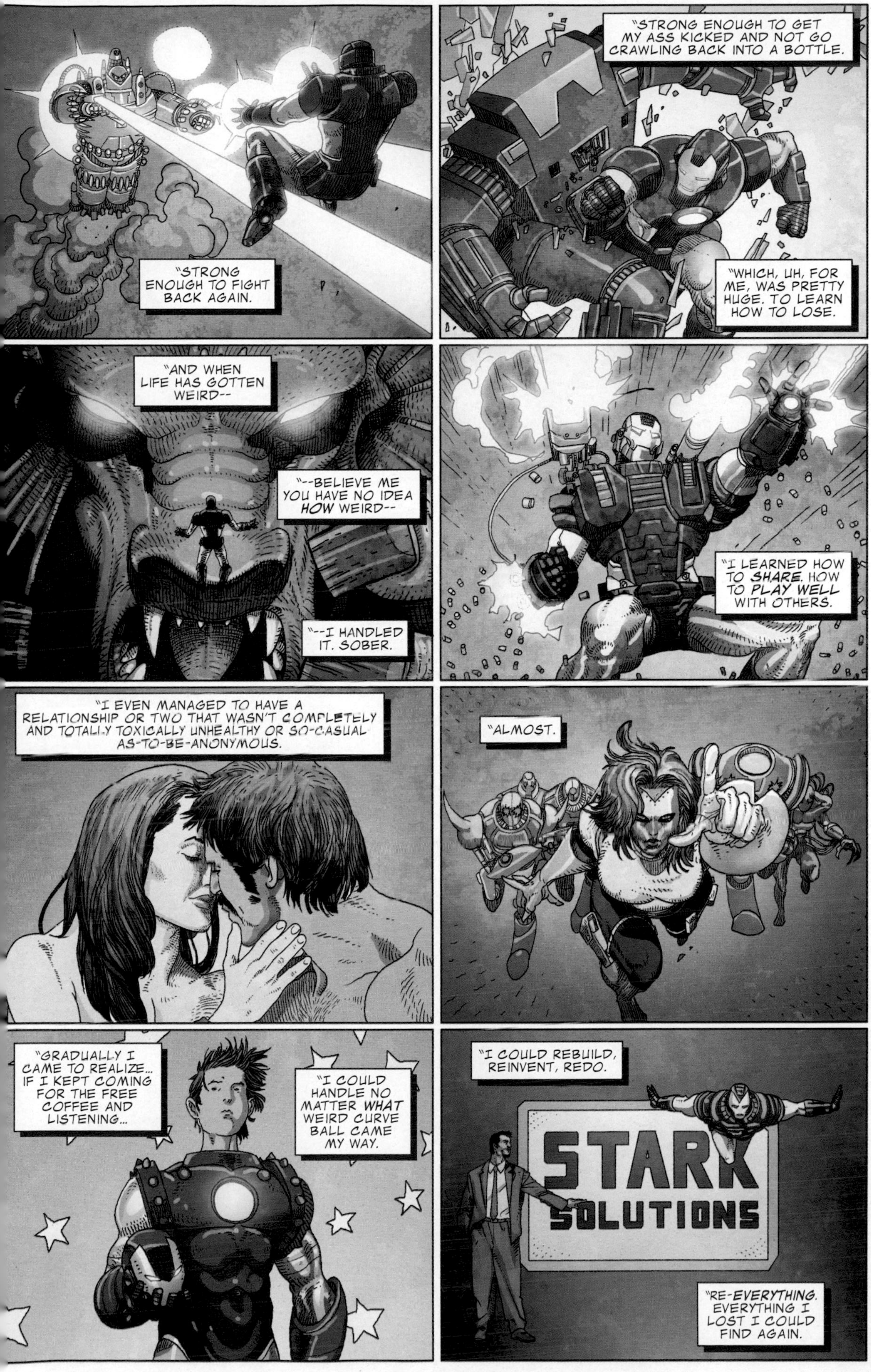
"STRONG ENOUGH TO FIGHT BACK AGAIN.
"STRONG ENOUGH TO GET MY ASS KICKED AND NOT GO CRAWLING BACK INTO A BOTTLE.
"WHICH, UH, FOR ME, WAS PRETTY HUGE. TO LEARN HOW TO LOSE.
"AND WHEN LIFE HAS GOTTEN WEIRD--
"--BELIEVE ME YOU HAVE NO IDEA HOW WEIRD--
"--I HANDLED IT. SOBER.
"I LEARNED HOW TO SHARE. HOW TO PLAY WELL WITH OTHERS.
"I EVEN MANAGED TO HAVE A RELATIONSHIP OR TWO THAT WASN'T COMPLETELY AND TOTALLY TOXICALLY UNHEALTHY OR SO-CASUAL AS-TO-BE-ANONYMOUS.
"ALMOST.
"GRADUALLY I CAME TO REALIZE... IF I KEPT COMING FOR THE FREE COFFEE AND LISTENING...
"I COULD HANDLE NO MATTER WHAT WEIRD CURVE BALL CAME MY WAY.
"I COULD REBUILD, REINVENT, REDO.
STARK SOLUTIONS
"RE-EVERYTHING. EVERYTHING I LOST I COULD FIND AGAIN.

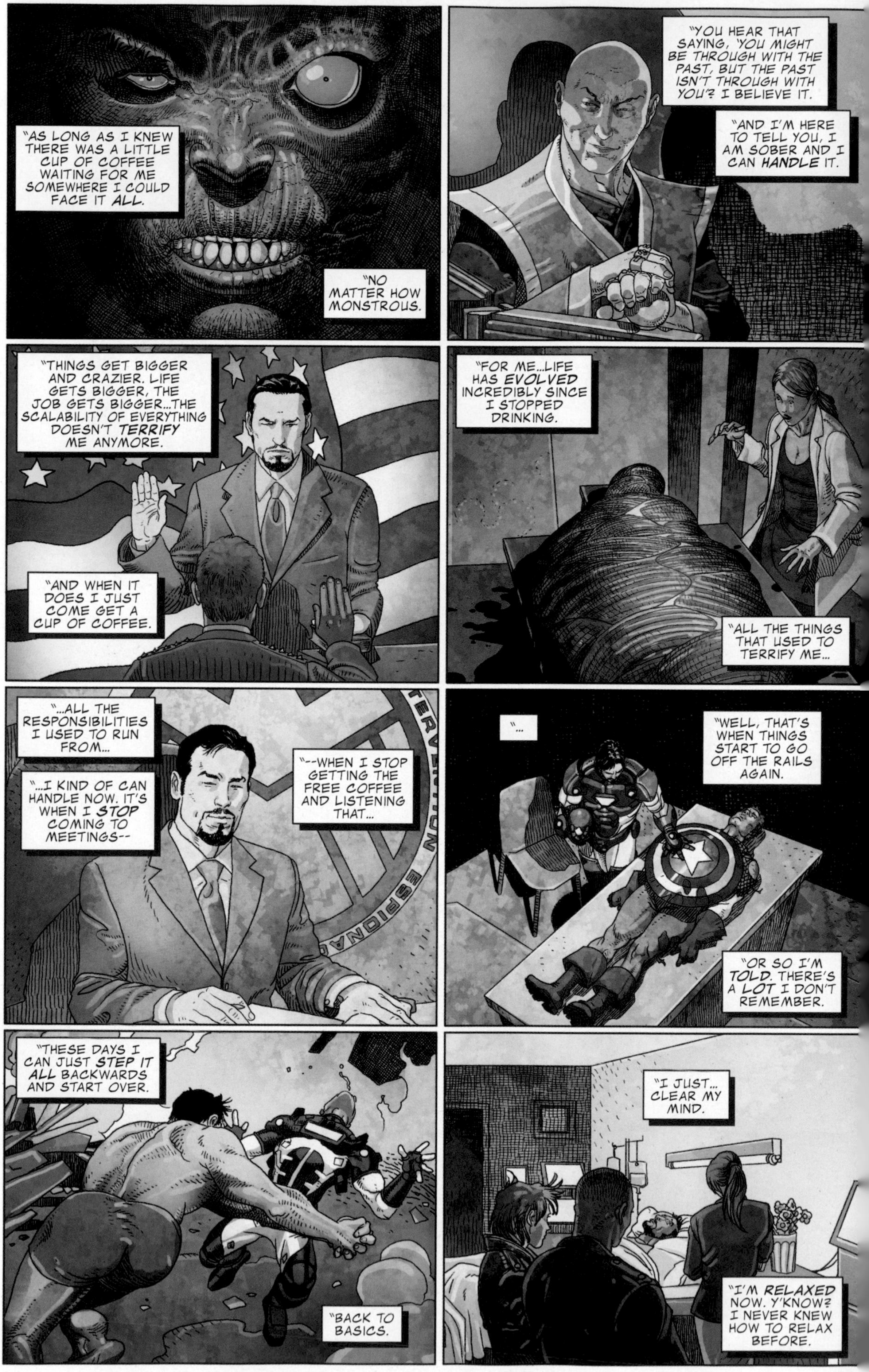

"AS LONG AS I KNEW THERE WAS A LITTLE CUP OF COFFEE WAITING FOR ME SOMEWHERE I COULD FACE IT ALL.
"NO MATTER HOW MONSTROUS.
"YOU HEAR THAT SAYING, 'YOU MIGHT BE THROUGH WITH THE PAST, BUT THE PAST ISN'T THROUGH WITH YOU'? I BELIEVE IT.
"AND I'M HERE TO TELL YOU, I AM SOBER AND I CAN HANDLE IT.
"THINGS GET BIGGER AND CRAZIER. LIFE GETS BIGGER, THE JOB GETS BIGGER...THE SCALABILITY OF EVERYTHING DOESN'T TERRIFY ME ANYMORE.
"AND WHEN IT DOES I JUST COME GET A CUP OF COFFEE.
"FOR ME...LIFE HAS EVOLVED INCREDIBLY SINCE I STOPPED DRINKING.
"ALL THE THINGS THAT USED TO TERRIFY ME...
"...ALL THE RESPONSIBILITIES I USED TO RUN FROM...
"...I KIND OF CAN HANDLE NOW. IT'S WHEN I STOP COMING TO MEETINGS--
"--WHEN I STOP GETTING THE FREE COFFEE AND LISTENING THAT...
"...
"WELL, THAT'S WHEN THINGS START TO GO OFF THE RAILS AGAIN.
"OR SO I'M TOLD. THERE'S A LOT I DON'T REMEMBER.
"THESE DAYS I CAN JUST STEP IT ALL BACKWARDS AND START OVER.
"BACK TO BASICS.
"I JUST... CLEAR MY MIND.
"I'M RELAXED NOW. Y'KNOW? I NEVER KNEW HOW TO RELAX BEFORE.

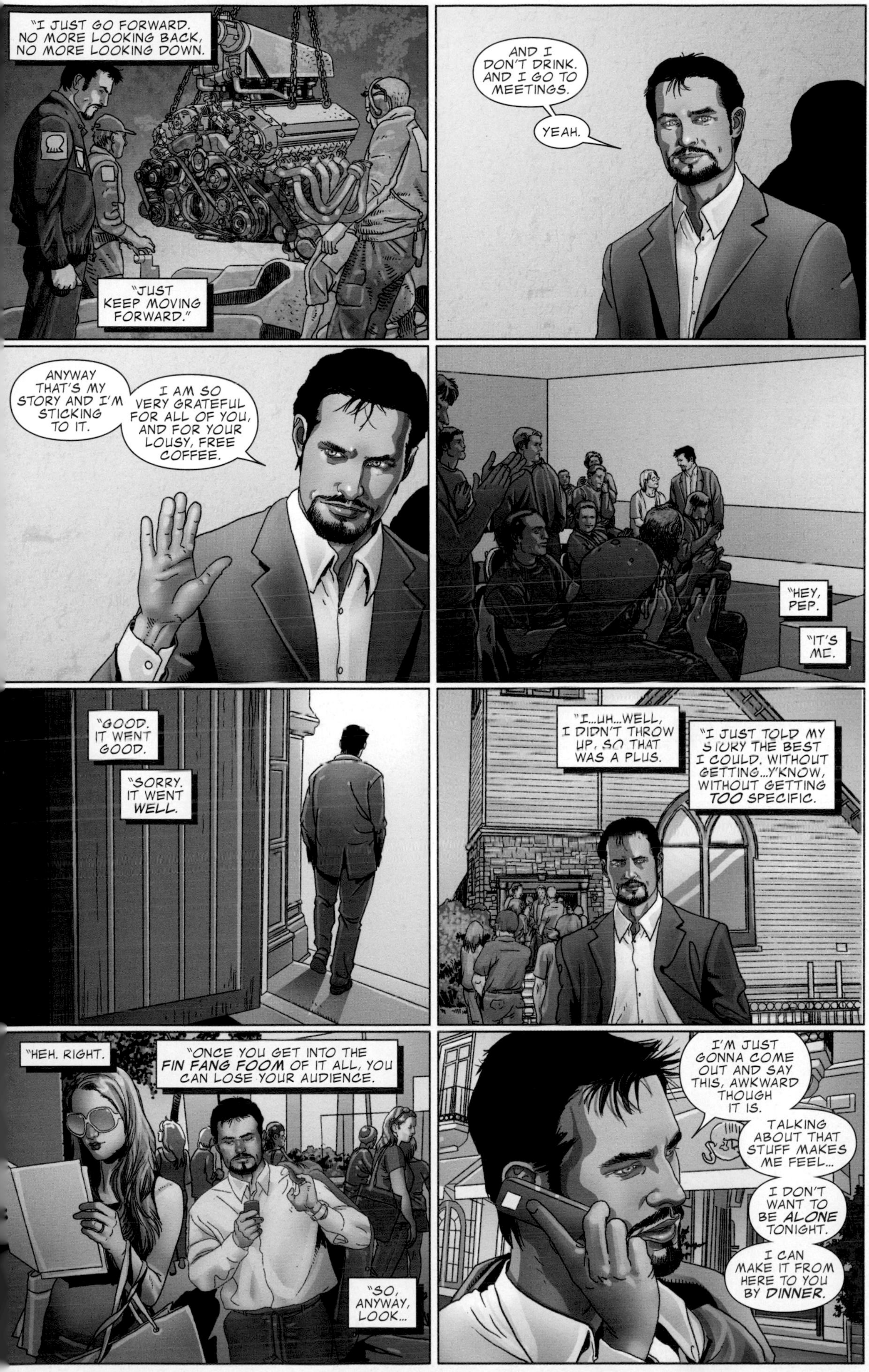
"I JUST GO FORWARD. NO MORE LOOKING BACK, NO MORE LOOKING DOWN.
"JUST KEEP MOVING FORWARD."
AND I DON'T DRINK. AND I GO TO MEETINGS.
YEAH.
ANYWAY THAT'S MY STORY AND I'M STICKING TO IT.
I AM SO VERY GRATEFUL FOR ALL OF YOU, AND FOR YOUR LOUSY, FREE COFFEE.
"HEY, PEP.
"IT'S ME.
"GOOD. IT WENT GOOD.
"SORRY. IT WENT WELL.
"I...UH...WELL, I DIDN'T THROW UP, SO THAT WAS A PLUS.
"I JUST TOLD MY STORY THE BEST I COULD. WITHOUT GETTING...Y'KNOW, WITHOUT GETTING TOO SPECIFIC.
"HEH. RIGHT.
"ONCE YOU GET INTO THE FIN FANG FOOM OF IT ALL, YOU CAN LOSE YOUR AUDIENCE.
"SO, ANYWAY, LOOK...
I'M JUST GONNA COME OUT AND SAY THIS, AWKWARD THOUGH IT IS.
TALKING ABOUT THAT STUFF MAKES ME FEEL...
I DON'T WANT TO BE ALONE TONIGHT.
I CAN MAKE IT FROM HERE TO YOU BY DINNER.

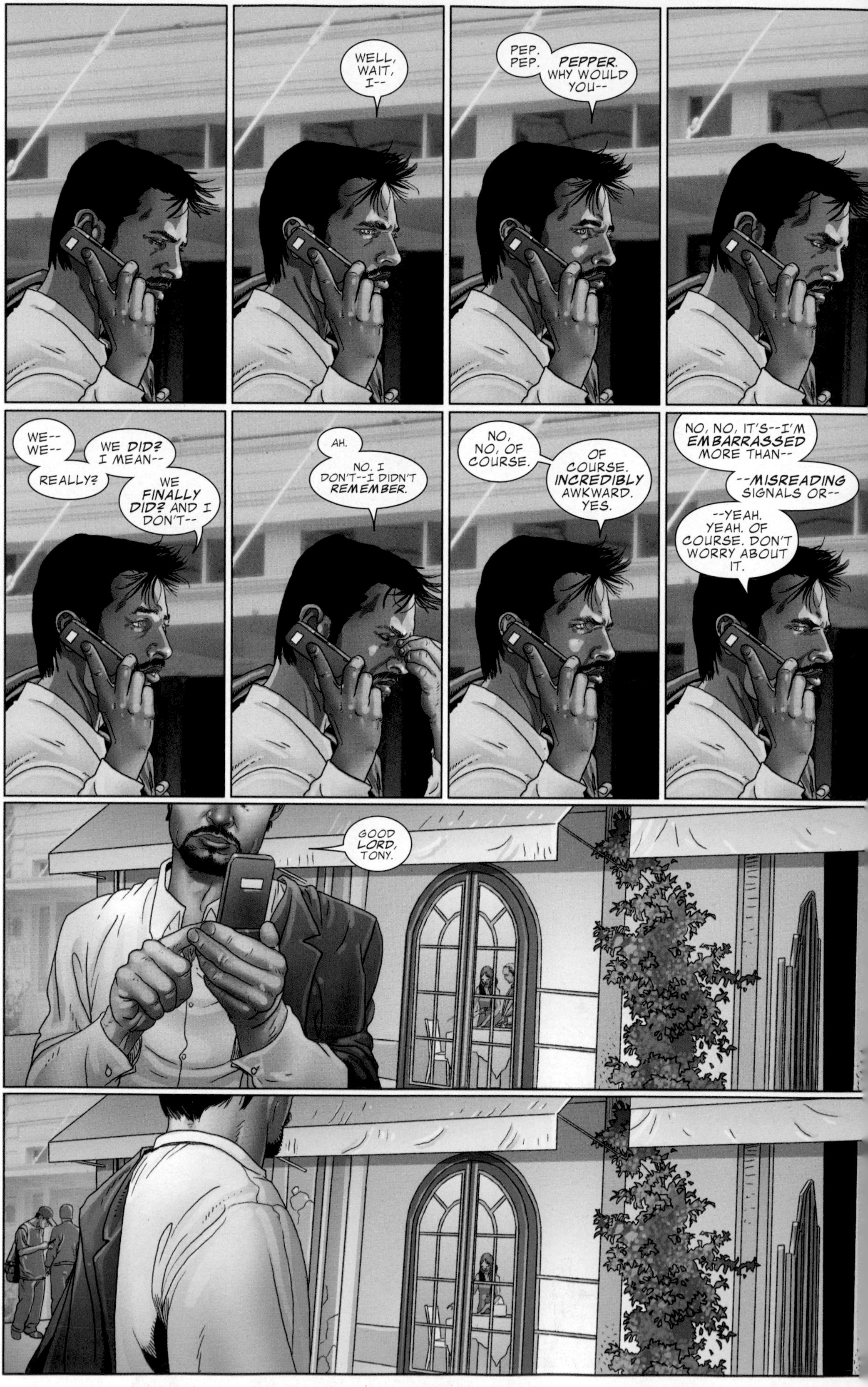
WELL, WAIT, I--
PEP. PEP.
PEPPER. WHY WOULD YOU--
WE-- WE--
WE DID? I MEAN--
REALLY?
WE FINALLY DID? AND I DON'T--
AH.
NO. I DON'T--I DIDN'T REMEMBER.
NO, NO, OF COURSE.
OF COURSE. INCREDIBLY AWKWARD. YES.
NO, NO, IT'S--I'M EMBARRASSED MORE THAN--
--MISREADING SIGNALS OR--
--YEAH. YEAH. OF COURSE. DON'T WORRY ABOUT IT.
GOOD LORD, TONY.

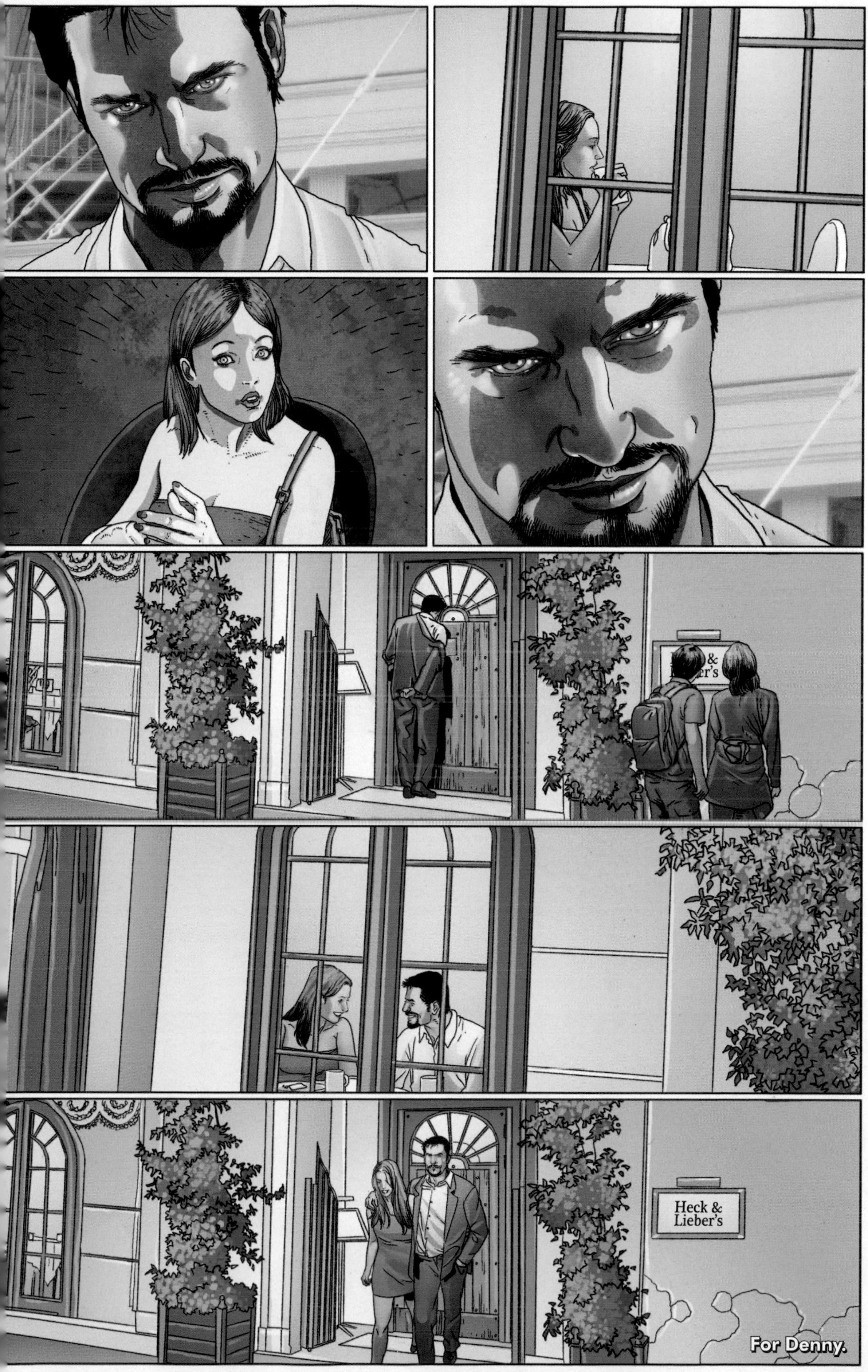
Heck &
Lieber's
For Denny.

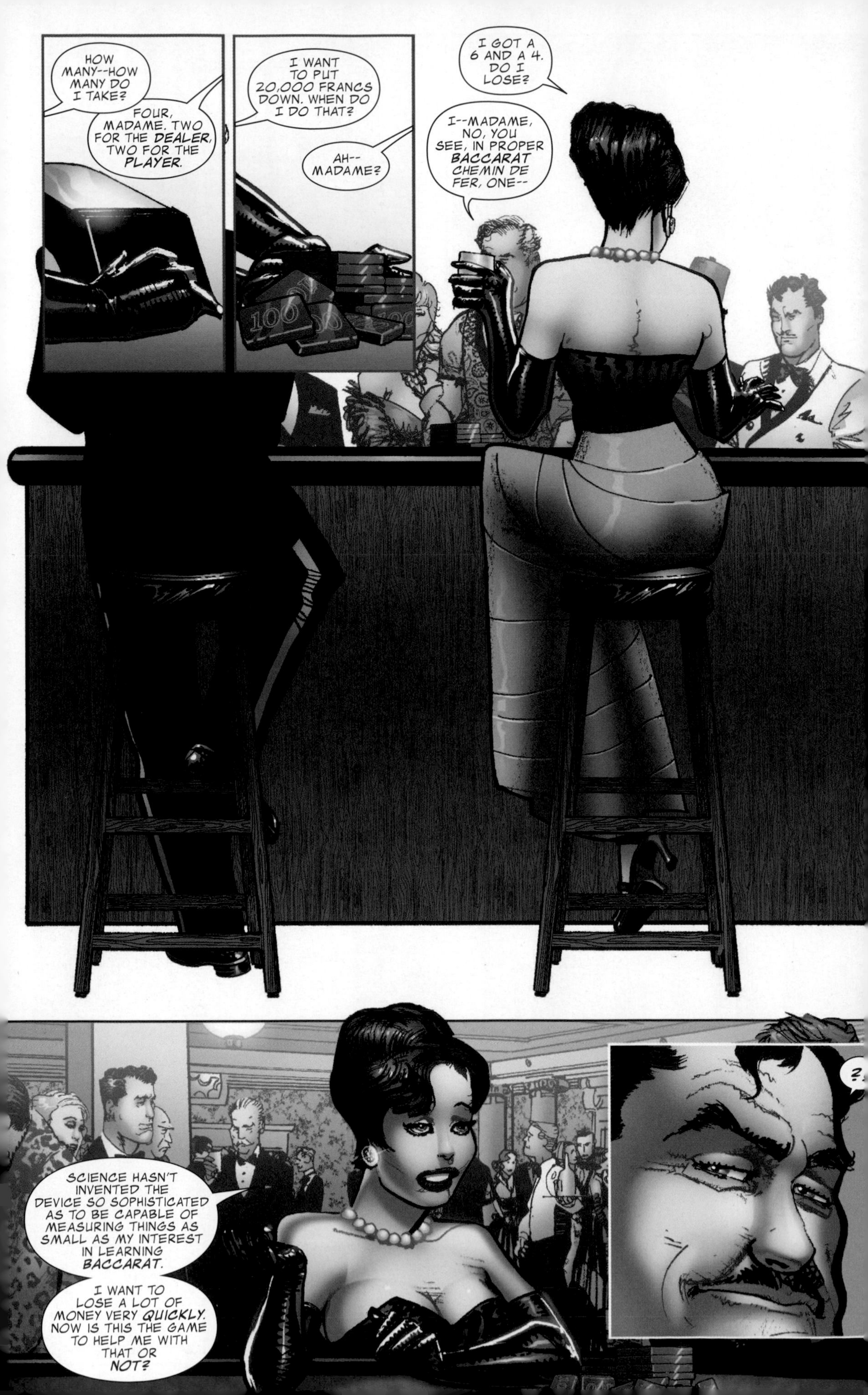
HOW MANY--HOW MANY DO I TAKE?
FOUR, MADAME. TWO FOR THE DEALER, TWO FOR THE PLAYER.
I WANT TO PUT 20,000 FRANCS DOWN. WHEN DO I DO THAT?
AH-- MADAME?
I GOT A 6 AND A 4. DO I LOSE?
I--MADAME, NO, YOU SEE, IN PROPER BACCARAT CHEMIN DE FER, ONE--
SCIENCE HASN'T INVENTED THE DEVICE SO SOPHISTICATED AS TO BE CAPABLE OF MEASURING THINGS AS SMALL AS MY INTEREST IN LEARNING BACCARAT.
I WANT TO LOSE A LOT OF MONEY VERY QUICKLY. NOW IS THIS THE GAME TO HELP ME WITH THAT OR NOT?
?!

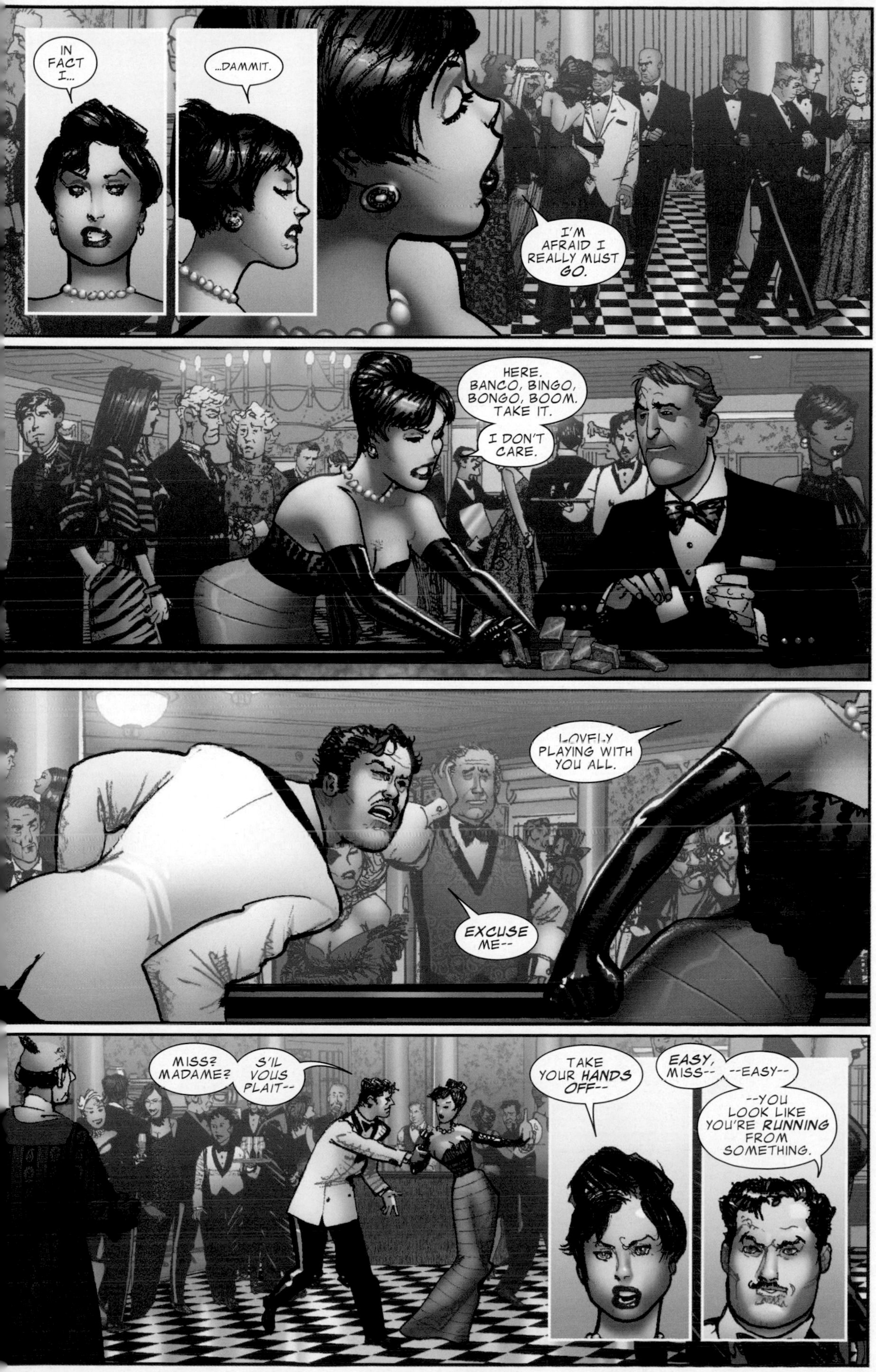
IN FACT I...
...DAMMIT.
I'M AFRAID I REALLY MUST GO.
HERE. BANCO, BINGO, BONGO, BOOM. TAKE IT.
I DON'T CARE.
LOVELY PLAYING WITH YOU ALL.
EXCUSE ME--
MISS? MADAME?
S'IL VOUS PLAIT--
TAKE YOUR HANDS OFF--
EASY, MISS--
--EASY--
--YOU LOOK LIKE YOU'RE RUNNING FROM SOMETHING.

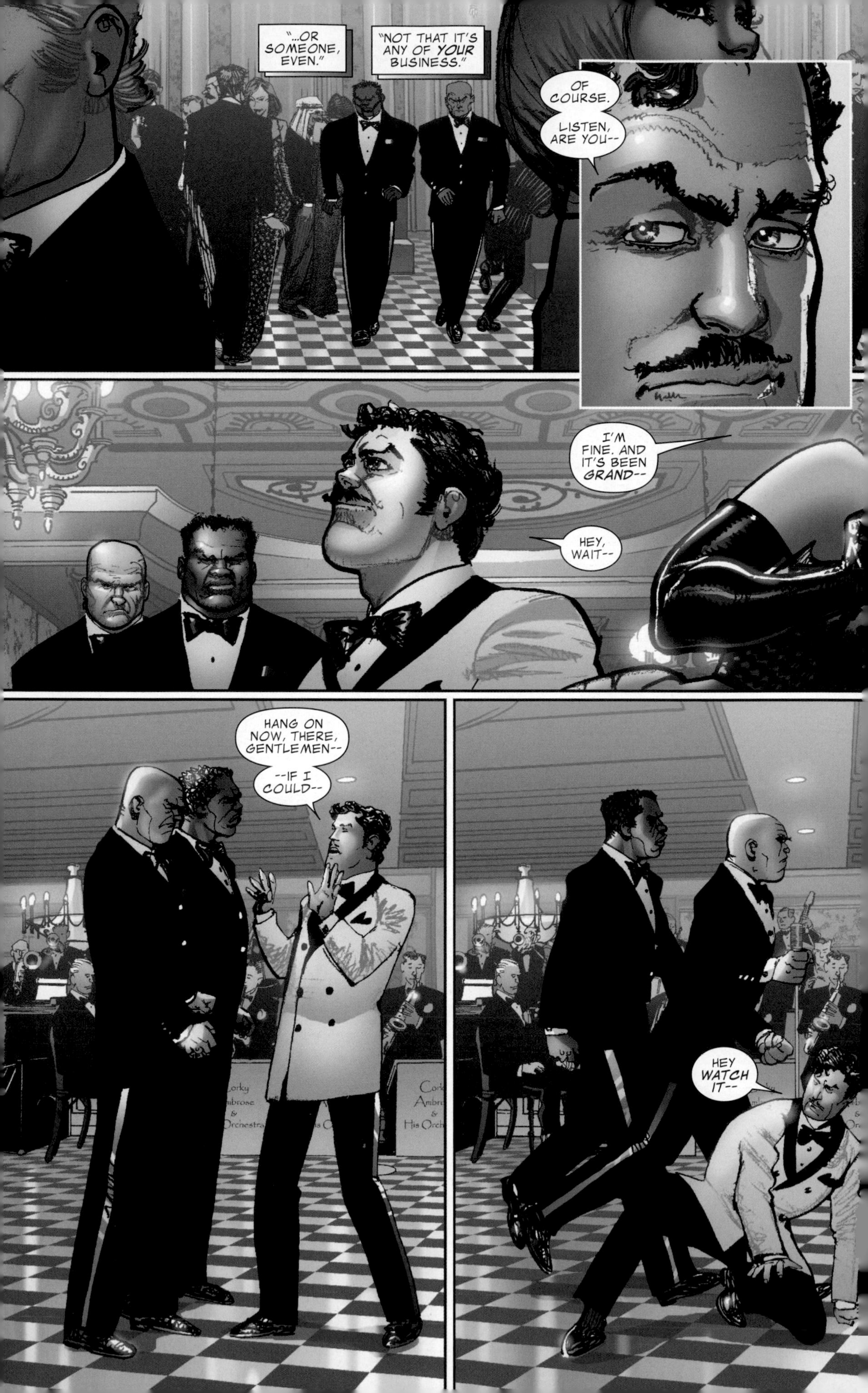
"...OR SOMEONE, EVEN."
"NOT THAT IT'S ANY OF YOUR BUSINESS."
OF COURSE.
LISTEN, ARE YOU--
I'M FINE. AND IT'S BEEN GRAND--
HEY, WAIT--
HANG ON NOW, THERE, GENTLEMEN--
--IF I COULD--
Corky Ambrose & His Orchestra
HEY WATCH IT--

WATCH YOUR *HEAD*, MA'AM--

SIR, STEP AWAY FROM--

GET YOUR HANDS *OFF* OF ME--

ARE YOU ALL *RIGHT?*

SIR--

I CAN HAVE *SECURITY* OUT HERE--

YOU DON'T HAVE TO GO ANYWHERE YOU DON'T *WANT* TO.

GO AHEAD. TELL HIM.

MY NAME IS *OBADIAH STANE.* THIS WOMAN IS WITH ME.

GO AHEAD. TELL HIM.

IT'S FINE. I'M FINE.

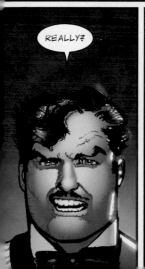

REALLY?

YES.

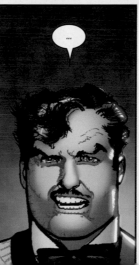

...

REALLY. IT'S FINE.

MR. STARK!

SIR, THE SECURITY CAMERAS SHOWED--

DAMMIT.

"OBADIAH STANE."

YOUR GIRLFRIEND LOST HER EARRING...

"BOYS, FIND OUT WHERE HE'S STAYING."

WHAT DO YOU MEAN, HE'S "BEEN DELAYED"?

WHAT KIND OF CRAP IS HE TRYING TO PULL?

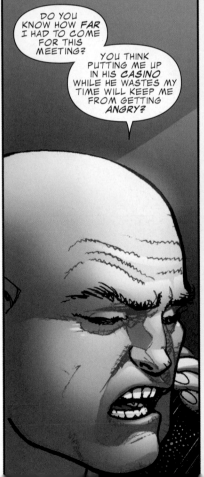

DO YOU KNOW HOW FAR I HAD TO COME FOR THIS MEETING?

YOU THINK PUTTING ME UP IN HIS CASINO WHILE HE WASTES MY TIME WILL KEEP ME FROM GETTING ANGRY?

TAP TAP

ONE MINUTE.

WHAT THE HELL--

SHH. HEY THERE.

HI.

23

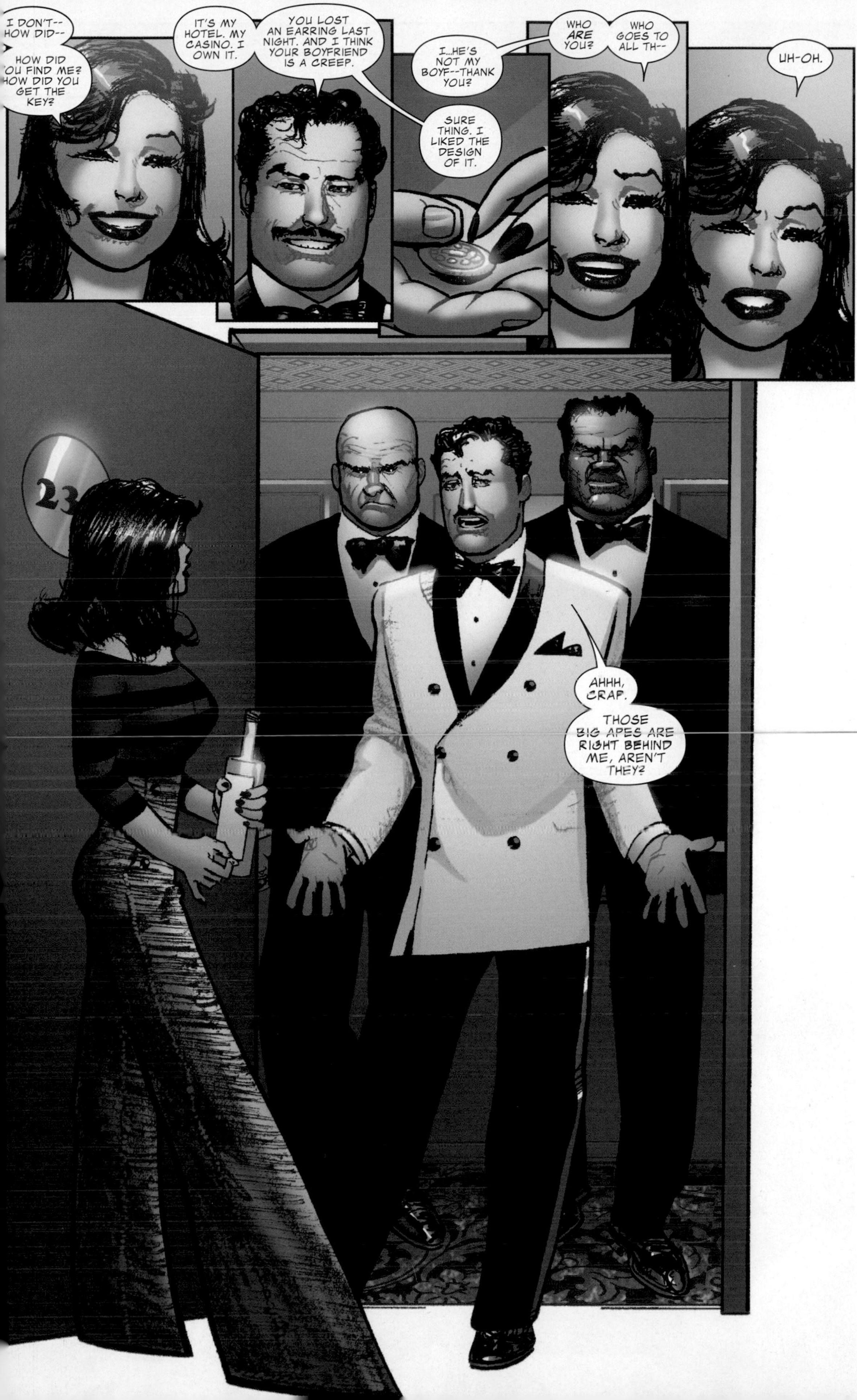
I DON'T-- HOW DID--
HOW DID YOU FIND ME? HOW DID YOU GET THE KEY?
IT'S MY HOTEL. MY CASINO. I OWN IT.
YOU LOST AN EARRING LAST NIGHT. AND I THINK YOUR BOYFRIEND IS A CREEP.
I...HE'S NOT MY BOYF--THANK YOU?
SURE THING. I LIKED THE DESIGN OF IT.
WHO ARE YOU?
WHO GOES TO ALL TH--
UH-OH.
AHHH, CRAP.
THOSE BIG APES ARE RIGHT BEHIND ME, AREN'T THEY?

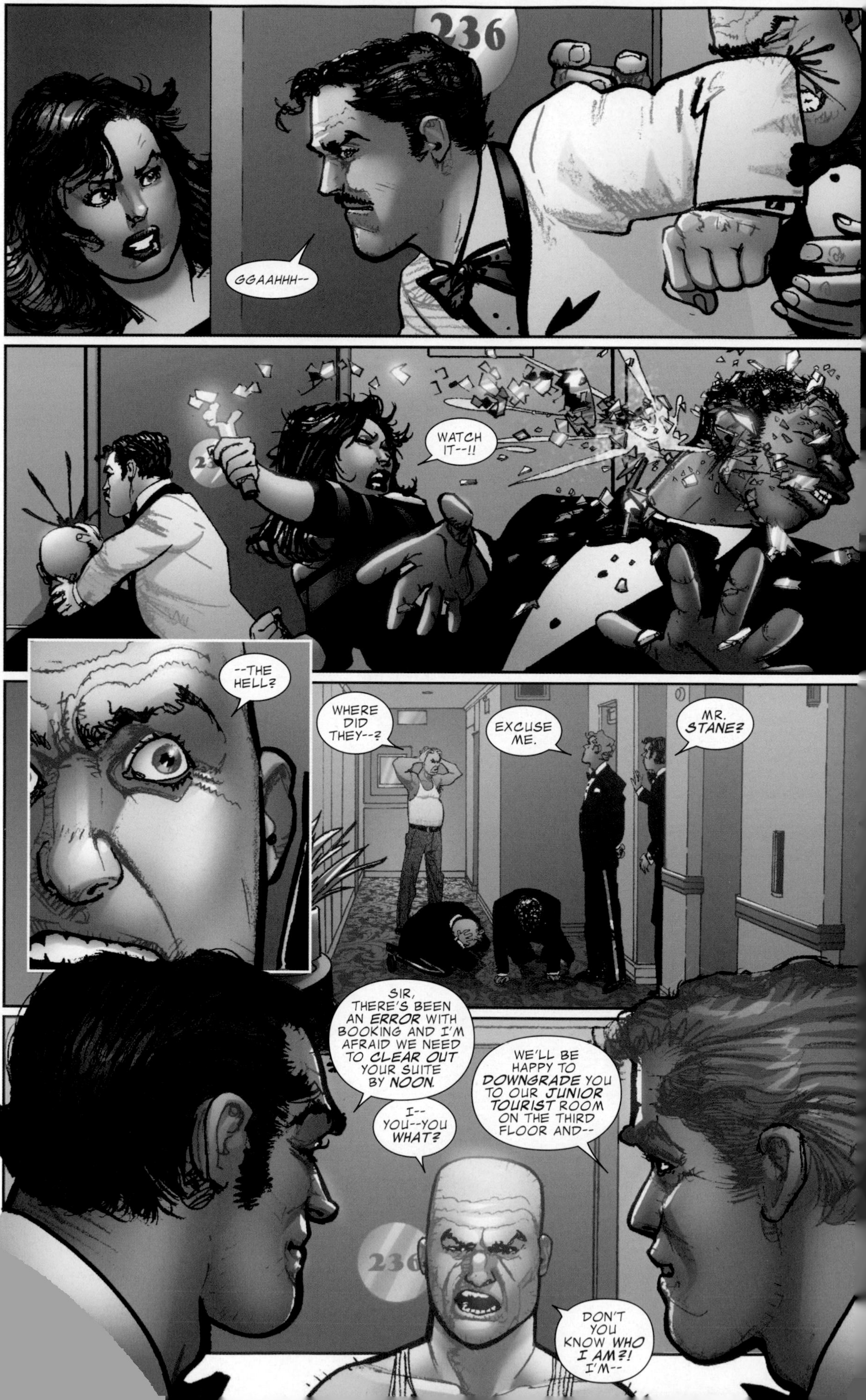
GGAAHHH--
WATCH IT--!!
--THE HELL?
WHERE DID THEY--?
EXCUSE ME.
MR. STANE?
SIR, THERE'S BEEN AN ERROR WITH BOOKING AND I'M AFRAID WE NEED TO CLEAR OUT YOUR SUITE BY NOON.
I-- YOU--YOU WHAT?
WE'LL BE HAPPY TO DOWNGRADE YOU TO OUR JUNIOR TOURIST ROOM ON THE THIRD FLOOR AND--
DON'T YOU KNOW WHO I AM?! I'M--
236

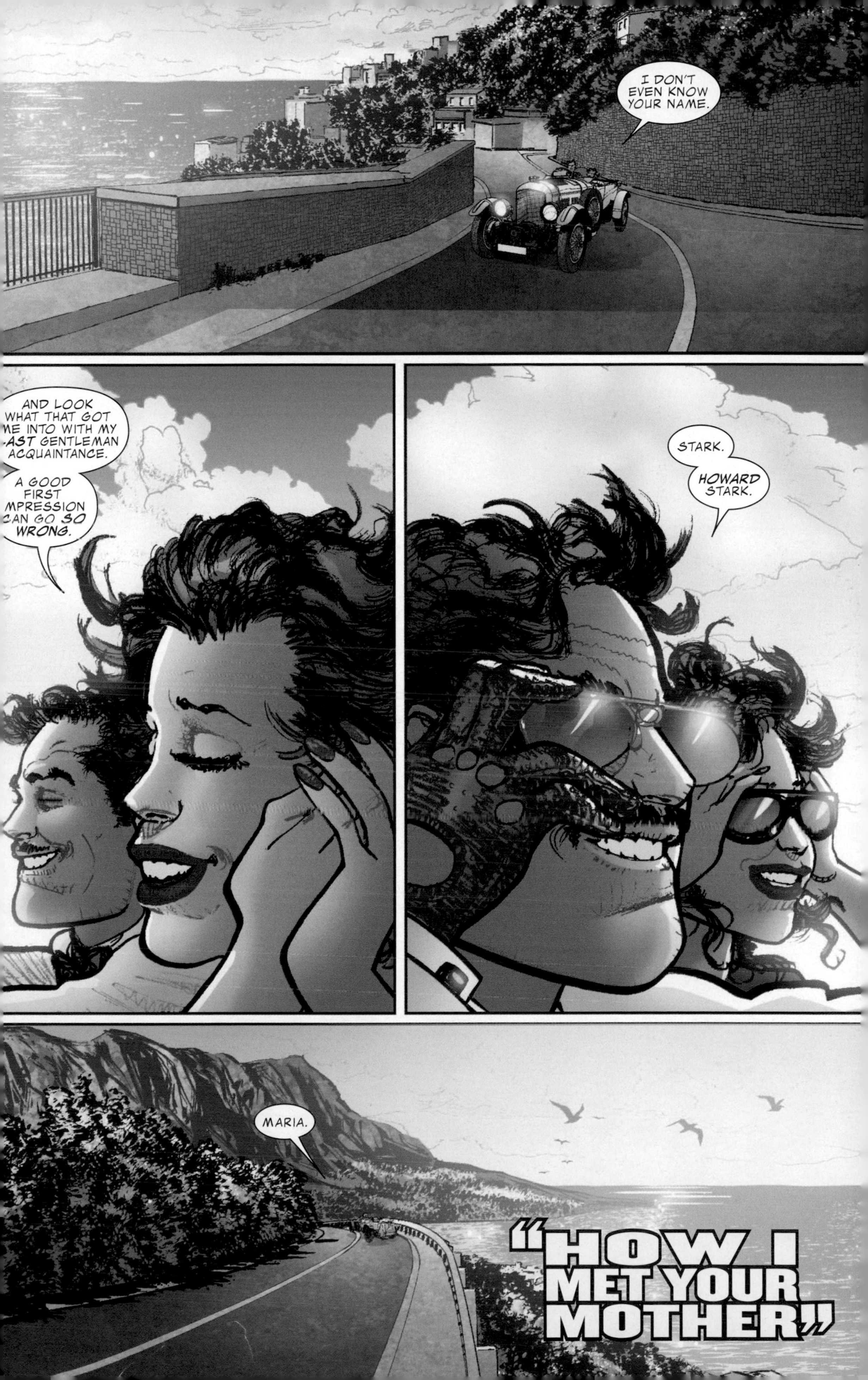
I DON'T EVEN KNOW YOUR NAME.
AND LOOK WHAT THAT GOT ME INTO WITH MY AST GENTLEMAN ACQUAINTANCE.
A GOOD FIRST MPRESSION CAN GO SO WRONG.
STARK.
HOWARD STARK.
MARIA.
"HOW I MET YOUR MOTHER"

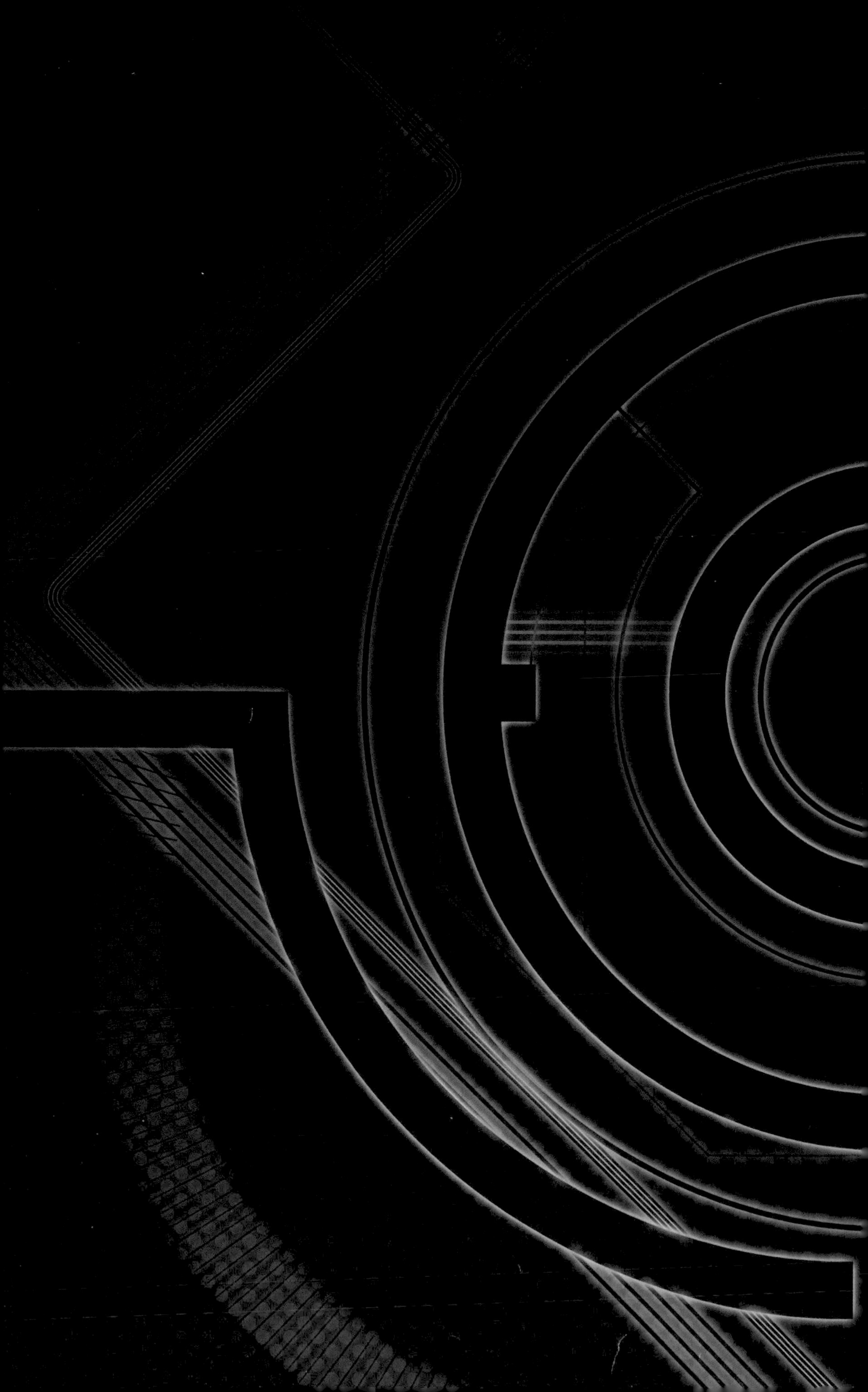

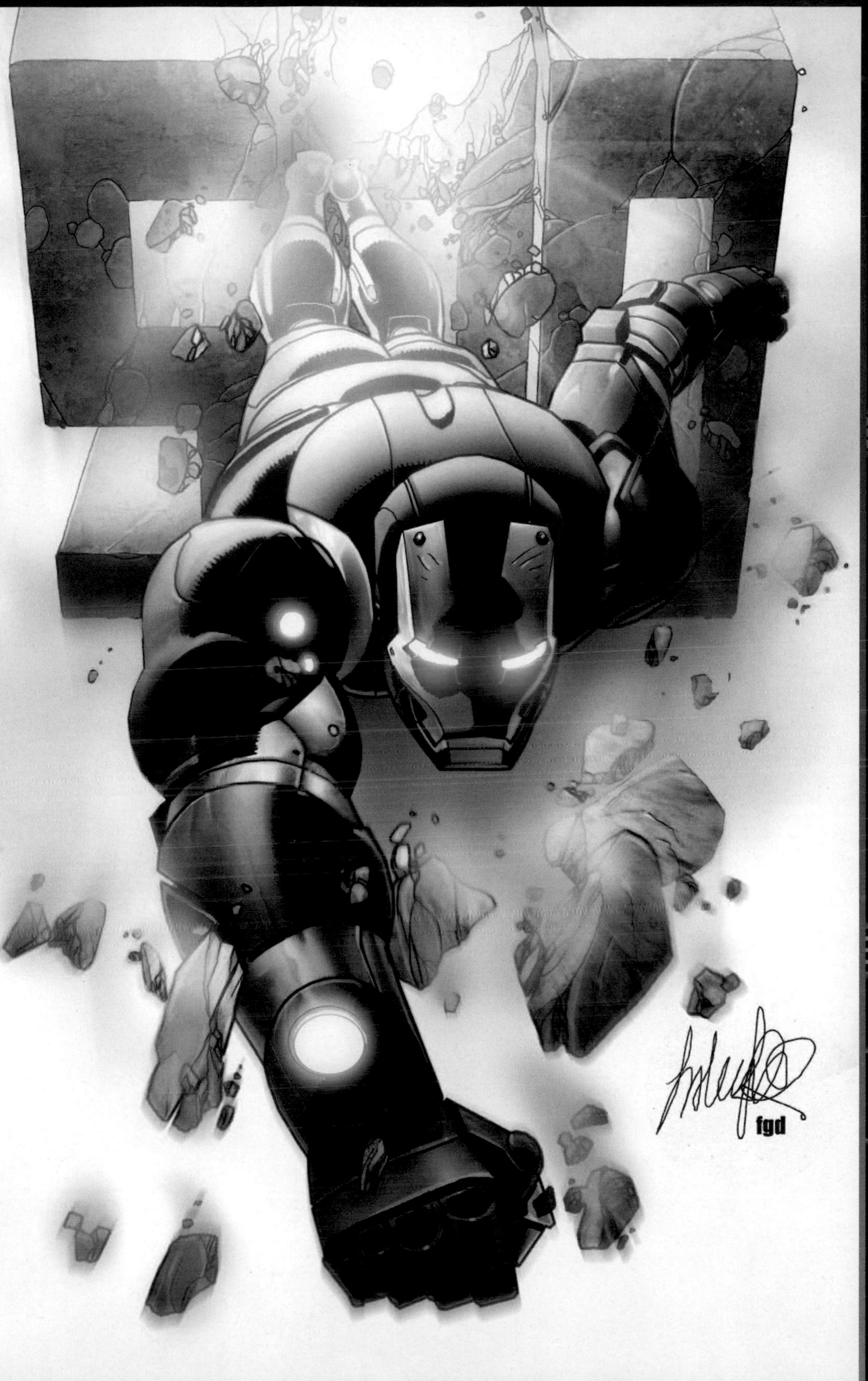
fgd

THE NEW IRON AGE 500

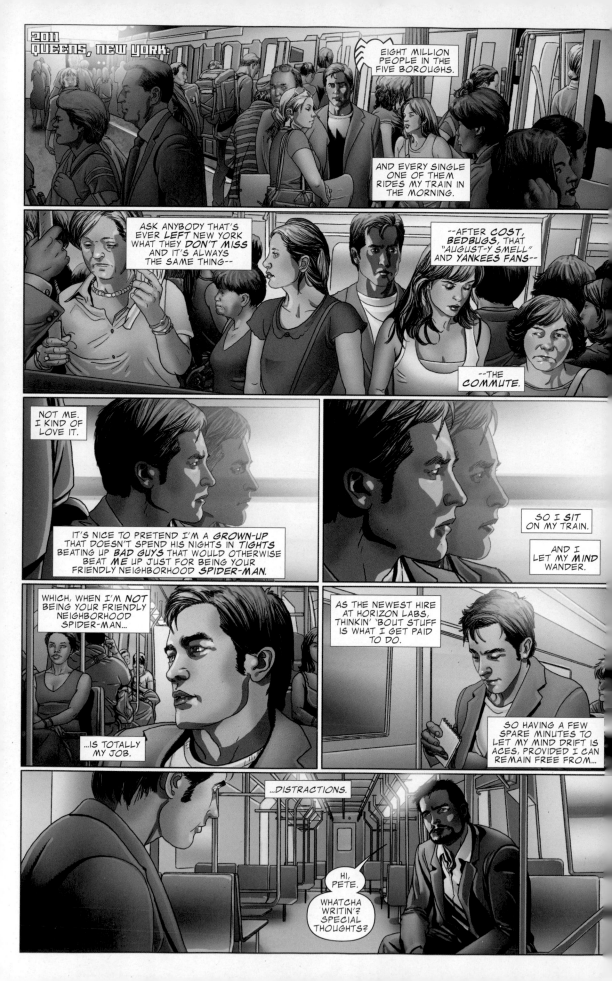

2011
QUEENS, NEW YORK:

EIGHT MILLION PEOPLE IN THE FIVE BOROUGHS.

AND EVERY SINGLE ONE OF THEM RIDES MY TRAIN IN THE MORNING.

ASK ANYBODY THAT'S EVER *LEFT* NEW YORK WHAT THEY *DON'T* MISS AND IT'S ALWAYS THE SAME THING--

--AFTER *COST*, *BEDBUGS*, THAT "*AUGUST-Y SMELL*" AND *YANKEES FANS*--

--THE *COMMUTE*.

NOT ME. I KIND OF LOVE IT.

IT'S NICE TO PRETEND I'M A *GROWN-UP* THAT DOESN'T SPEND HIS NIGHTS IN *TIGHTS* BEATING UP *BAD GUYS* THAT WOULD OTHERWISE BEAT *ME* UP JUST FOR BEING YOUR FRIENDLY NEIGHBORHOOD *SPIDER-MAN*.

SO I *SIT* ON MY TRAIN.

AND I LET MY *MIND* WANDER.

WHICH, WHEN I'M *NOT* BEING YOUR FRIENDLY NEIGHBORHOOD SPIDER-MAN...

...IS TOTALLY MY JOB.

AS THE NEWEST HIRE AT HORIZON LABS, THINKIN' 'BOUT STUFF IS WHAT I GET PAID TO DO.

SO HAVING A FEW SPARE MINUTES TO LET MY MIND DRIFT IS ACES, PROVIDED I CAN REMAIN FREE FROM...

...DISTRACTIONS.

HI, PETE.
WHATCHA WRITIN'? SPECIAL THOUGHTS?

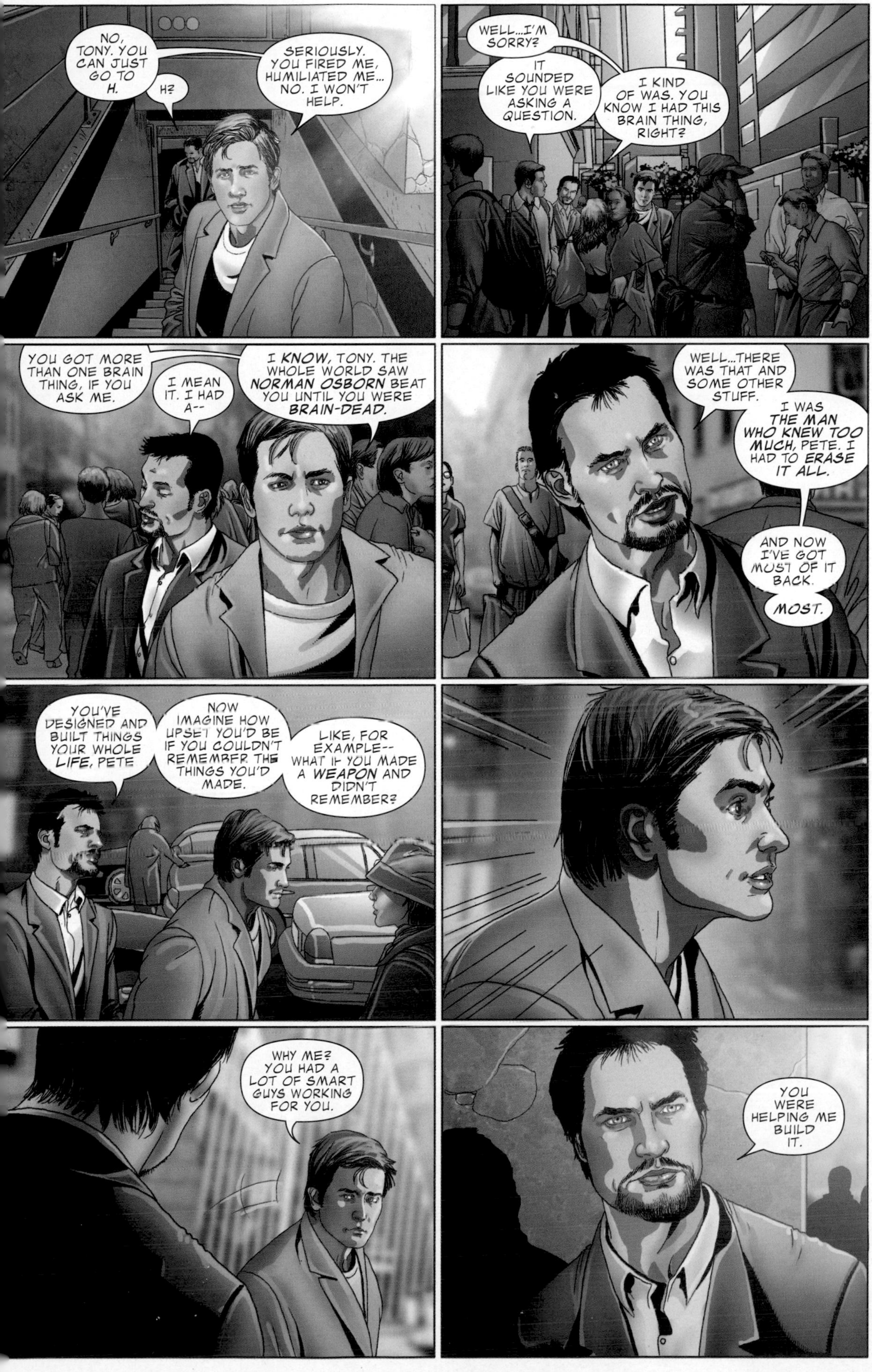
NO, TONY. YOU CAN JUST GO TO H.
H?
SERIOUSLY. YOU FIRED ME, HUMILIATED ME... NO. I WON'T HELP.
WELL...I'M SORRY?
IT SOUNDED LIKE YOU WERE ASKING A QUESTION.
I KIND OF WAS. YOU KNOW I HAD THIS BRAIN THING, RIGHT?
YOU GOT MORE THAN ONE BRAIN THING, IF YOU ASK ME.
I MEAN IT. I HAD A--
I KNOW, TONY. THE WHOLE WORLD SAW NORMAN OSBORN BEAT YOU UNTIL YOU WERE BRAIN-DEAD.
WELL...THERE WAS THAT AND SOME OTHER STUFF.
I WAS THE MAN WHO KNEW TOO MUCH, PETE. I HAD TO ERASE IT ALL.
AND NOW I'VE GOT MOST OF IT BACK.
MOST.
YOU'VE DESIGNED AND BUILT THINGS YOUR WHOLE LIFE, PETE
NOW IMAGINE HOW UPSET YOU'D BE IF YOU COULDN'T REMEMBER THE THINGS YOU'D MADE.
LIKE, FOR EXAMPLE-- WHAT IF YOU MADE A WEAPON AND DIDN'T REMEMBER?
WHY ME? YOU HAD A LOT OF SMART GUYS WORKING FOR YOU.
YOU WERE HELPING ME BUILD IT.

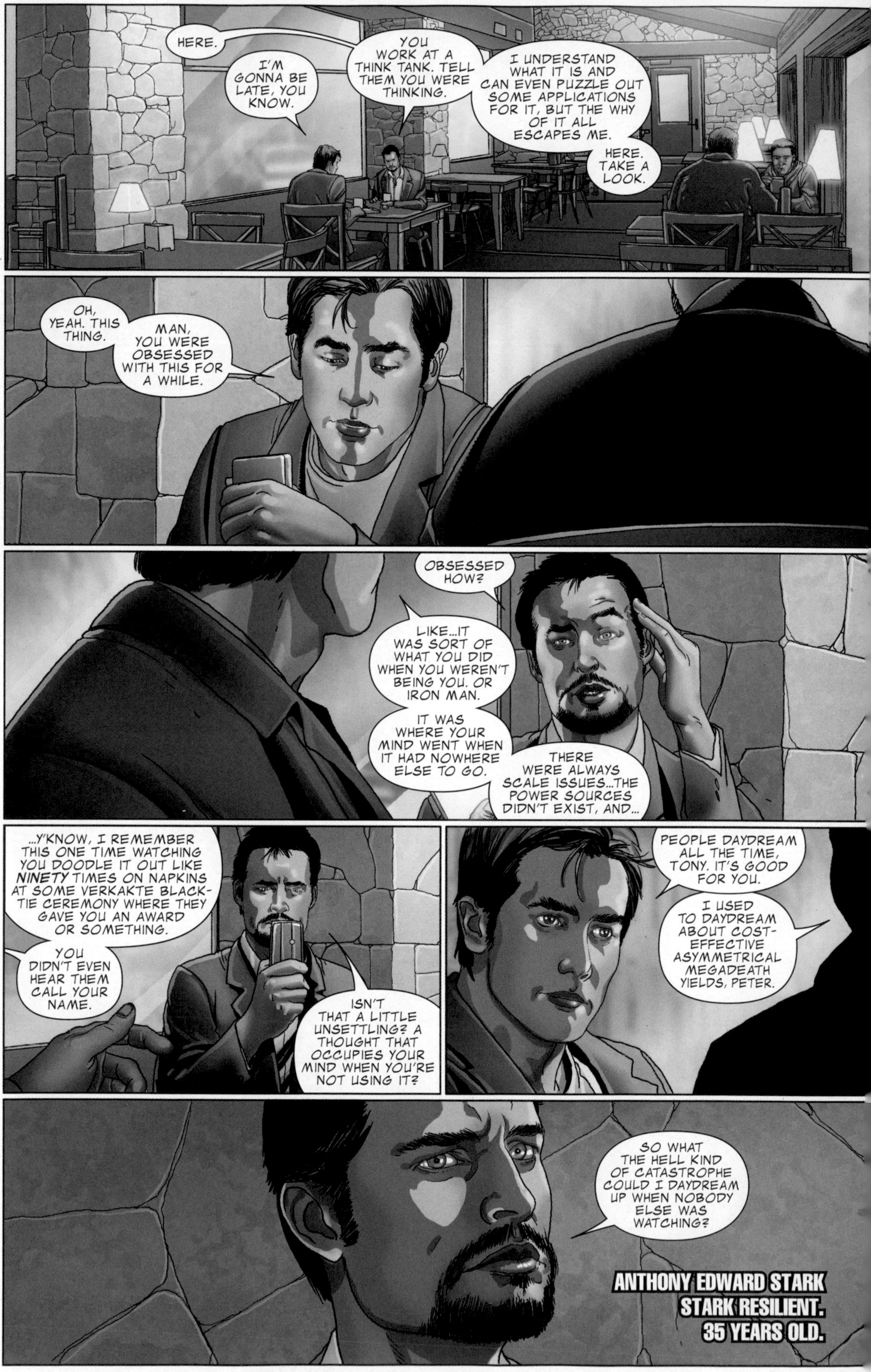
HERE.
I'M GONNA BE LATE, YOU KNOW.
YOU WORK AT A THINK TANK. TELL THEM YOU WERE THINKING.
I UNDERSTAND WHAT IT IS AND CAN EVEN PUZZLE OUT SOME APPLICATIONS FOR IT, BUT THE WHY OF IT ALL ESCAPES ME.
HERE. TAKE A LOOK.
OH, YEAH. THIS THING.
MAN, YOU WERE OBSESSED WITH THIS FOR A WHILE.
OBSESSED HOW?
LIKE...IT WAS SORT OF WHAT YOU DID WHEN YOU WEREN'T BEING YOU. OR IRON MAN.
IT WAS WHERE YOUR MIND WENT WHEN IT HAD NOWHERE ELSE TO GO.
THERE WERE ALWAYS SCALE ISSUES...THE POWER SOURCES DIDN'T EXIST, AND...
...Y'KNOW, I REMEMBER THIS ONE TIME WATCHING YOU DOODLE IT OUT LIKE NINETY TIMES ON NAPKINS AT SOME VERKAKTE BLACK-TIE CEREMONY WHERE THEY GAVE YOU AN AWARD OR SOMETHING.
YOU DIDN'T EVEN HEAR THEM CALL YOUR NAME.
ISN'T THAT A LITTLE UNSETTLING? A THOUGHT THAT OCCUPIES YOUR MIND WHEN YOU'RE NOT USING IT?
PEOPLE DAYDREAM ALL THE TIME, TONY. IT'S GOOD FOR YOU.
I USED TO DAYDREAM ABOUT COST-EFFECTIVE ASYMMETRICAL MEGADEATH YIELDS, PETER.
SO WHAT THE HELL KIND OF CATASTROPHE COULD I DAYDREAM UP WHEN NOBODY ELSE WAS WATCHING?
ANTHONY EDWARD STARK
STARK RESILIENT.
35 YEARS OLD.

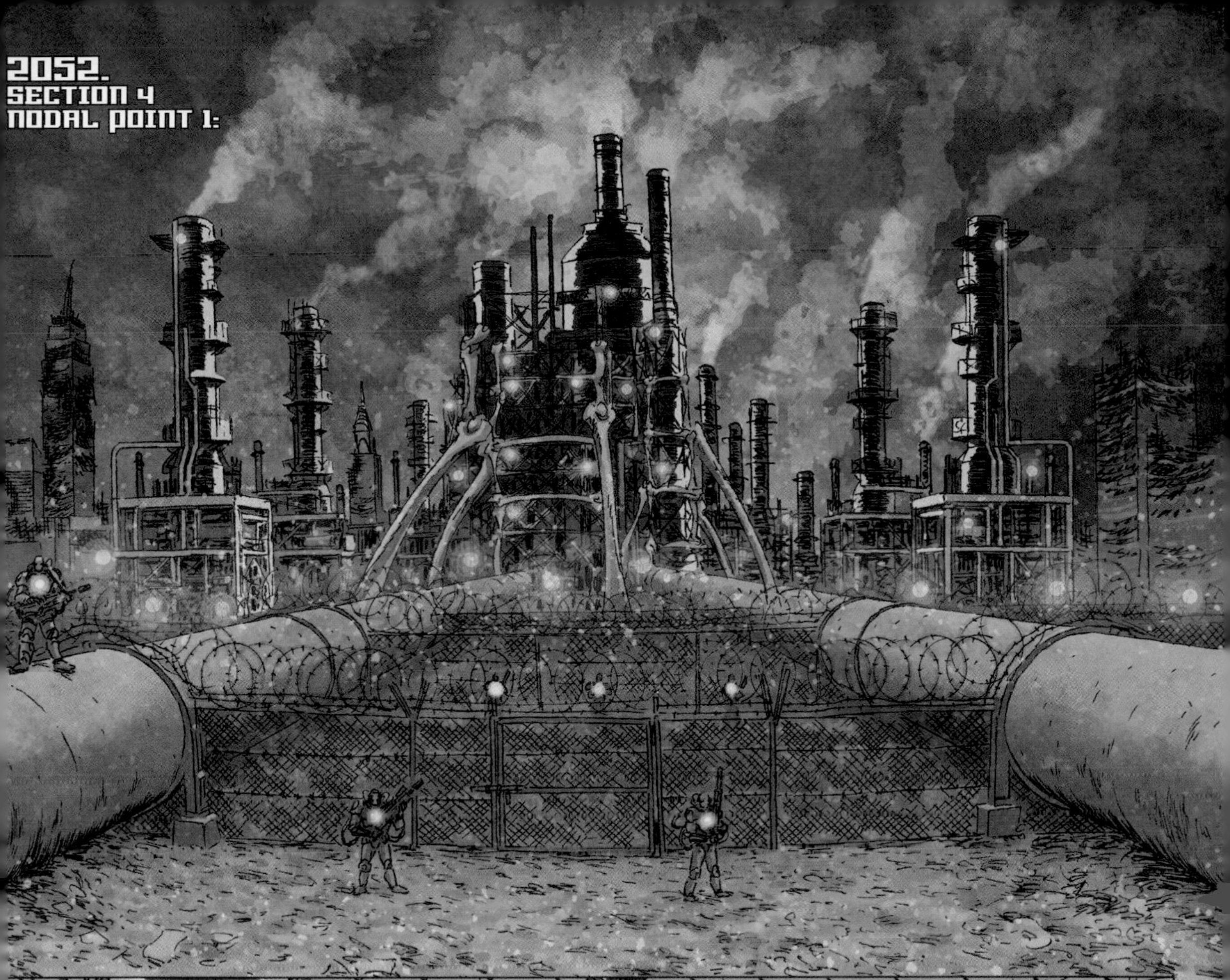
2052.
SECTION 4
NODAL POINT 1:

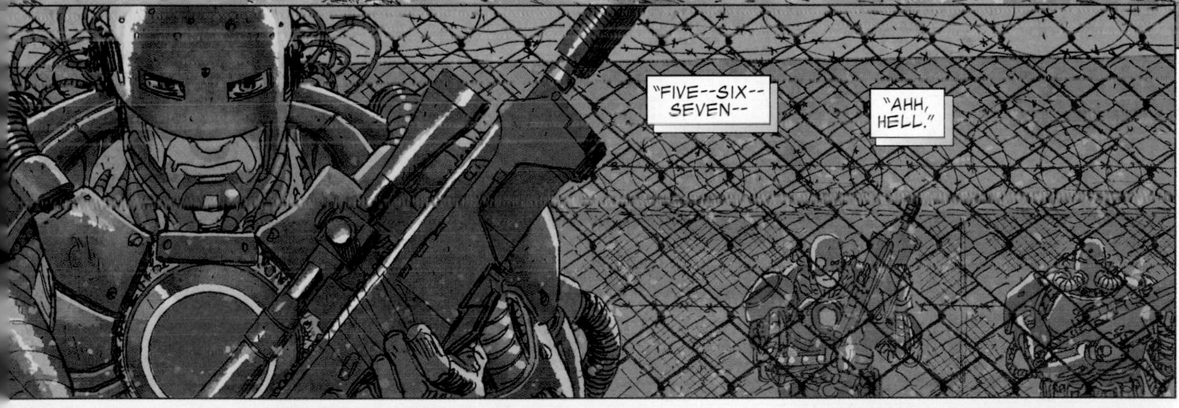
"FIVE--SIX--SEVEN--
"AHH, HELL."

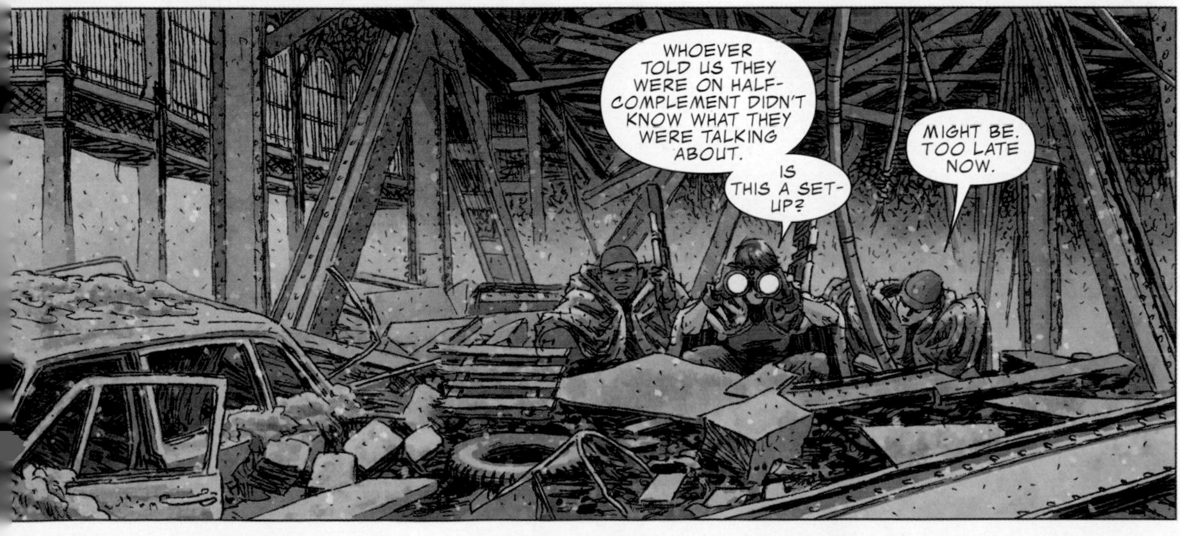
WHOEVER TOLD US THEY WERE ON HALF-COMPLEMENT DIDN'T KNOW WHAT THEY WERE TALKING ABOUT.
IS THIS A SET-UP?
MIGHT BE. TOO LATE NOW.

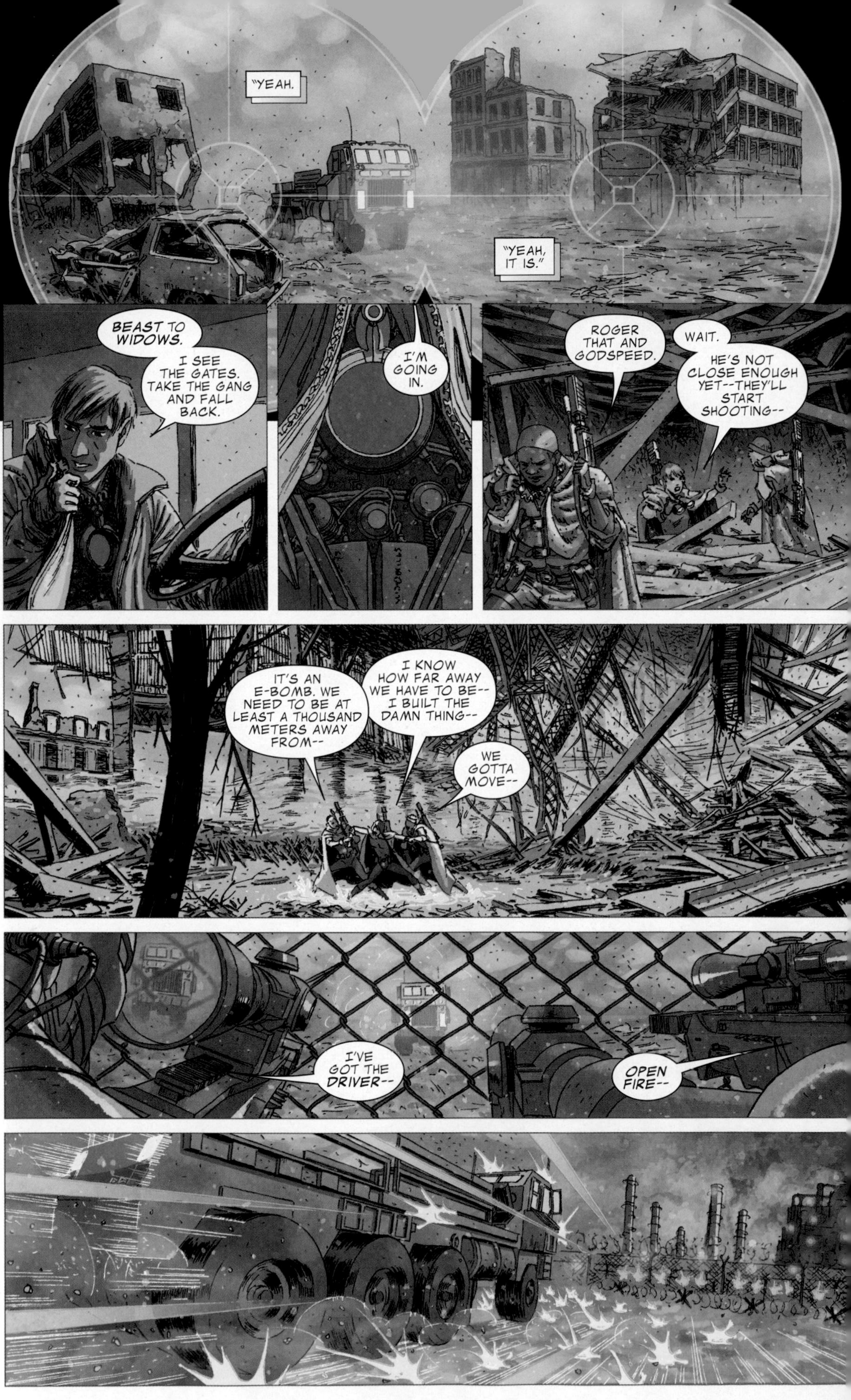
"YEAH.
"YEAH, IT IS."
BEAST TO WIDOWS.
I SEE THE GATES. TAKE THE GANG AND FALL BACK.
I'M GOING IN.
ROGER THAT AND GODSPEED.
WAIT.
HE'S NOT CLOSE ENOUGH YET--THEY'LL START SHOOTING--
IT'S AN E-BOMB. WE NEED TO BE AT LEAST A THOUSAND METERS AWAY FROM--
I KNOW HOW FAR AWAY WE HAVE TO BE--I BUILT THE DAMN THING--
WE GOTTA MOVE--
I'VE GOT THE DRIVER--
OPEN FIRE--

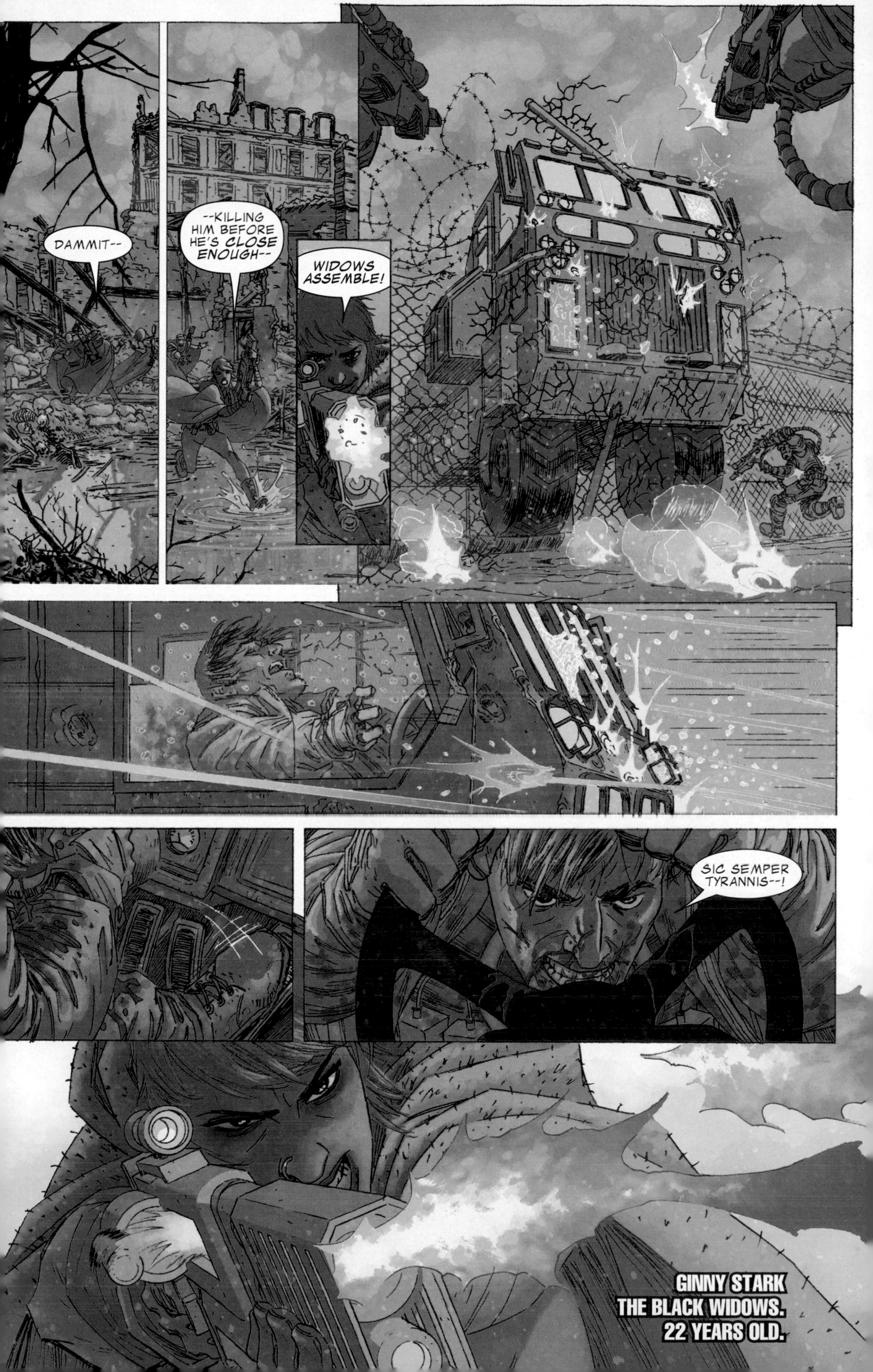
DAMMIT--
--KILLING HIM BEFORE HE'S CLOSE ENOUGH--
WIDOWS ASSEMBLE!
SIC SEMPER TYRANNIS--!
GINNY STARK
THE BLACK WIDOWS.
22 YEARS OLD.

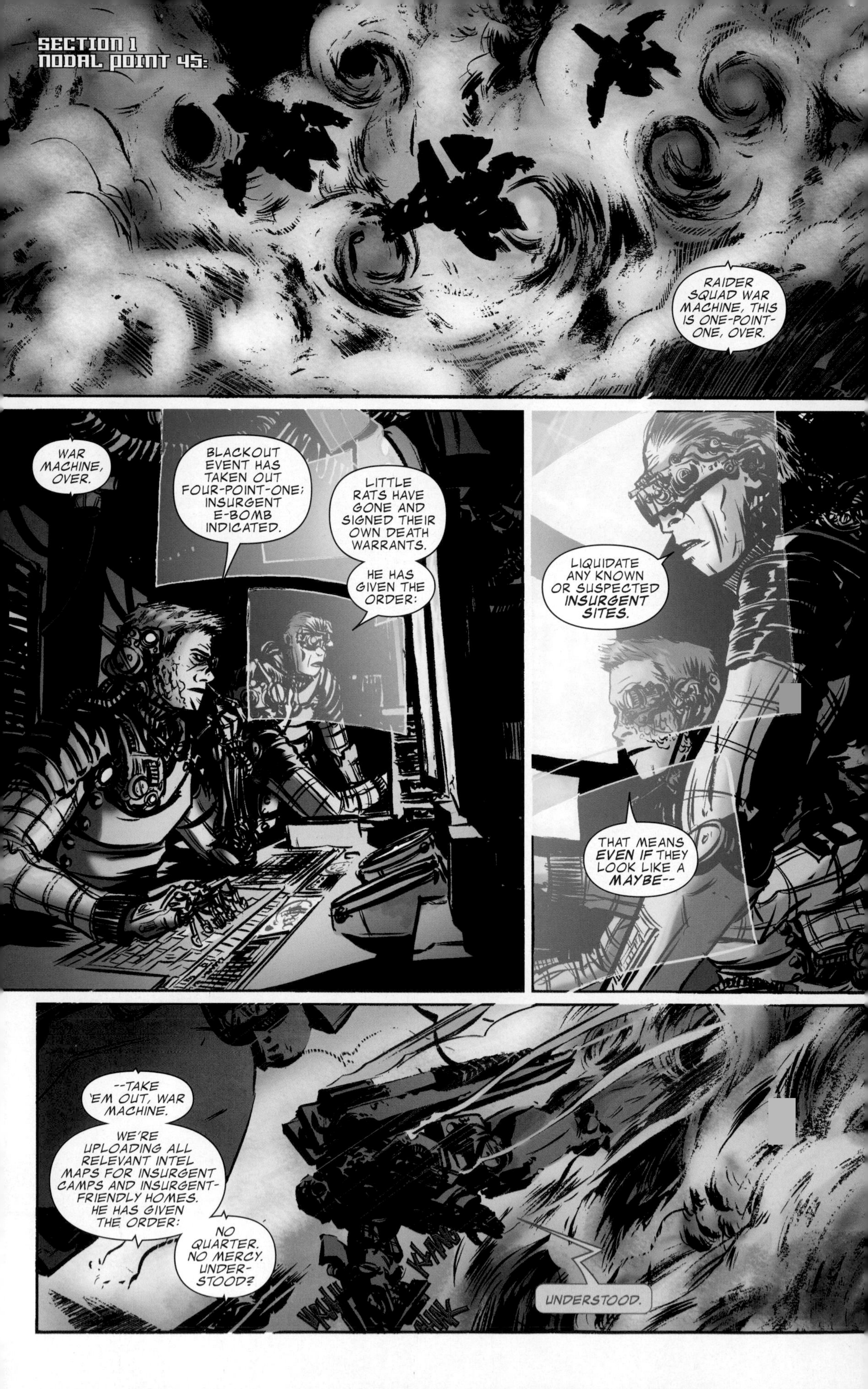
SECTION 1
NODAL POINT 45:
RAIDER SQUAD WAR MACHINE, THIS IS ONE-POINT-ONE, OVER.
WAR MACHINE, OVER.
BLACKOUT EVENT HAS TAKEN OUT FOUR-POINT-ONE; INSURGENT E-BOMB INDICATED.
LITTLE RATS HAVE GONE AND SIGNED THEIR OWN DEATH WARRANTS.
HE HAS GIVEN THE ORDER:
LIQUIDATE ANY KNOWN OR SUSPECTED INSURGENT SITES.
THAT MEANS EVEN IF THEY LOOK LIKE A MAYBE--
--TAKE 'EM OUT, WAR MACHINE.
WE'RE UPLOADING ALL RELEVANT INTEL MAPS FOR INSURGENT CAMPS AND INSURGENT-FRIENDLY HOMES. HE HAS GIVEN THE ORDER:
NO QUARTER. NO MERCY. UNDER-STOOD?
UNDERSTOOD.

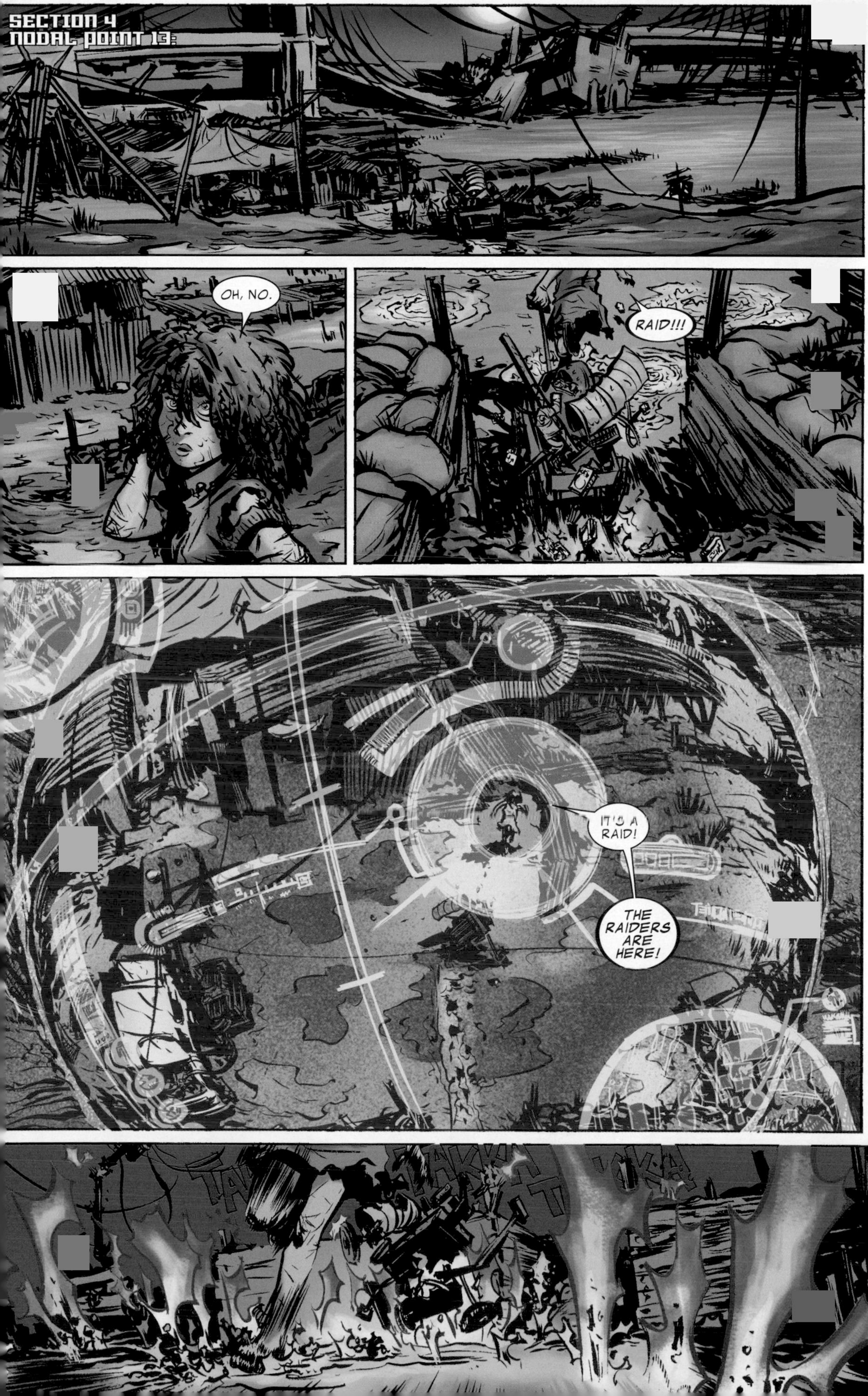
SECTION 4
NODAL POINT 13:
OH, NO.
RAID!!!
IT'S A RAID!
THE RAIDERS ARE HERE!

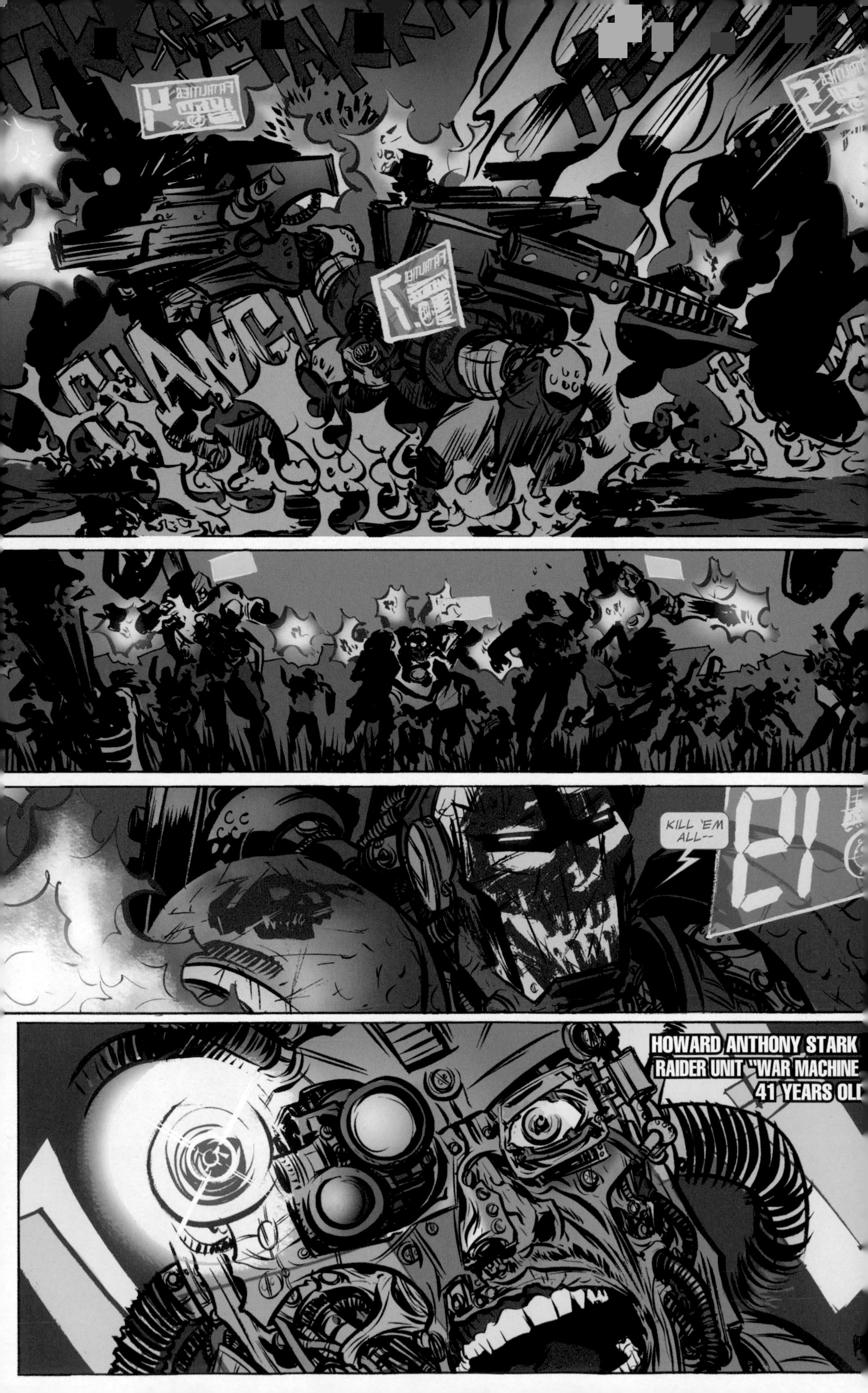
KILL 'EM ALL--
21
HOWARD ANTHONY STARK
RAIDER UNIT "WAR MACHINE
41 YEARS OL

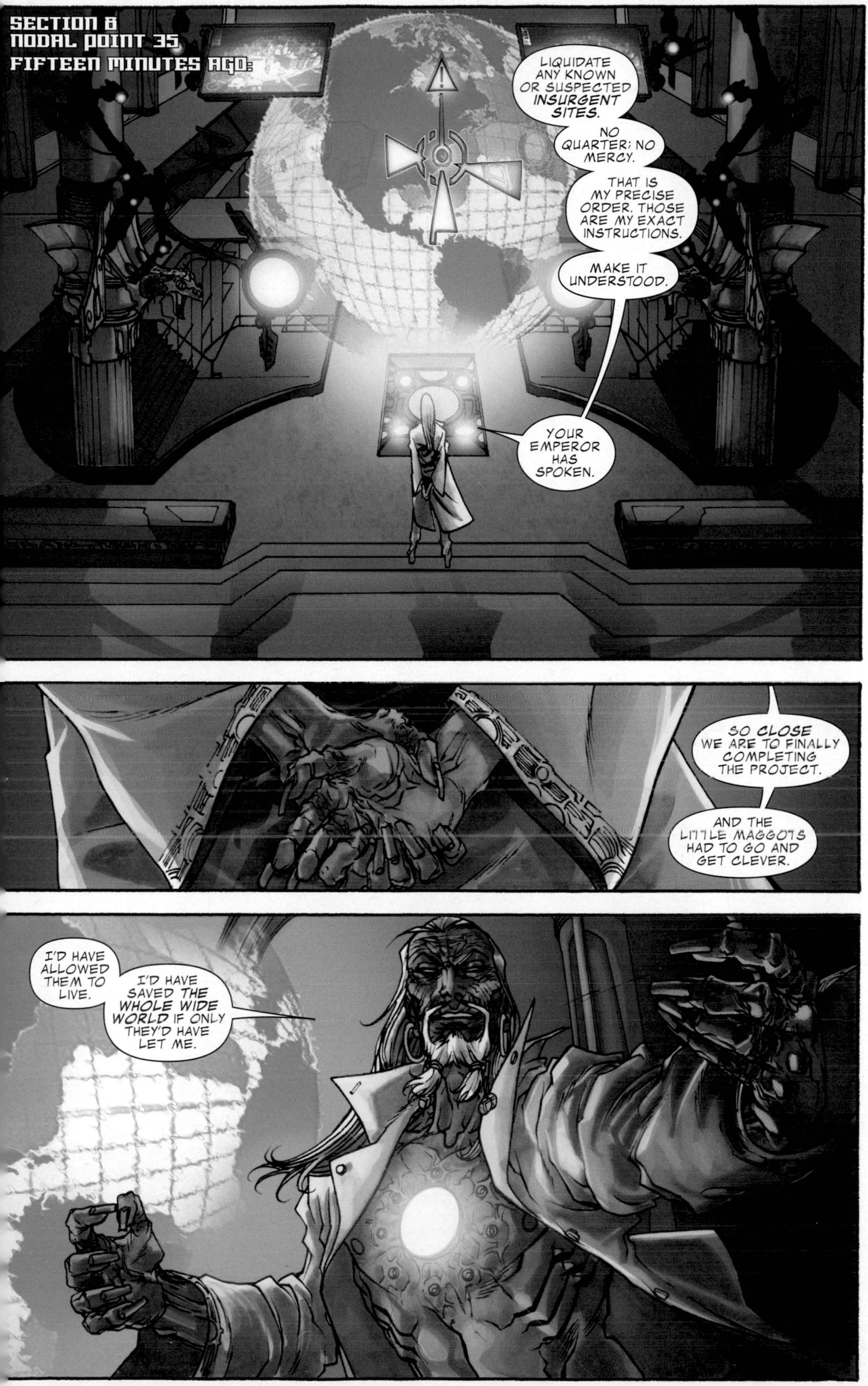
SECTION 6
NODAL POINT 35
FIFTEEN MINUTES AGO:
LIQUIDATE ANY KNOWN OR SUSPECTED INSURGENT SITES.
NO QUARTER; NO MERCY.
THAT IS MY PRECISE ORDER. THOSE ARE MY EXACT INSTRUCTIONS.
MAKE IT UNDERSTOOD.
YOUR EMPEROR HAS SPOKEN.
SO CLOSE WE ARE TO FINALLY COMPLETING THE PROJECT.
AND THE LITTLE MAGGOTS HAD TO GO AND GET CLEVER.
I'D HAVE ALLOWED THEM TO LIVE.
I'D HAVE SAVED THE WHOLE WIDE WORLD IF ONLY THEY'D HAVE LET ME.

EH?

AH. YES. OF COURSE.

HOW MAY I BE OF SERVICE?

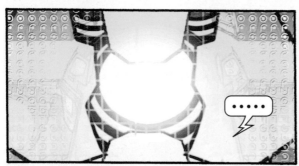

.....

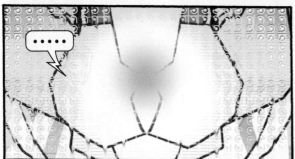

YES.

I GAVE THE ORDER. THEY SHALL BE LIQUIDATED. NO FURTHER DELAYS WILL BE SUFFERED OR TOLERATED.

.....

AH.

"OR TOLERATED...

"MASTER."

"MASTER."

TCH.

PIG!

PIG, COME HERE. I NEED YOU.

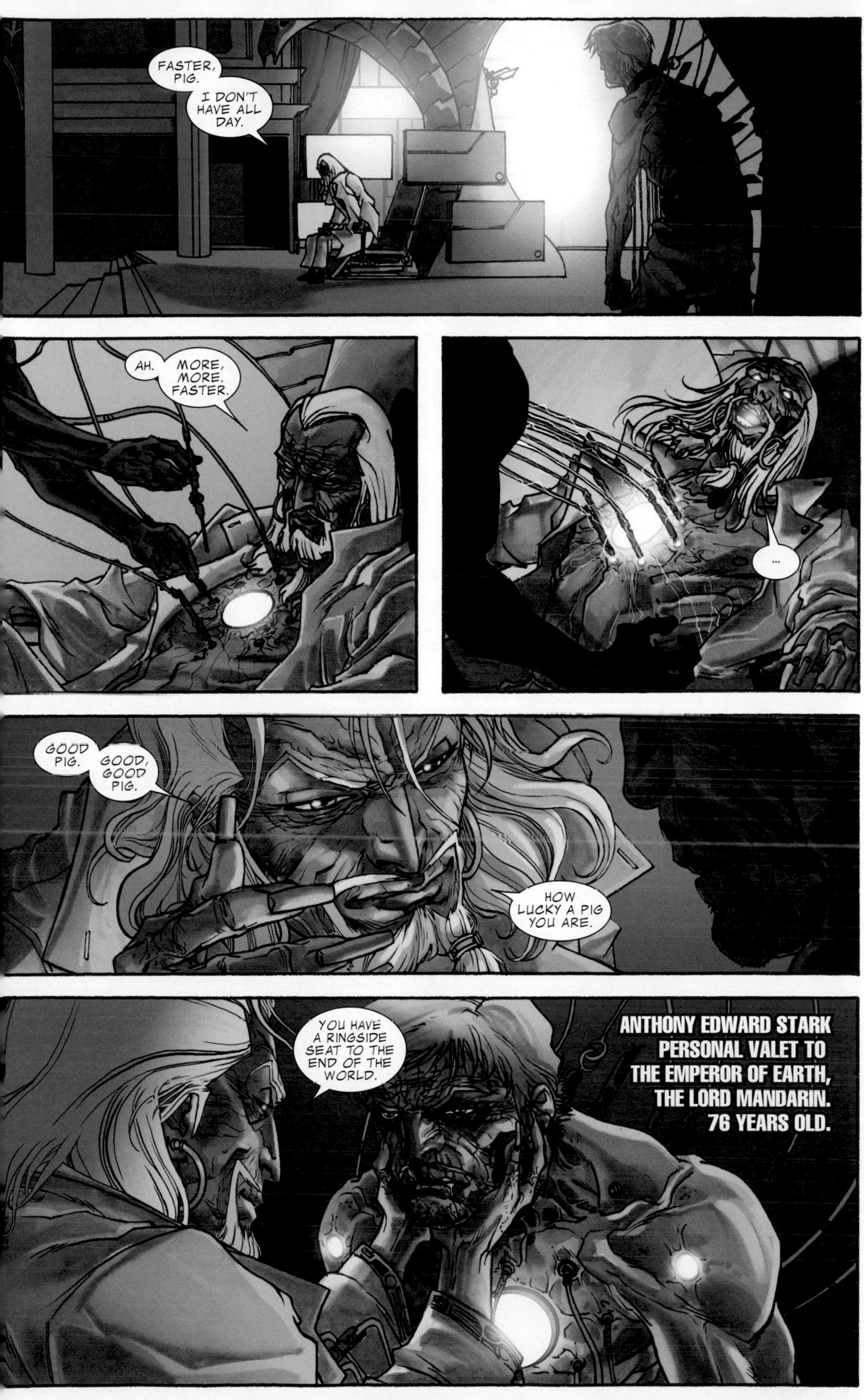
FASTER, PIG.
I DON'T HAVE ALL DAY.
AH.
MORE, MORE. FASTER.
...
GOOD PIG.
GOOD, GOOD PIG.
HOW LUCKY A PIG YOU ARE.
YOU HAVE A RINGSIDE SEAT TO THE END OF THE WORLD.
ANTHONY EDWARD STARK
PERSONAL VALET TO
THE EMPEROR OF EARTH,
THE LORD MANDARIN.
76 YEARS OLD.

IT'S SUCH A *SPECIFIC* AND *WEIRD* THING TO HAVE *NO MEMORY* OF, Y'KNOW?

YEAH.

I DON'T EVEN SEE WHAT GOOD IT COULD SERVE. OR WHY.

YEAH.

YOU'RE JUST SAYING "YEAH" AFTER EVERYTHING I SAY, AREN'T YOU?

YEAH. SO, LOOK--

WHY YOU DESIGNED THIS THING--AND WANTED *HELP* WITH IT--ISN'T A MEMORY THAT WILL MAGICALLY *RETURN* TO YOU.

YOU COULD'VE BEEN BORED. BEEN LOOKING FOR A CHALLENGE. BEEN IN A BAD MOOD.

WE DON'T, WON'T, AND *CAN'T* KNOW WHY. DOESN'T MATTER.

THE *SCARY* QUESTION IS, "FOR *WHAT?*"

ASKING, "WHAT IS THE *NATURE* OF THE *DEVICE*" WILL LEAD US TO *WHO* COULD WANT SUCH A THING.

THEN THE "*WHY*" SHOULD BE PRETTY OBVIOUS.

THERE ARE NO GOOD ANSWERS TO ANY OF THOSE QUESTIONS, PETER.

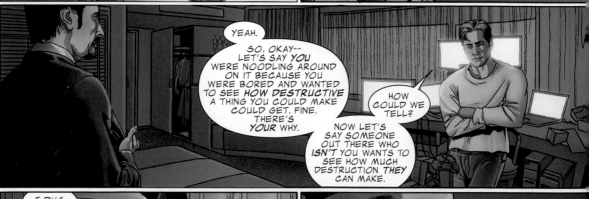

YEAH.

SO, OKAY-- LET'S SAY *YOU* WERE NOODLING AROUND ON IT BECAUSE YOU WERE BORED AND WANTED TO SEE *HOW DESTRUCTIVE* A THING YOU COULD MAKE COULD GET. FINE. THERE'S *YOUR* WHY.

NOW LET'S SAY SOMEONE OUT THERE WHO *ISN'T* YOU WANTS TO SEE HOW MUCH DESTRUCTION *THEY* CAN MAKE.

HOW COULD WE TELL?

I DUG AROUND.

I CAN'T TELL IF THEY WERE SPECIFICALLY *SOUGHT OUT* OR JUST DUMPED WITH THE REST OF THE STARK DATA THAT LEAKED DURING YOUR *FALL*, BUT...

YOU'VE NOT ONLY DESIGNED A POTENTIAL SUPERWEAPON OF MASS DESTRUCTION BUT SOMEBODY OUT THERE MIGHT BE TRYING TO *BUILD* IT.

MAKE A LIST OF POSSIBLE CANDIDATES THAT HAVE PRODUCTION CAPABILITIES.

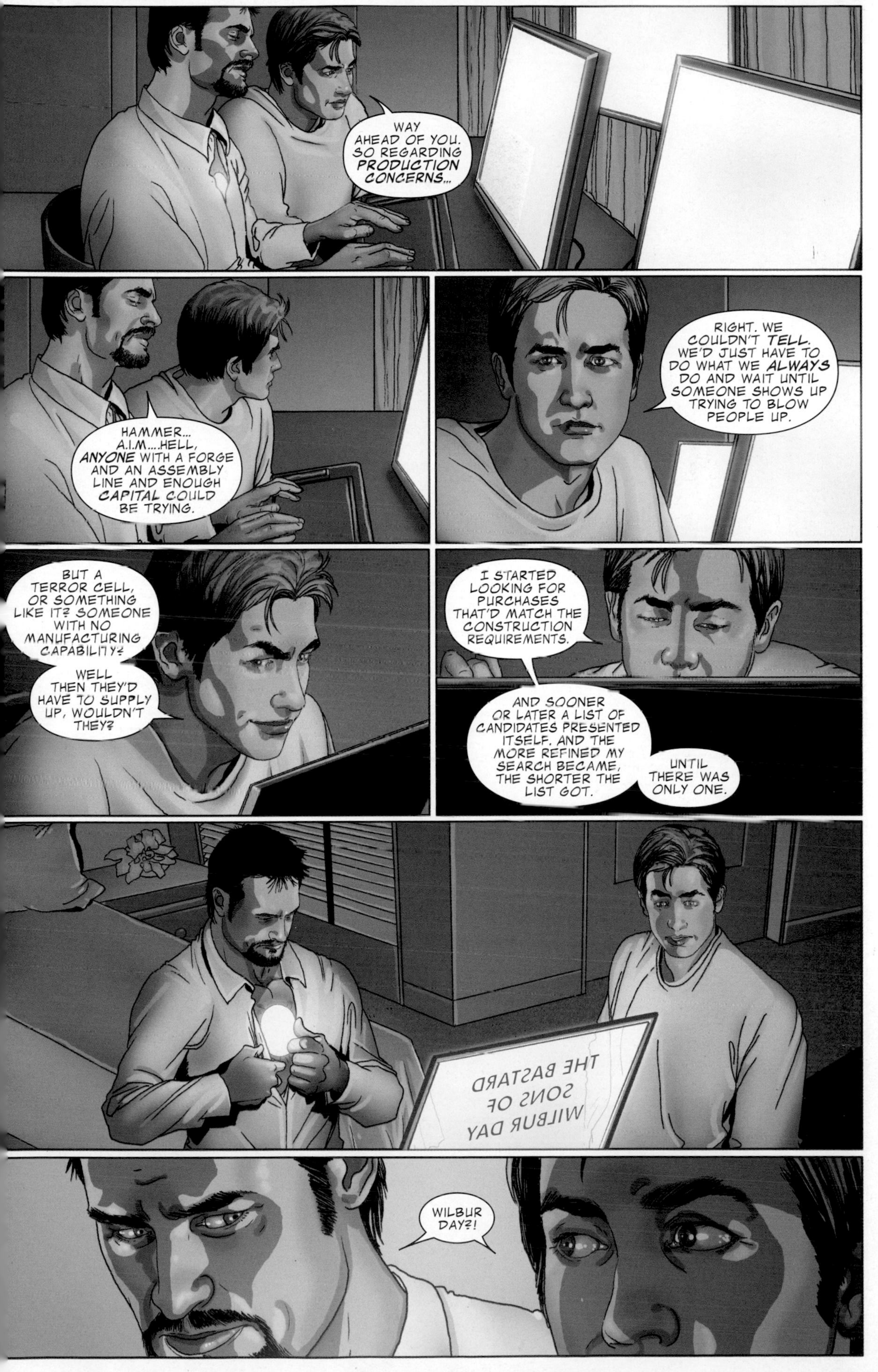

WAY AHEAD OF YOU. SO REGARDING *PRODUCTION CONCERNS*...
HAMMER... A.I.M....HELL, *ANYONE* WITH A FORGE AND AN ASSEMBLY LINE AND ENOUGH *CAPITAL* COULD BE TRYING.
RIGHT. WE COULDN'T *TELL*. WE'D JUST HAVE TO DO WHAT WE *ALWAYS* DO AND WAIT UNTIL SOMEONE SHOWS UP TRYING TO BLOW PEOPLE UP.
BUT A TERROR CELL, OR SOMETHING LIKE IT? SOMEONE WITH NO MANUFACTURING CAPABILITY?
WELL THEN THEY'D HAVE TO SUPPLY UP, WOULDN'T THEY?
I STARTED LOOKING FOR PURCHASES THAT'D MATCH THE CONSTRUCTION REQUIREMENTS.
AND SOONER OR LATER A LIST OF CANDIDATES PRESENTED ITSELF. AND THE MORE REFINED MY SEARCH BECAME, THE SHORTER THE LIST GOT.
UNTIL THERE WAS ONLY ONE.
THE BASTARD SONS OF WILBUR DAY
WILBUR DAY?!

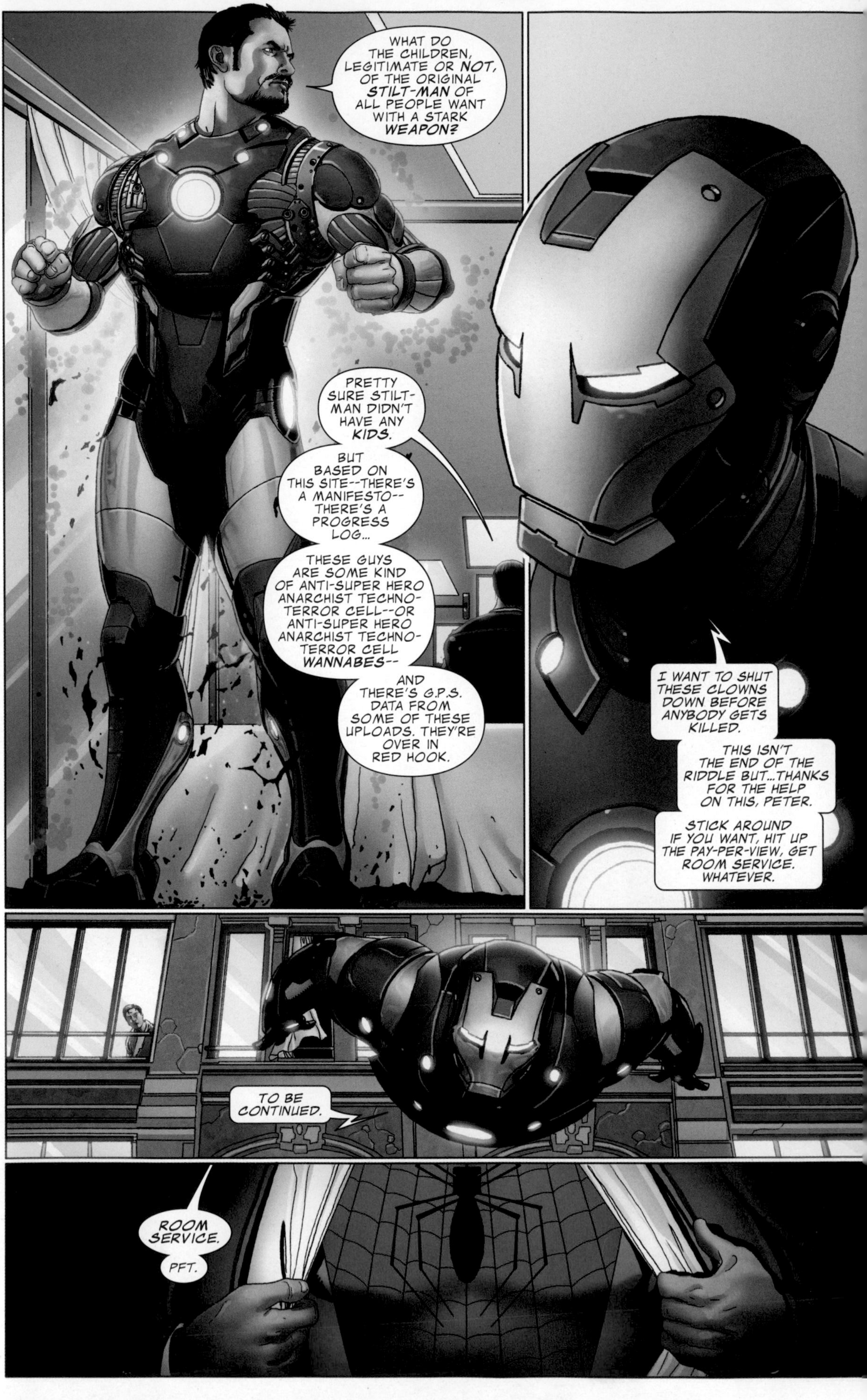
WHAT DO THE CHILDREN, LEGITIMATE OR NOT, OF THE ORIGINAL STILT-MAN OF ALL PEOPLE WANT WITH A STARK WEAPON?
PRETTY SURE STILT-MAN DIDN'T HAVE ANY KIDS.
BUT BASED ON THIS SITE--THERE'S A MANIFESTO--THERE'S A PROGRESS LOG...
THESE GUYS ARE SOME KIND OF ANTI-SUPER HERO ANARCHIST TECHNO-TERROR CELL--OR ANTI-SUPER HERO ANARCHIST TECHNO-TERROR CELL WANNABES--
AND THERE'S G.P.S. DATA FROM SOME OF THESE UPLOADS. THEY'RE OVER IN RED HOOK.
I WANT TO SHUT THESE CLOWNS DOWN BEFORE ANYBODY GETS KILLED.
THIS ISN'T THE END OF THE RIDDLE BUT...THANKS FOR THE HELP ON THIS, PETER.
STICK AROUND IF YOU WANT, HIT UP THE PAY-PER-VIEW, GET ROOM SERVICE. WHATEVER.
TO BE CONTINUED.
ROOM SERVICE.
PFT.

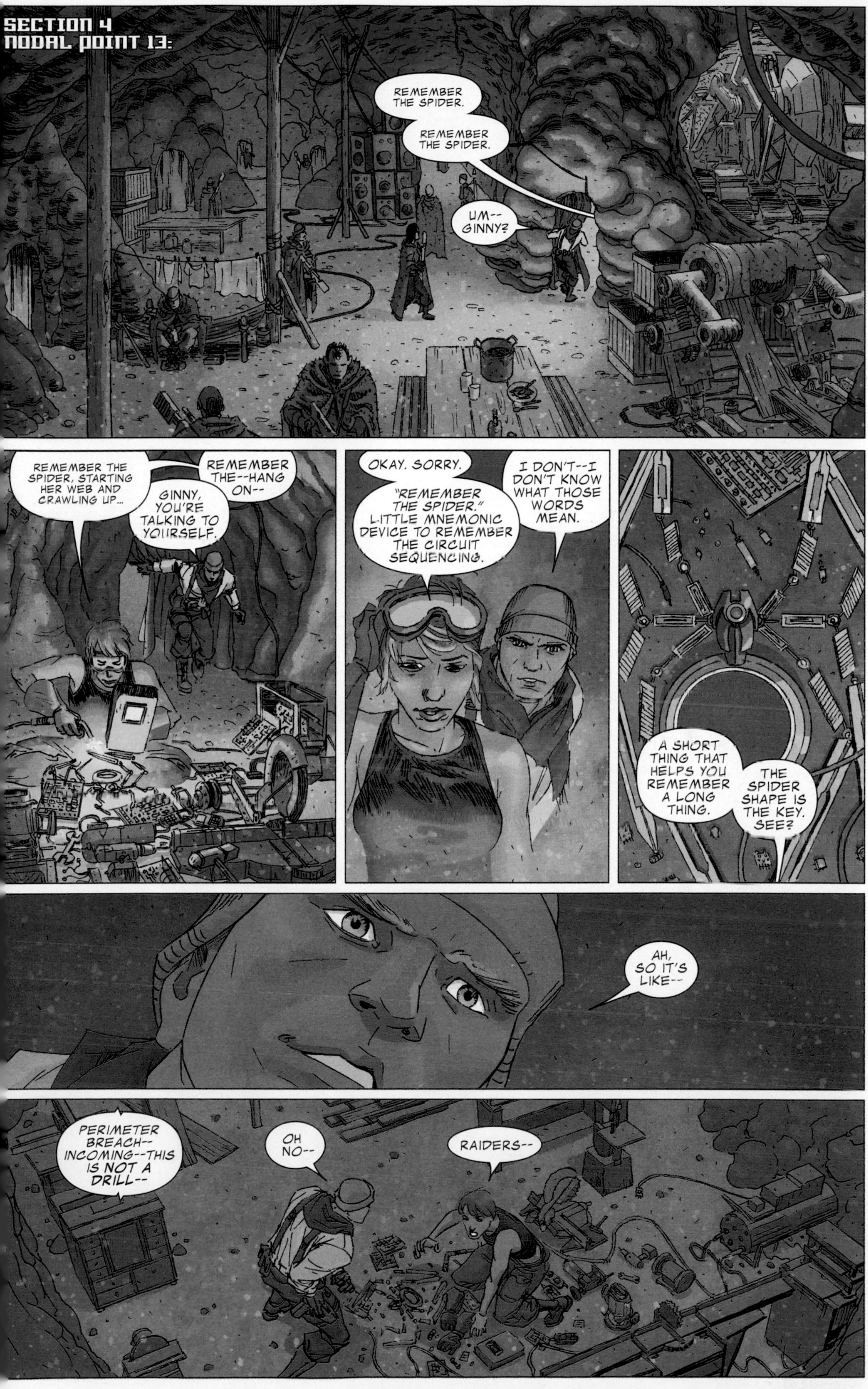
SECTION 4
NODAL POINT 13:
REMEMBER THE SPIDER.
REMEMBER THE SPIDER.
UM-- GINNY?
REMEMBER THE SPIDER, STARTING HER WEB AND CRAWLING UP...
REMEMBER THE--HANG ON--
GINNY, YOU'RE TALKING TO YOURSELF.
OKAY. SORRY.
"REMEMBER THE SPIDER." LITTLE MNEMONIC DEVICE TO REMEMBER THE CIRCUIT SEQUENCING.
I DON'T--I DON'T KNOW WHAT THOSE WORDS MEAN.
A SHORT THING THAT HELPS YOU REMEMBER A LONG THING.
THE SPIDER SHAPE IS THE KEY. SEE?
AH, SO IT'S LIKE--
PERIMETER BREACH--INCOMING--THIS IS NOT A DRILL--
OH NO--
RAIDERS--

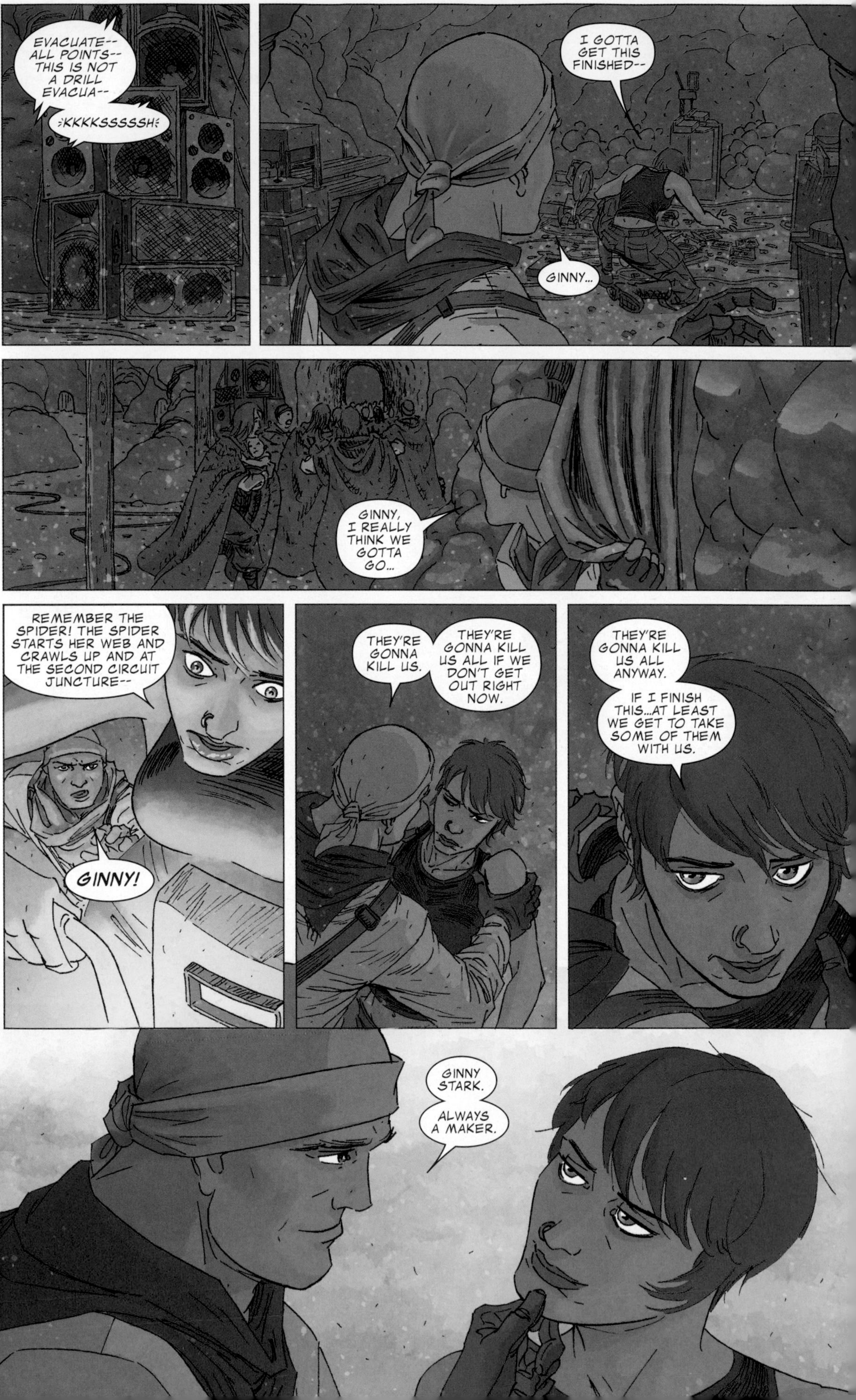
EVACUATE-- ALL POINTS-- THIS IS NOT A DRILL EVACUA--
KKKKSSSSSH
I GOTTA GET THIS FINISHED--
GINNY...
GINNY, I REALLY THINK WE GOTTA GO...
REMEMBER THE SPIDER! THE SPIDER STARTS HER WEB AND CRAWLS UP AND AT THE SECOND CIRCUIT JUNCTURE--
GINNY!
THEY'RE GONNA KILL US.
THEY'RE GONNA KILL US ALL IF WE DON'T GET OUT RIGHT NOW.
THEY'RE GONNA KILL US ALL ANYWAY.
IF I FINISH THIS...AT LEAST WE GET TO TAKE SOME OF THEM WITH US.
GINNY STARK.
ALWAYS A MAKER.

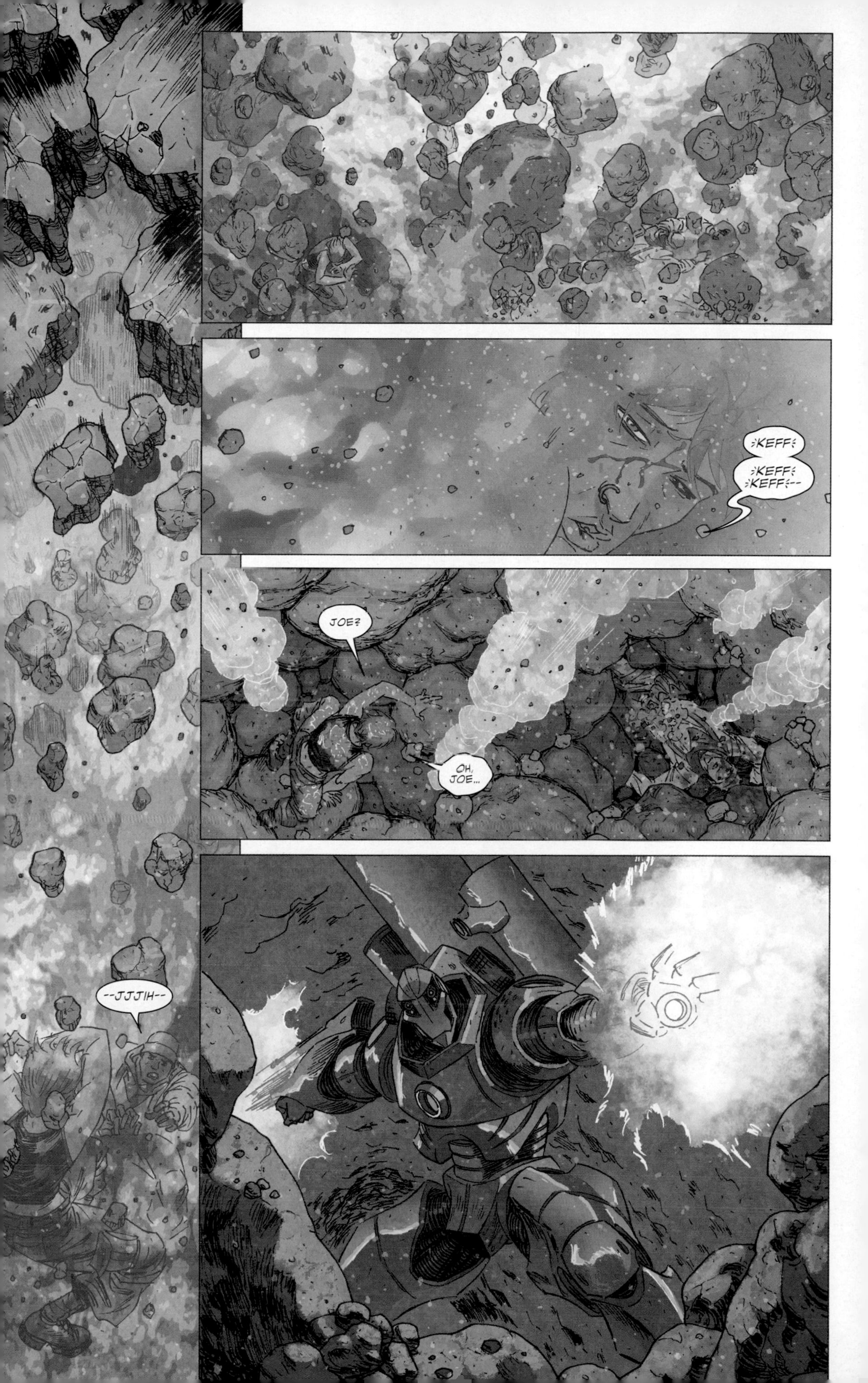

KEFF
KEFF KEFF--
JOE?
OH, JOE...
--JJJIH--

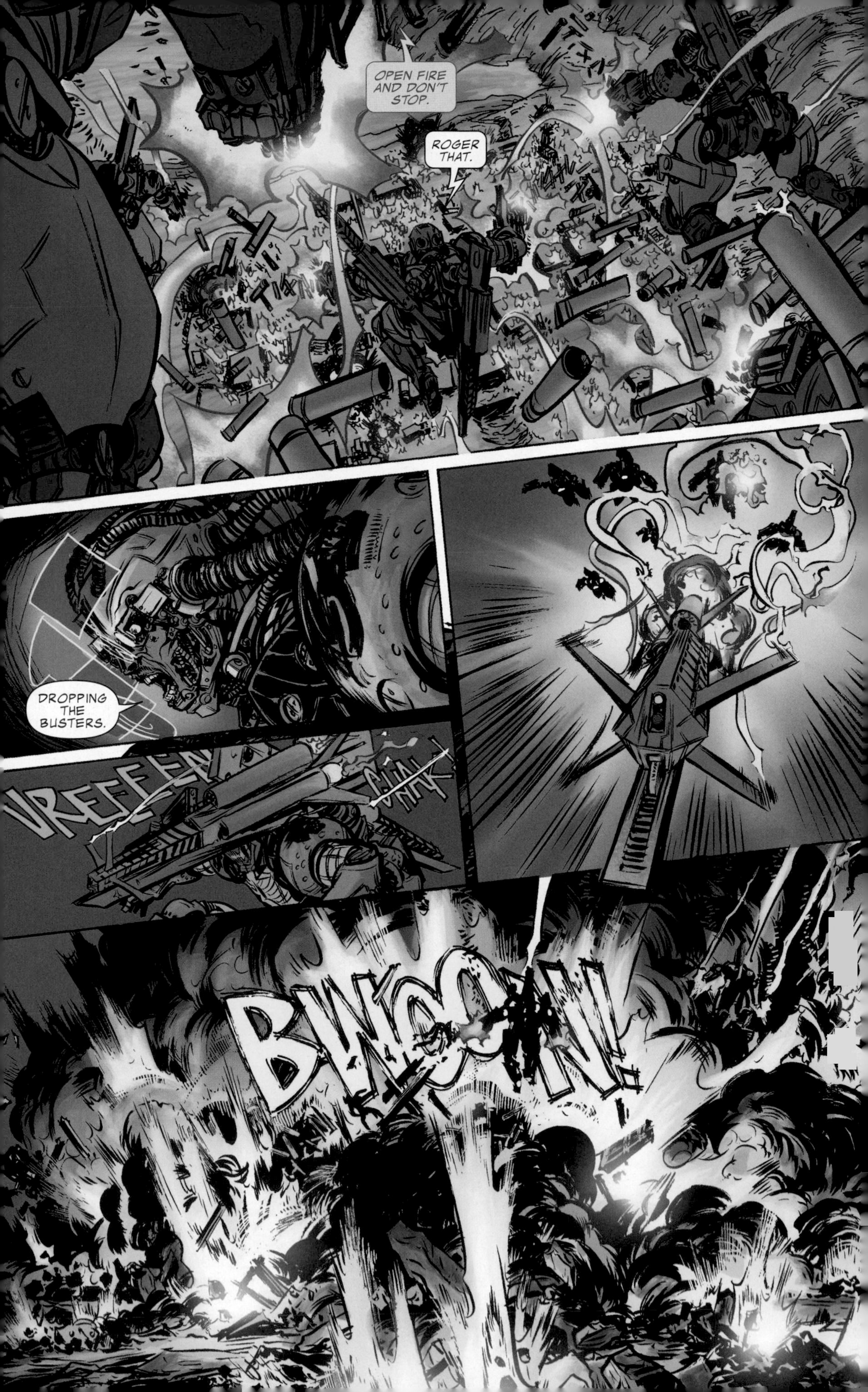
OPEN FIRE AND DON'T STOP.
ROGER THAT.
DROPPING THE BUSTERS.
VREEEEE
CHAK
BWOOM!

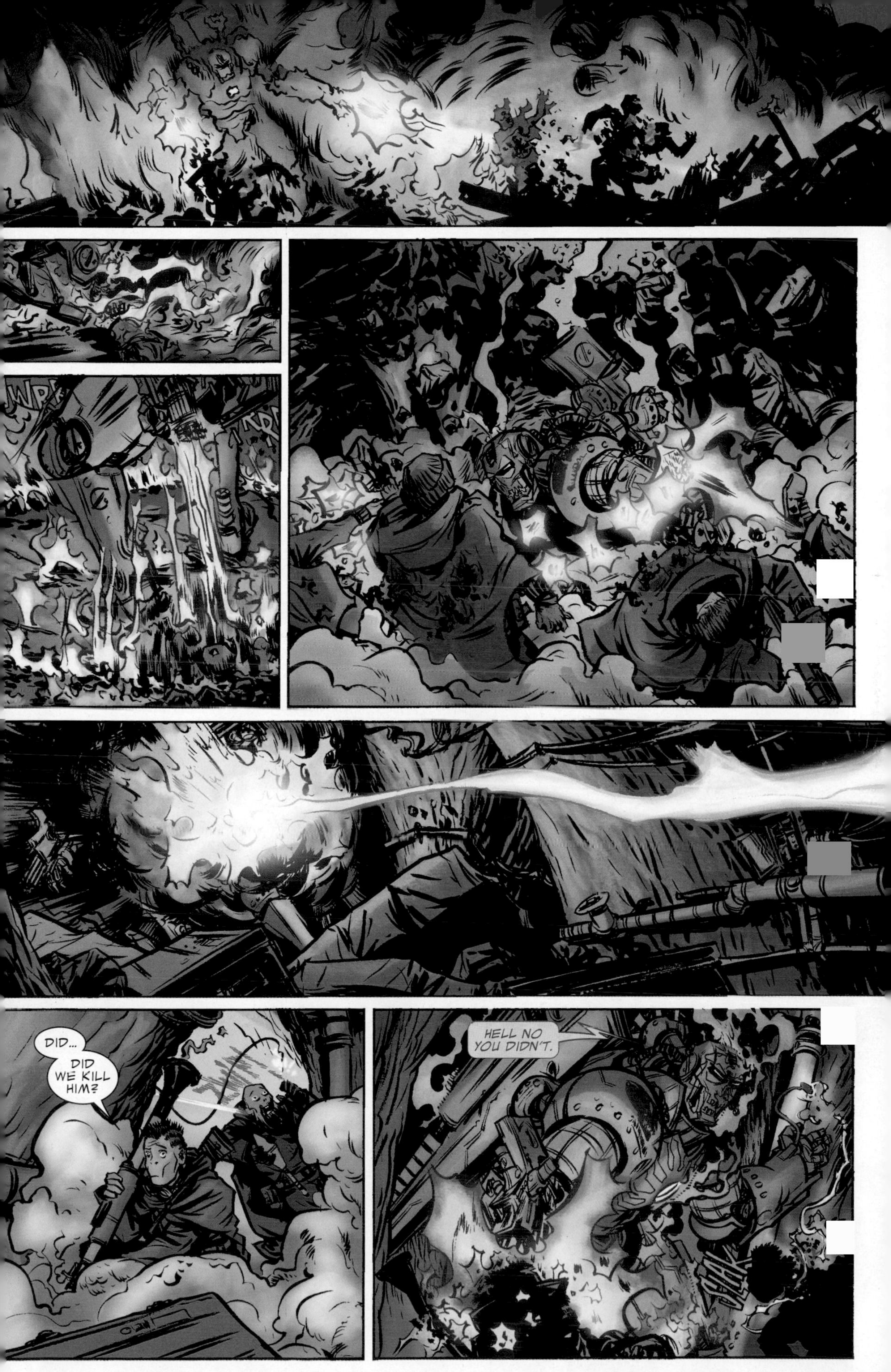
DID...
DID WE KILL HIM?
HELL NO YOU DIDN'T.

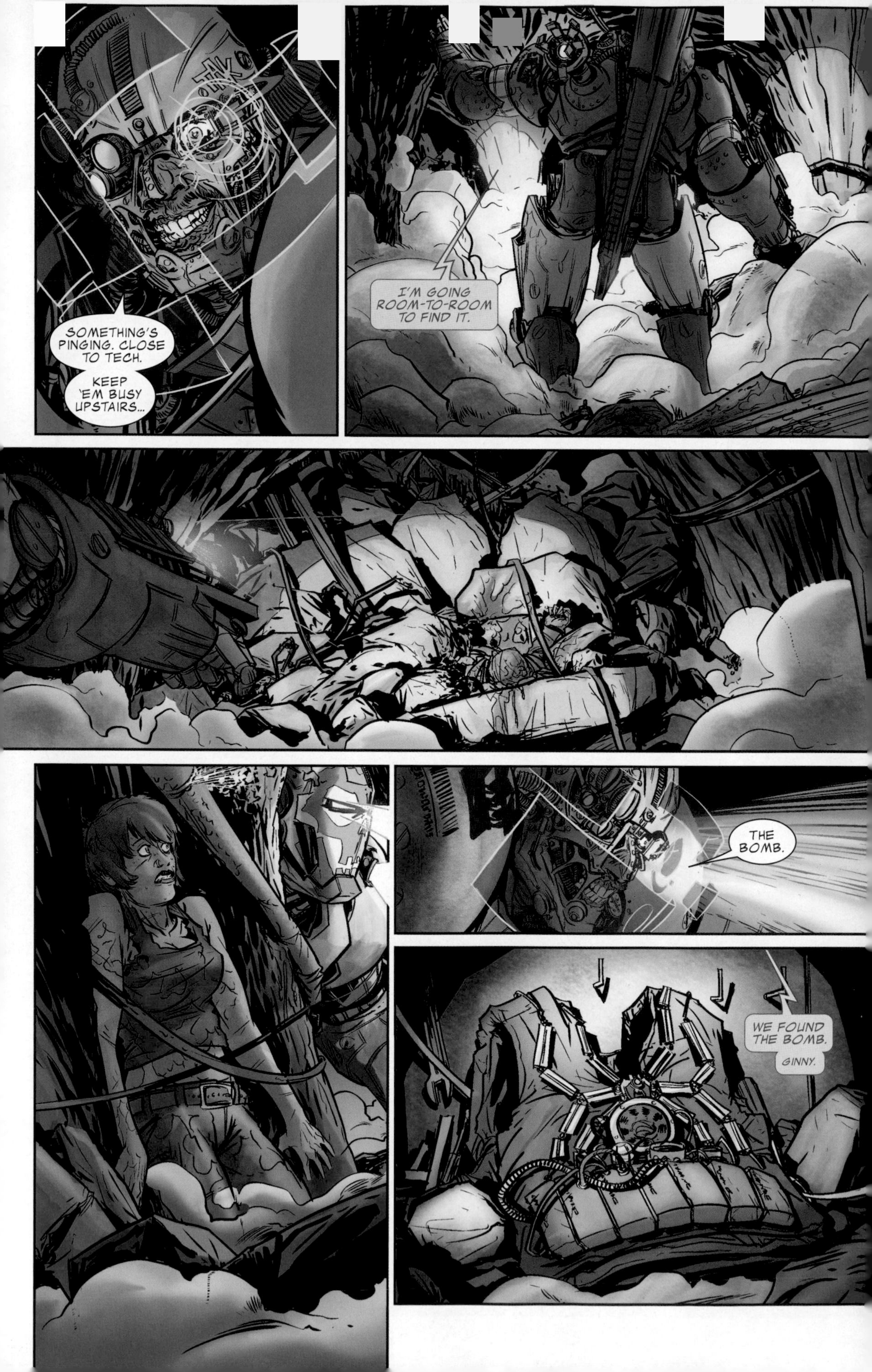

SOMETHING'S PINGING. CLOSE TO TECH.
KEEP 'EM BUSY UPSTAIRS...
I'M GOING ROOM-TO-ROOM TO FIND IT.
THE BOMB.
WE FOUND THE BOMB.
GINNY.

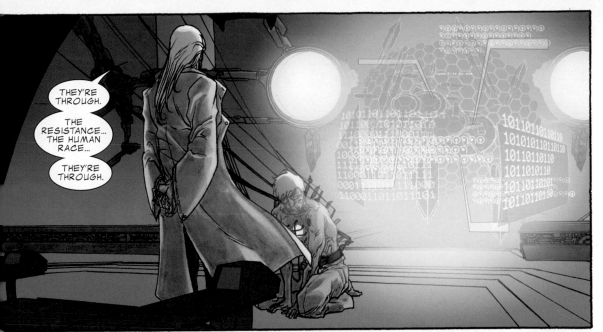

THEY'RE THROUGH.

THE RESISTANCE... THE HUMAN RACE...

THEY'RE THROUGH.

WE WON.

NO IRON MAN TO SAVE THE DAY.

NO AVENGERS TO SWOOP IN AND FIX THINGS FOR YOU.

WRITE DOWN THE DATE. WRITE DOWN THE TIME.

I BEAT YOU, STARK. I BEAT EVERYONE.

WE ARE ABOUT TO LEAVE THIS PLACE ONCE AND FOR ALL. EXHAUSTED, EXTINGUISHED AND, FINALLY, ABANDONED.

WE ARE CRACKING THE EARTH TO ITS CORE AND THEY HAVE THE NERVE TO TRY AND STOP US?

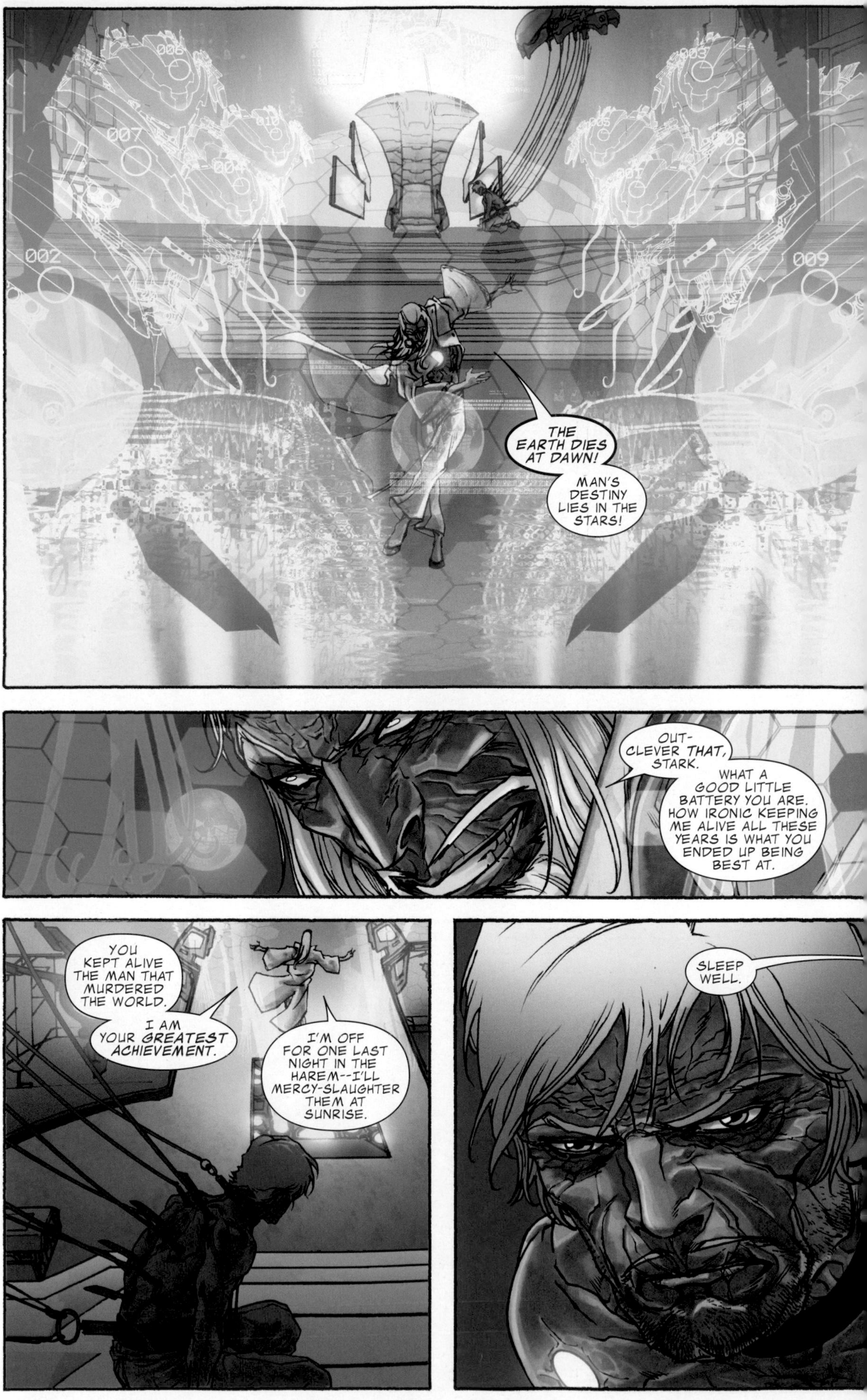
THE EARTH DIES AT DAWN!
MAN'S DESTINY LIES IN THE STARS!
OUT-CLEVER THAT, STARK.
WHAT A GOOD LITTLE BATTERY YOU ARE. HOW IRONIC KEEPING ME ALIVE ALL THESE YEARS IS WHAT YOU ENDED UP BEING BEST AT.
YOU KEPT ALIVE THE MAN THAT MURDERED THE WORLD.
I AM YOUR GREATEST ACHIEVEMENT.
I'M OFF FOR ONE LAST NIGHT IN THE HAREM--I'LL MERCY-SLAUGHTER THEM AT SUNRISE.
SLEEP WELL.

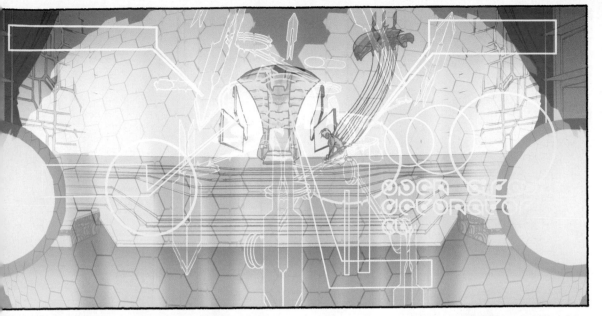

I...

...REMEMBER...

"REMEMBER THE SPIDER."

OH, GOD, GINNY...I...I REMEMBER NOW.

GINNY. HOWARD.

DON'T LET ME BE *TOO* LATE.

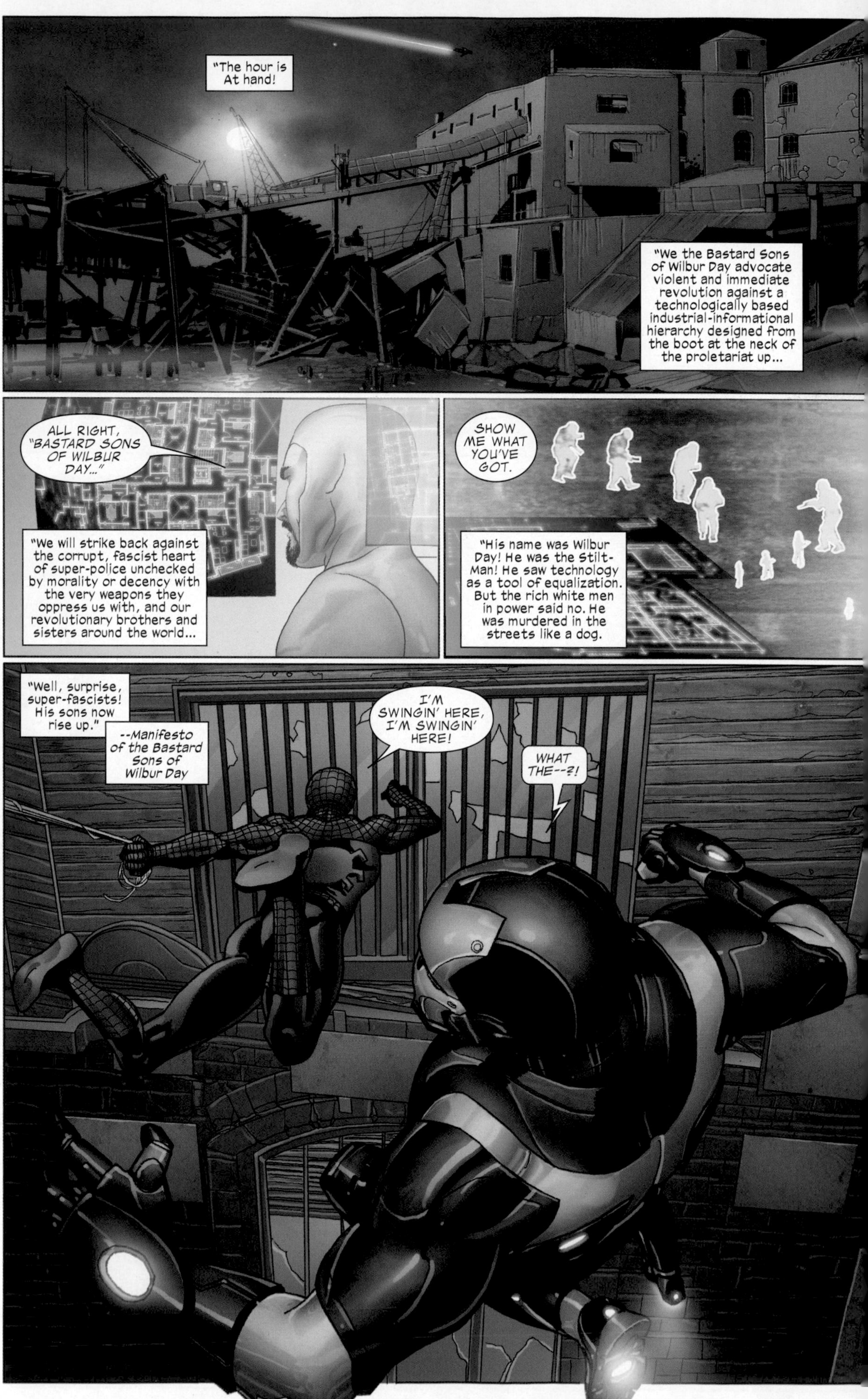
"The hour is At hand!
"We the Bastard Sons of Wilbur Day advocate violent and immediate revolution against a technologically based industrial-informational hierarchy designed from the boot at the neck of the proletariat up...
ALL RIGHT, "BASTARD SONS OF WILBUR DAY..."
"We will strike back against the corrupt, fascist heart of super-police unchecked by morality or decency with the very weapons they oppress us with, and our revolutionary brothers and sisters around the world...
SHOW ME WHAT YOU'VE GOT.
"His name was Wilbur Day! He was the Stilt-Man! He saw technology as a tool of equalization. But the rich white men in power said no. He was murdered in the streets like a dog.
"Well, surprise, super-fascists! His sons now rise up."
--Manifesto of the Bastard Sons of Wilbur Day
I'M SWINGIN' HERE, I'M SWINGIN' HERE!
WHAT THE--?!

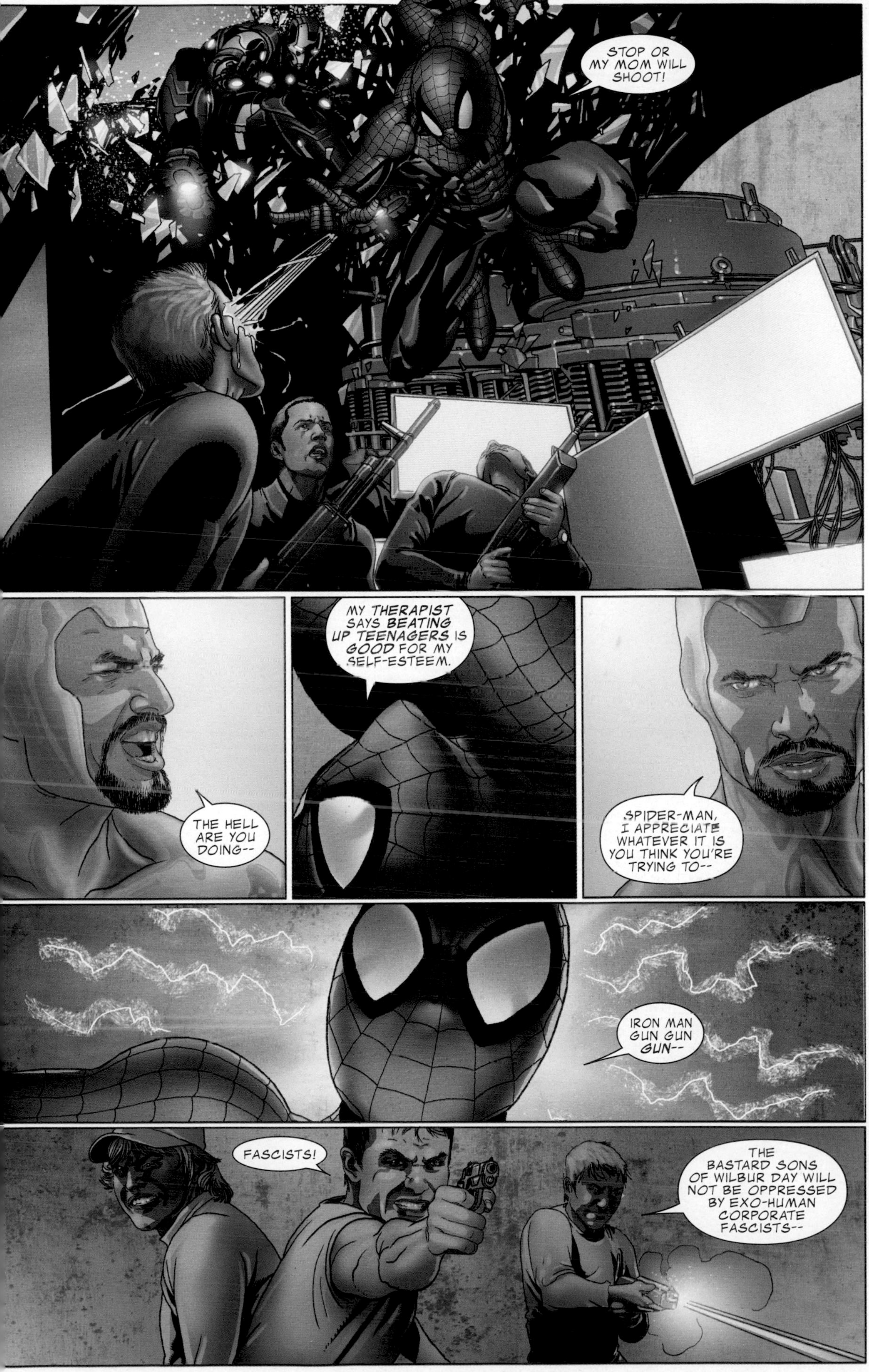
STOP OR MY MOM WILL SHOOT!
THE HELL ARE YOU DOING--
MY THERAPIST SAYS BEATING UP TEENAGERS IS GOOD FOR MY SELF-ESTEEM.
SPIDER-MAN, I APPRECIATE WHATEVER IT IS YOU THINK YOU'RE TRYING TO--
IRON MAN GUN GUN GUN--
FASCISTS!
THE BASTARD SONS OF WILBUR DAY WILL NOT BE OPPRESSED BY EXO-HUMAN CORPORATE FASCISTS--

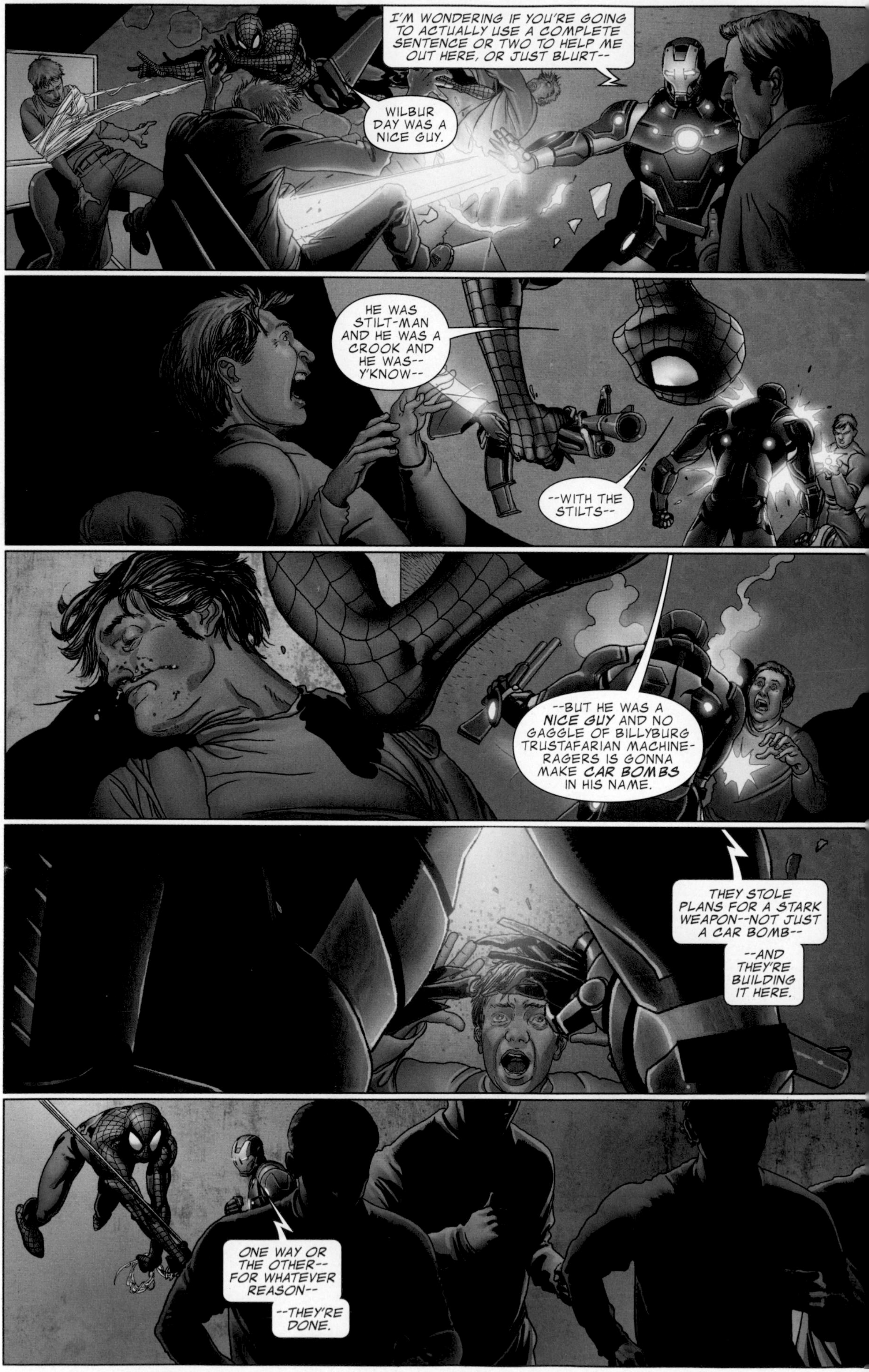
I'M WONDERING IF YOU'RE GOING TO ACTUALLY USE A COMPLETE SENTENCE OR TWO TO HELP ME OUT HERE, OR JUST BLURT--
WILBUR DAY WAS A NICE GUY.
HE WAS STILT-MAN AND HE WAS A CROOK AND HE WAS-- Y'KNOW--
--WITH THE STILTS--
--BUT HE WAS A NICE GUY AND NO GAGGLE OF BILLYBURG TRUSTAFARIAN MACHINE-RAGERS IS GONNA MAKE CAR BOMBS IN HIS NAME.
THEY STOLE PLANS FOR A STARK WEAPON--NOT JUST A CAR BOMB--
--AND THEY'RE BUILDING IT HERE.
ONE WAY OR THE OTHER-- FOR WHATEVER REASON--
--THEY'RE DONE.

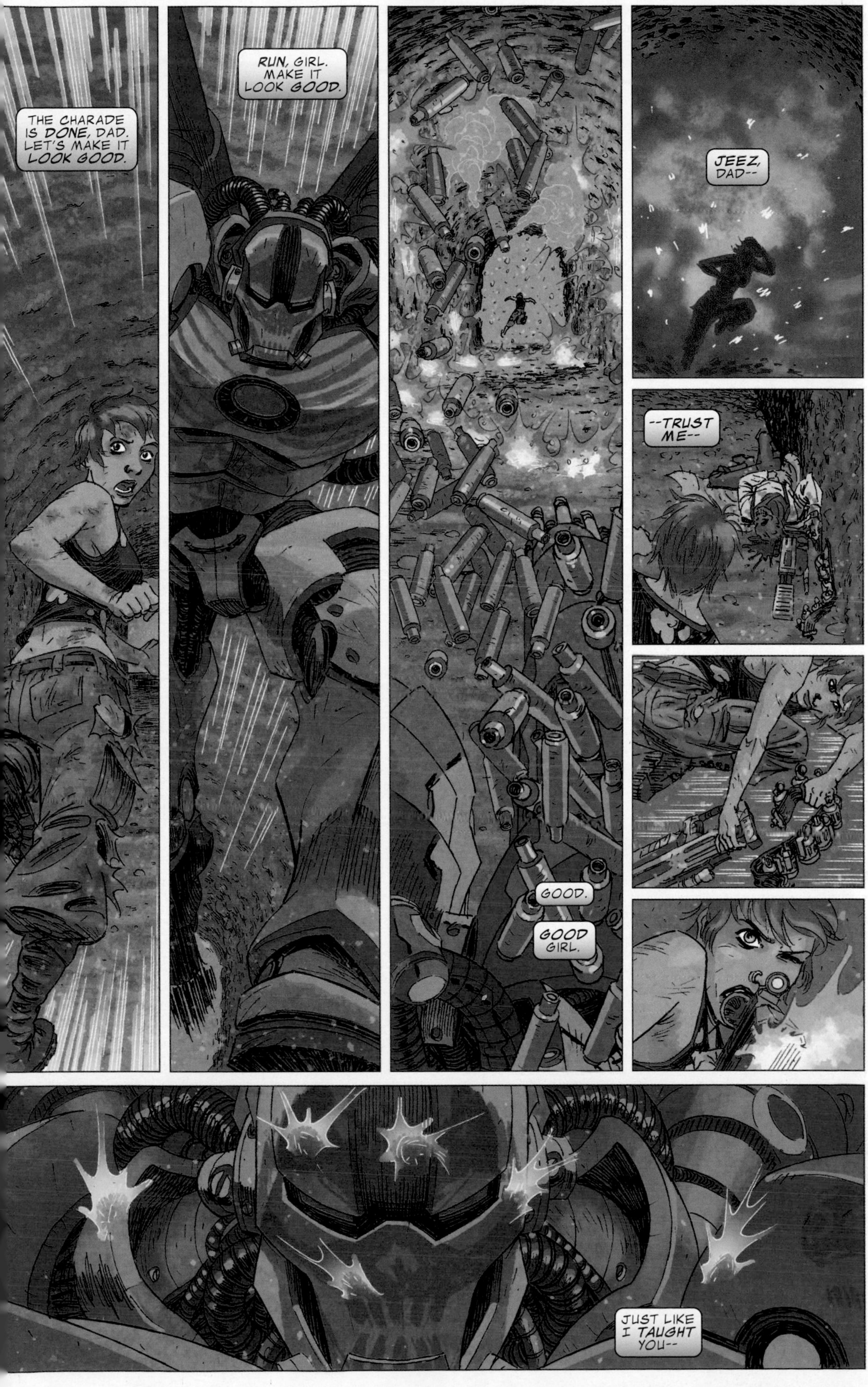
THE CHARADE IS DONE, DAD. LET'S MAKE IT LOOK GOOD.
RUN, GIRL. MAKE IT LOOK GOOD.
JEEZ, DAD--
--TRUST ME--
GOOD.
GOOD GIRL.
JUST LIKE I TAUGHT YOU--

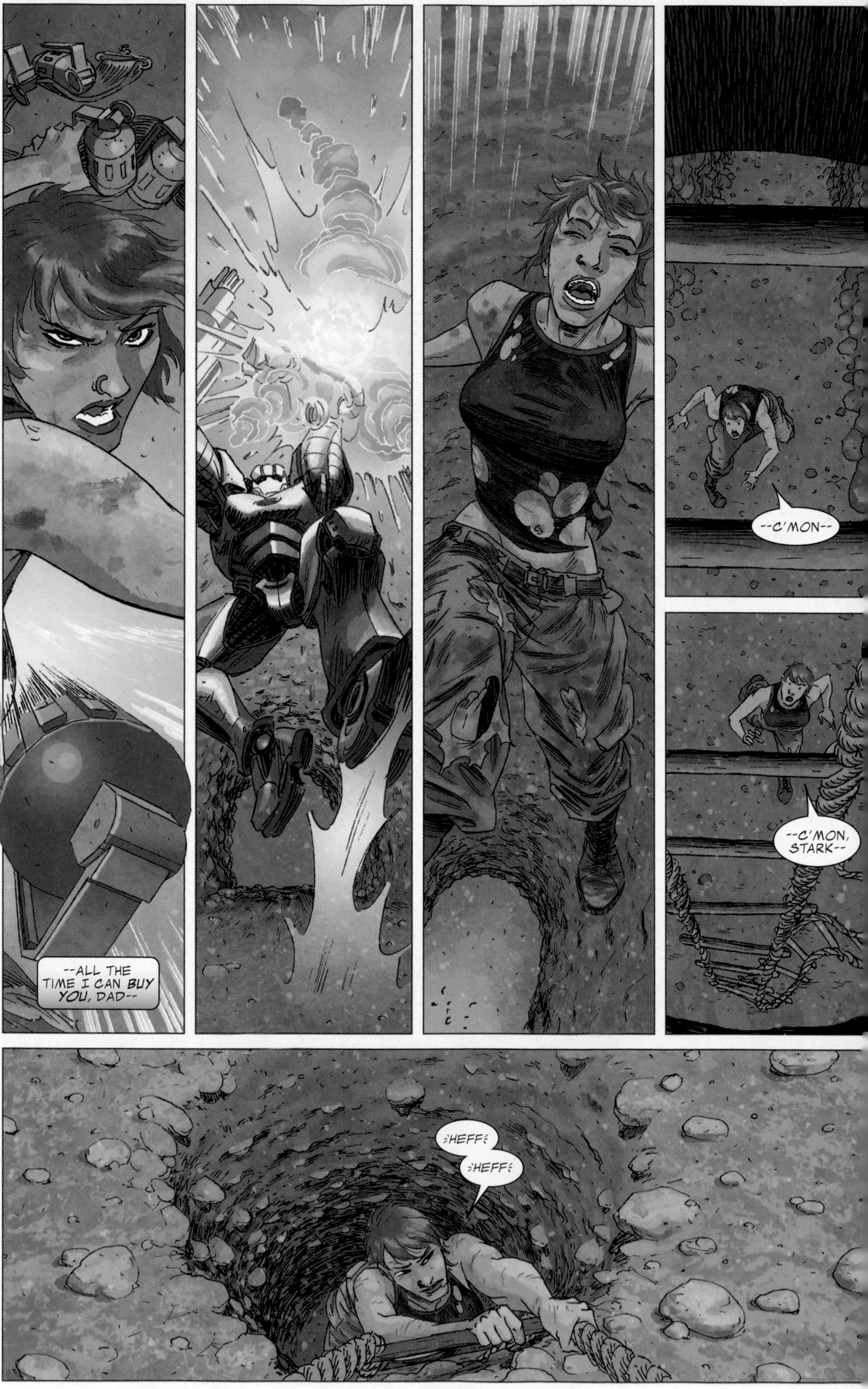
--ALL THE TIME I CAN BUY YOU, DAD--
--C'MON--
--C'MON, STARK--
HEFF
HEFF

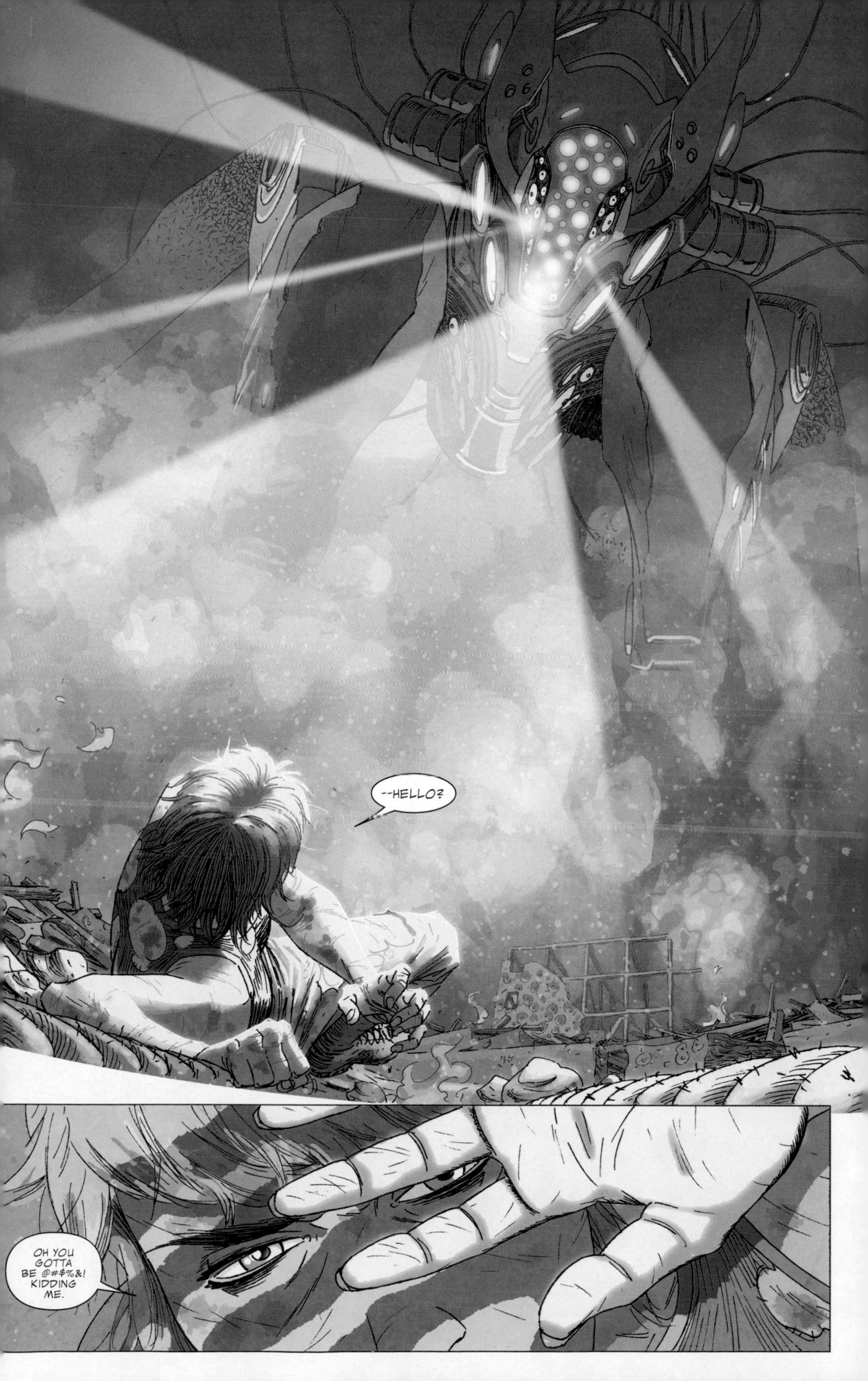
--HELLO?
OH YOU GOTTA BE @#$%&! KIDDING ME.

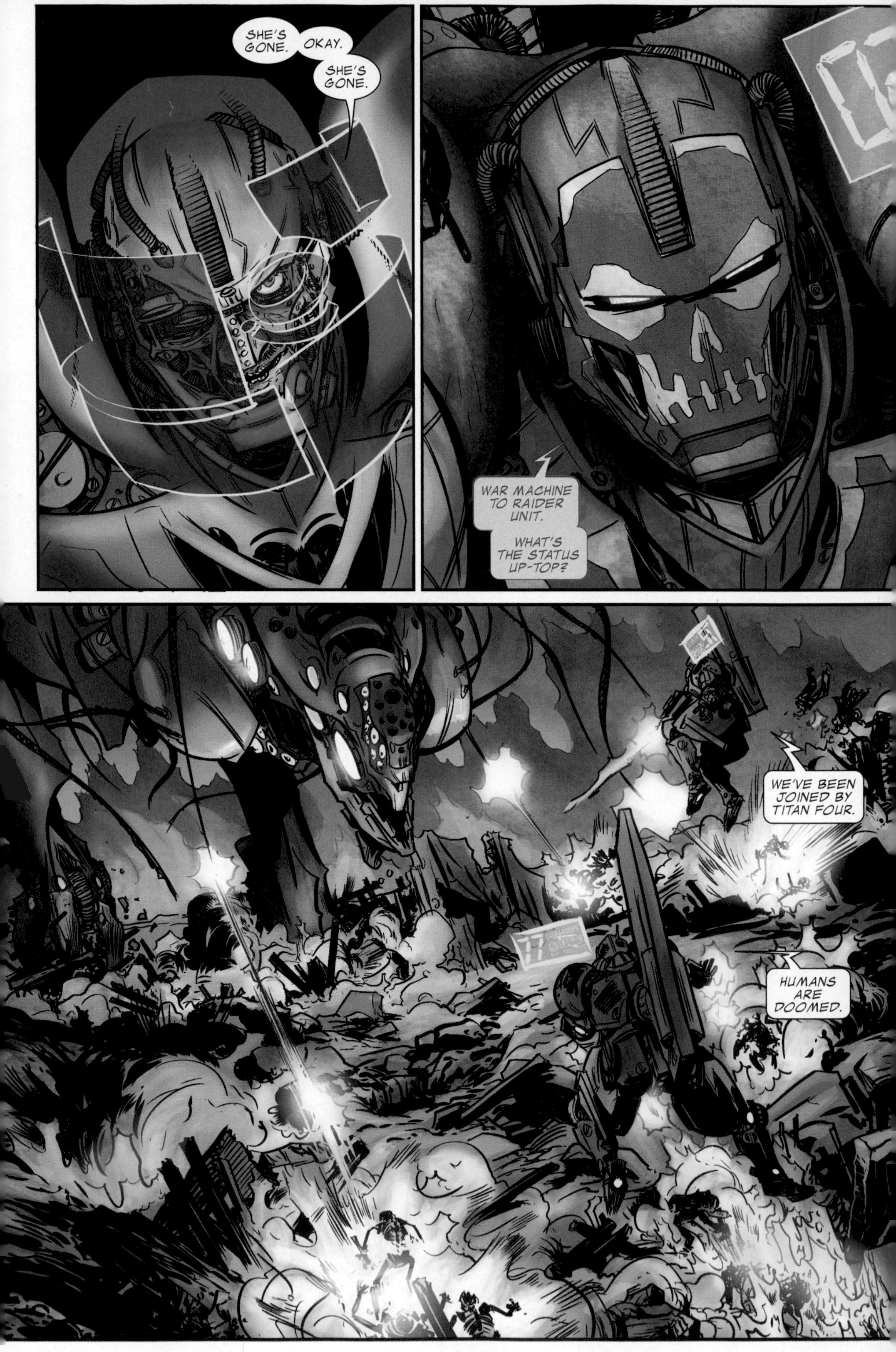
SHE'S GONE.
OKAY.
SHE'S GONE.
WAR MACHINE TO RAIDER UNIT.
WHAT'S THE STATUS UP-TOP?
WE'VE BEEN JOINED BY TITAN FOUR.
HUMANS ARE DOOMED.

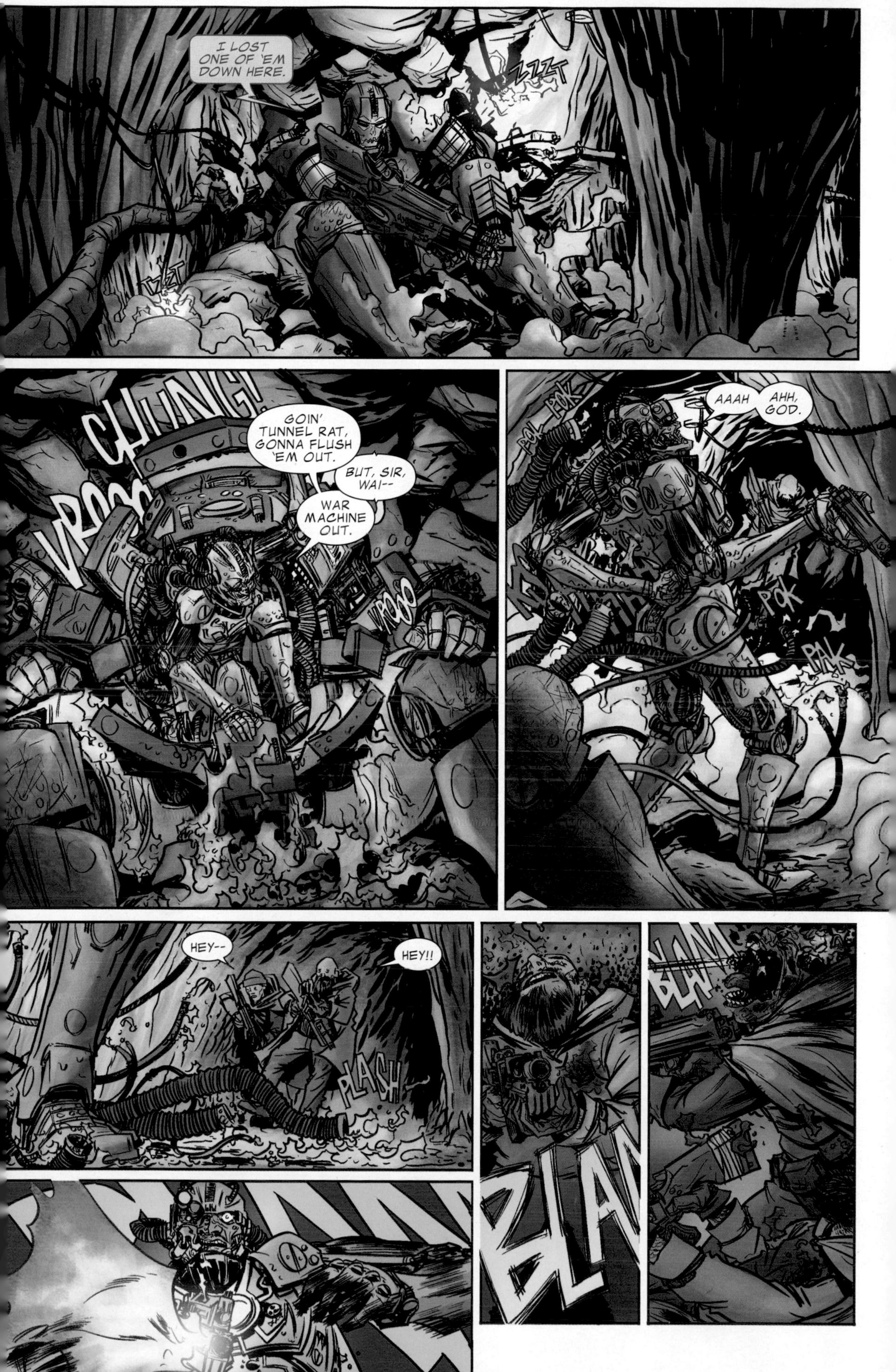
I LOST ONE OF 'EM DOWN HERE.
CHUNG!
GOIN' TUNNEL RAT, GONNA FLUSH 'EM OUT.
BUT, SIR, WAI--
WAR MACHINE OUT.
AAAH
AHH, GOD.
POK
PAK
HEY--
HEY!!
PLASH
BLAM

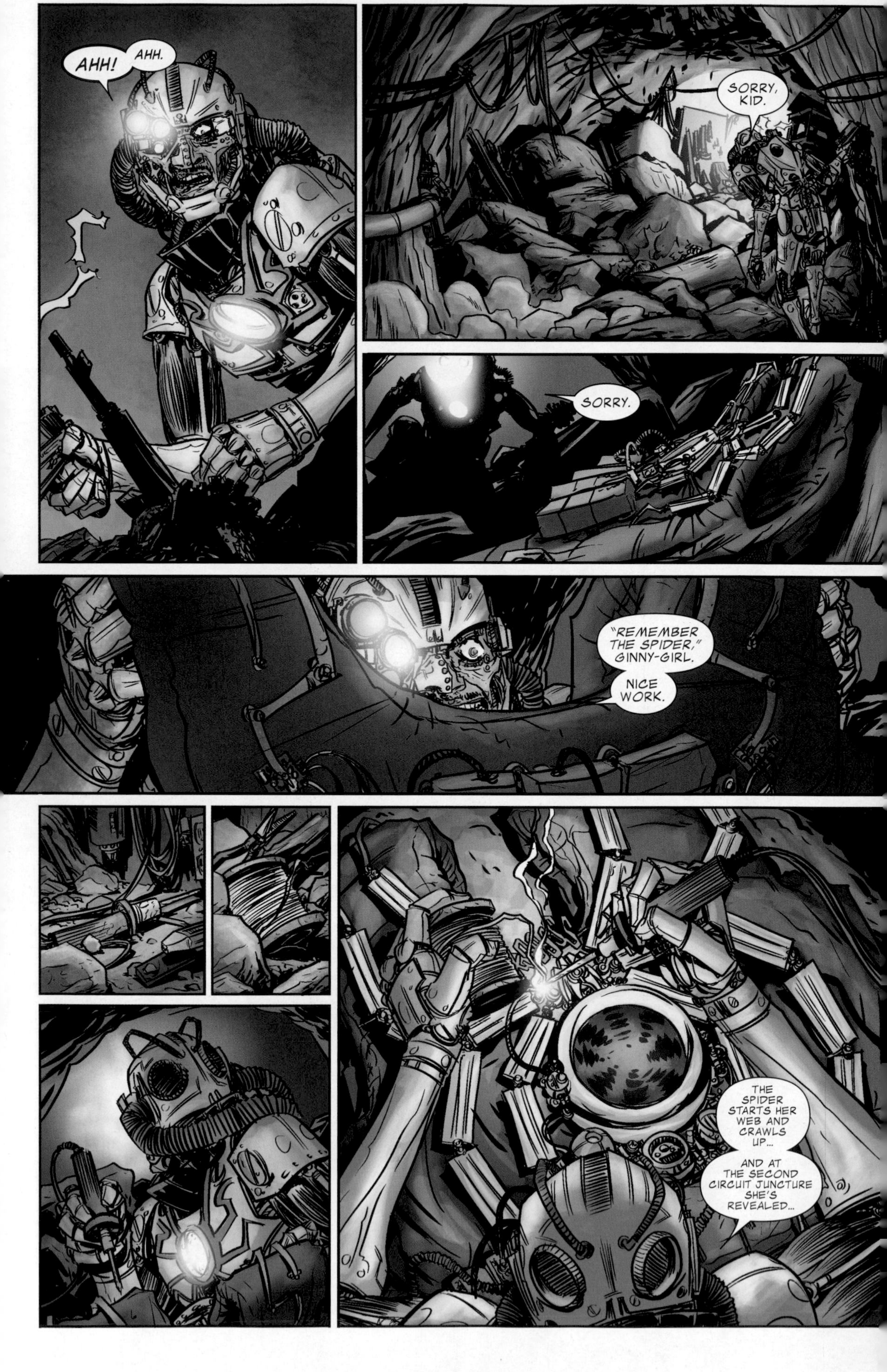
AHH!
AHH.
SORRY, KID.
SORRY.
"REMEMBER THE SPIDER," GINNY-GIRL.
NICE WORK.
THE SPIDER STARTS HER WEB AND CRAWLS UP...
AND AT THE SECOND CIRCUIT JUNCTURE SHE'S REVEALED...

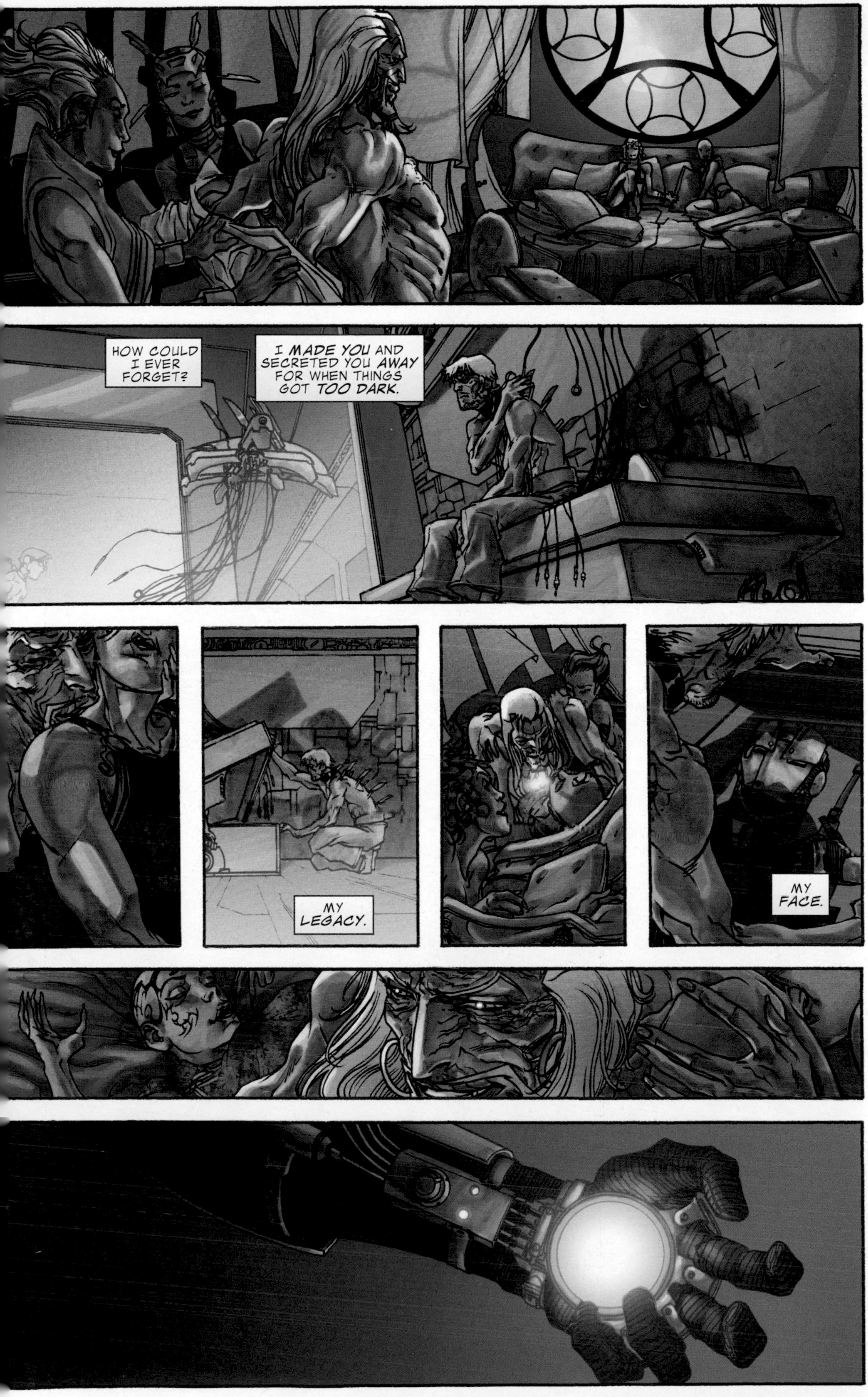
HOW COULD I EVER FORGET?
I MADE YOU AND SECRETED YOU AWAY FOR WHEN THINGS GOT TOO DARK.
MY LEGACY.
MY FACE.

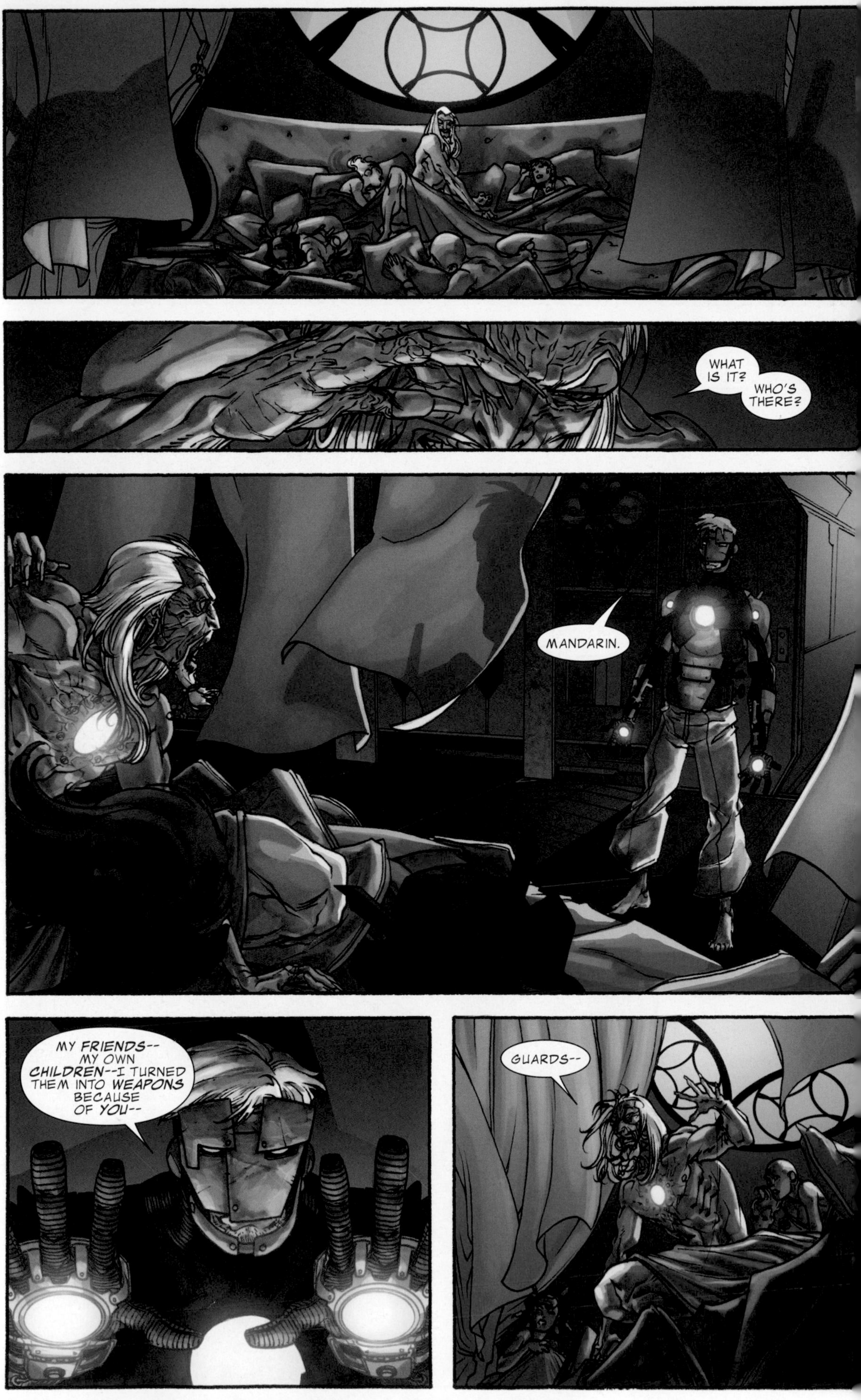
WHAT IS IT? WHO'S THERE?
MANDARIN.
MY FRIENDS-- MY OWN CHILDREN--I TURNED THEM INTO WEAPONS BECAUSE OF YOU--
GUARDS--

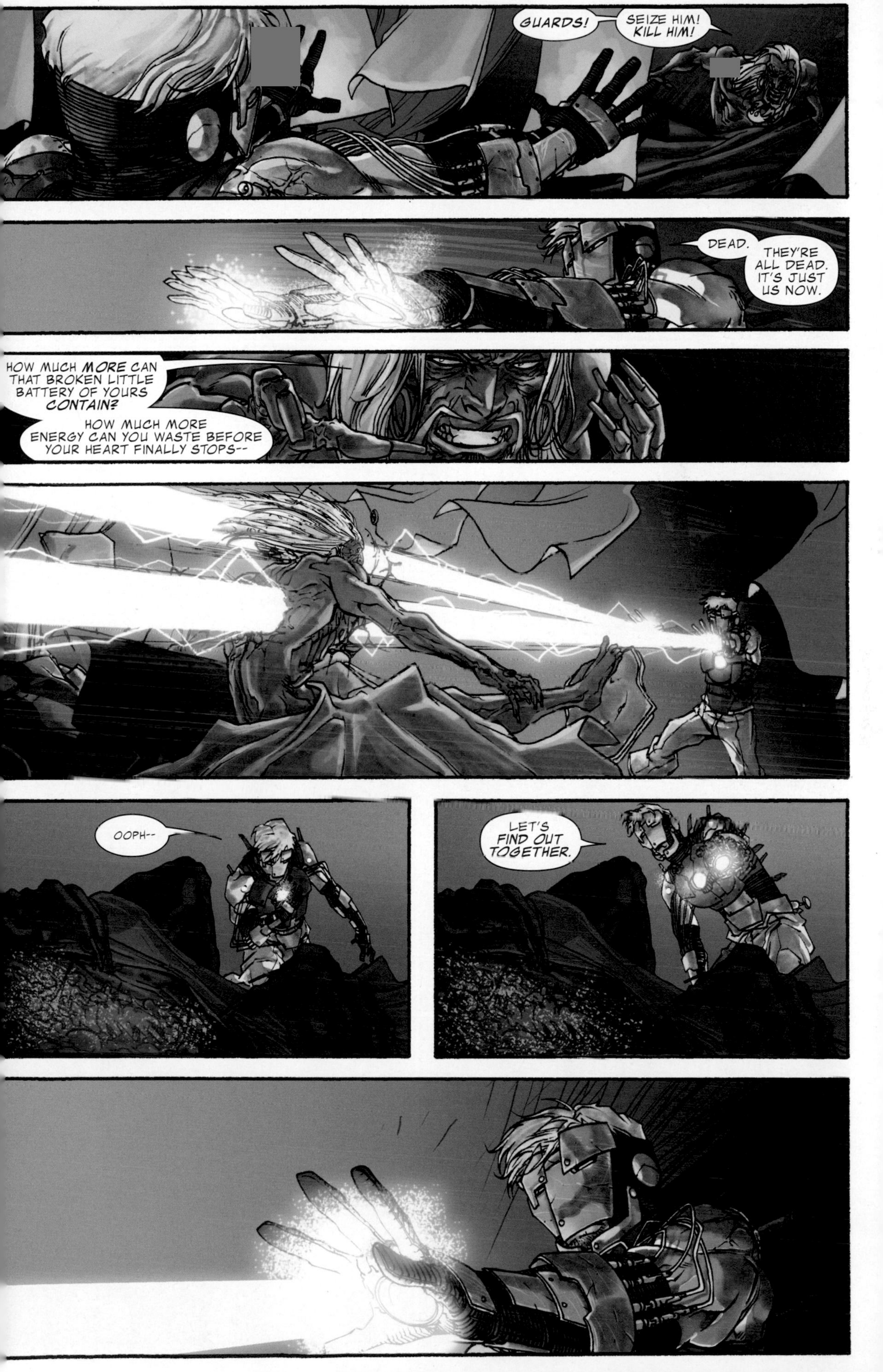
GUARDS!
SEIZE HIM! KILL HIM!
DEAD.
THEY'RE ALL DEAD. IT'S JUST US NOW.
HOW MUCH **MORE** CAN THAT BROKEN LITTLE BATTERY OF YOURS **CONTAIN?**
HOW MUCH MORE ENERGY CAN YOU WASTE BEFORE YOUR HEART FINALLY STOPS--
OOPH--
LET'S **FIND OUT TOGETHER.**

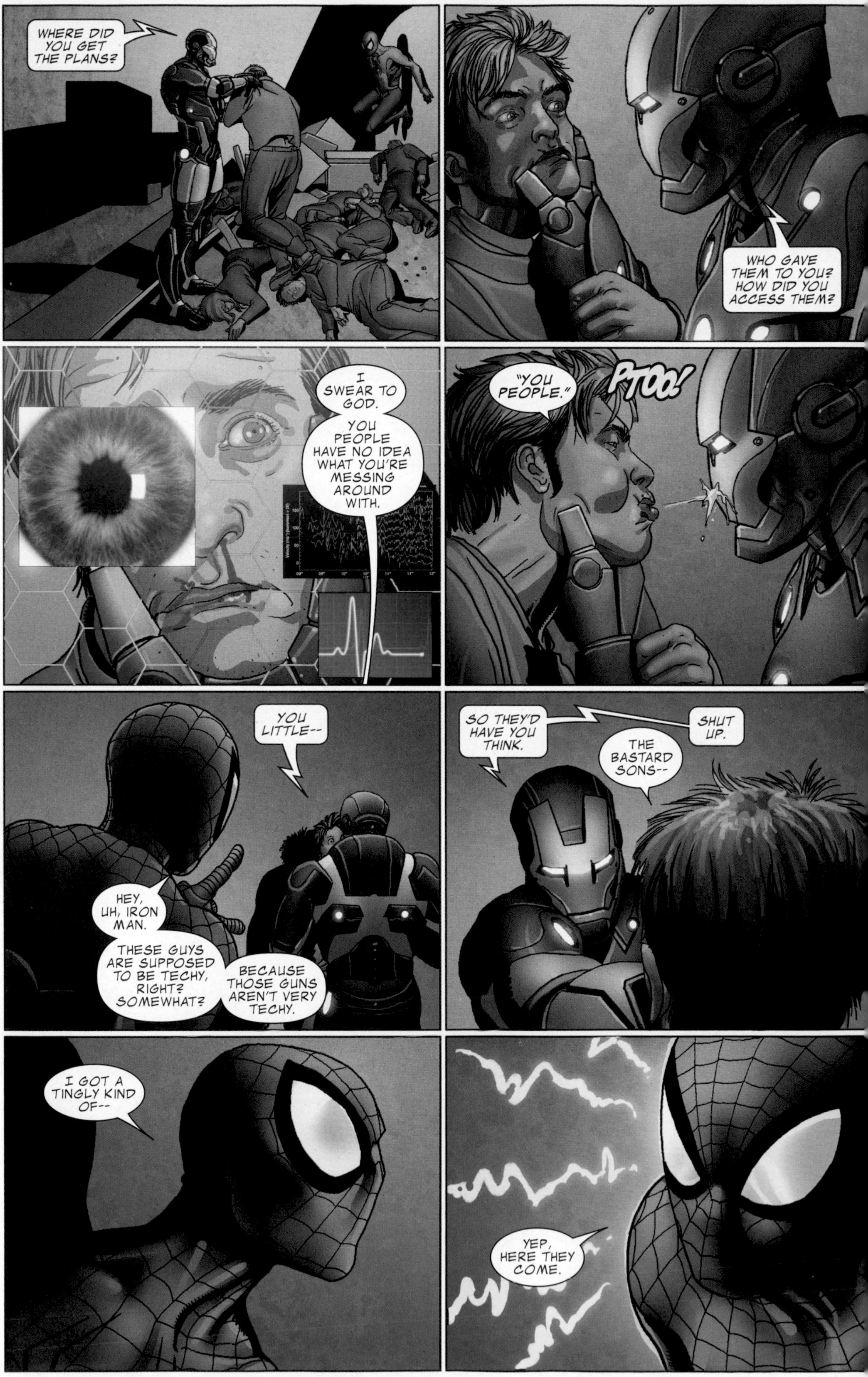
WHERE DID YOU GET THE PLANS?
WHO GAVE THEM TO YOU? HOW DID YOU ACCESS THEM?
I SWEAR TO GOD.
YOU PEOPLE HAVE NO IDEA WHAT YOU'RE MESSING AROUND WITH.
"YOU PEOPLE."
PTOO!
YOU LITTLE--
HEY, UH, IRON MAN.
THESE GUYS ARE SUPPOSED TO BE TECHY, RIGHT? SOMEWHAT?
BECAUSE THOSE GUNS AREN'T VERY TECHY.
SO THEY'D HAVE YOU THINK.
THE BASTARD SONS--
SHUT UP.
I GOT A TINGLY KIND OF--
YEP, HERE THEY COME.

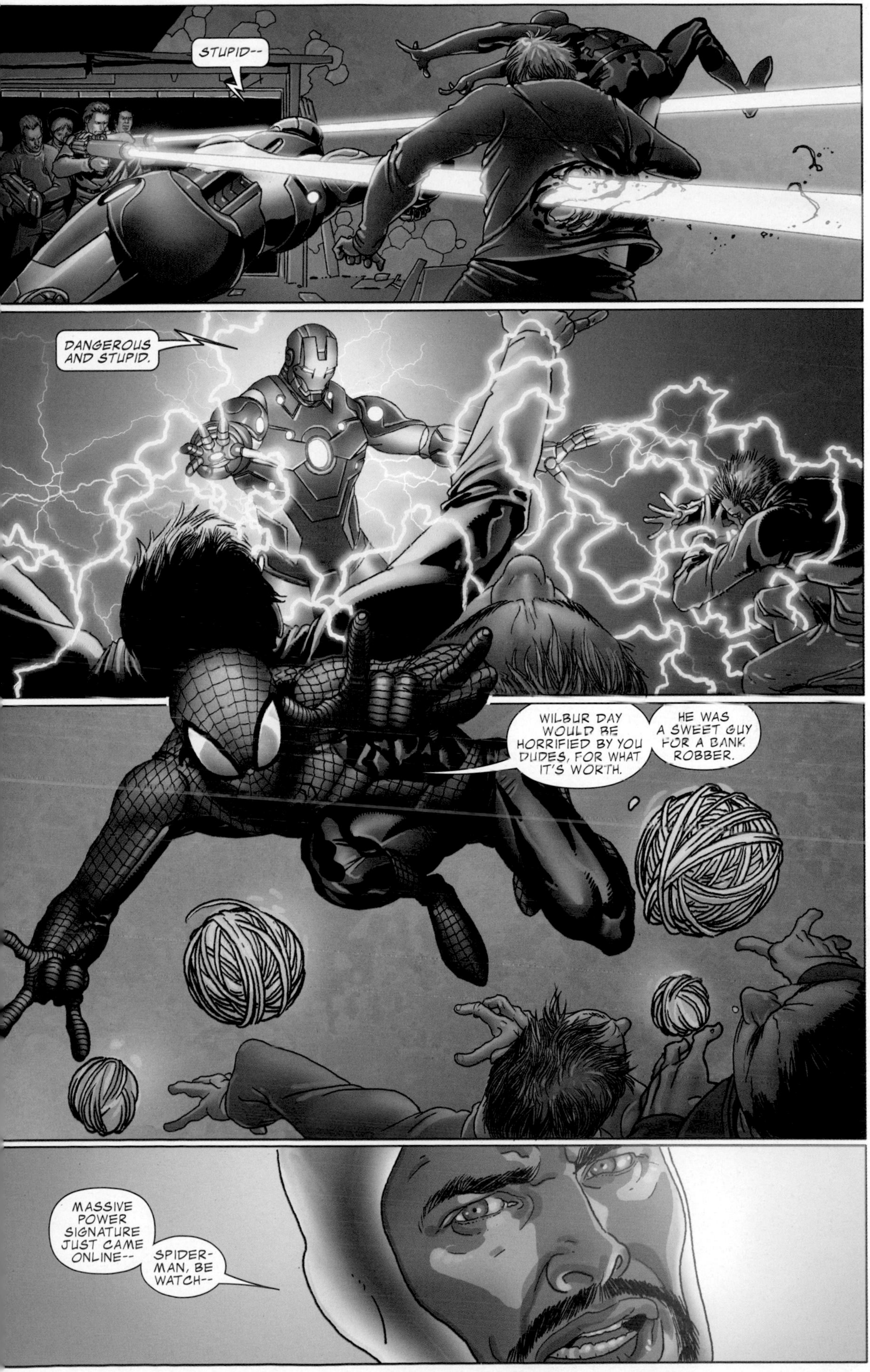
STUPID--
DANGEROUS AND STUPID.
WILBUR DAY WOULD BE HORRIFIED BY YOU DUDES, FOR WHAT IT'S WORTH.
HE WAS A SWEET GUY FOR A BANK ROBBER.
MASSIVE POWER SIGNATURE JUST CAME ONLINE--
SPIDER-MAN, BE WATCH--

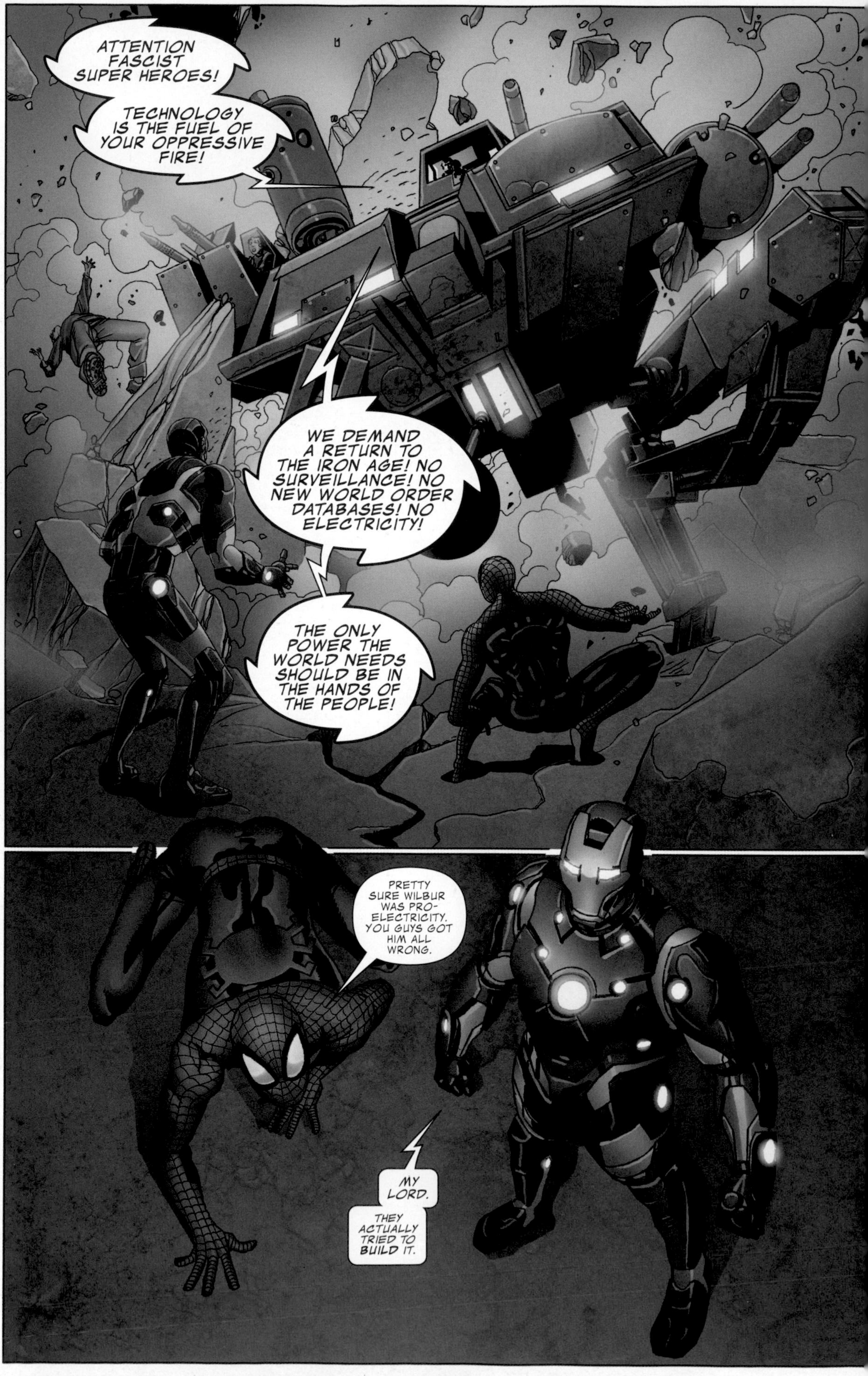
ATTENTION FASCIST SUPER HEROES!
TECHNOLOGY IS THE FUEL OF YOUR OPPRESSIVE FIRE!
WE DEMAND A RETURN TO THE IRON AGE! NO SURVEILLANCE! NO NEW WORLD ORDER DATABASES! NO ELECTRICITY!
THE ONLY POWER THE WORLD NEEDS SHOULD BE IN THE HANDS OF THE PEOPLE!
PRETTY SURE WILBUR WAS PRO-ELECTRICITY. YOU GUYS GOT HIM ALL WRONG.
MY LORD.
THEY ACTUALLY TRIED TO BUILD IT.

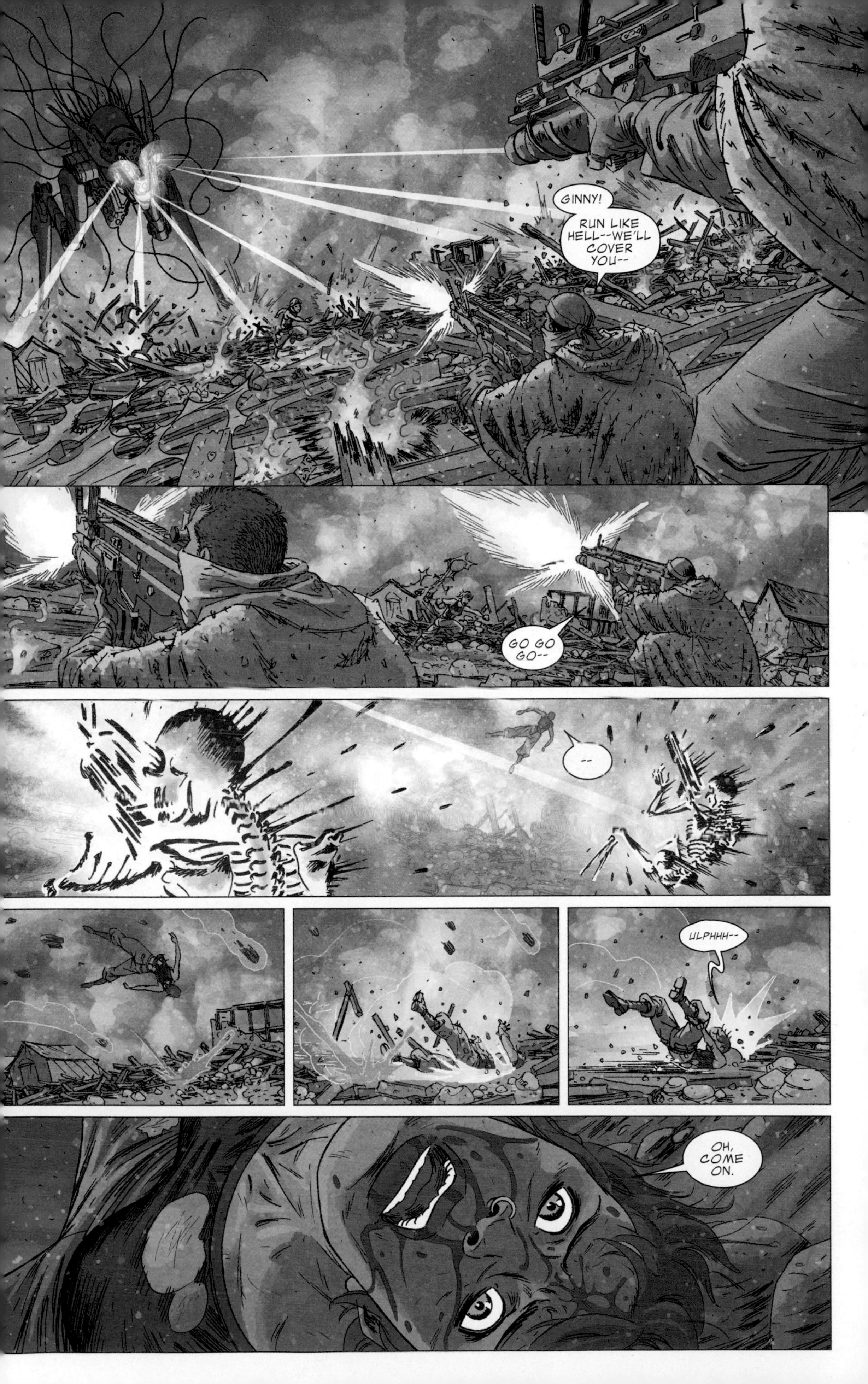
GINNY!
RUN LIKE HELL--WE'LL COVER YOU--
GO GO GO--
--
ULPHHH--
OH, COME ON.

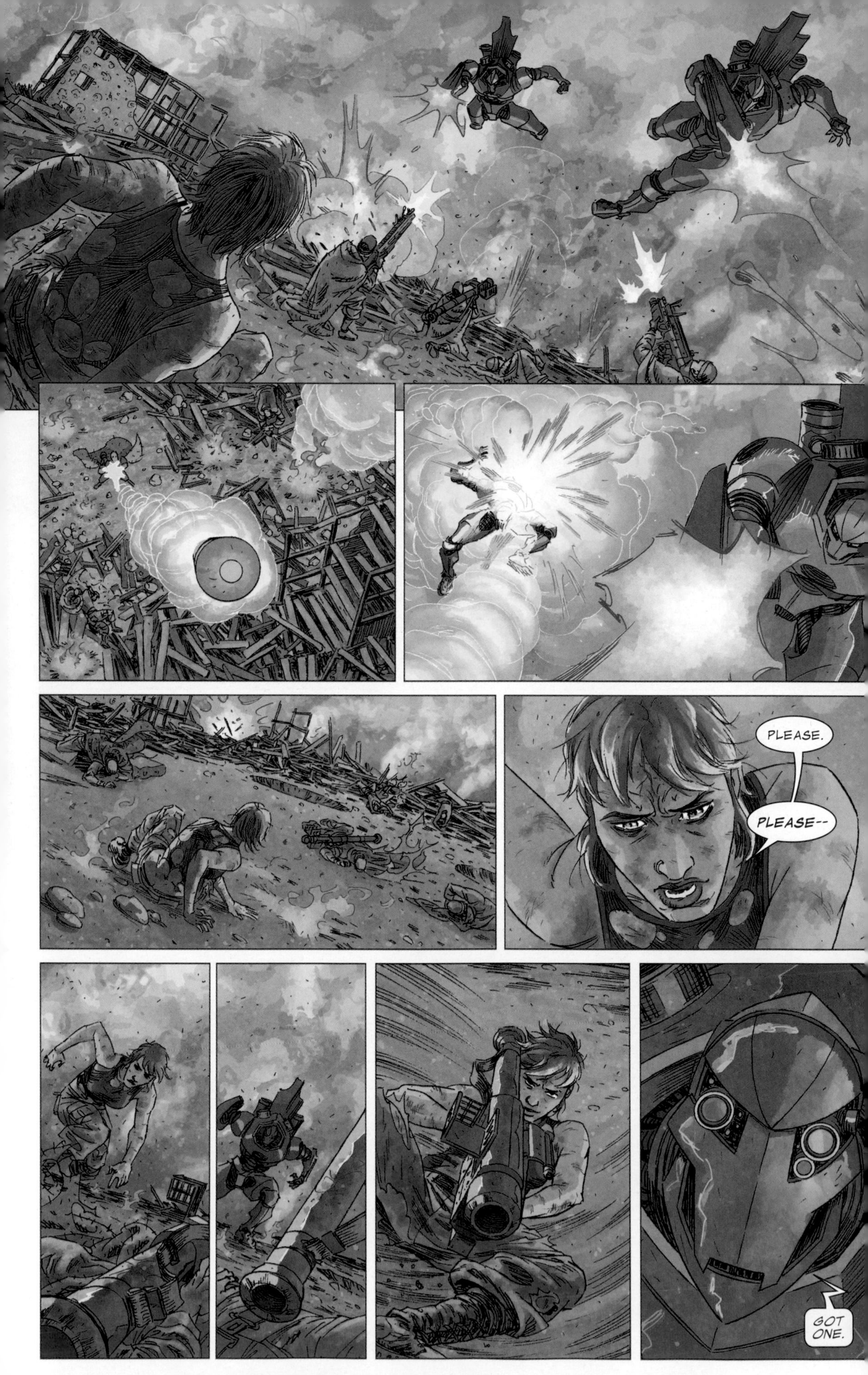
PLEASE.
PLEASE--
GOT ONE.

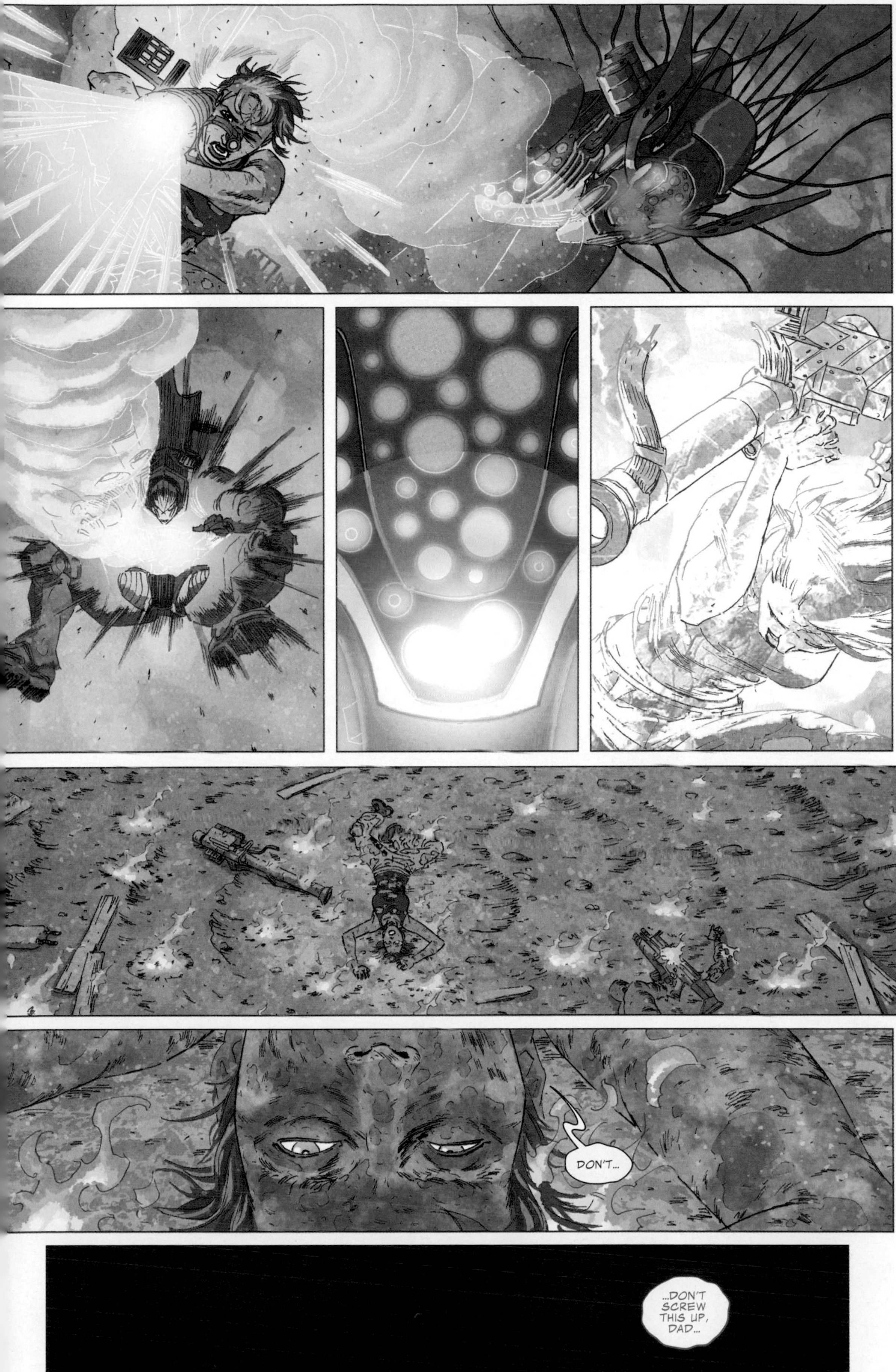
DON'T...
...DON'T SCREW THIS UP, DAD...

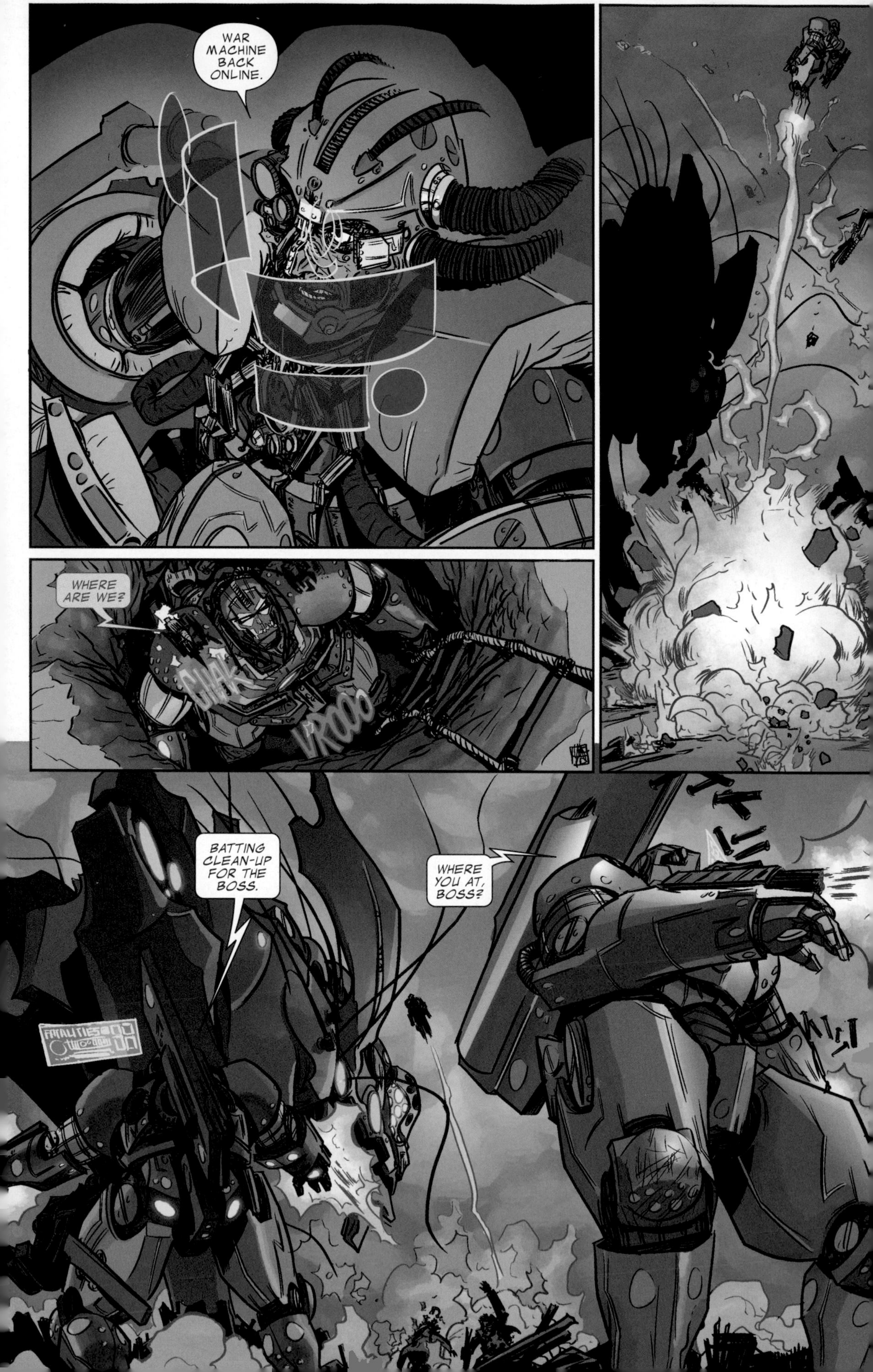
WAR MACHINE BACK ONLINE.
WHERE ARE WE?
GHAK
VROOOO
BATTING CLEAN-UP FOR THE BOSS.
WHERE YOU AT, BOSS?

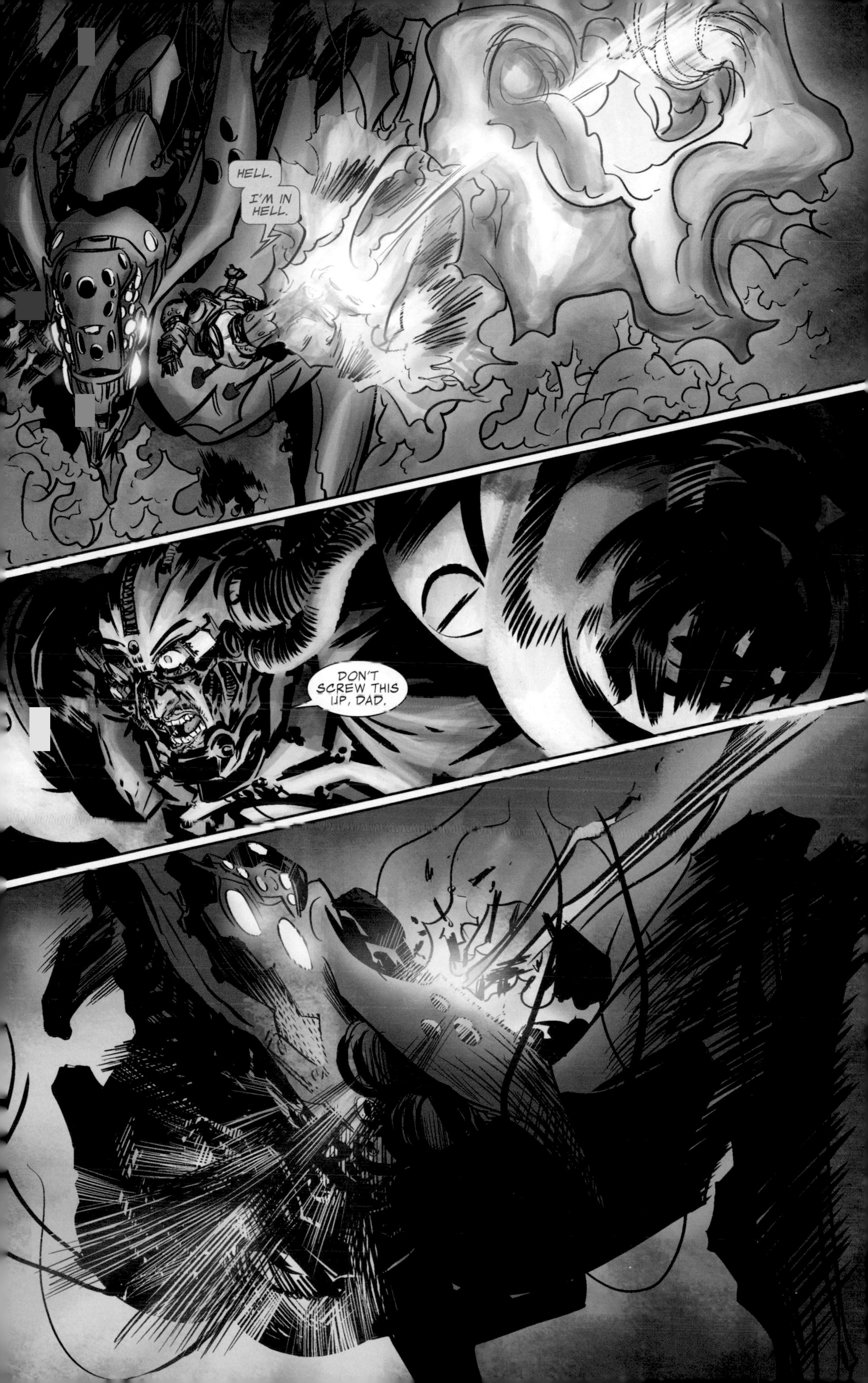
HELL.
I'M IN HELL.
DON'T SCREW THIS UP, DAD.

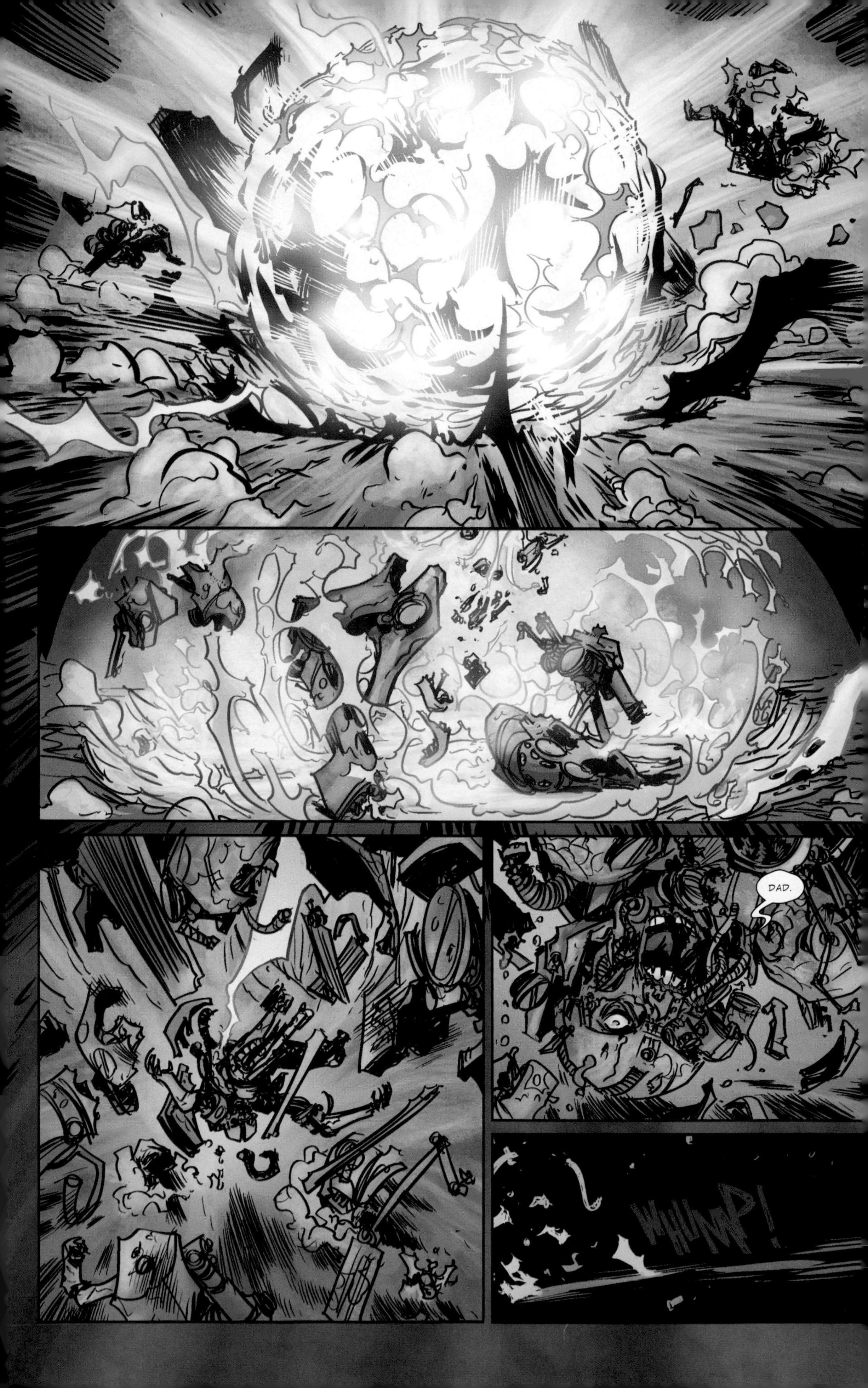
DAD.
WHUMP!

OOPH.

C'MON, OLD MAN.

ALMOST FINISHED.

TOOK ME A WHILE TO REMEMBER AFTER EVERYTHING YOU *DID* TO ME, MANDARIN.

SHOCK. TORTURE.

BUT I REMEMBERED. DIDN'T I?

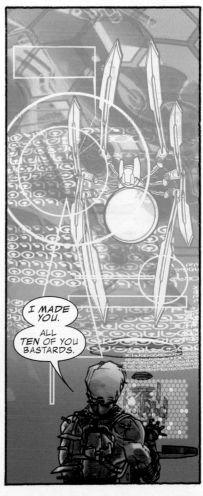

I MADE YOU.

ALL TEN OF YOU BASTARDS.

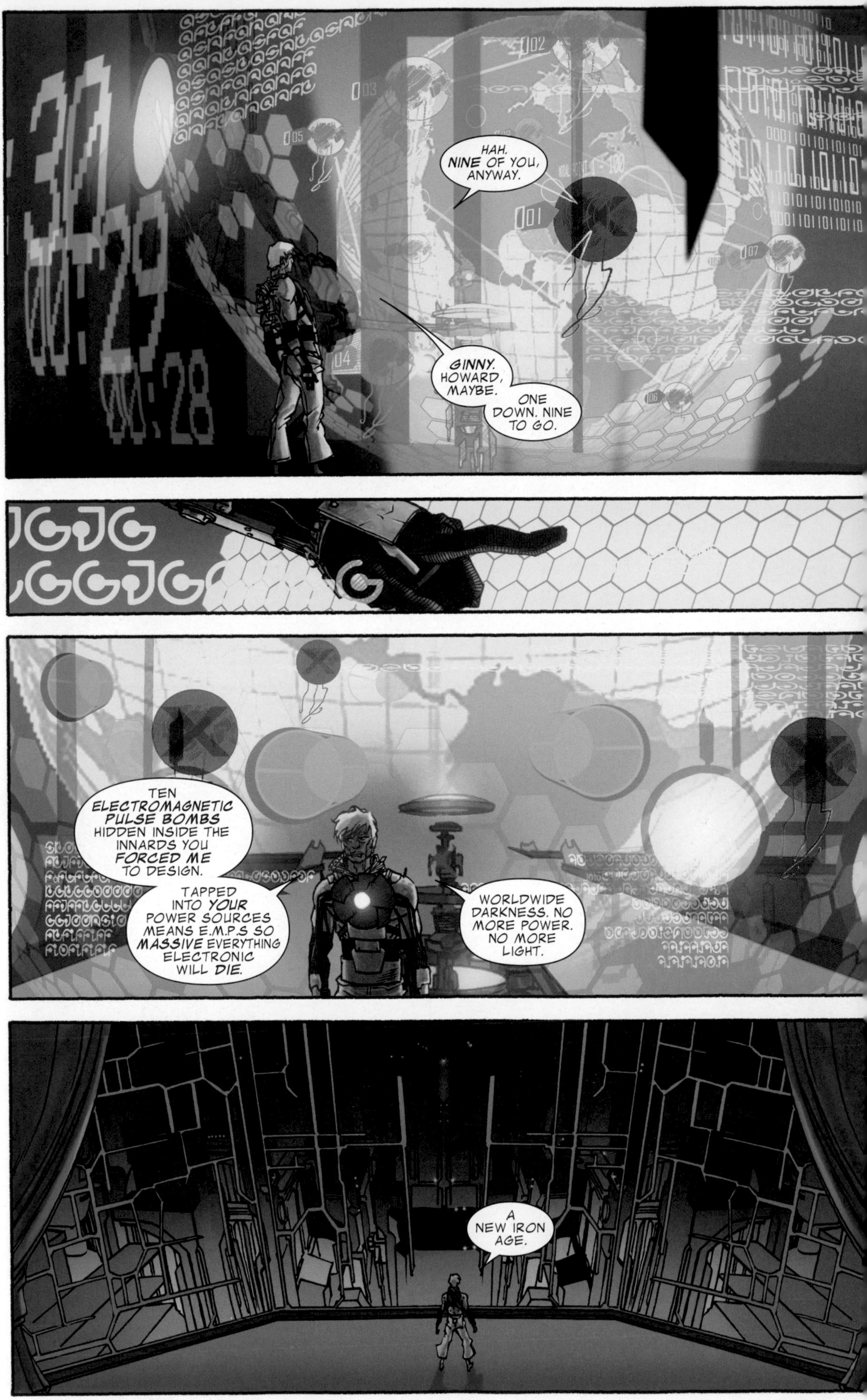
HAH. NINE OF YOU, ANYWAY.
GINNY. HOWARD, MAYBE.
ONE DOWN. NINE TO GO.
TEN ELECTROMAGNETIC PULSE BOMBS HIDDEN INSIDE THE INNARDS YOU FORCED ME TO DESIGN.
TAPPED INTO YOUR POWER SOURCES MEANS E.M.P.S SO MASSIVE EVERYTHING ELECTRONIC WILL DIE.
WORLDWIDE DARKNESS. NO MORE POWER. NO MORE LIGHT.
A NEW IRON AGE.

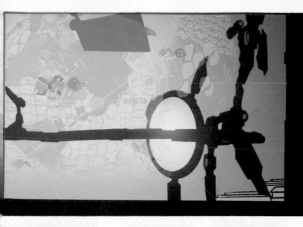

UH-OH.

THAT'S... THAT'S IT?

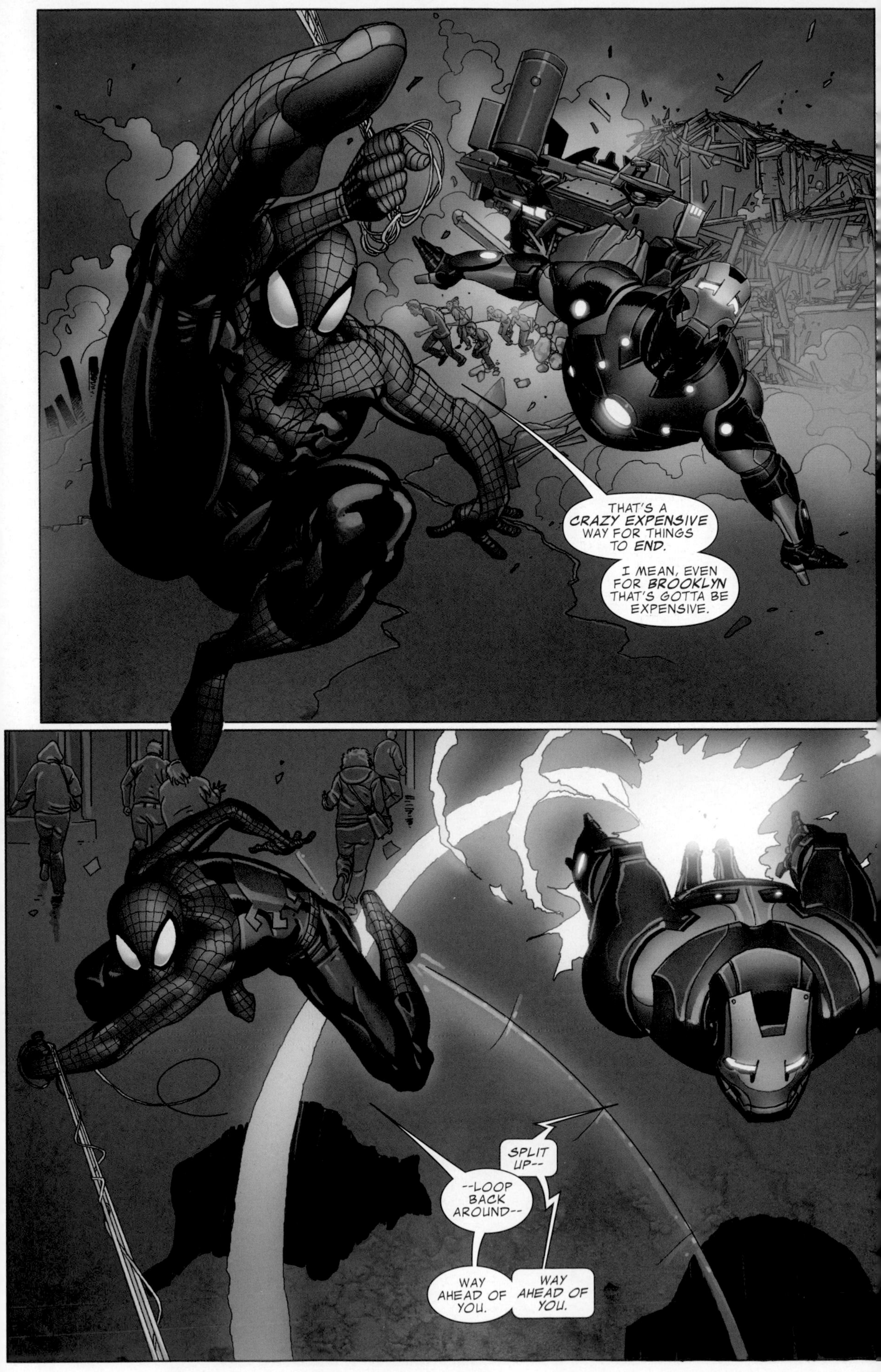
THAT'S A CRAZY EXPENSIVE WAY FOR THINGS TO END.
I MEAN, EVEN FOR BROOKLYN THAT'S GOTTA BE EXPENSIVE.
SPLIT UP--
--LOOP BACK AROUND--
WAY AHEAD OF YOU.
WAY AHEAD OF YOU.

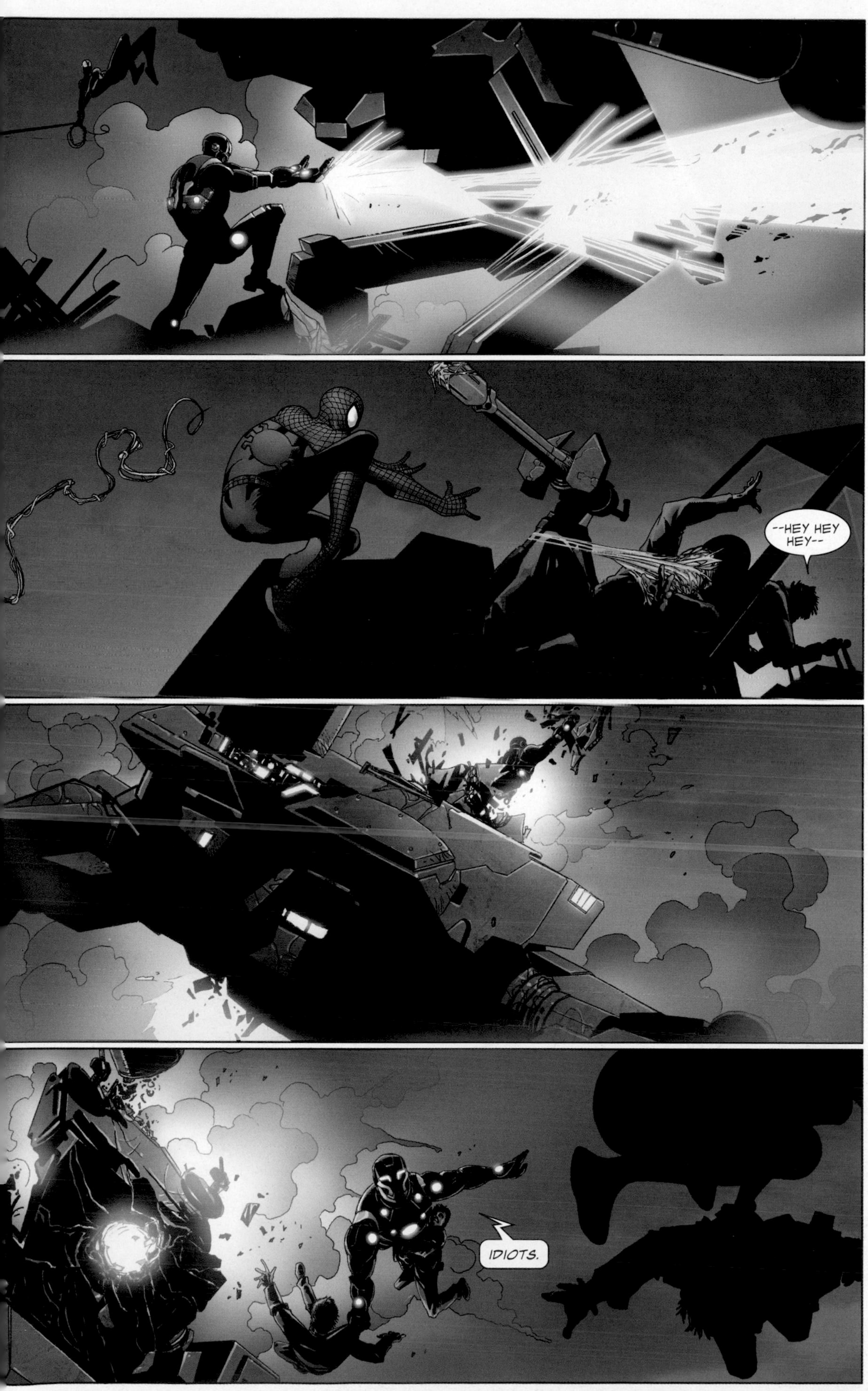
--HEY HEY HEY--
IDIOTS.

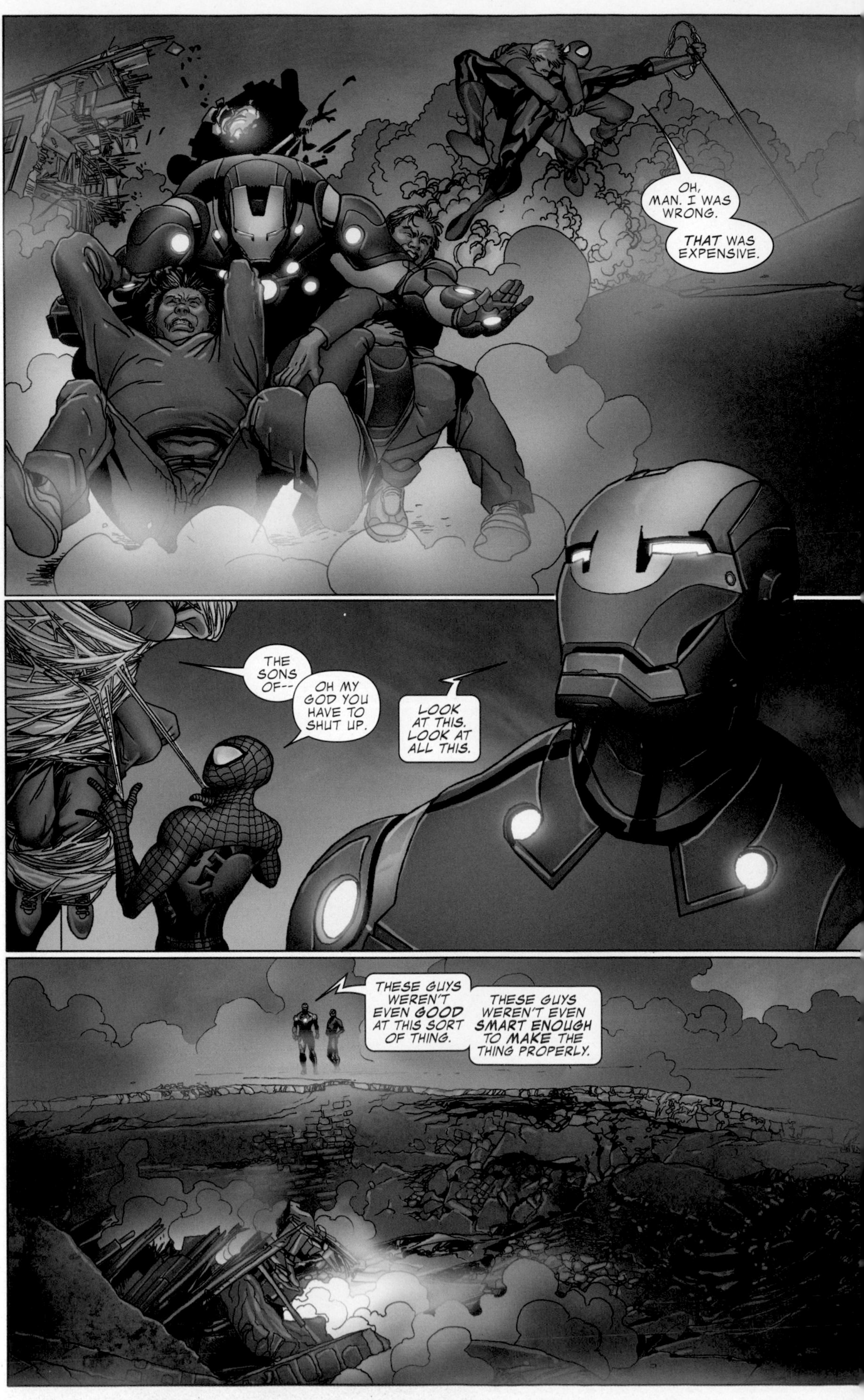
OH, MAN. I WAS WRONG.
THAT WAS EXPENSIVE.
THE SONS OF--
OH MY GOD YOU HAVE TO SHUT UP.
LOOK AT THIS. LOOK AT ALL THIS.
THESE GUYS WEREN'T EVEN GOOD AT THIS SORT OF THING.
THESE GUYS WEREN'T EVEN SMART ENOUGH TO MAKE THE THING PROPERLY.

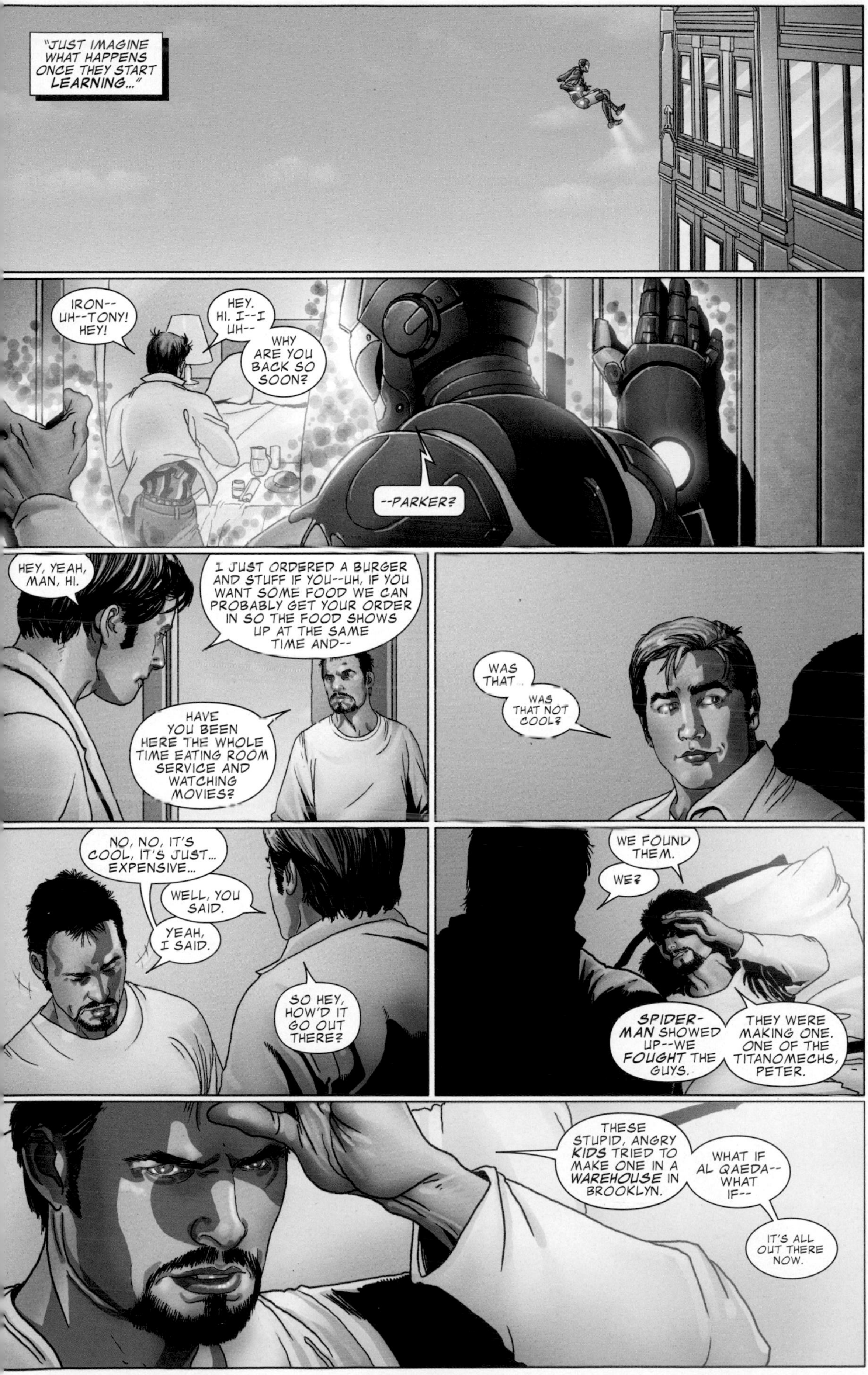
"JUST IMAGINE WHAT HAPPENS ONCE THEY START LEARNING..."
IRON-- UH--TONY! HEY!
HEY. HI. I--I UH--
WHY ARE YOU BACK SO SOON?
--PARKER?
HEY, YEAH, MAN, HI.
I JUST ORDERED A BURGER AND STUFF IF YOU--UH, IF YOU WANT SOME FOOD WE CAN PROBABLY GET YOUR ORDER IN SO THE FOOD SHOWS UP AT THE SAME TIME AND--
HAVE YOU BEEN HERE THE WHOLE TIME EATING ROOM SERVICE AND WATCHING MOVIES?
WAS THAT...
WAS THAT NOT COOL?
NO, NO, IT'S COOL, IT'S JUST... EXPENSIVE...
WELL, YOU SAID.
YEAH, I SAID.
SO HEY, HOW'D IT GO OUT THERE?
WE FOUND THEM.
WE?
SPIDER-MAN SHOWED UP--WE FOUGHT THE GUYS.
THEY WERE MAKING ONE. ONE OF THE TITANOMECHS, PETER.
THESE STUPID, ANGRY KIDS TRIED TO MAKE ONE IN A WAREHOUSE IN BROOKLYN.
WHAT IF AL QAEDA-- WHAT IF--
IT'S ALL OUT THERE NOW.

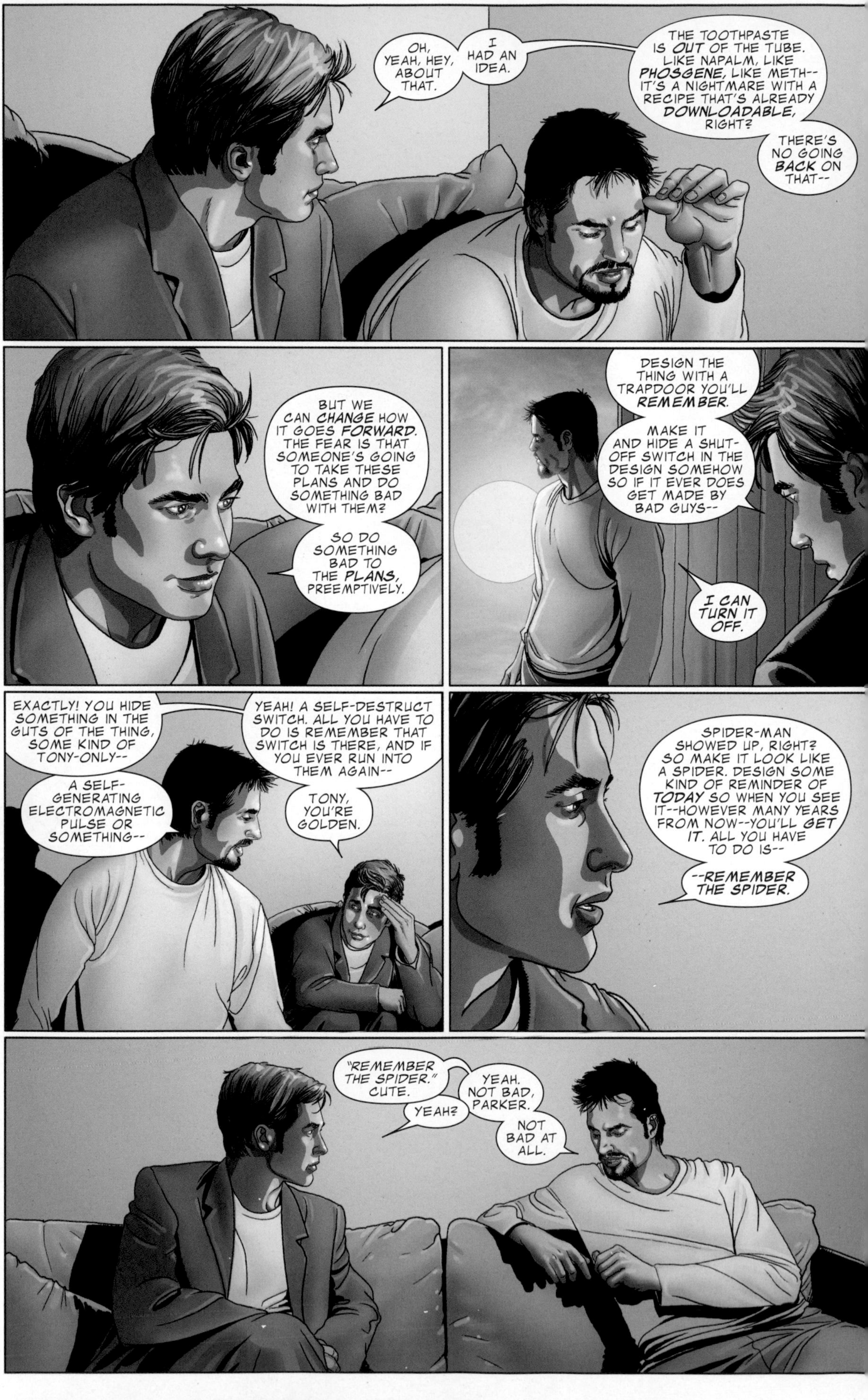
OH, YEAH, HEY, ABOUT THAT.
I HAD AN IDEA.
THE TOOTHPASTE IS OUT OF THE TUBE. LIKE NAPALM, LIKE PHOSGENE, LIKE METH-- IT'S A NIGHTMARE WITH A RECIPE THAT'S ALREADY DOWNLOADABLE, RIGHT?
THERE'S NO GOING BACK ON THAT--
BUT WE CAN CHANGE HOW IT GOES FORWARD. THE FEAR IS THAT SOMEONE'S GOING TO TAKE THESE PLANS AND DO SOMETHING BAD WITH THEM?
SO DO SOMETHING BAD TO THE PLANS, PREEMPTIVELY.
DESIGN THE THING WITH A TRAPDOOR YOU'LL REMEMBER.
MAKE IT AND HIDE A SHUT-OFF SWITCH IN THE DESIGN SOMEHOW SO IF IT EVER DOES GET MADE BY BAD GUYS--
I CAN TURN IT OFF.
EXACTLY! YOU HIDE SOMETHING IN THE GUTS OF THE THING, SOME KIND OF TONY-ONLY--
A SELF-GENERATING ELECTROMAGNETIC PULSE OR SOMETHING--
YEAH! A SELF-DESTRUCT SWITCH. ALL YOU HAVE TO DO IS REMEMBER THAT SWITCH IS THERE, AND IF YOU EVER RUN INTO THEM AGAIN--
TONY, YOU'RE GOLDEN.
SPIDER-MAN SHOWED UP, RIGHT? SO MAKE IT LOOK LIKE A SPIDER. DESIGN SOME KIND OF REMINDER OF TODAY SO WHEN YOU SEE IT--HOWEVER MANY YEARS FROM NOW--YOU'LL GET IT. ALL YOU HAVE TO DO IS--
--REMEMBER THE SPIDER.
"REMEMBER THE SPIDER." CUTE.
YEAH?
YEAH. NOT BAD, PARKER.
NOT BAD AT ALL.

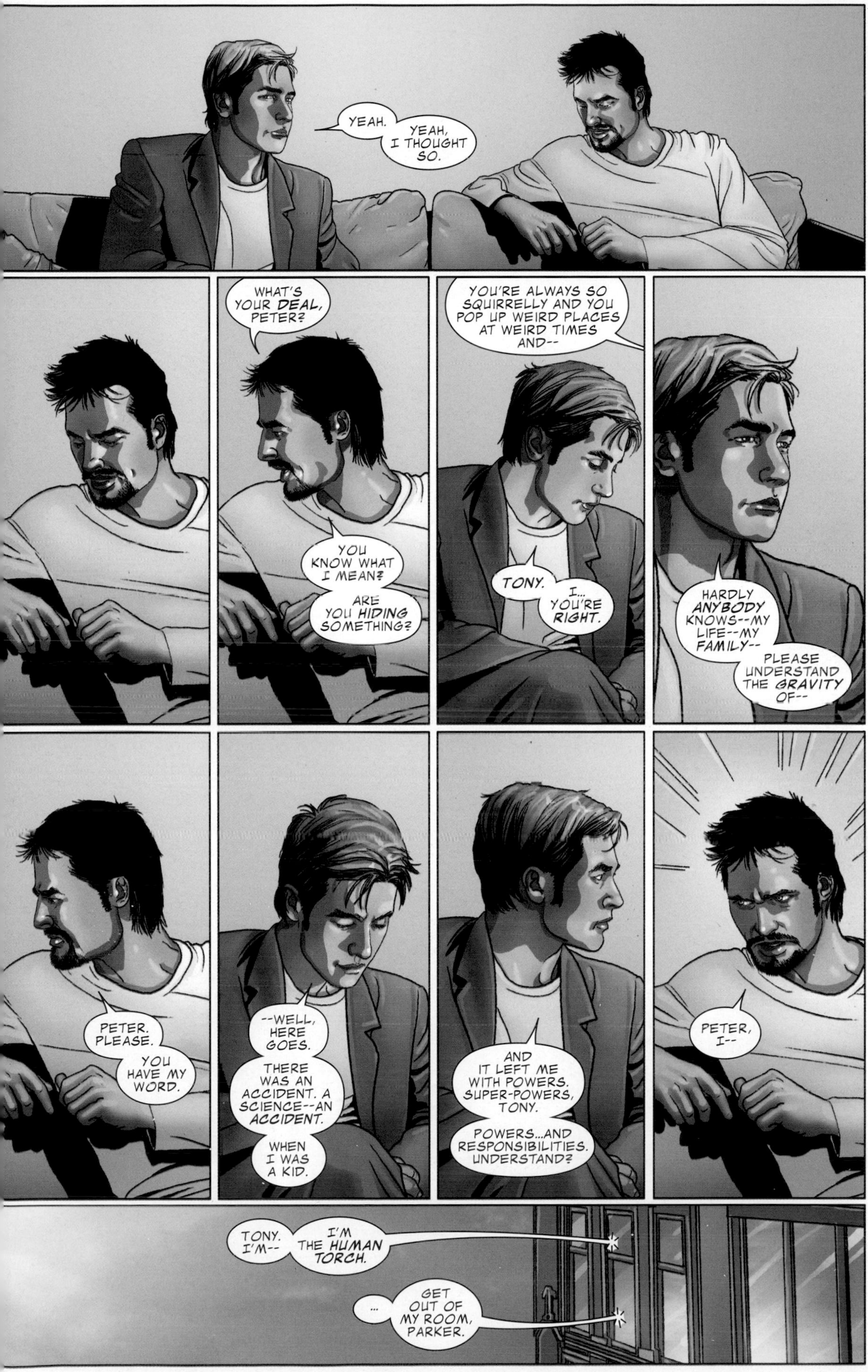
YEAH.
YEAH, I THOUGHT SO.
WHAT'S YOUR DEAL, PETER?
YOU KNOW WHAT I MEAN?
ARE YOU HIDING SOMETHING?
YOU'RE ALWAYS SO SQUIRRELLY AND YOU POP UP WEIRD PLACES AT WEIRD TIMES AND--
TONY.
I... YOU'RE RIGHT.
HARDLY ANYBODY KNOWS--MY LIFE--MY FAMILY--
PLEASE UNDERSTAND THE GRAVITY OF--
PETER. PLEASE.
YOU HAVE MY WORD.
--WELL, HERE GOES.
THERE WAS AN ACCIDENT. A SCIENCE--AN ACCIDENT.
WHEN I WAS A KID.
AND IT LEFT ME WITH POWERS. SUPER-POWERS, TONY.
POWERS...AND RESPONSIBILITIES. UNDERSTAND?
PETER, I--
TONY. I'M--
I'M THE HUMAN TORCH.
...
GET OUT OF MY ROOM, PARKER.

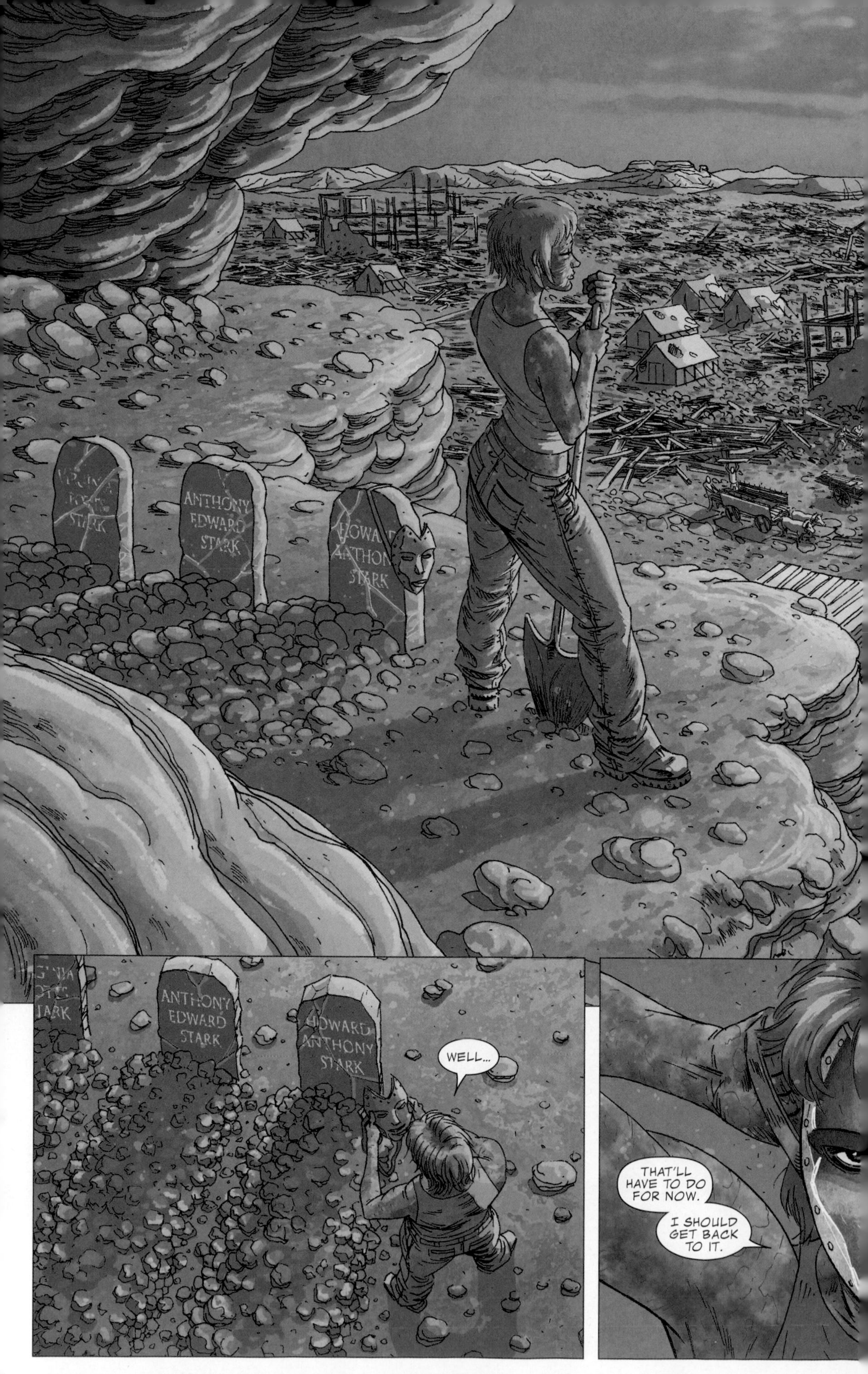
ANTHONY EDWARD STARK
HOWARD ANTHONY STARK
WELL...
THAT'LL HAVE TO DO FOR NOW.
I SHOULD GET BACK TO IT.

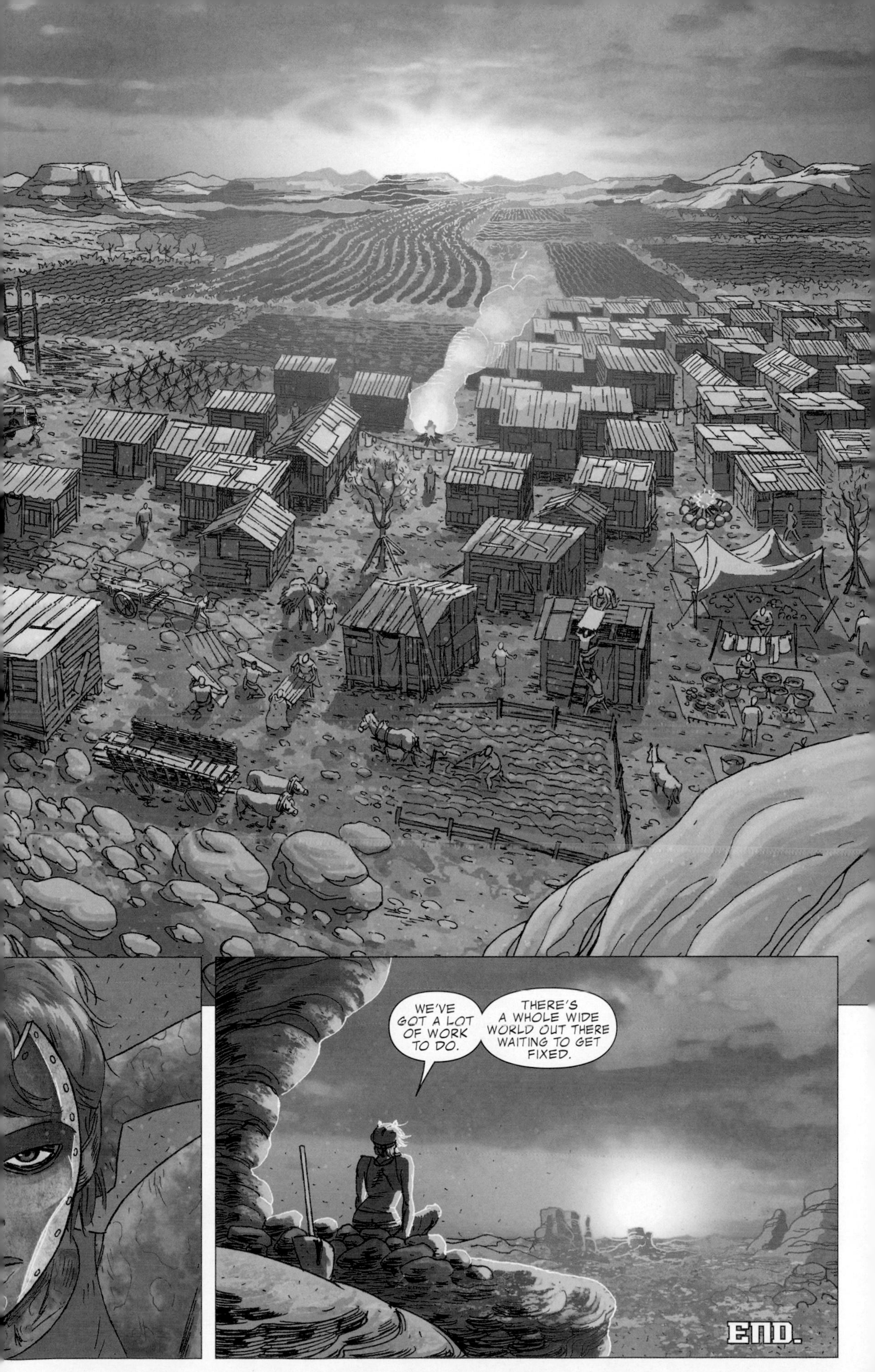
WE'VE GOT A LOT OF WORK TO DO.
THERE'S A WHOLE WIDE WORLD OUT THERE WAITING TO GET FIXED.
END.

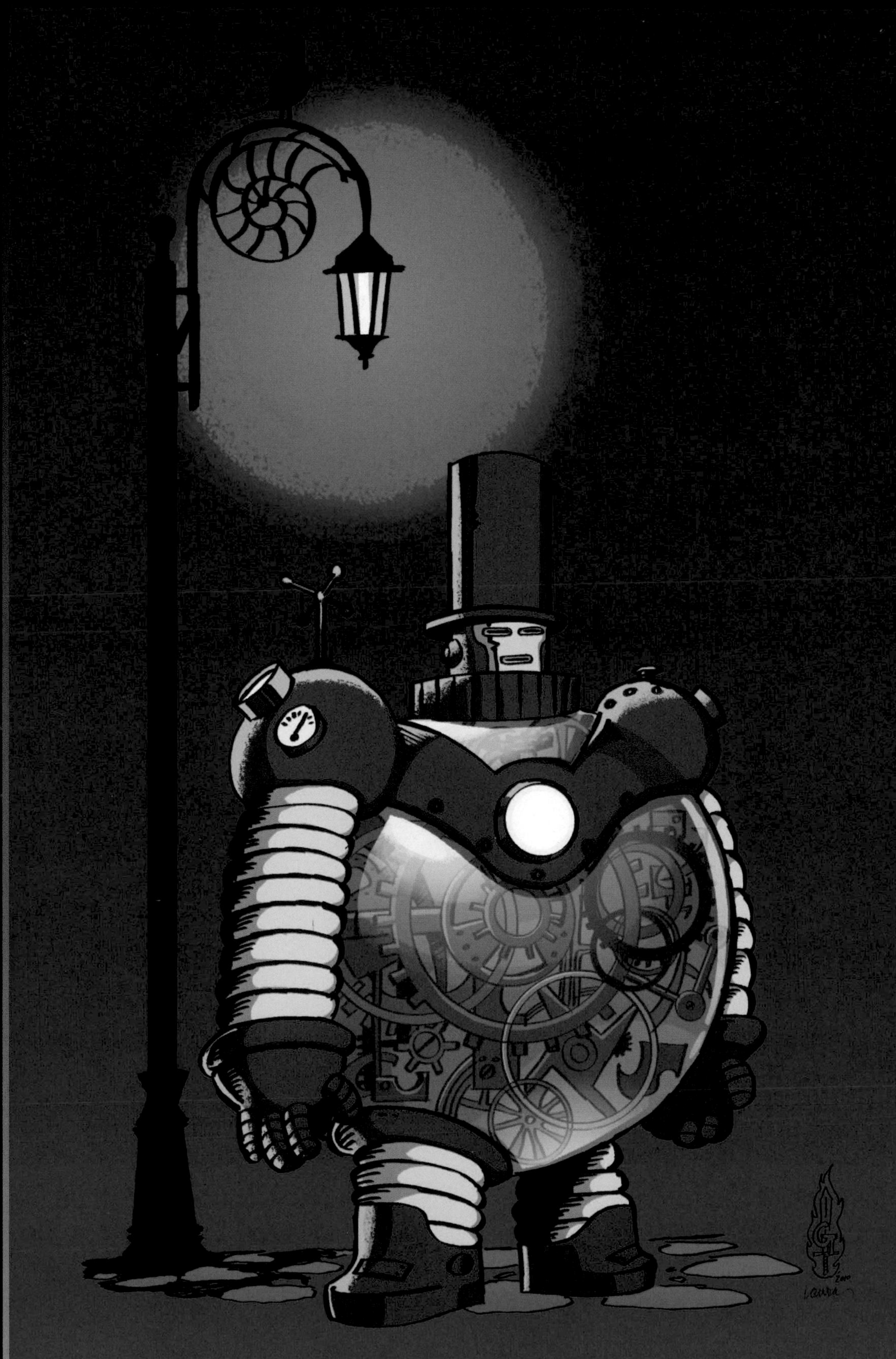

ANNUAL #1 IRON MAN BY DESIGN VARIANT
BY GENNEDY TARTAKOVSKY & LAURA MARTIN

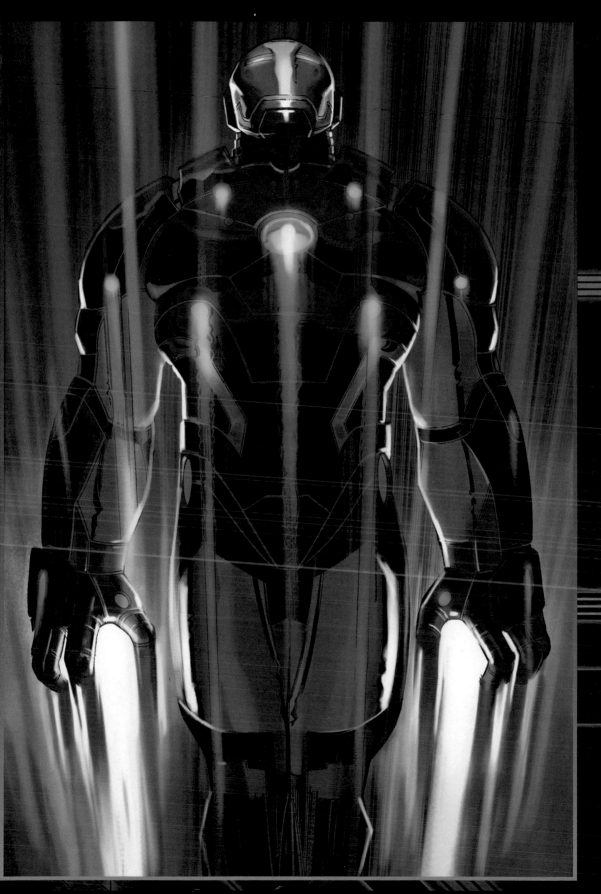

#500 VARIANT
BY JOHN ROMITA JR., KLAUS JANSON & DEAN WHITE

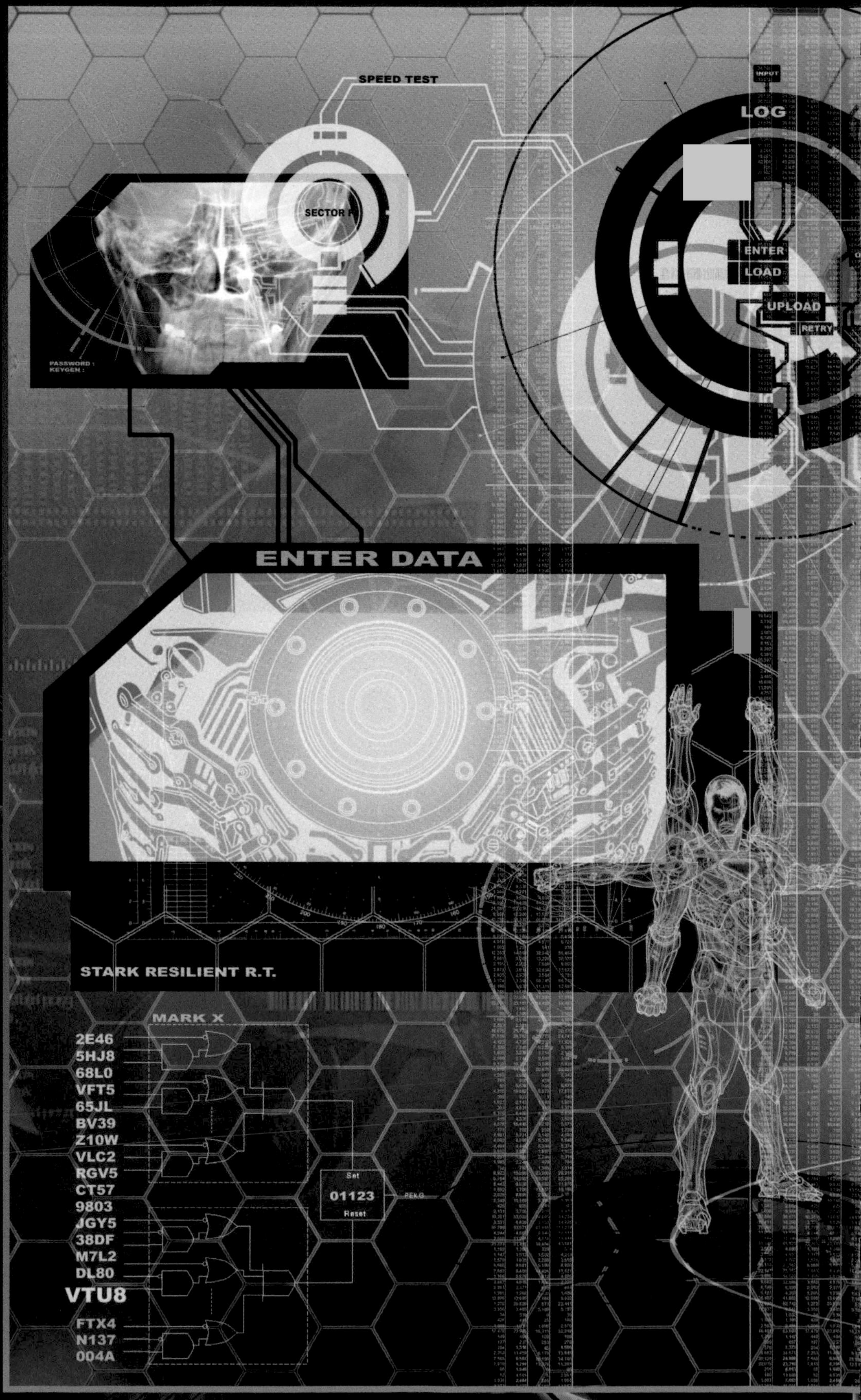
SPEED TEST
SECTOR R
PASSWORD :
KEYGEN :
INPUT
LOG
ENTER
LOAD
UPLOAD
RETRY
ENTER DATA
STARK RESILIENT R.T.
MARK X
2E46
5HJ8
68L0
VFT5
65JL
BV39
Z10W
VLC2
RGV5
CT57
9803
JGY5
38DF
M7L2
DL80
VTU8
FTX4
N137
004A
Set
01123
Reset

#500 VARIANT
BY SALVADOR LARROCA

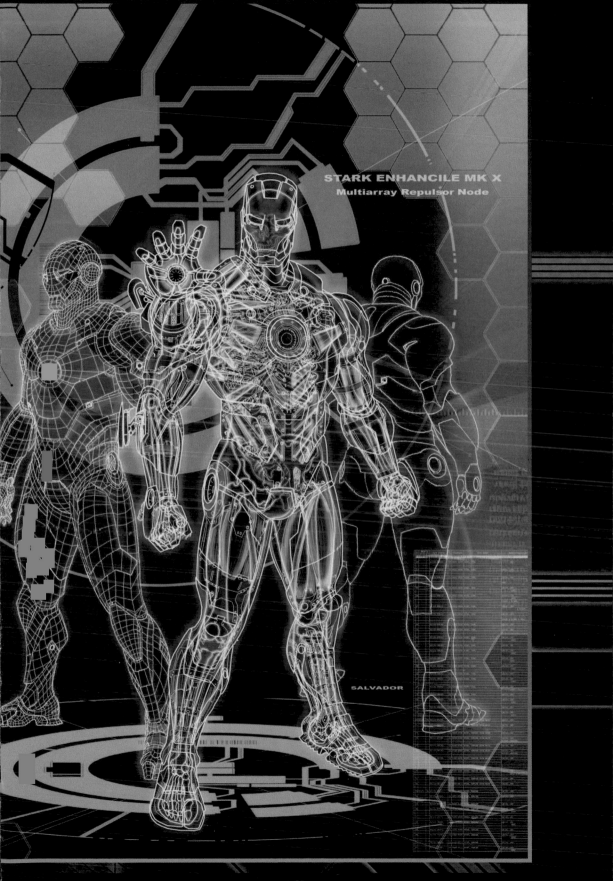

STARK ENHANCILE MK X
Multiarray Repulsor Node

SALVADOR

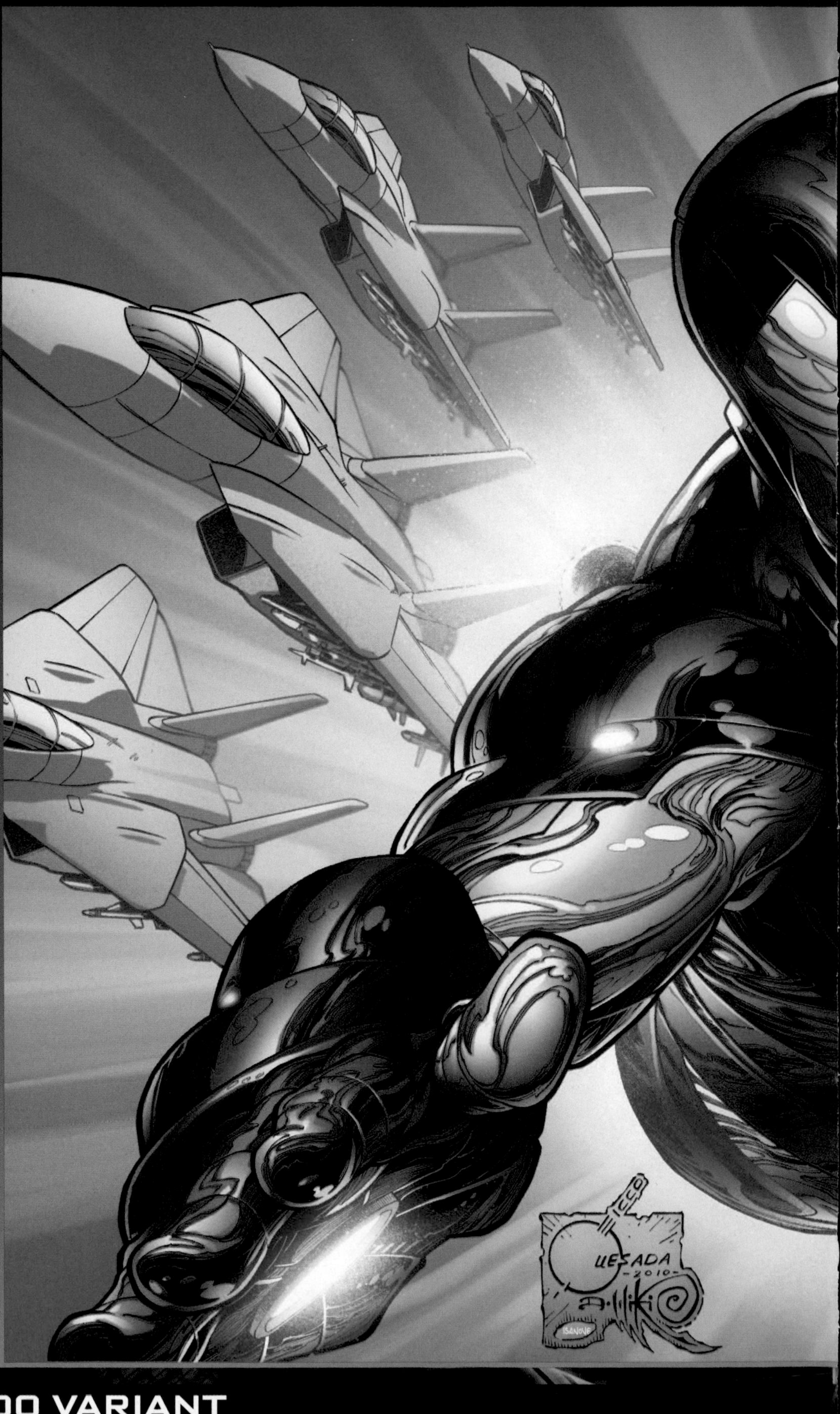
QUESADA
-2010-
ISANOVE

#500 VARIANT

BY JOE QUESADA, DANNY MIKI & RICHARD ISANOVE

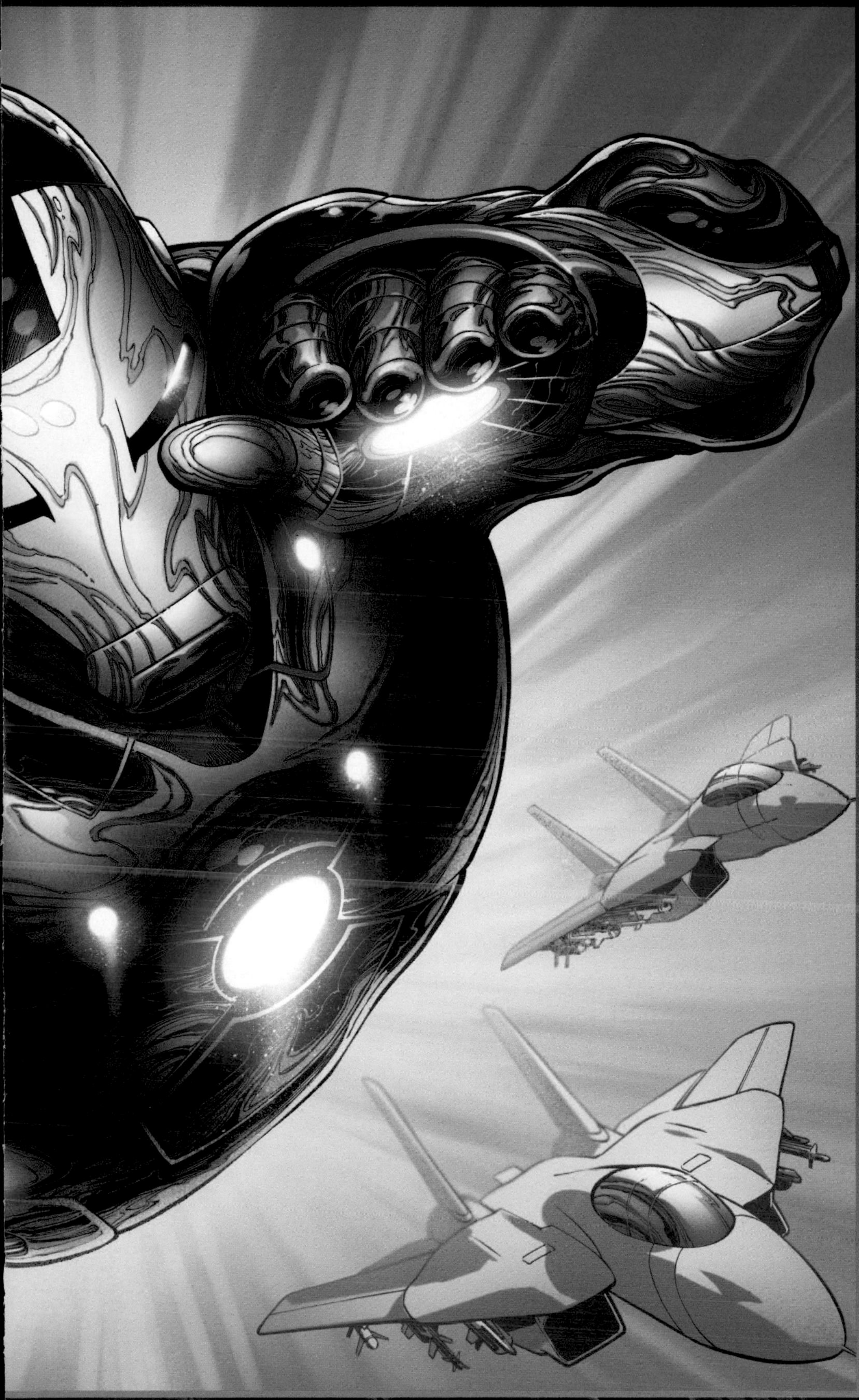

INVINCIBLE IRON MAN #500-502
& IRON MAN 2.0 #1-3

COMBINED VARIANT COVERS
BY MARKO DJURDJEVIC

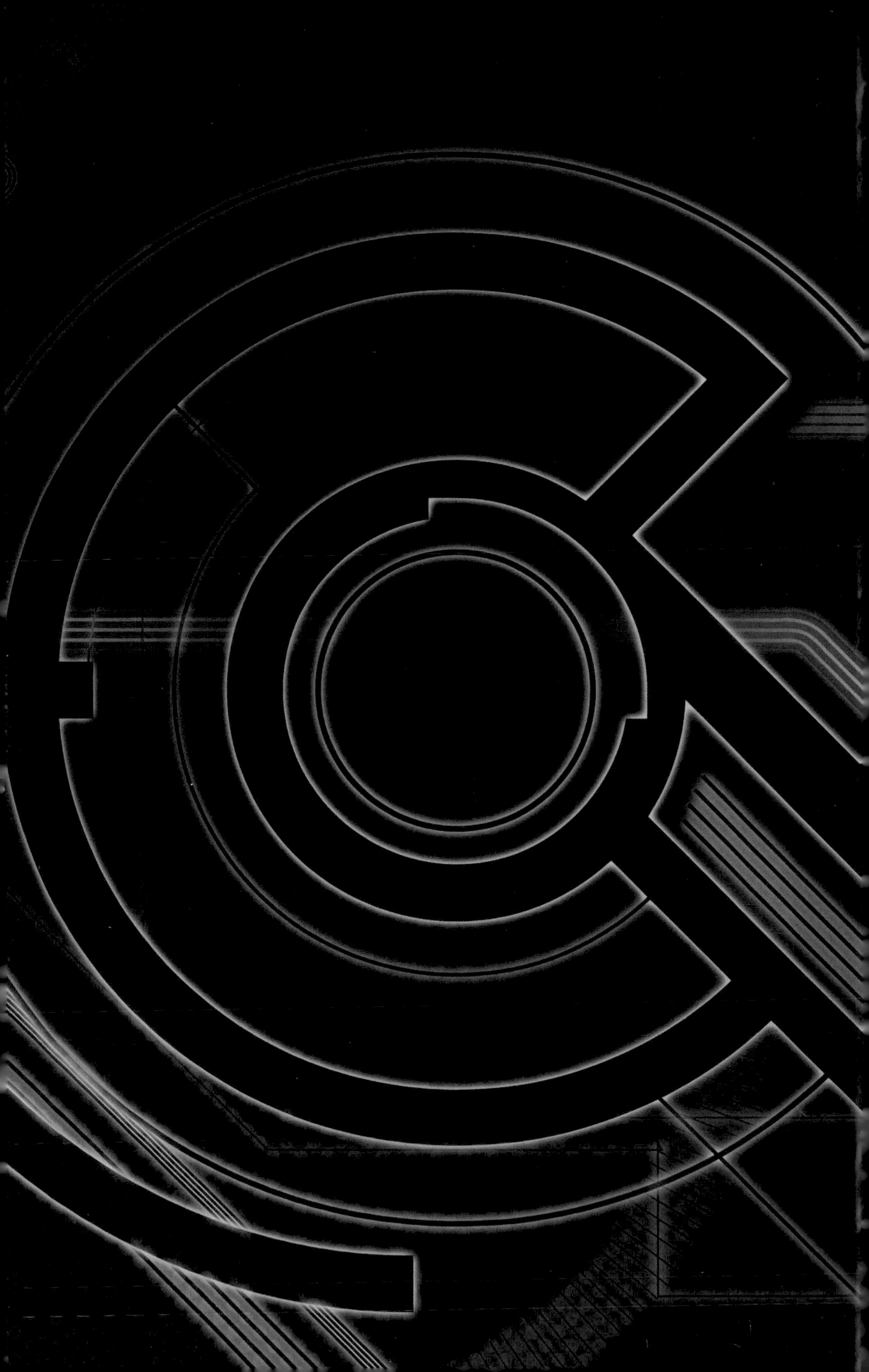